HISTORIC PHOTOS OF
VERMONT

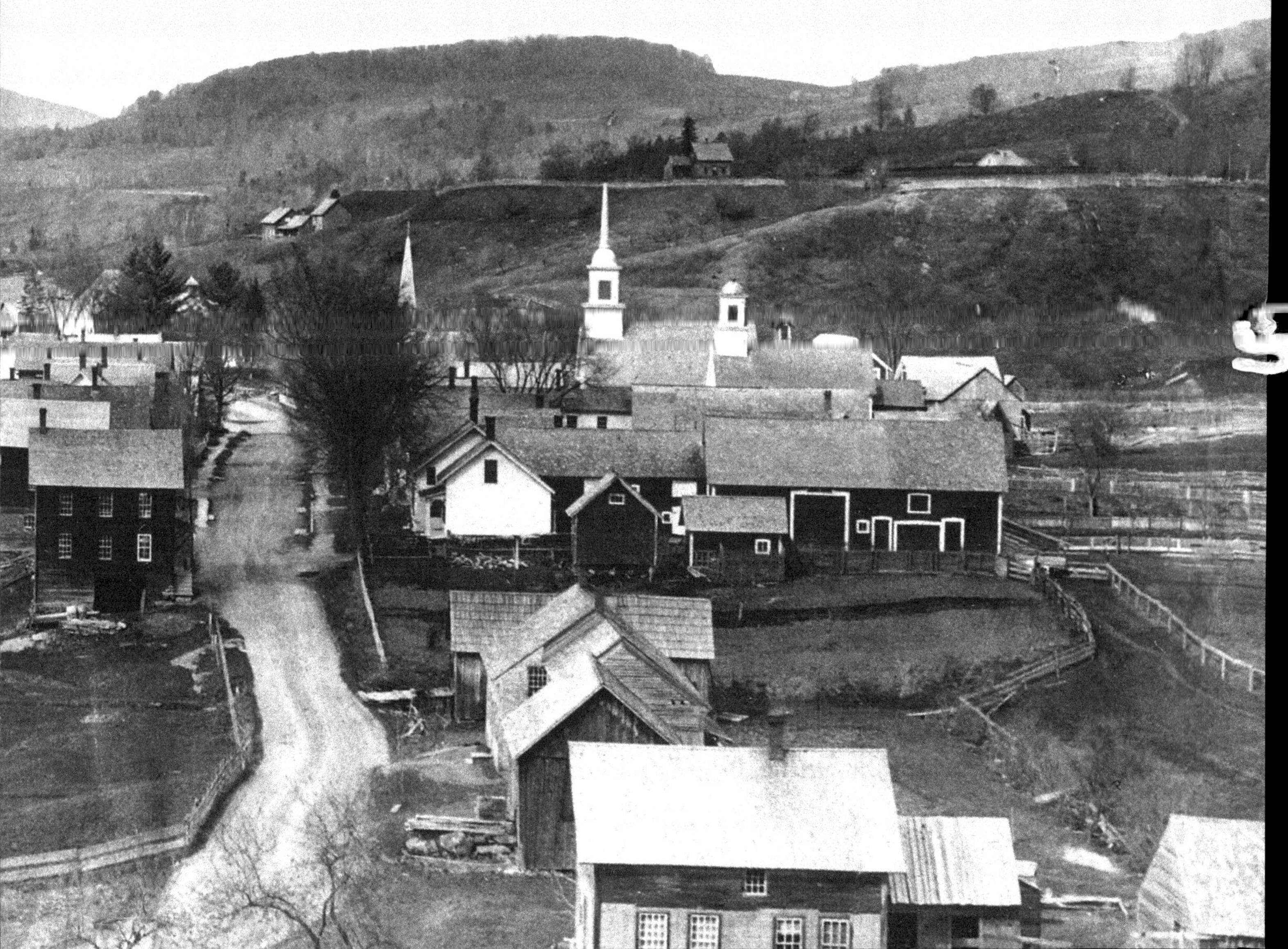

Turner Publishing Company
www.turnerpublishing.com

Historic Photos of Vermont

Library of Congress Control Number: 2008921532

ISBN-13: 978-1-59652-449-1

Printed in the United States of America

ISBN 978-1-68442-031-5 (hc)

Contents

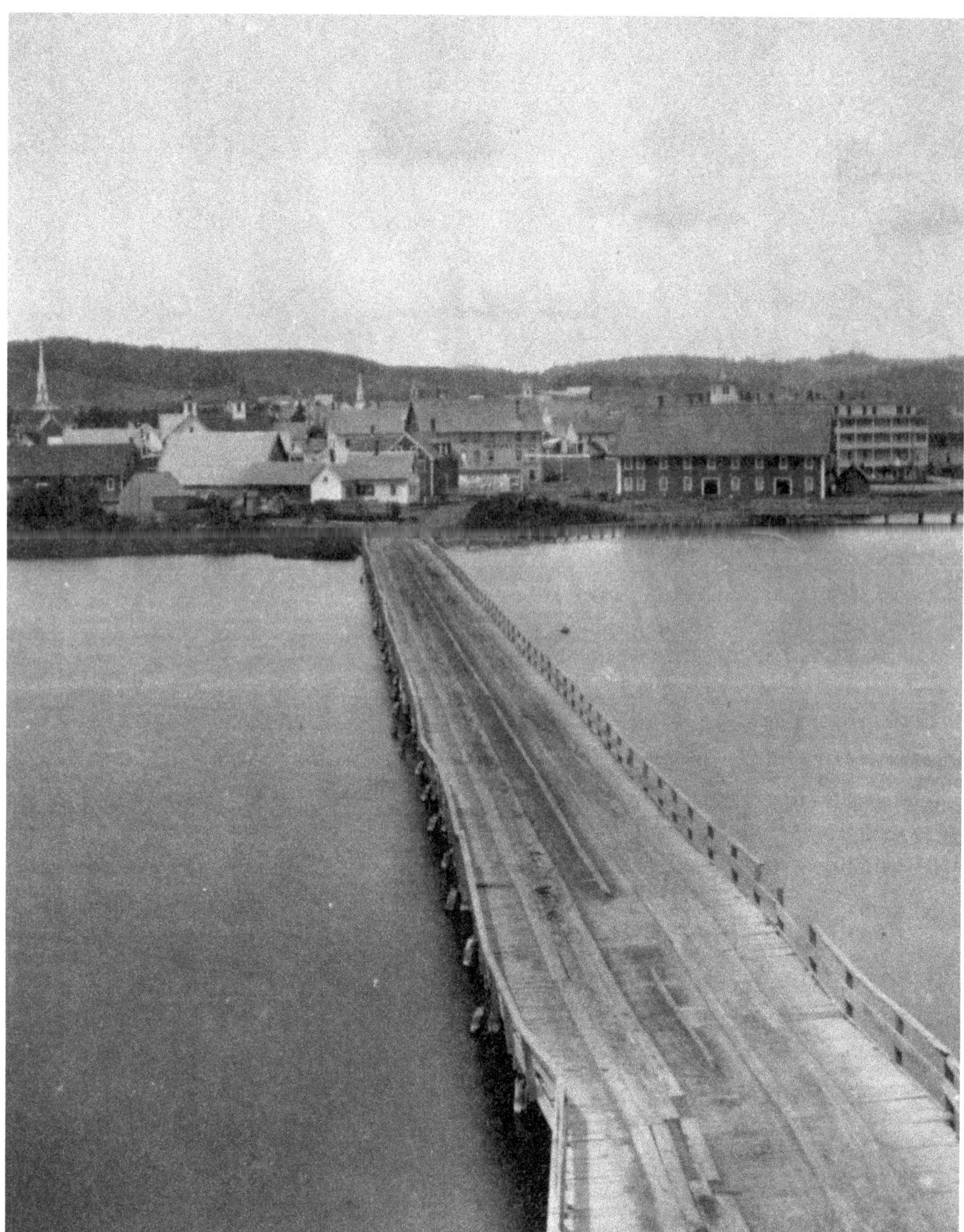

View of Newport from West Derby along the Long Bridge. Because boats provided the only early connection between these two towns, residents who needed Dr. Newcomb, the towns' only physician, fetched him by rowboat. Residents built the first bridges connecting the two towns in the 1830s and completed the Long Bridge in 1863.

ACKNOWLEDGMENTS

This volume, *Historic Photos of Vermont,* is the result of the cooperation and efforts of many individuals, organizations, and corporations. It is with great thanks that we acknowledge the valuable contribution of the following for their generous support:

Bailey/Howe Special Collections, University of Vermont
Bixby Memorial Free Library, Vergennes
Brattleboro Historical Society
Bristol Historical Society
Cabot Historical Society
Jericho Historical Society
League of Local Historical Societies
Library of Congress
Floyd and Vesta McLaughlin
Moretown Historical Society
Noyes House Museum, Morristown Historical Society
Richmond Historical Society
Shoreham Historical Society
Shrewsbury Historical Society of Cuttingsville, Vermont
University of Vermont Landscape Change Program
Vermont Department of Libraries
Vermont State Archives
Jane Vincent
Williston Historical Society

Special thanks to Ginger Isham, John Carnahan, Christie Carter, Joann Nichols, and Gregory Sanford for their on-the-spot, save-the-day, quick-turnaround answers to my many questions.

Finally, my heartfelt appreciation and admiration for Scott A. McLaughlin, for his outstanding and welcome ability to come up with the right phrase at the right time, and to make stories out of mere words.

With the exception of touching up imperfections caused by the vicissitudes of time and cropping where necessary, no other changes have been made. The focus and clarity of many images is limited to the technology and the ability of the photographer at the time they were recorded.

PREFACE

If you are one of those people who moved to Vermont in the last few years—and goodness knows there are many—then you have probably been dubbed a "flatlander" at one time or another. This is the term that longtime residents use when speaking of newcomers who were born outside the Green Mountain State. Perhaps you have chatted with your neighbor at a summer barbecue and listened to her count back how many generations her family has lived in Vermont. Conversations like these underscore the pride that comes with being a native "Vermonter."

These conversations also hint at the tensions given rise to by the influx of the many new residents who now call Vermont home. Many "flatlanders" were once summer vacationers who had purchased second homes in Vermont and eventually decided to live here. The result has been that the number of people in Vermont has increased by more than 200,000 since 1960, and state population growth has outpaced national increases for the first time since the early 1800s. Vermonters remember that, not too long ago, Williston's Walmart was a cow pasture and Interstate 91 was nonexistent. They remind us that a national chain store put their uncle's stationery shop out of business. With these dynamics in mind, it is no wonder that flatlanders have a bad reputation in Vermont.

Native Vermonters have long demonstrated the habit of rebuffing outsiders. The most familiar example dates back to Ethan Allen's Green Mountain Boys, who chased New York residents out of the region during the land disputes of the late eighteenth century. Even today, the Vermont Air National Guard carries the nickname "Green Mountain Boys" and has painted that moniker in billboard-sized letters on the Guard hangar at Burlington Airport. Vermonters have a history of warning outsiders to stay on their best behavior.

A similar insider-versus-outsider dynamic was evident in attitudes toward immigrants who worked in Rutland's quarries and Bennington's mills during the late nineteenth century. Tensions toward outsiders also rose against national labor union representatives, who stirred up political unrest in Vermont's urban areas. Objections to outsider intervention have been at times so strong that Vermonters have refused the intrusiveness of federal aid for local projects.

Over time, as more outsiders made their way into the state, many Vermonters dug in their heels and mounted defenses against whatever changes the outsiders might bring. They hugged more tightly a local identity rooted in traditional values. As Vermont hosted more foreign-language immigrants in the late nineteenth century, for example, Ferrisburg author Rowland E. Robinson memorialized Vermont's original dialects in his short stories. As Vermont's youth departed the state for better economic opportunities, towns put their histories on paper and hosted "Old Home" Weeks, reminding their departed sons and daughters of the rich Vermont heritage they had left behind. The result was that Vermonters gained a greater fondness for those things that signify old Vermont.

The idea of "Old Vermont" lives on, particularly in the state's tourism and marketing. Vermont-made food products such as maple syrup and handmade breads, covered bridges, and refurbished round barns have become the language for marketing the state. It is one of the ironies of old Vermont that today the state's heritage survives largely to satisfy the appetites of the outsiders who visit. Another is that changes to the state have indeed been wrought by the flatlanders, particularly in recent decades. It is the business of history to record such changes, leaving to posterity to sift the evidence for what may have been gained and what lost.

—Ginger Gellman

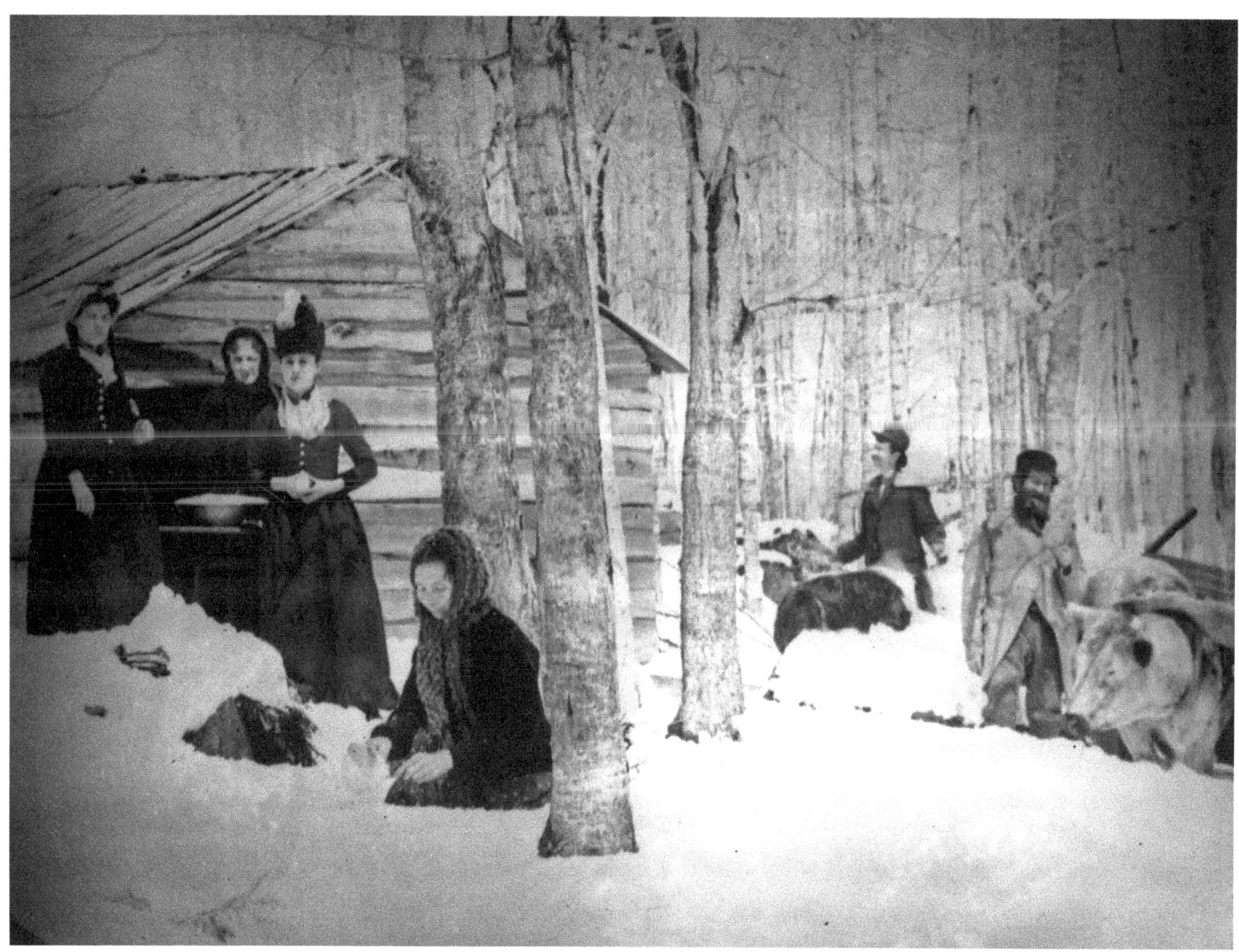

The Bentley family returns to the sugarhouse with sap from the family property in Jericho. At right, one relative dons his snowshoes and shoulder neck yoke, while another leads a team of oxen that are drawing a bobsled loaded with the sap tank. At left, the Bentley women prepare sugar-on-snow. Vermont's maple sugaring tradition dates back to the Abenaki Indians. As early as 1890, the state led the nation in syrup production.

Old Yankee Country

(1860–1899)

Prototypical of Vermont communities in the nineteenth century, Moretown aptly illustrates the successes and challenges faced by many Vermont towns. Like other communities around the state, Moretown enjoyed population gains of 50 percent and higher in the decades following the Revolutionary War and Vermont's statehood in 1791. By 1830, the community was home to six carpenters, two millers, five wheelwrights, three shoemakers, six blacksmiths, two coopers, a physician, a jeweler, and two ministers. Farmers composed much of the remaining population, and agriculture was the mainstay of daily living. Farmers used their surpluses to barter in town for cloth, spices, wagon wheels, or perhaps a new clock. Like many Vermont towns, Moretown became a success story in self-sufficiency, but was also subject to repeated challenges to that success.

During the nineteenth century, agriculture remained the economic core of Moretown and other communities. Farmers began the century harvesting wheat, then grazed sheep, and finally turned to dairy farming in the post–Civil War era. Most protected their financial welfare by diversifying into maple sugar, apples, or potatoes. Some communities sought out other ways to sustain themselves. A good number found success in lumbering, mining, manufacturing, and commerce. None of these ventures was hazard-proof.

For Vermonters, the nineteenth century was a search for the best ways to earn a living—and given the promise of wealth farther west, many native-born sons chose to seek their fortunes elsewhere. As early as the 1820s, some Vermonters were packing up their belongings and heading west in search of better opportunities. Young people were most apt to leave. By 1850, nearly half the people born in Vermont lived someplace else. By 1900, it had become an old local adage among Vermonters that the state's "best exports" were its children.

How the residents who remained tackled economic challenges is a happier thread in the narrative. One welcome consequence of their determination was a growing sense of community pride, which led to newly written town histories, community-funded military bands, book clubs, social organizations, opera houses, and athletic clubs. These activities replenished the void left by economic and demographic instability and served to create an "idea" of community that bound residents together during hard times.

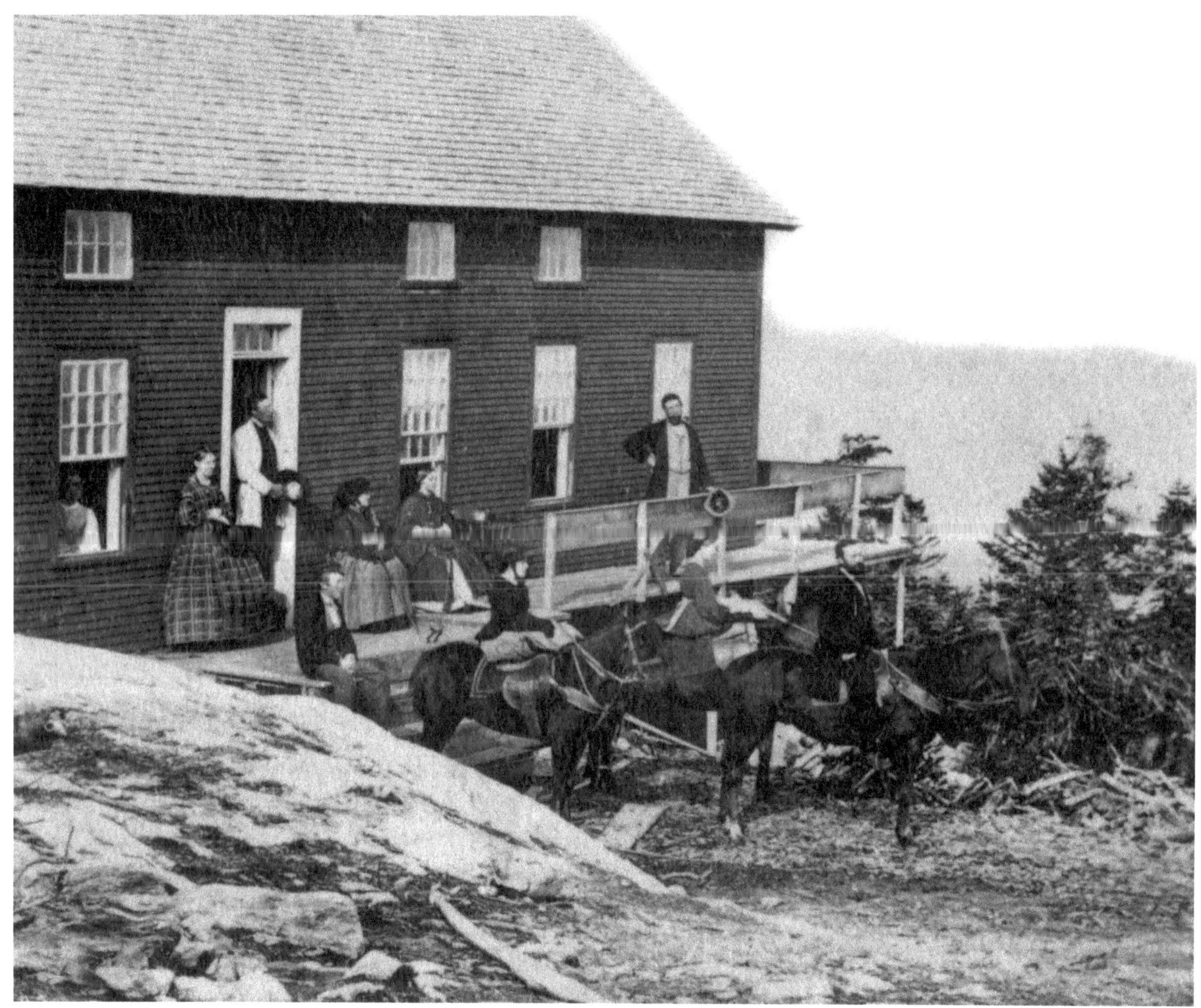

A group at the Summit House on Mount Mansfield, 1865. Mount Mansfield attracted business as a resort destination as early as the 1850s. A carriage road was built in 1853, and the Summit House, a "posh mountain hotel" situated just below the Nose, opened in 1858. A year later, the hotel owner sold the surrounding land to the University of Vermont—ostensibly to preserve a wilderness that helped attract out-of-state visitors.

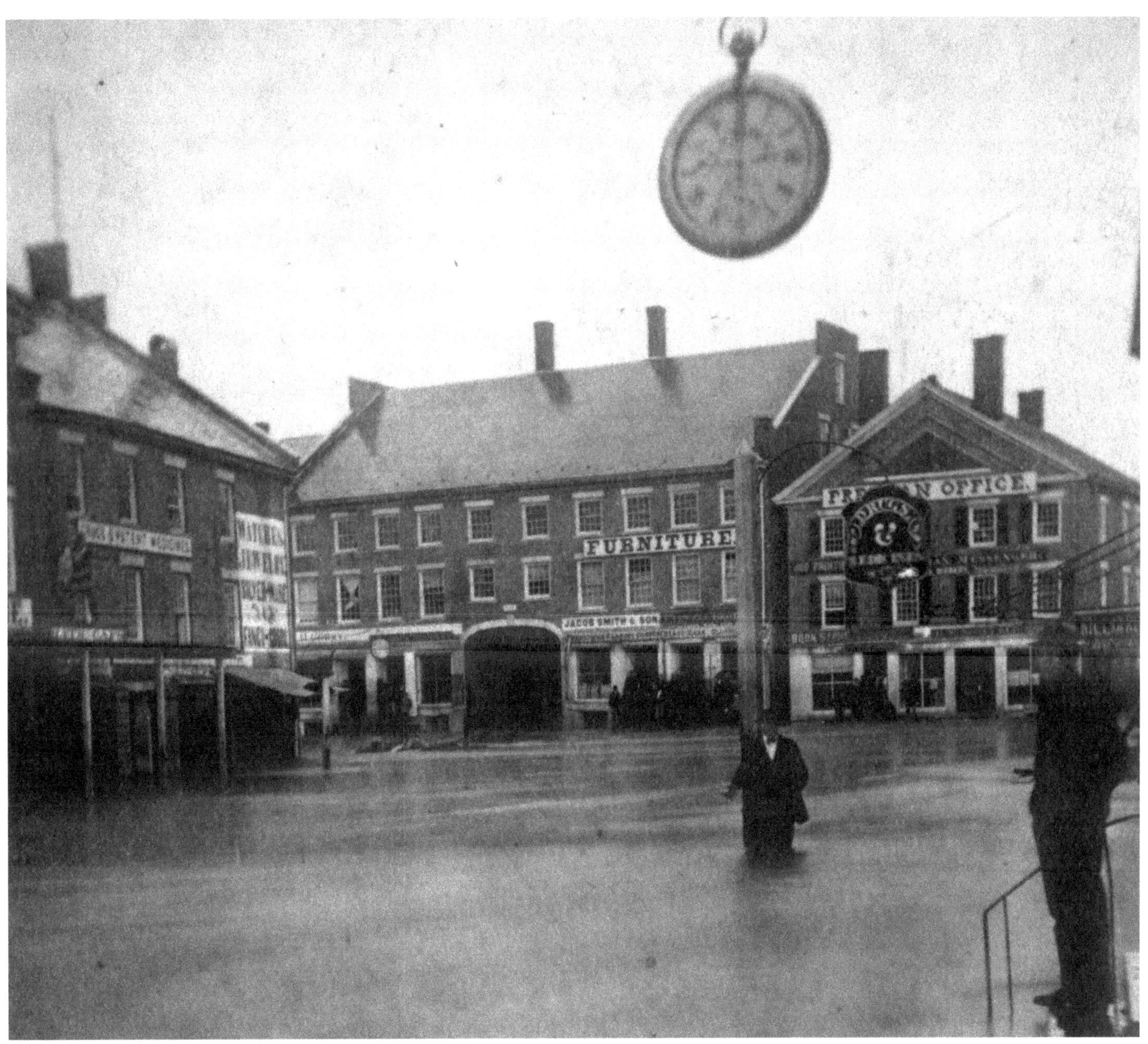

In Montpelier, residents regularly expected the Winooski River to reach its banks, and it frequently did, often overflowing. Among the town's many deluges were an 1810 flood (when Main and State streets were submerged), another in 1828 (when two bridges and a barn were swept away), and one in 1830 (when water flowed up to the lower windows along State Street). This photograph depicts an 1860 flood, when water reportedly ran four feet deep in the street.

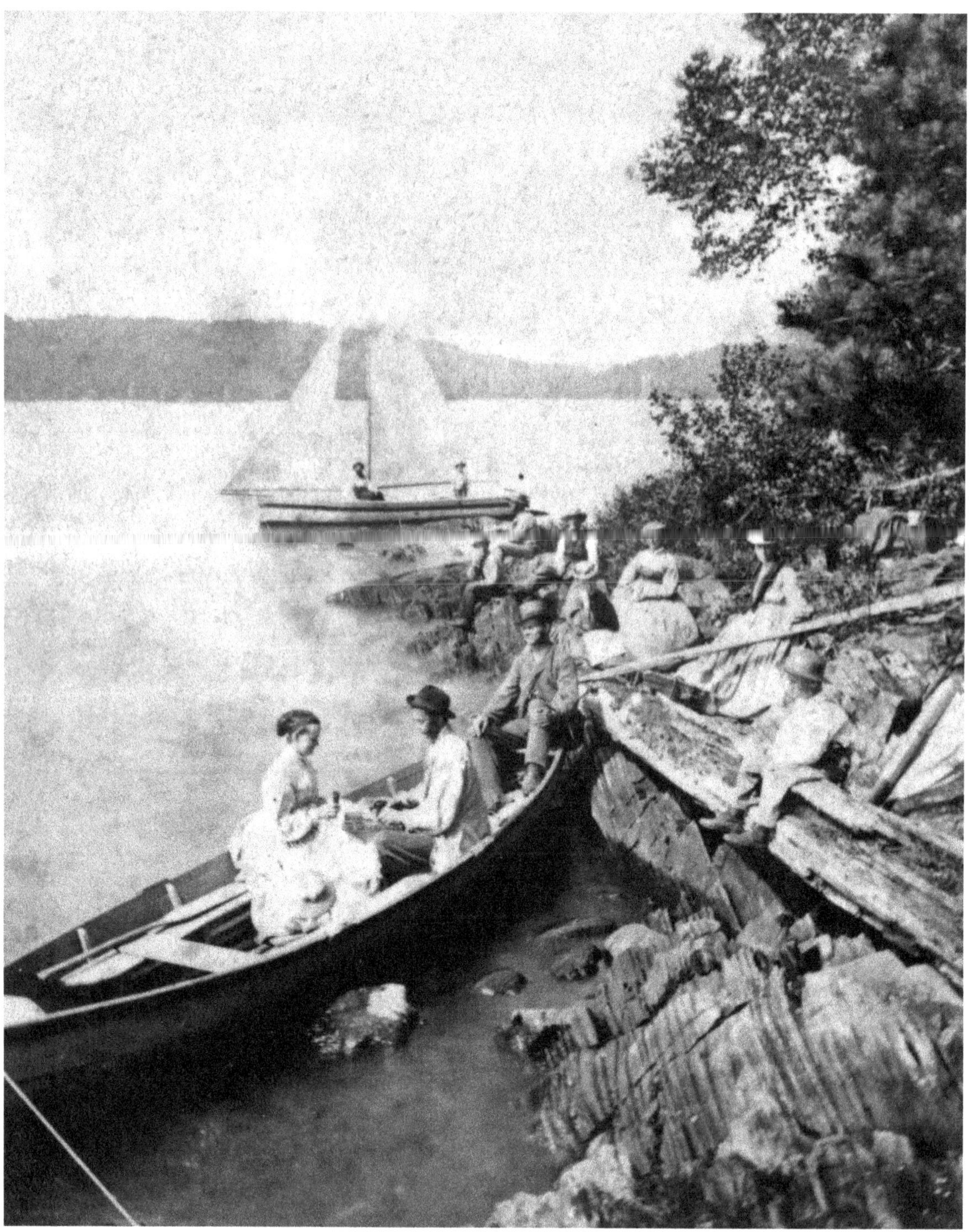

A camping party rests on Lake Memphremagog's Long Island in 1865. One of 15 islands on the Canadian side of the border, Long Island was a favorite resort area, particularly during blueberry season. A guidebook of the era advised female visitors not to dress "in a gorgeous way" when coming to the region to hike or boat, since "the worse you attire, the better you'll feel."

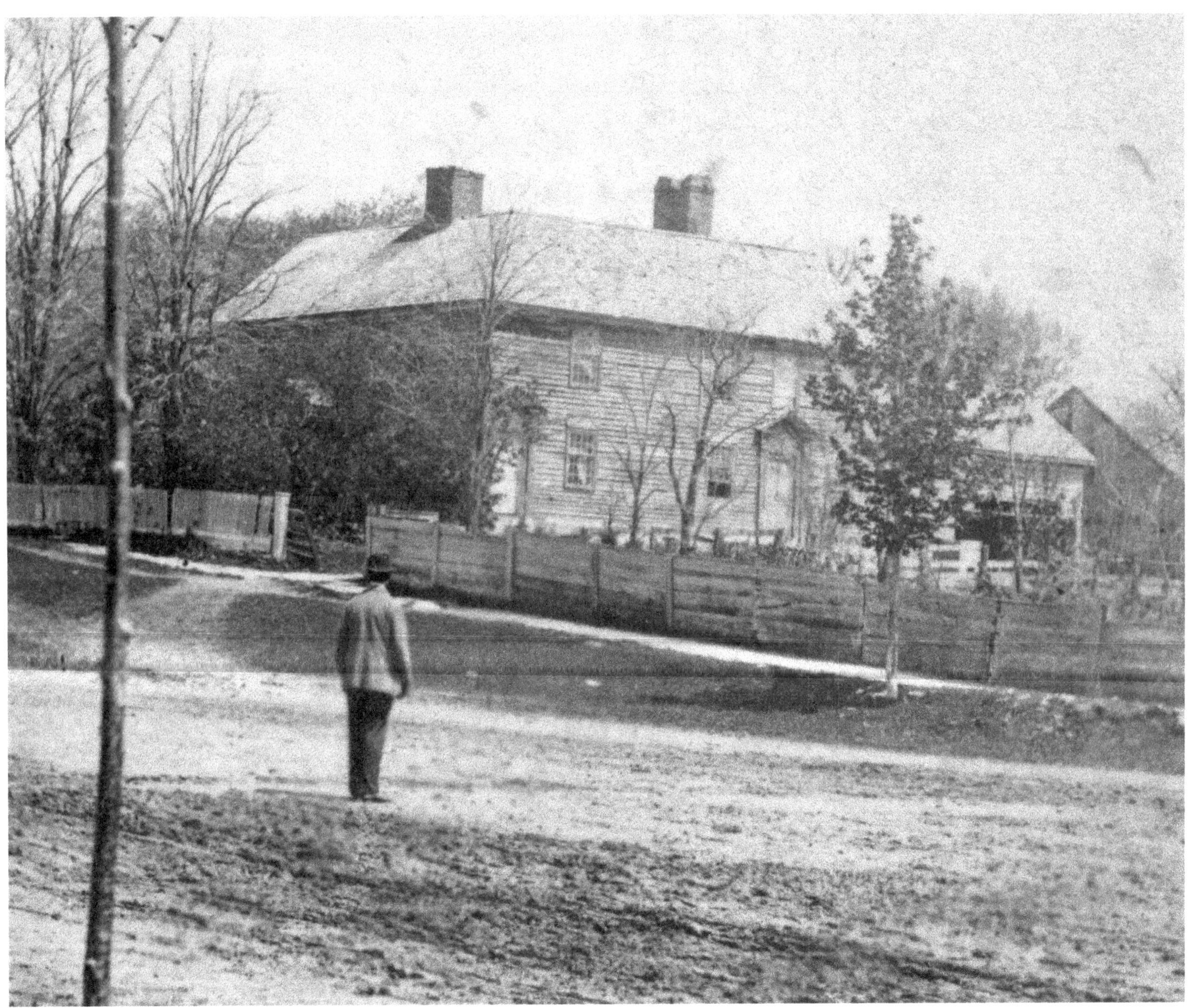

Catamount Tavern, Bennington. Built in the late 1760s, the Catamount Tavern was the perennial meeting place of Ethan Allen and the Green Mountain Boys, a group of Revolution-era vigilante settlers who chased the "Yorkers" from Vermont lands. The tavern continued to operate until it burned in 1871. Six years later, Bennington residents unveiled a design for another tribute to the Revolution: the Bennington Monument, which would stand just up the hill from the old tavern.

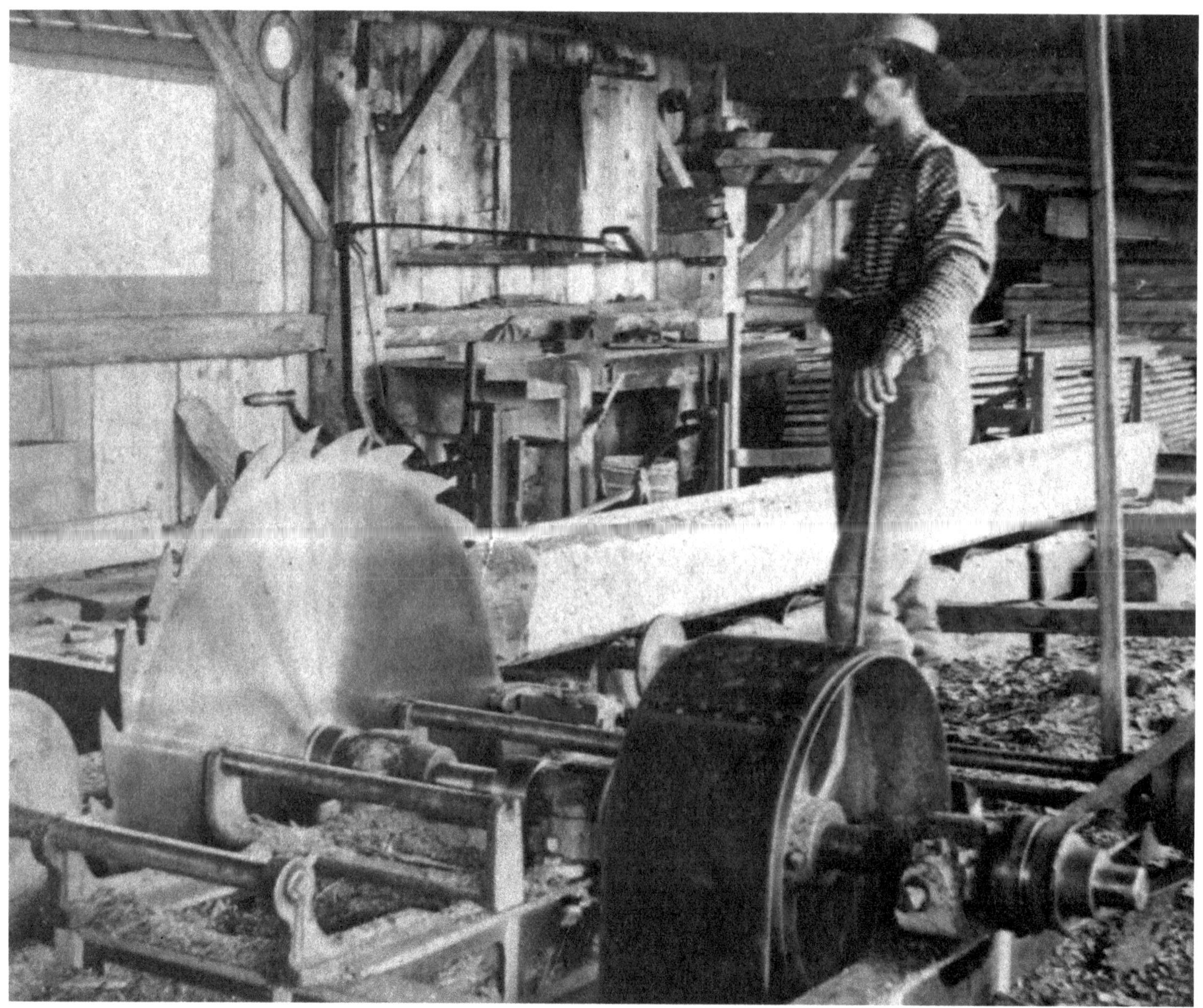

Water-powered sawmills made good business in Vermont throughout the nineteenth century. Logging became Vermont's largest nonagricultural industry by the 1820s, capitalizing on the native timber felled for new settlements. By the 1840s, much of Vermont's timber had been cut, leaving behind a bare countryside. Vermont's sawmills were once again in use by the 1850s—but this time with timber imported from Canada by way of the Richelieu River and Lake Champlain.

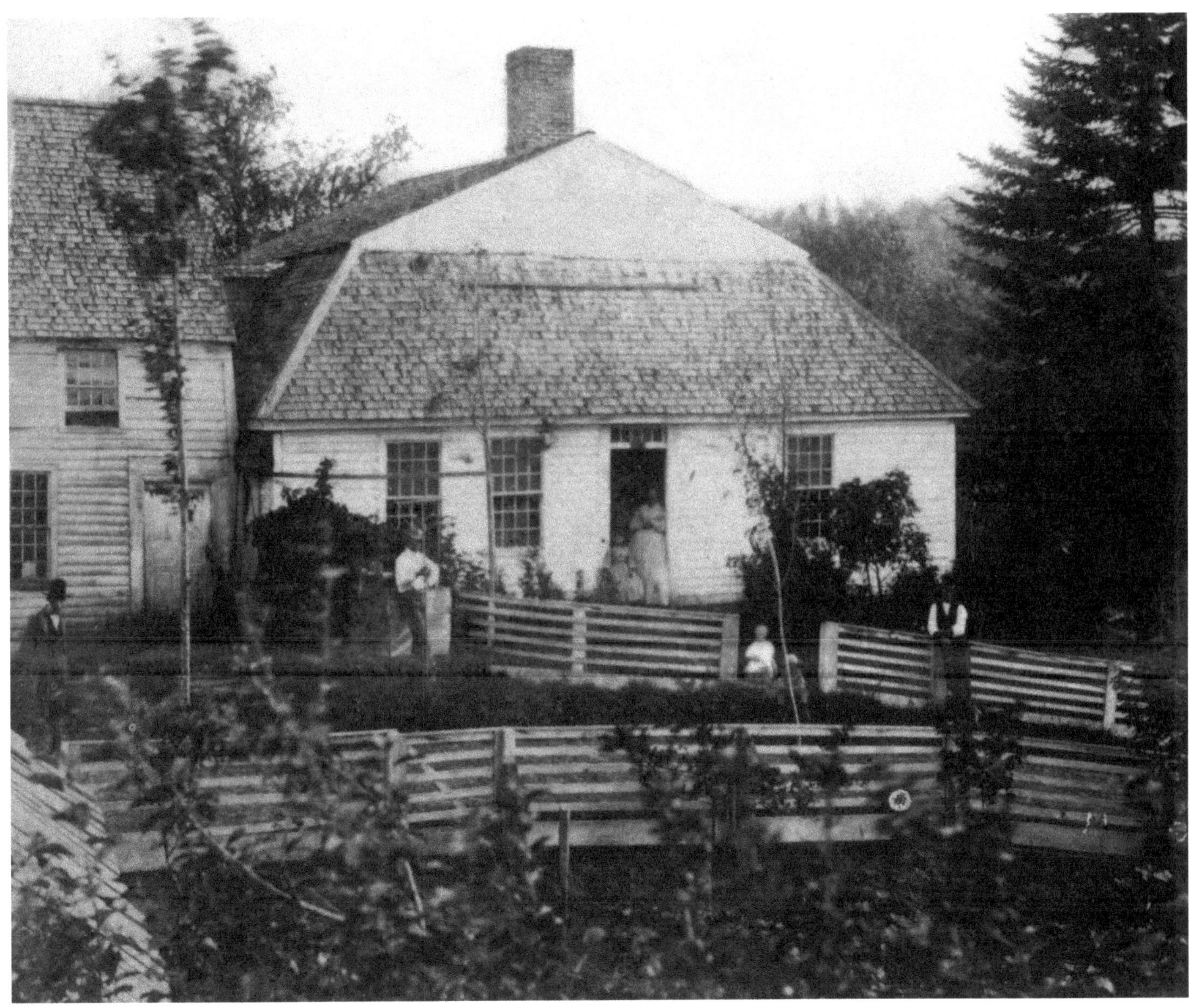

Hiram Powers, sculptor of the famed *Greek Slave,* which was displayed at London's Crystal Palace, was born in 1805 on this Woodstock farm. When Hiram was 13, his family lost their home, suffered crop failure and famine, and headed for Ohio. The experience of the Powers family mirrors a statewide trend, in which native-born sons left the state to find opportunities farther west. Vermonters struggled with population drift throughout the century.

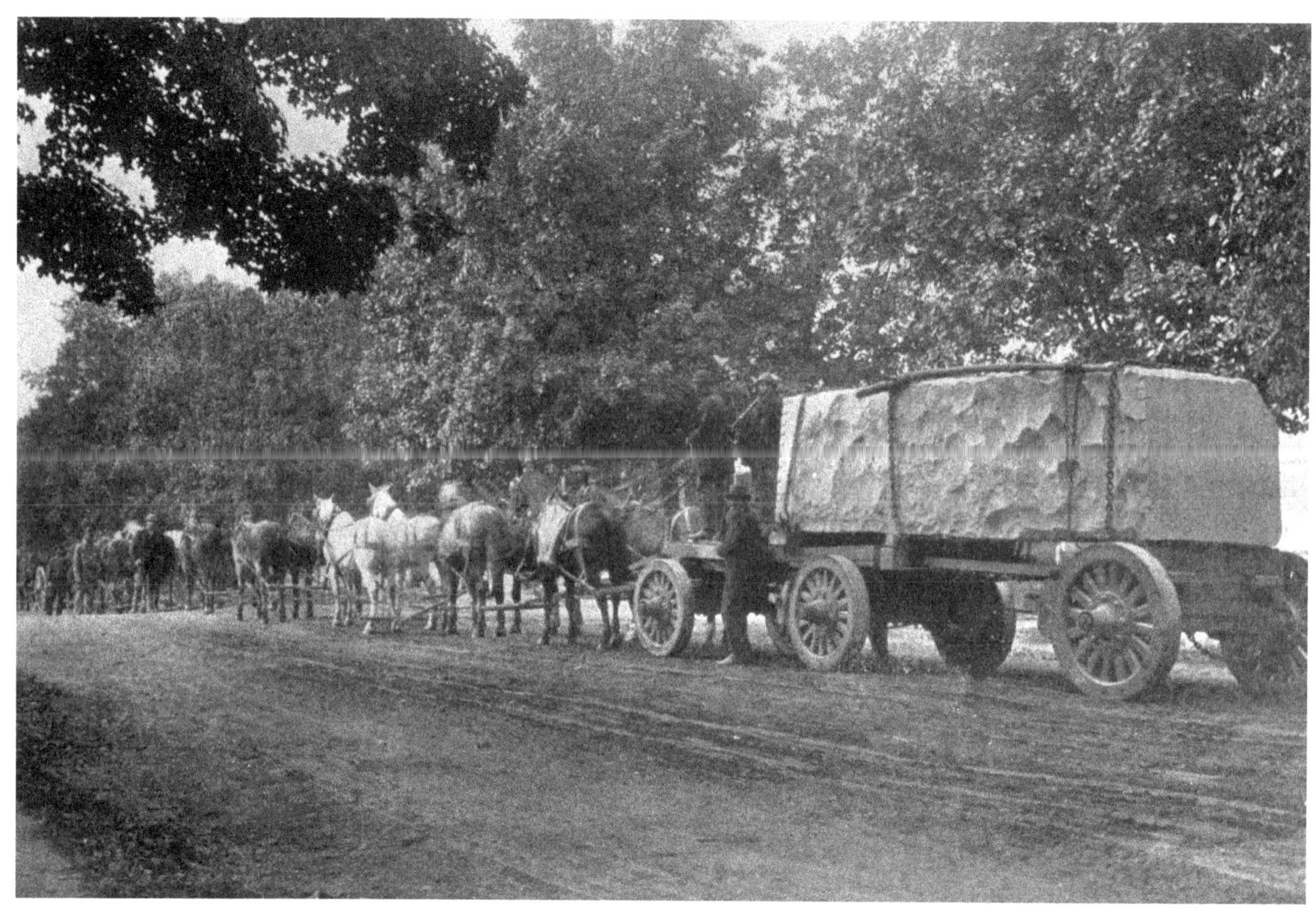

Stonecutters in Barre prepare an enormous block of stone for transport. Before the advent of Vermont railroads, quarries in Massachusetts and Maine had a competitive advantage owing to their access to low-cost coastal water transportation. The granite industry was fraught with dangers for quarrymen, who blasted out and moved these large stones. Silica dust posed the greatest danger. When inhaled by stonecutters, the dust caused lung damage known as "Stonecutters TB."

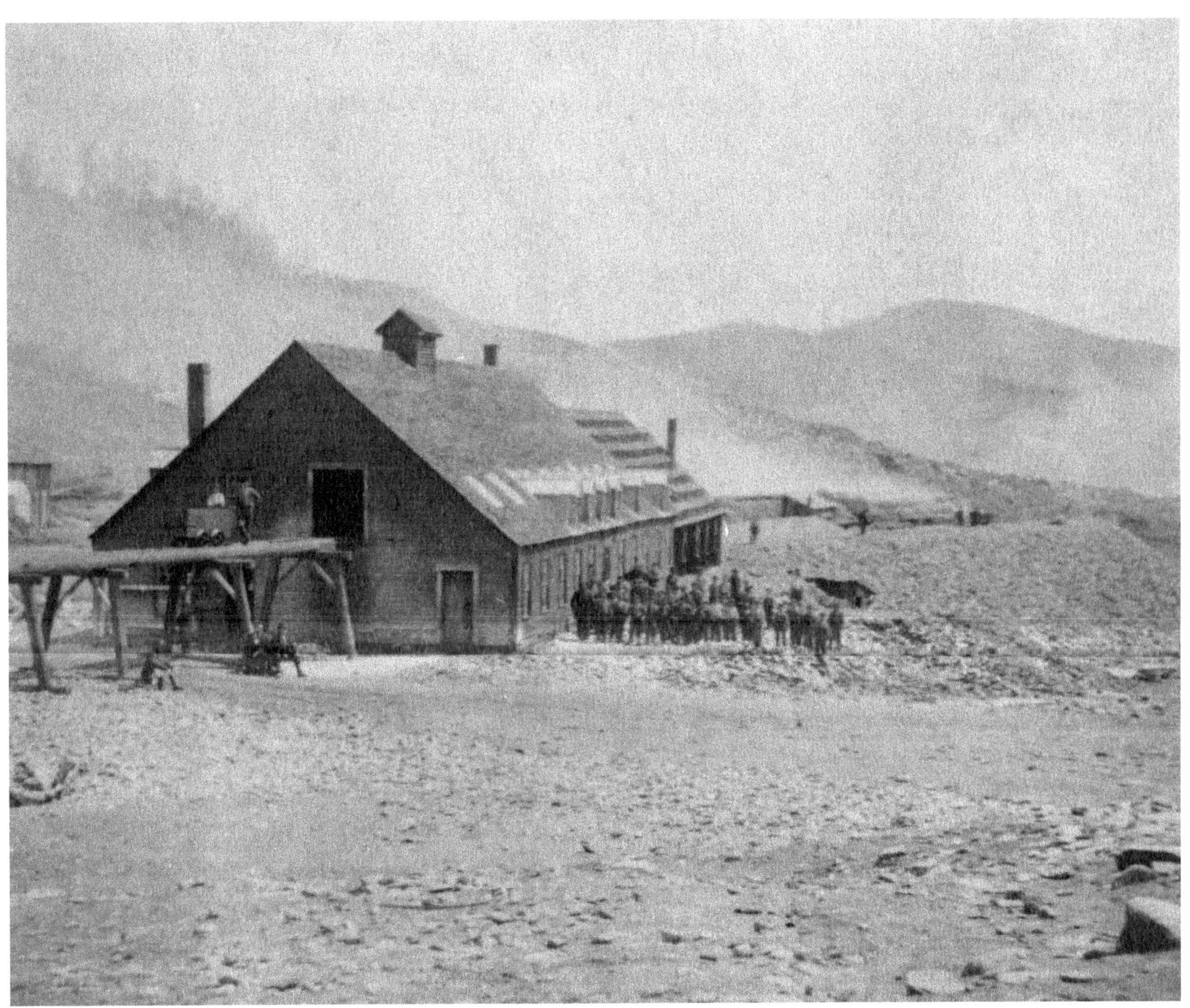

The washhouse at the Vermont Copper Mines, Vershire. After a yearlong delay in paying workers, this indebted mine closed in 1883. The miners, incensed that the company had not paid their overdue wages, invaded the village in protest. The town doctor observed that "these—Irishmen" would blow up and "destroy every dollar's worth of property" if they did not receive their money, but he also condemned the company's actions.

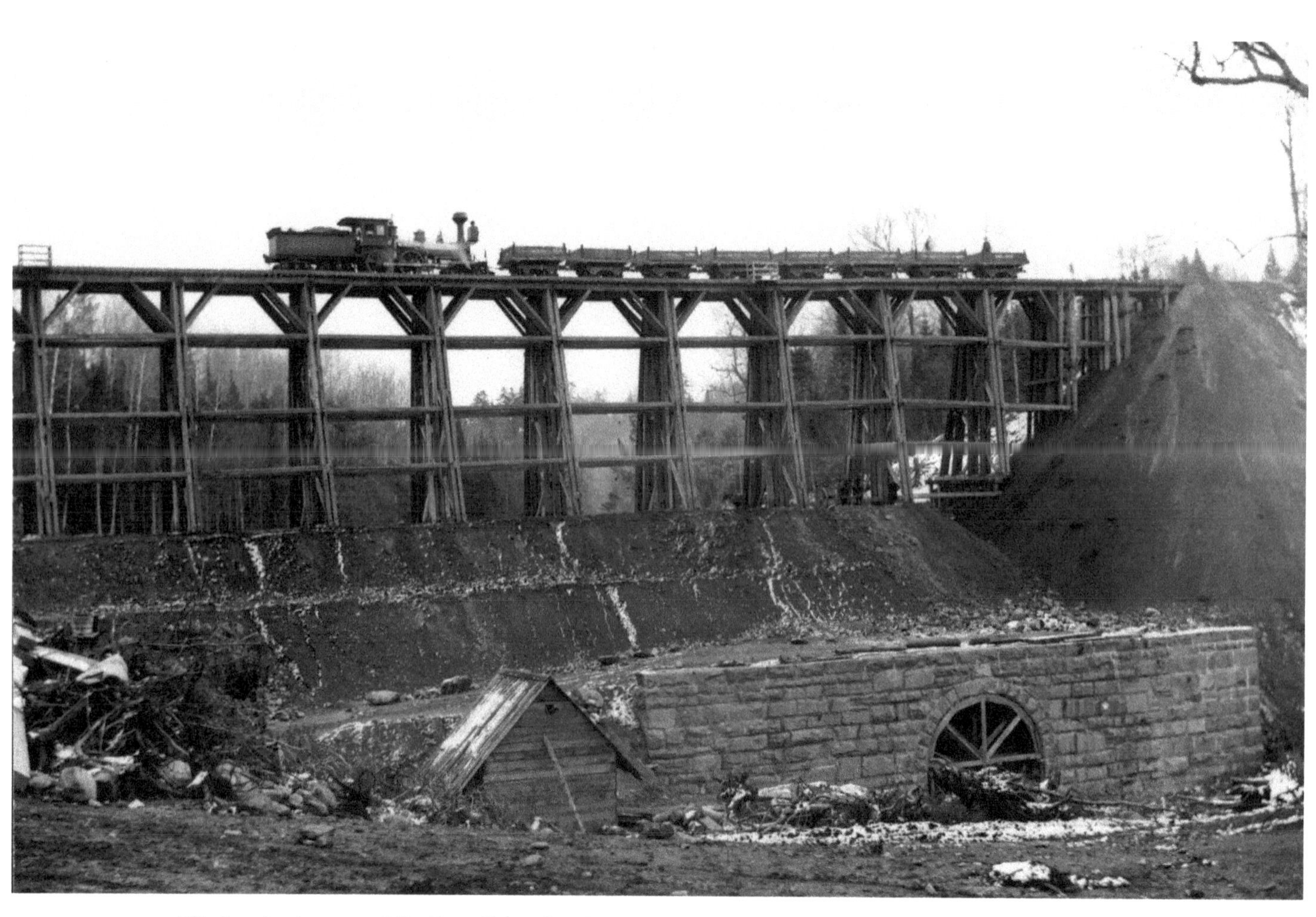

Workers broke ground for Danville's railroad in spring 1870, part of Horace Fairbanks' proposal for a railroad connecting Portland, Maine, with Ogdensburg, New York—and, eventually, with the Great Lakes. When the first engine reached Danville in September 1871, the newspaper reported that Danville was now "the end of the world" and that the town would enjoy "that exalted position during the whole night," until trackmen resumed extending the line come morning.

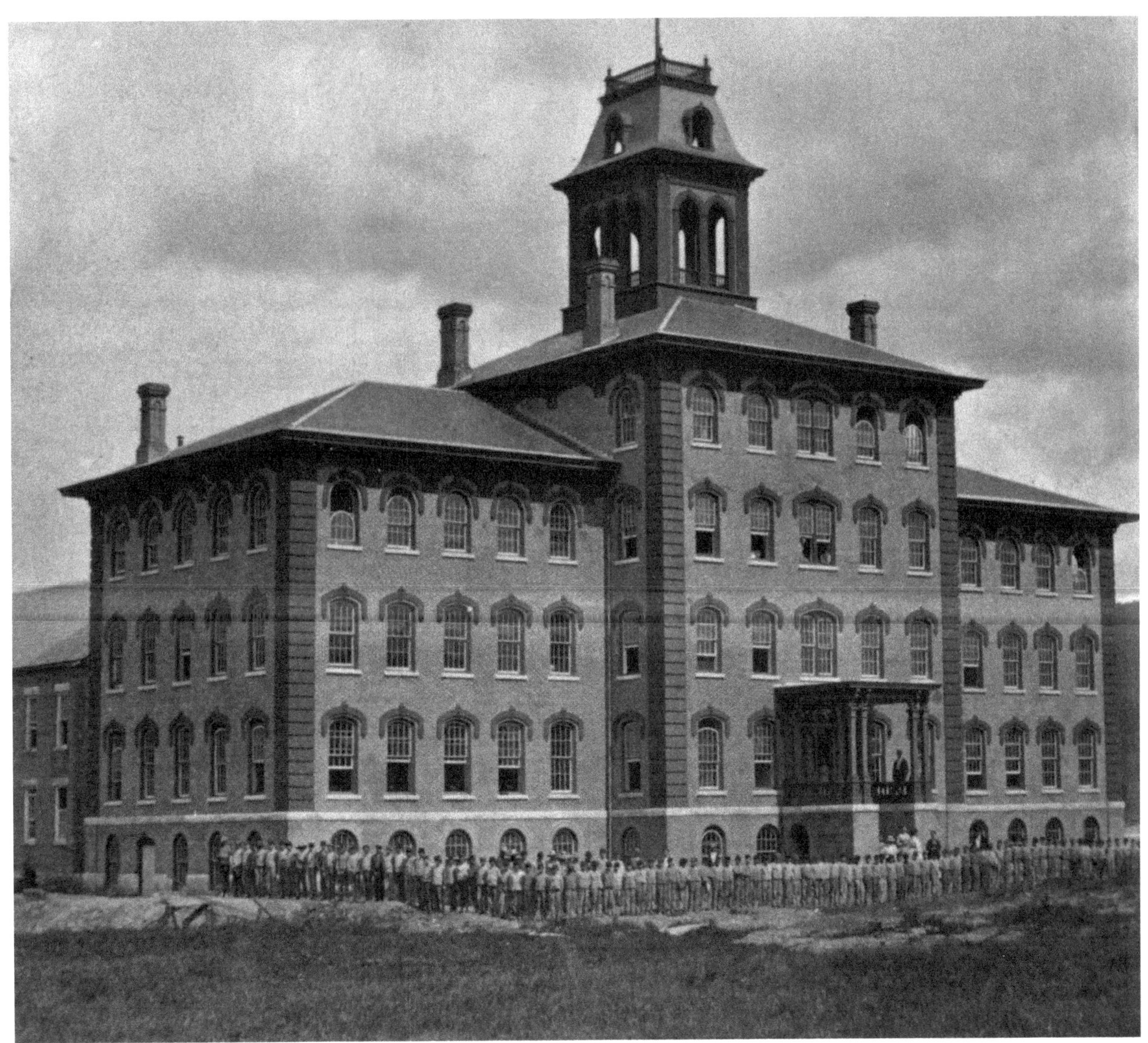

The State Reform School at Waterbury. When a committee selected a site for the state's first reform school, they hoped for a location where "the boys, wherever they are at work on the farm, are never out of sight or hearing." The Reform School in this photograph was built in 1871 at a cost of $50,000. The facility burned just three short years after it opened.

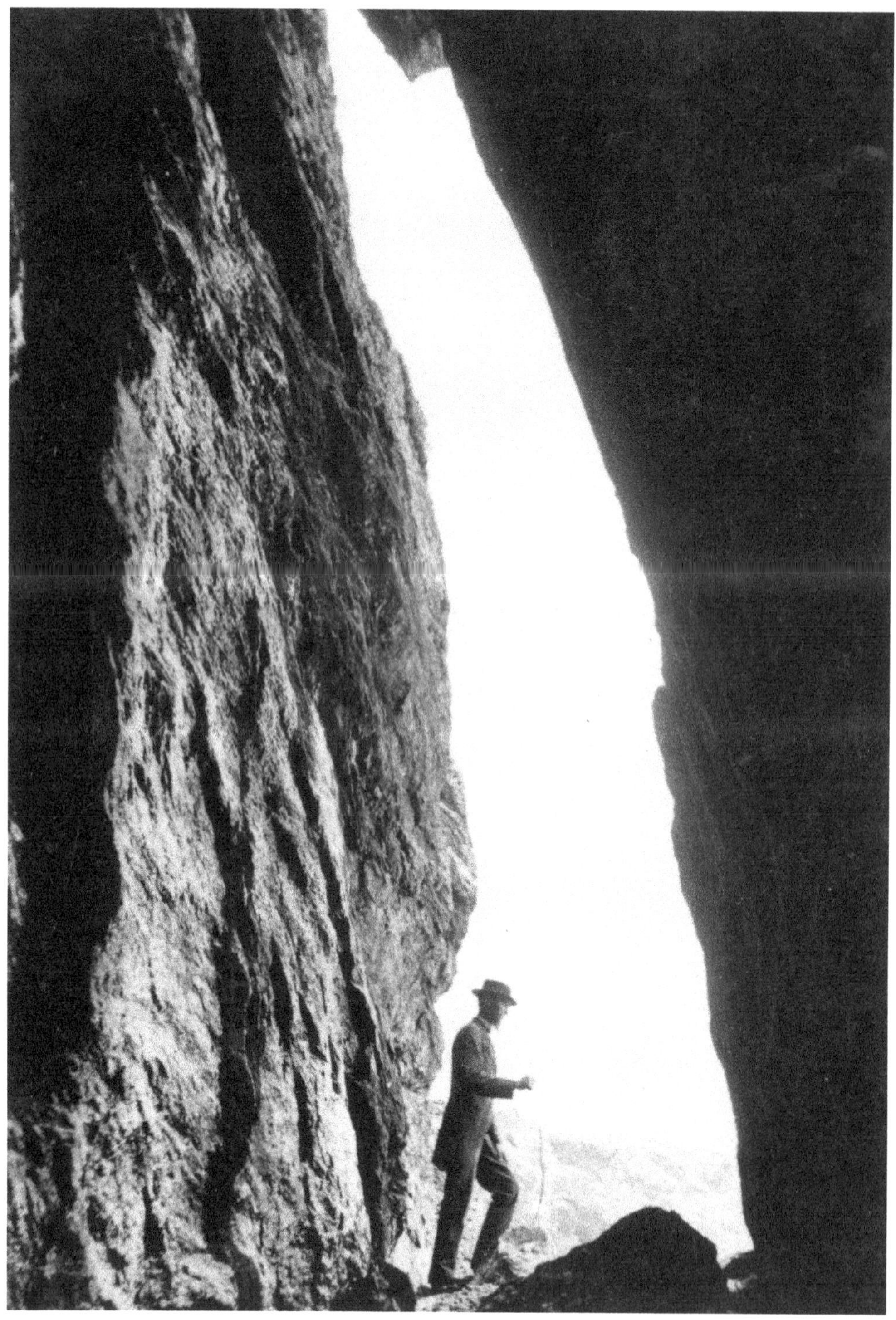

A view from Smuggler's Cave on Mount Mansfield, about 1875. Vermont towns competed vigorously for bragging rights throughout the nineteenth century. Peaks like Mount Mansfield became the stomping ground for their debates, with squabblers from different towns laying claim to the state's highest peak. In 1901, newspapers from three different towns claimed three different mountains to be Vermont's highest. The debate continued until 1924, when Mount Mansfield won official recognition.

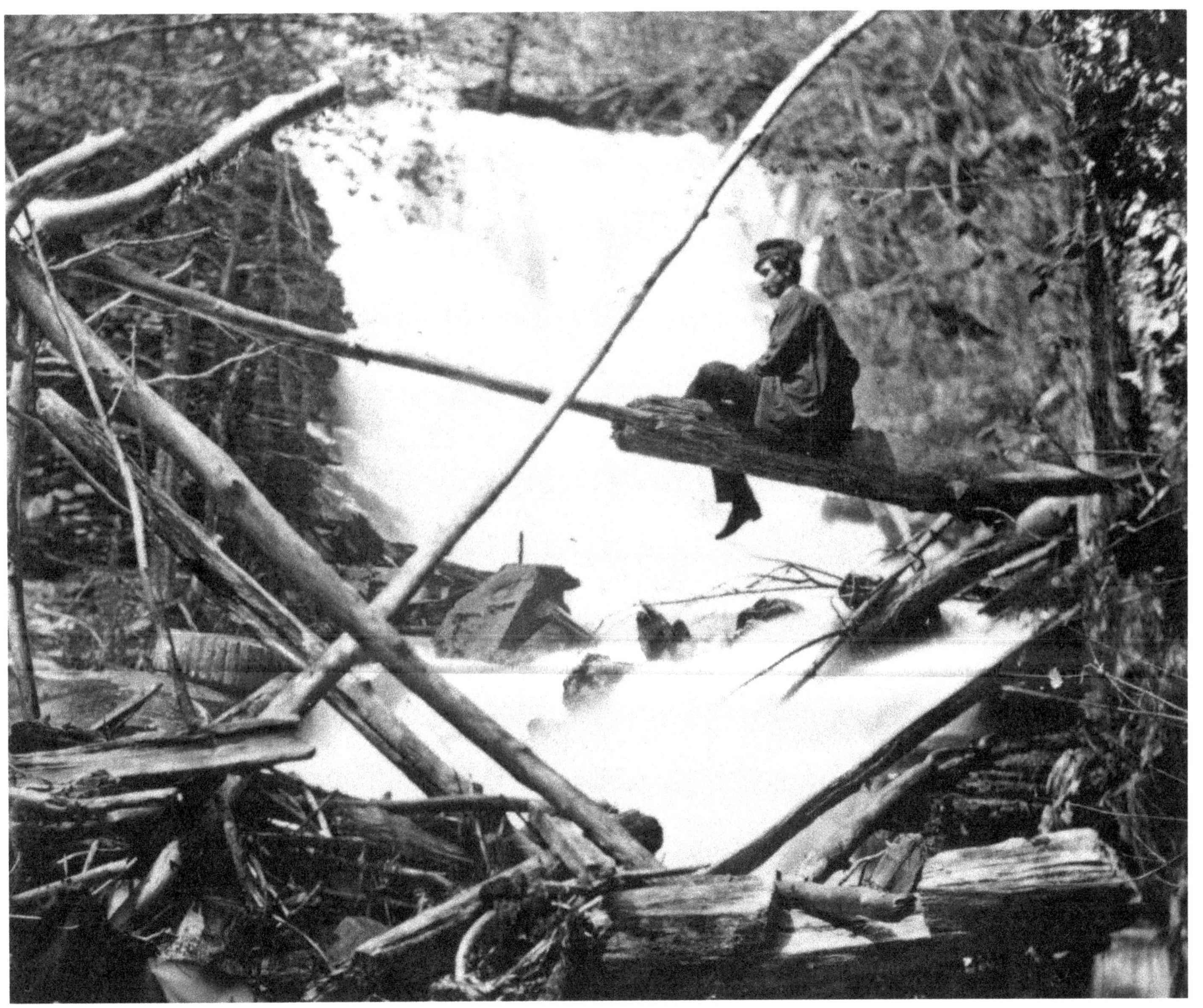

A view of the cascades at Berlin in 1875. This photograph shows the fragility of many Vermont businesses in the late nineteenth century. Now a site for daydreaming, this area below the falls was once home to a gristmill. A fallen beam and discarded millstone in the lower half of the photograph are evidence of the mill.

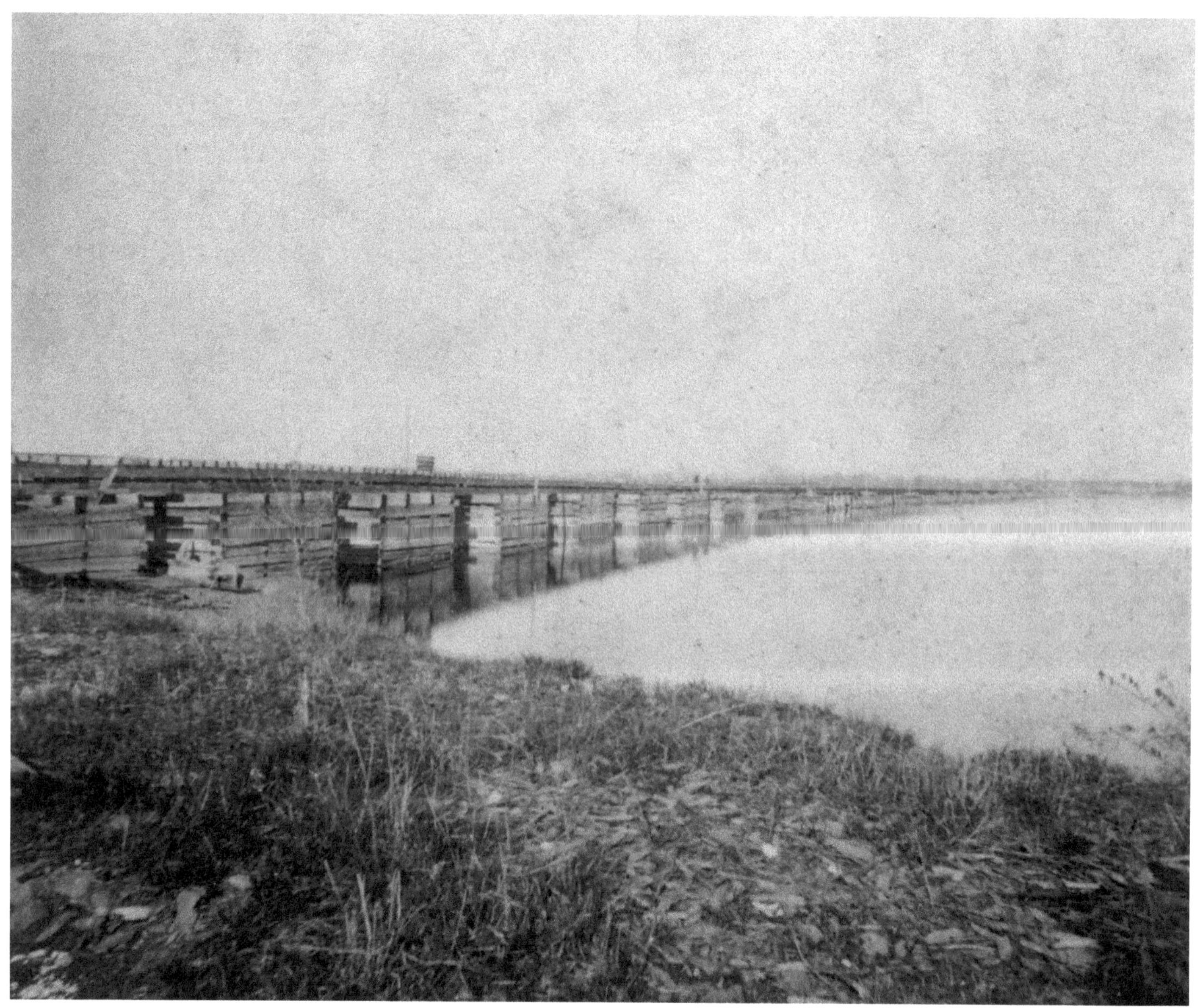

The East Alburgh railroad trestle. Built in 1850, this bridge crossed Lake Champlain from Swanton to Alburgh (then spelled Alburg). The wooden cribs in the photograph are filled with rocks and reach to the lake floor. The bridge included a floating "drawboat," a hinged arm that permitted boat traffic passage to and from Canada. The drawboat—approximately 70 feet in length—pulled aside to create an opening wide enough to accommodate the lake's large paddlewheel steamboats.

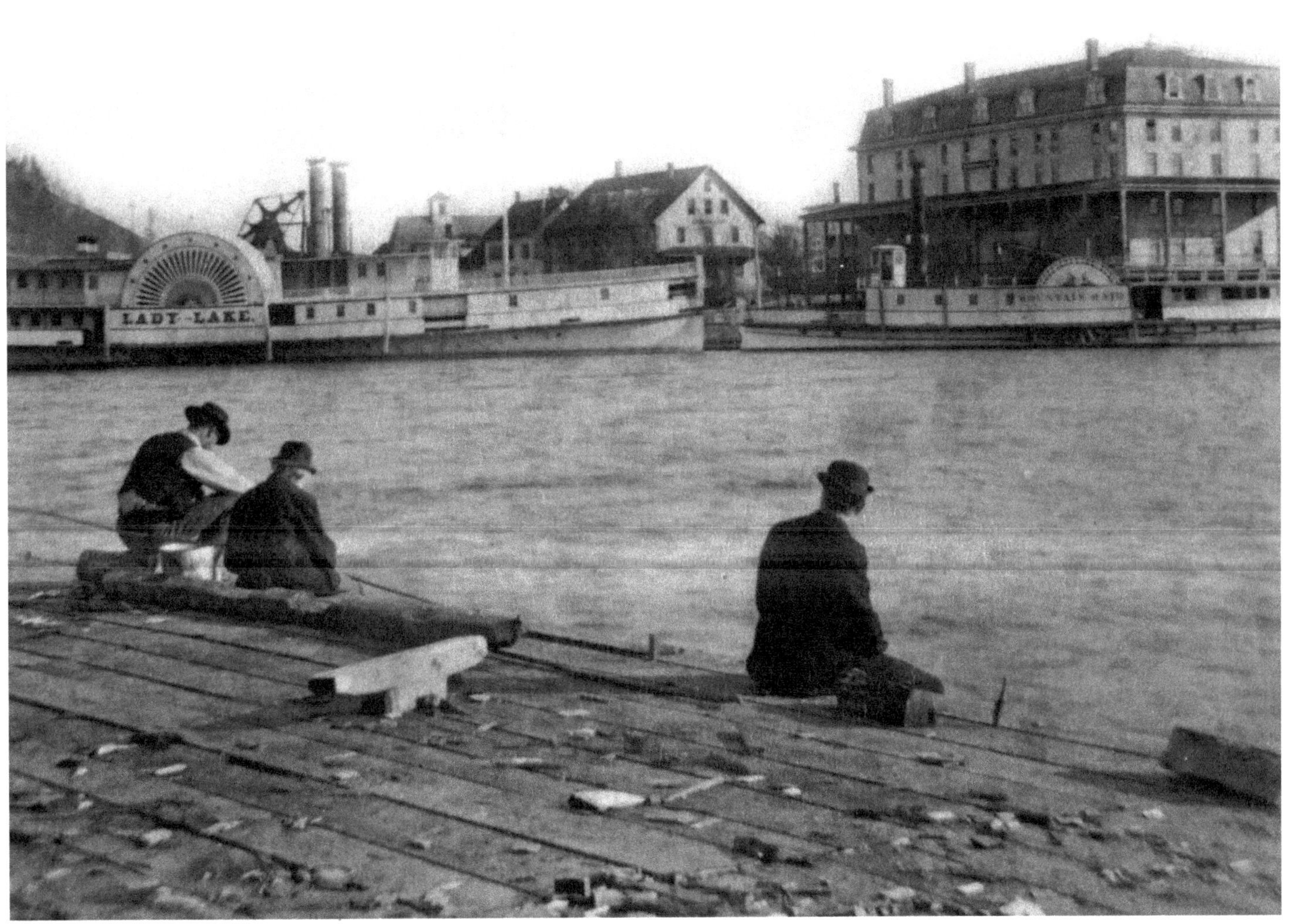

A view from the steamboat wharf on Lake Memphremagog, at Newport. Lake Memphremagog was a travelers' destination in the mid–nineteenth century. This image shows the Memphremagog House, built in 1838. Also visible are the steamboats *Lady Lake* (left) and *Mountain Maid* (right). *Mountain Maid* was the lake's first steamer. Its boiler arrived after a 24-day haul from Montreal.

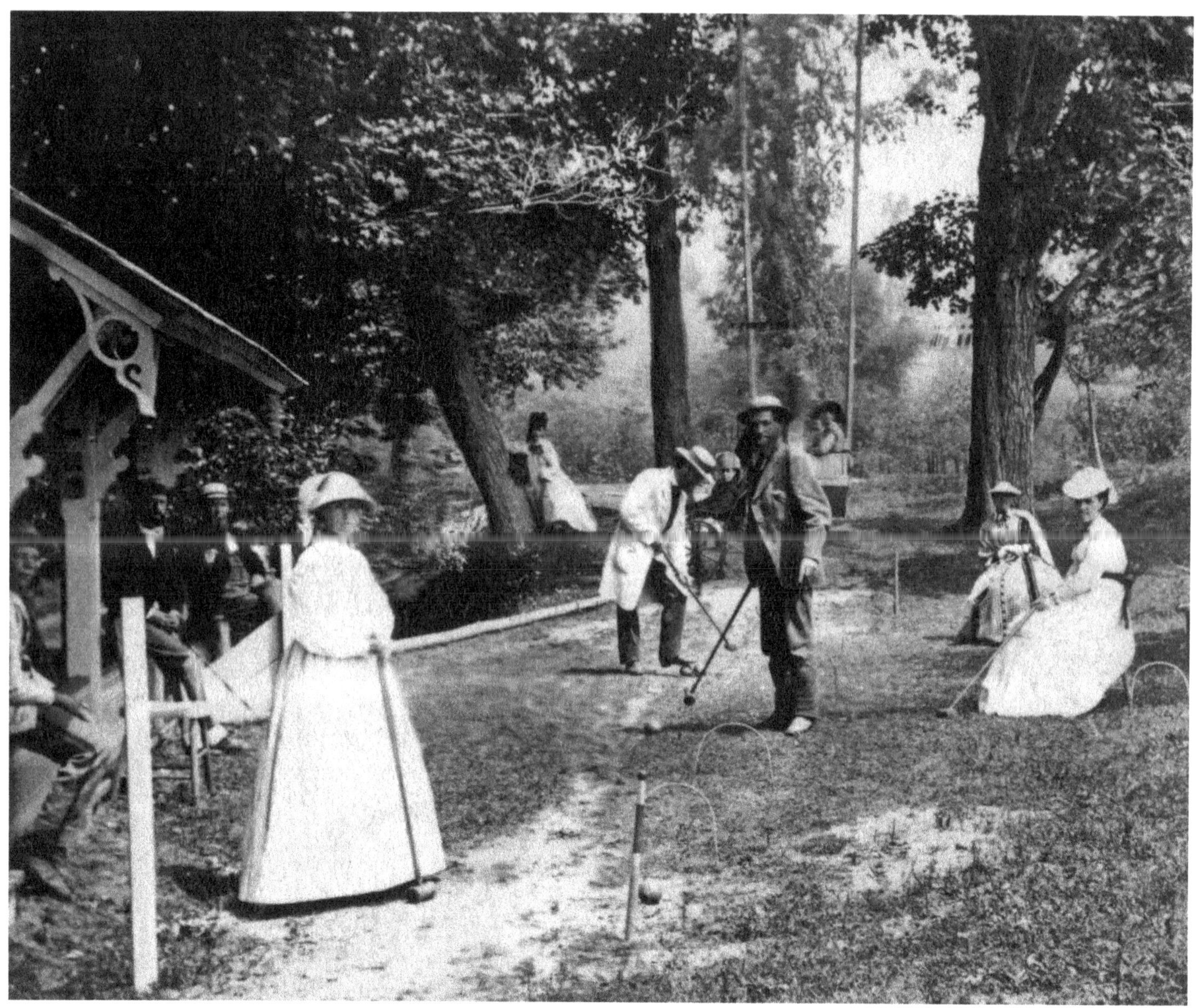

Playing croquet at Middletown Springs, 1875. People from the mid-Atlantic and southern states flocked to Vermont's elevated mountain air to visit spas and springs purporting to offer relief from various ailments. The Middletown Hotel Springs Company numbered its springs according to the illness that each claimed to cure: "No. 1" for piles, "No. 2" for asthma, and a drink from "No. 2 or 3," followed by a drink from "No. 1," for dyspepsia.

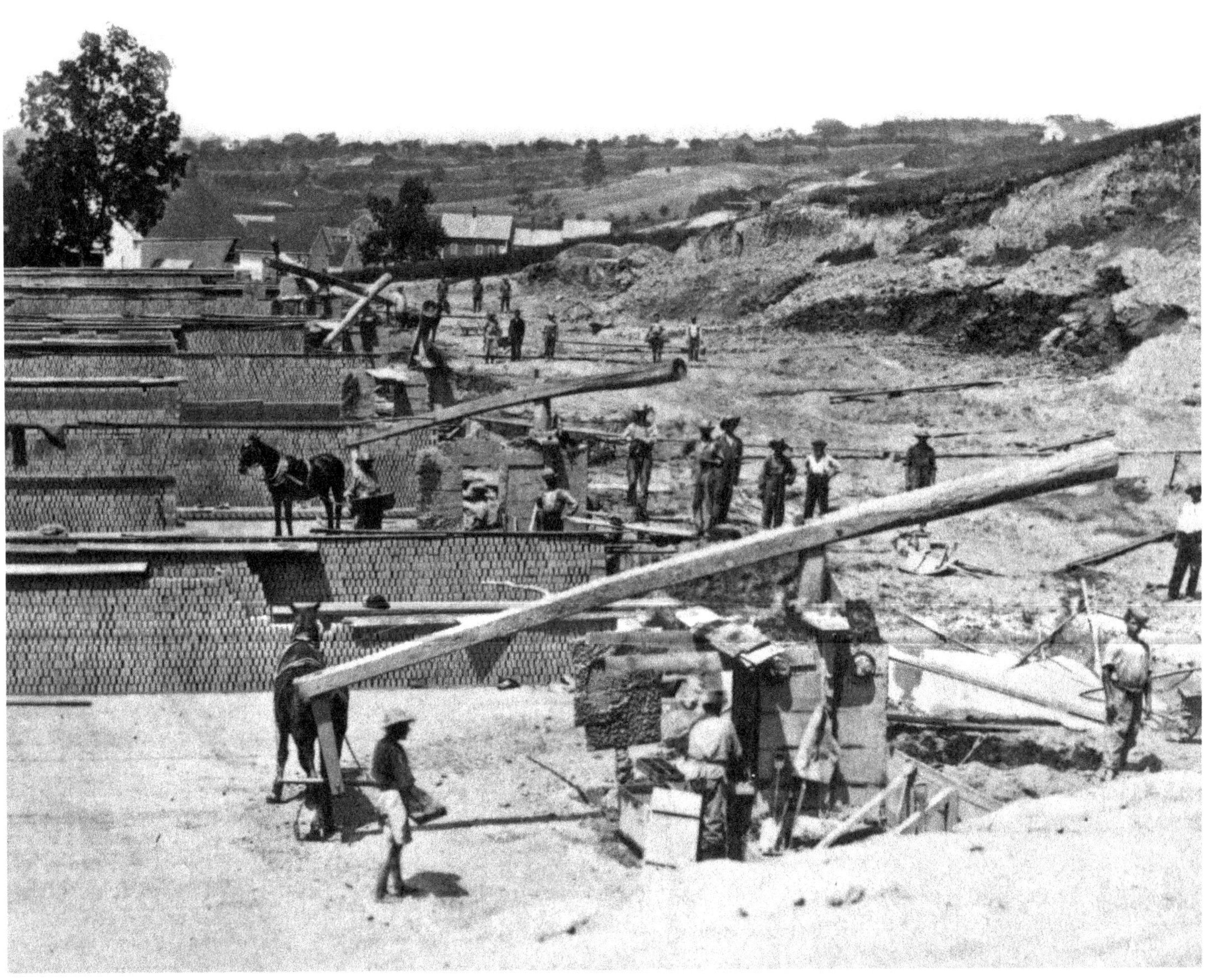

A nineteenth-century brickyard. The contraption in this photograph is a pug mill, also called a mud mill, used to temper newly harvested clay before molding it into bricks. The brick maker added clay and water to the mill and mixed it to achieve an even consistency. Smaller brick operations were less inclined to own pug mills; they did the same work by stomping on the mixture, much like crushing grapes when making wine.

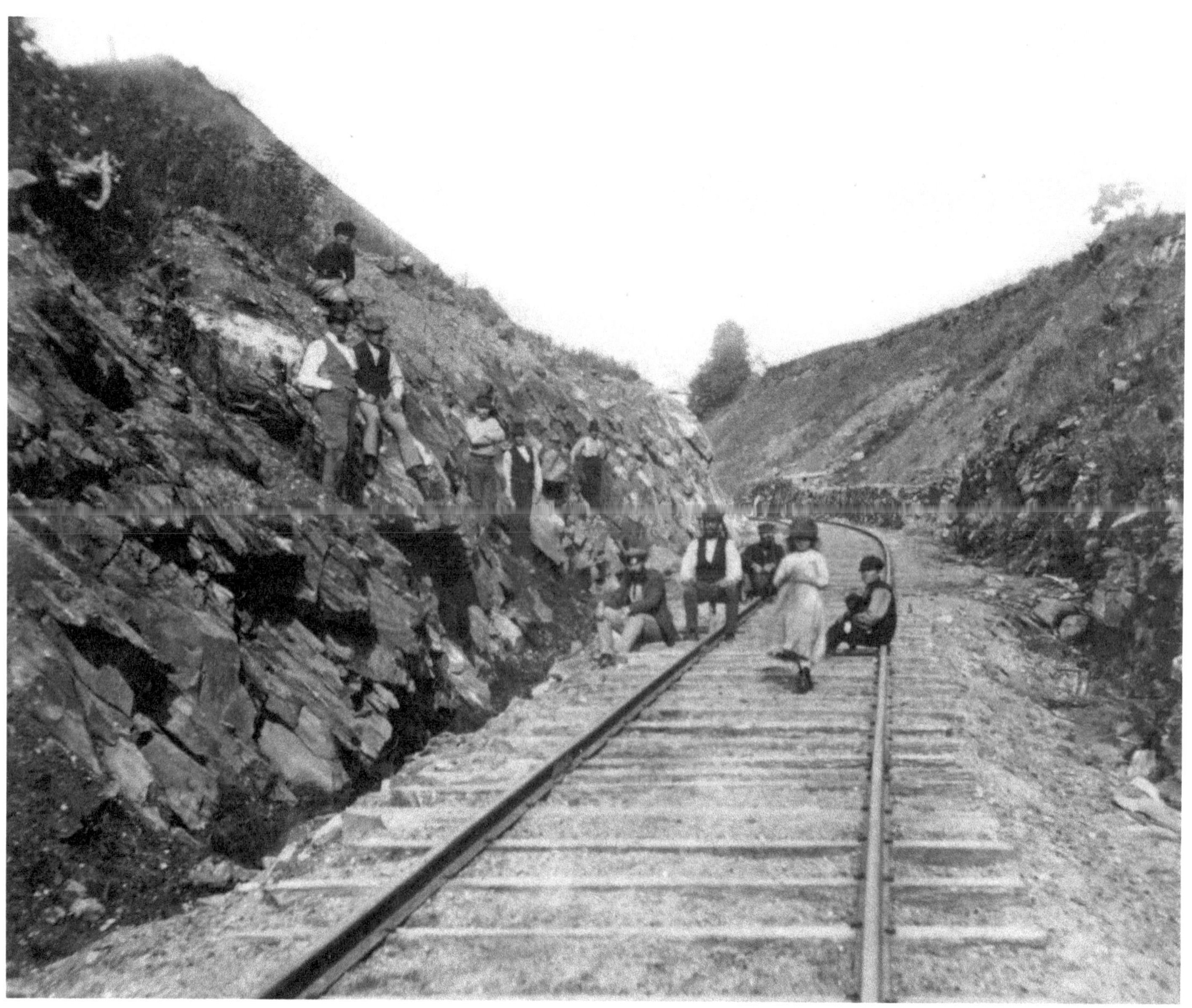

Railroad cut at Shallies Hill, Woodstock. The Woodstock Railway, a 14-mile track to White River Junction, was one of many spur lines connecting communities to the state's main rail routes. The railway drew an audience during construction—to watch a daredevil rail worker perform handstands on a pine tree 190 feet above the ground. Once completed, the tracks also provided a welcome walking trail for some of the local residents as they traveled to and from town.

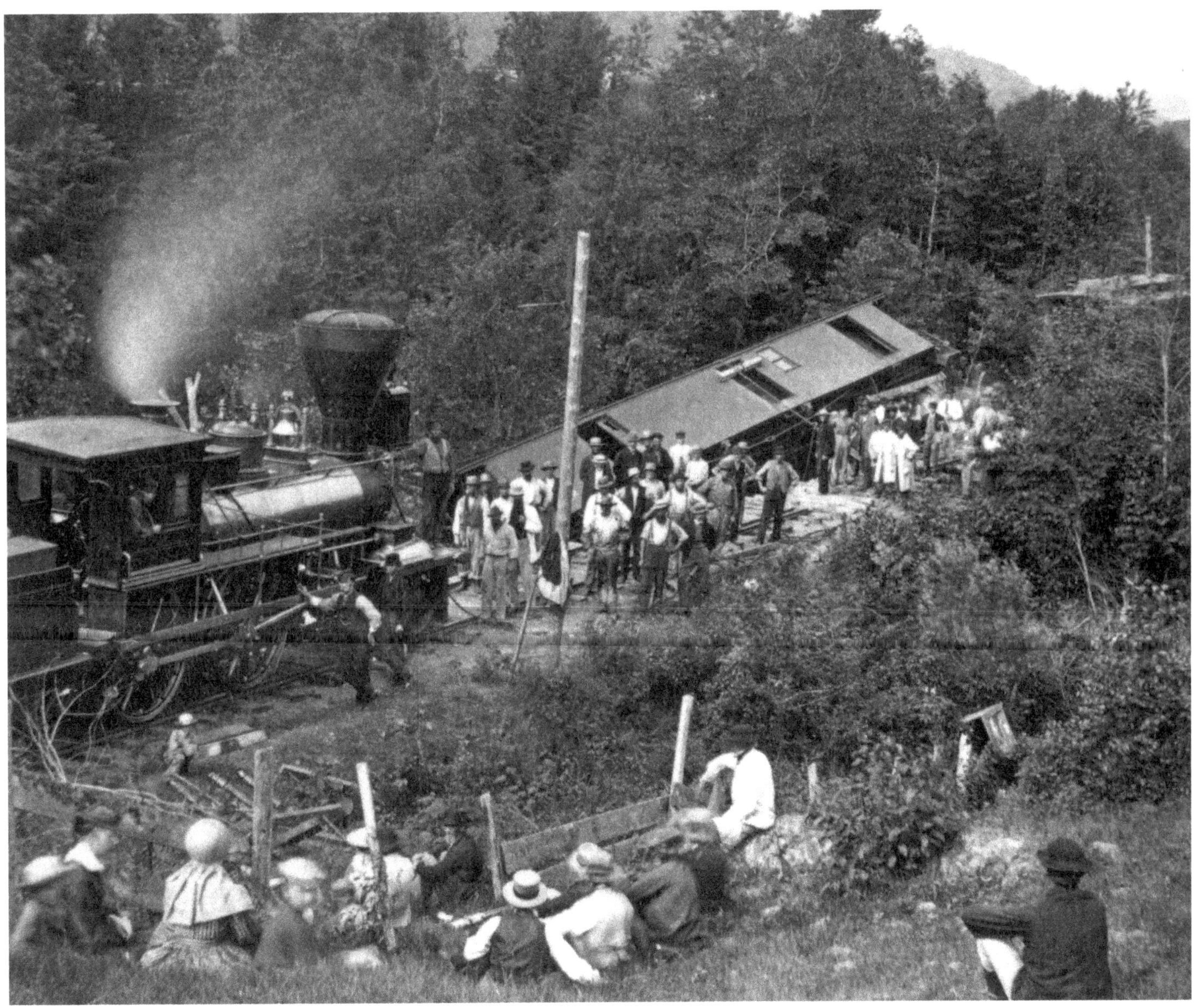

Train wreck near the village of Brockway Mills in Rockingham, 1869. When this locomotive derailed and nearly toppled off the 80-foot bridge, it was the second accident in a decade. Passengers crawled out of the rear cars, which lay precariously at the bridge's edge, fearing their weight would send the wreckage plummeting. In this photograph, spectators make bleachers of the nearby hill to watch the rescue.

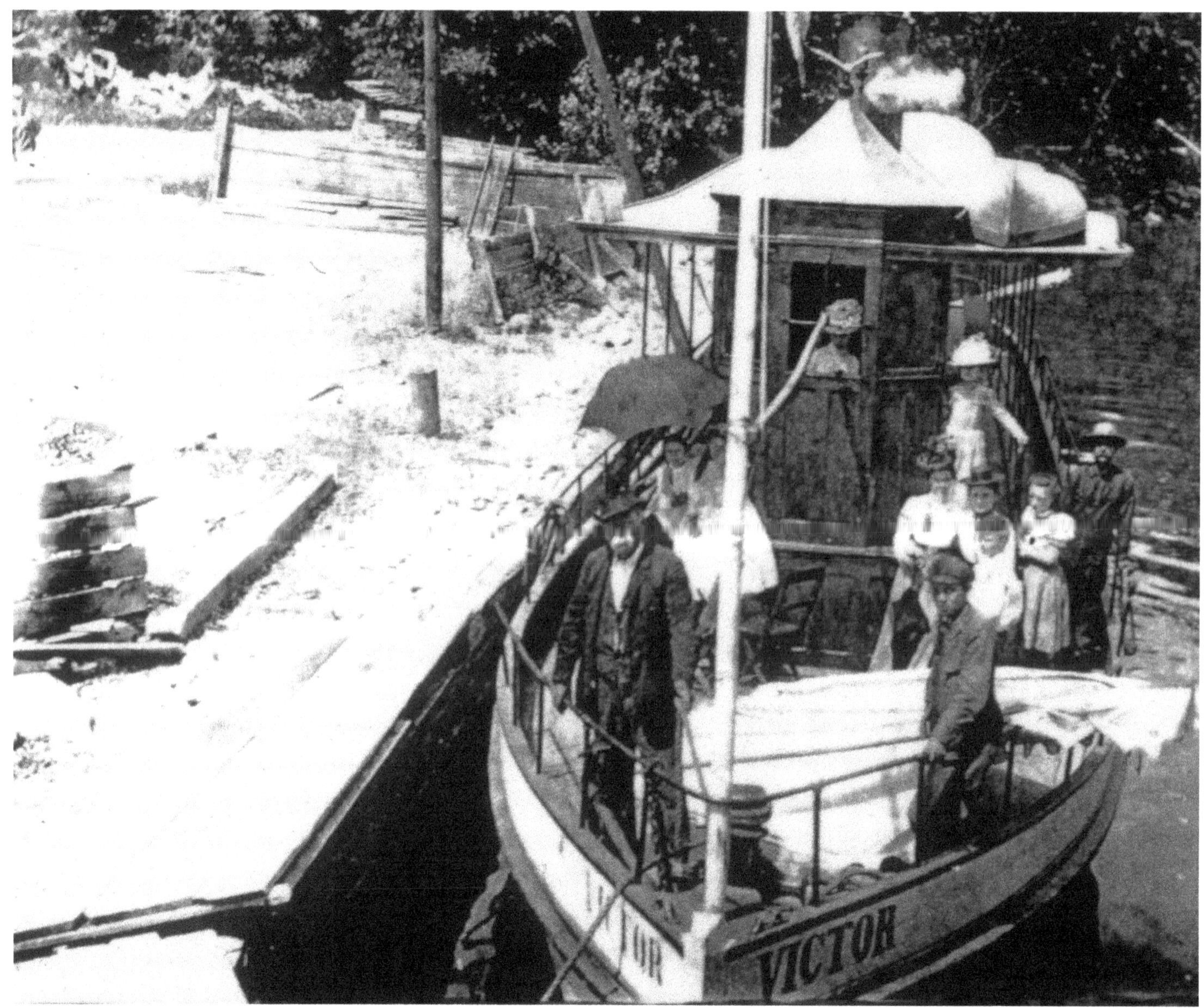

Philomene Daniels (in the pilothouse) was the first woman in the world to acquire a steamboat pilot's license. With her husband and two sons, Philomene cruised between New York and Vergennes on her tugboats, where her boiler room call and rustling skirts became a study in contrasts. By 1916, Philomene's ferries would be put out of business by automobile ferries. One of the Daniels' boats was used for firewood and the other became part of the Burlington breakwater.

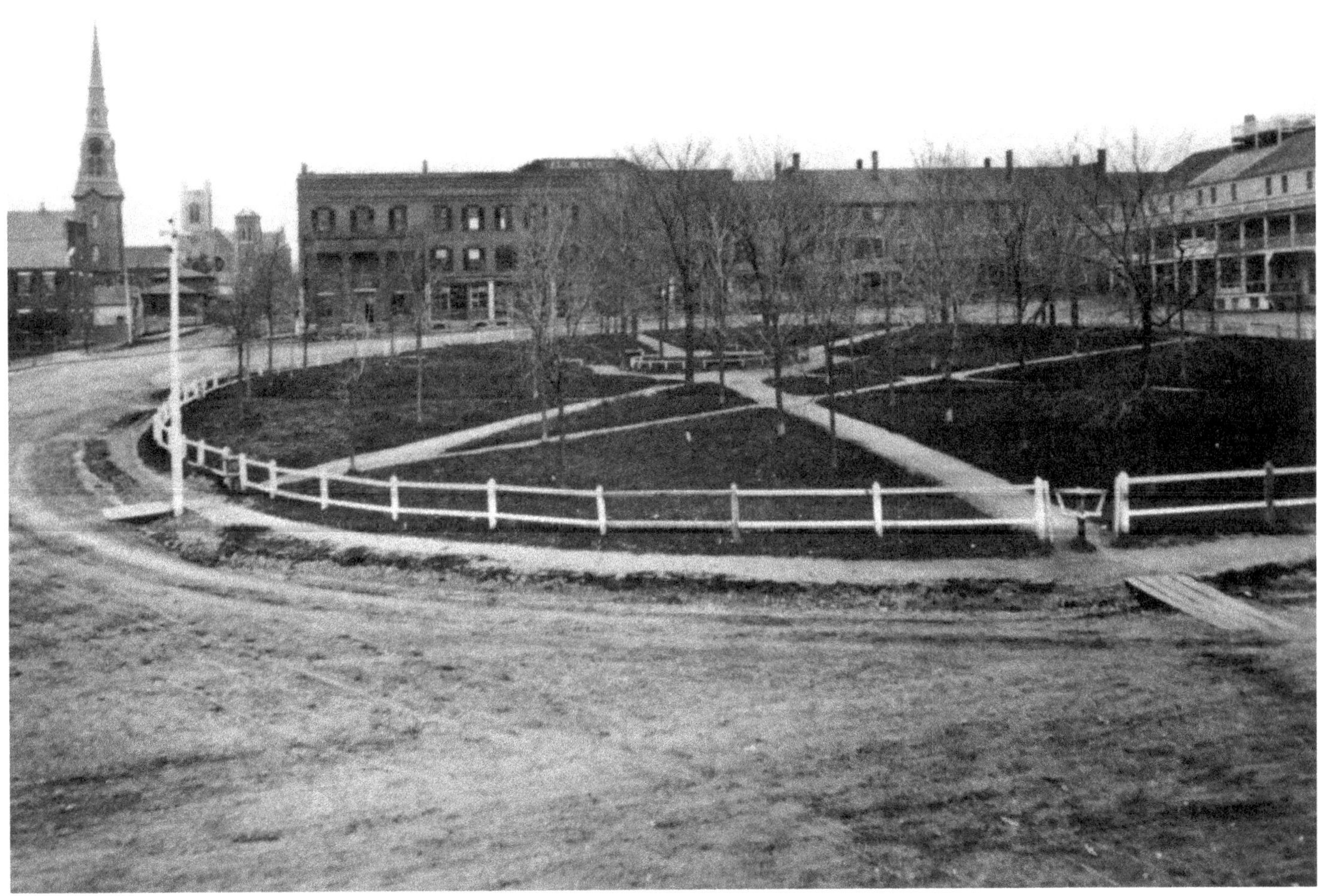

City Hall Park, Burlington. This section of Burlington had been the village green since the 1780s. Known as Courthouse Square, the area quickly became a business center with a bookstore and printer, two tailors, saddlers, a tin shop, attorney's office, and at least three general stores—all before 1810. Like Charlotte, St. Albans, and Vergennes, Burlington served as a commercial hub for Champlain Valley farmers and manufacturers who shipped their goods by steamer or railroad.

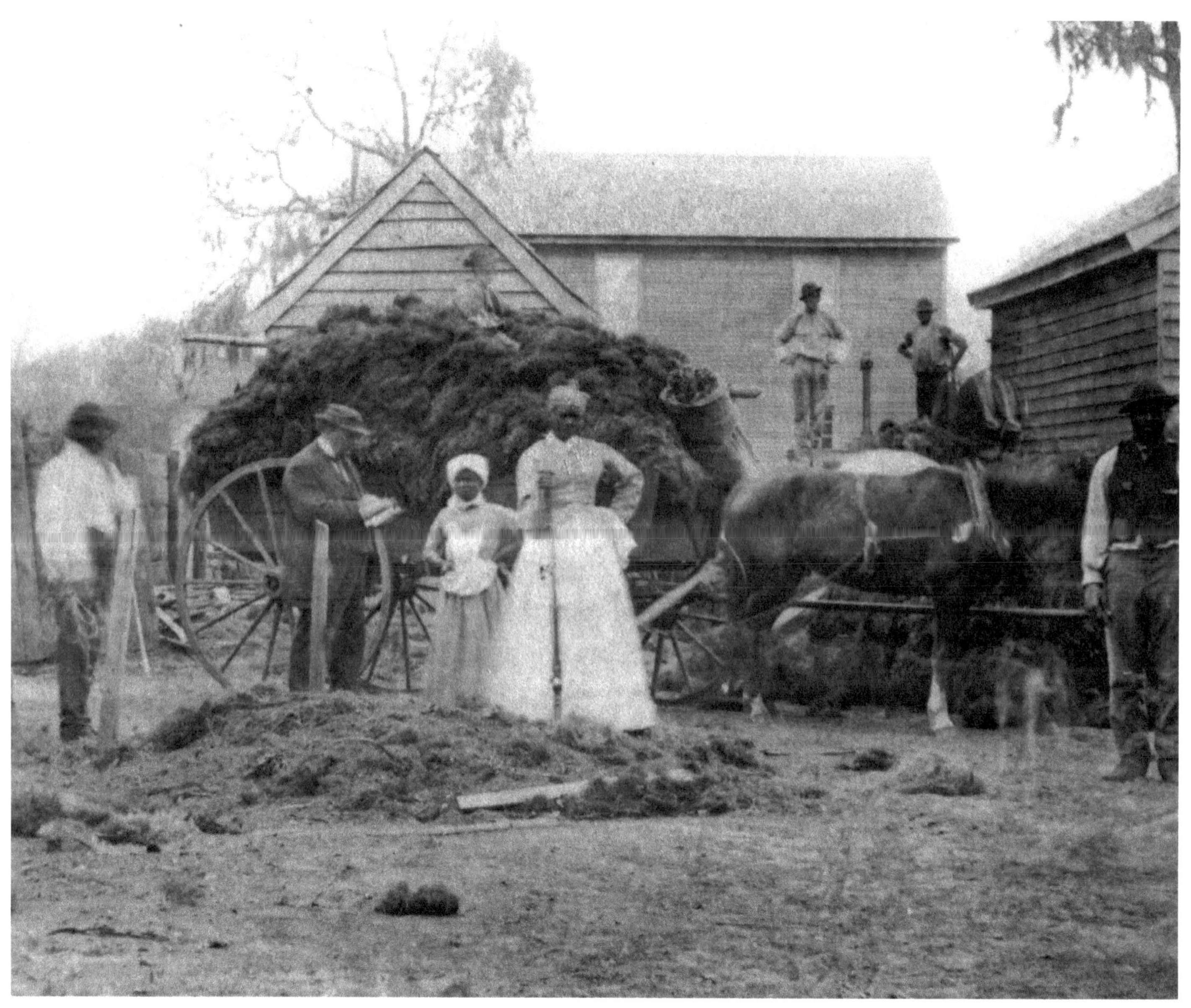

According to the label on the back of this nineteenth-century image, this family made a living dealing in moss. Vermont's African-American population experienced limited social and economic mobility, often working in unskilled jobs as laborers, domestic servants, cooks, and porters. Opportunity was not universally limited: by 1880, Burlington was home to an African-American carpenter, printer, shoemaker, and dressmaker.

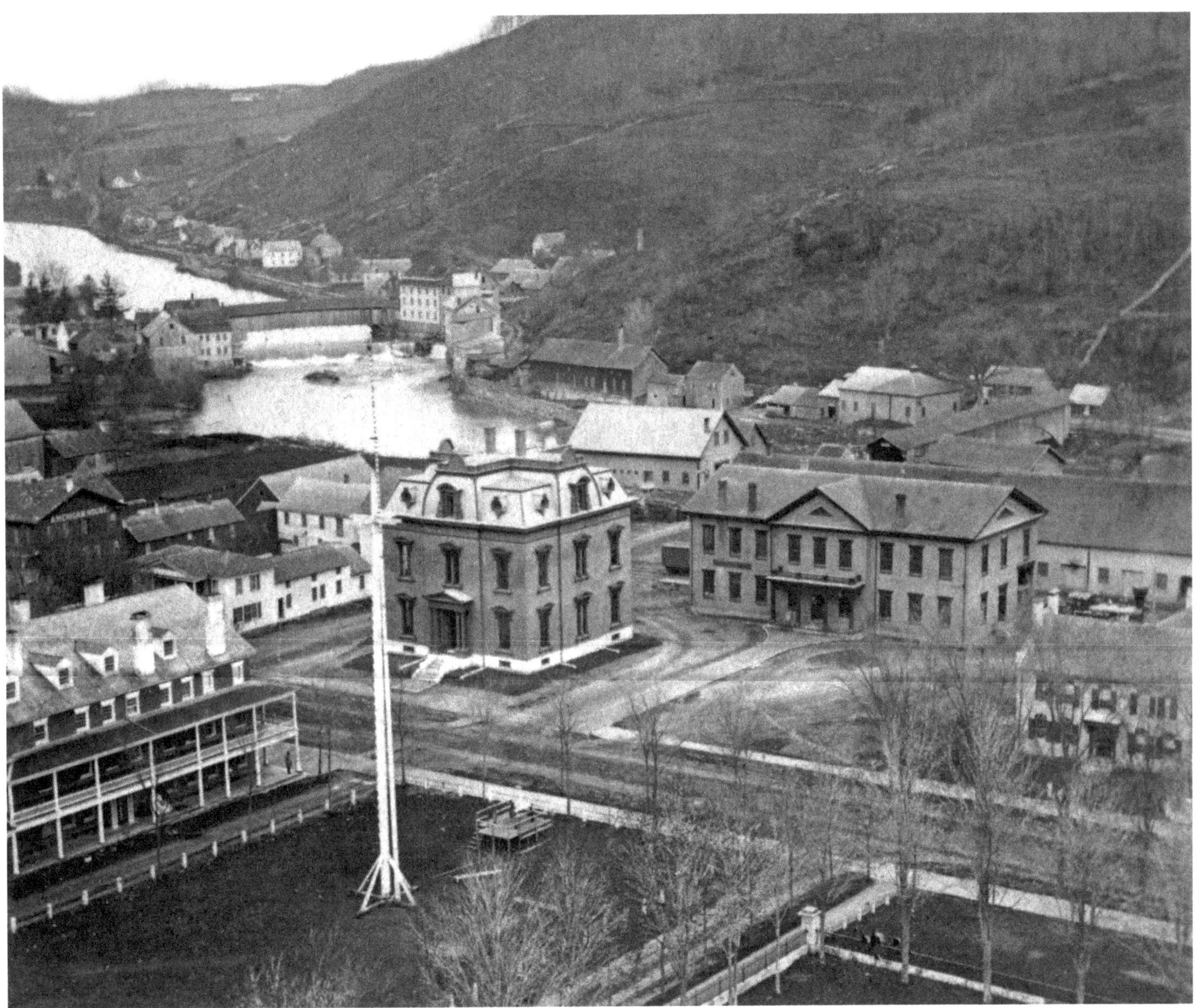

A view from the State House. Early on, Vermont's capital rotated through more than 12 towns around the state. In 1805, the legislature selected Montpelier as the permanent capital—in part as "a measure of peace" to quell competition among upstart towns. With no funds raised as of 1808, Montpelier residents voted a land tax of four cents to pay for the building. They paid two parts of the tax in grain and one part in cash.

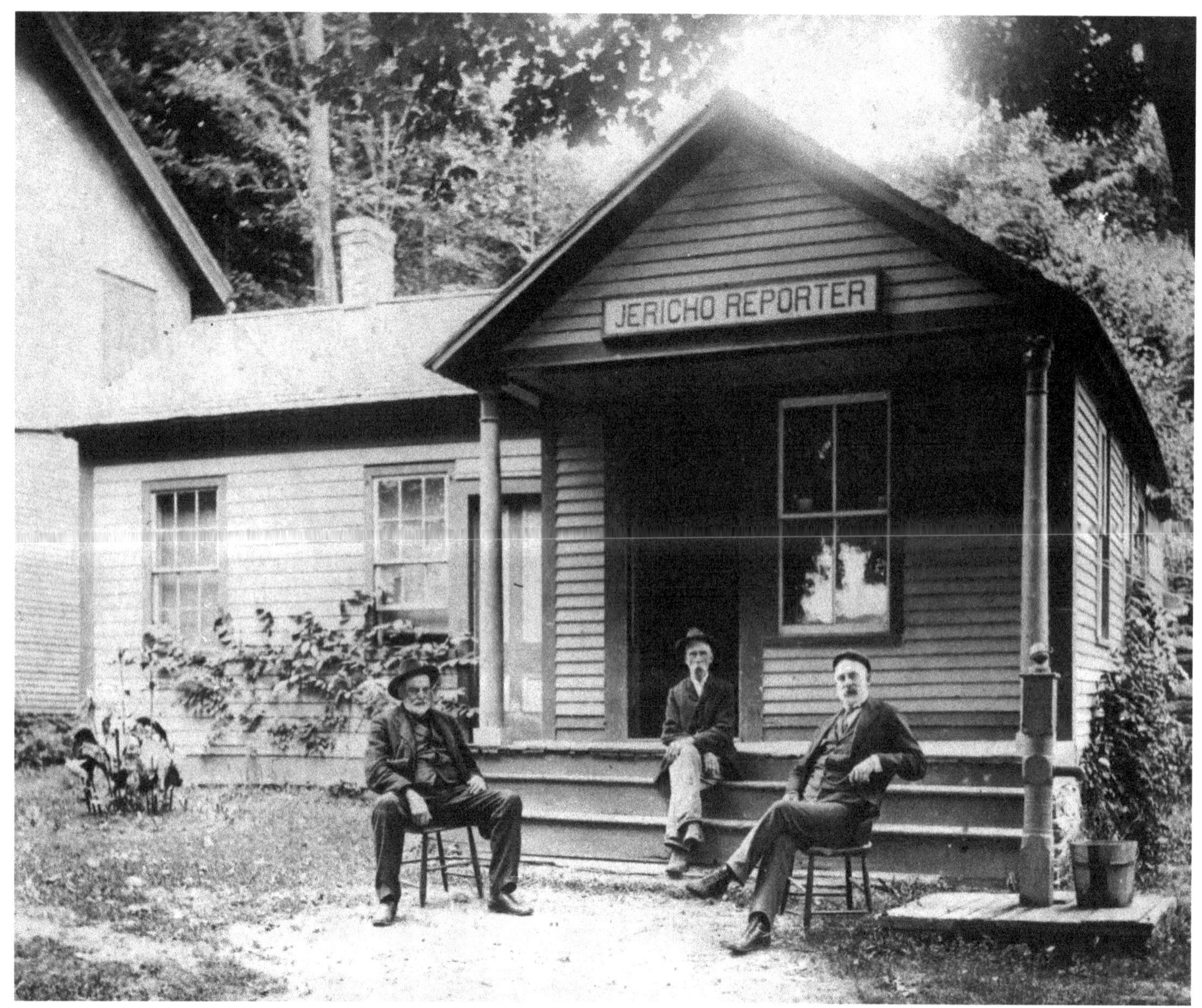

Staff of the *Jericho Reporter* pose here for a group shot. This "Live Local Paper for the Family" was one of many town newspapers that began publication in the 1880s. The paper pumped news into the local community, from headlines that included "What Colors to Wear" and "How to Cook a Turkey," to notices that "D. E. Rood and his wife are off on Orchard Beach excursion today" and "A. B. Barney has a horse sick with pinkeye."

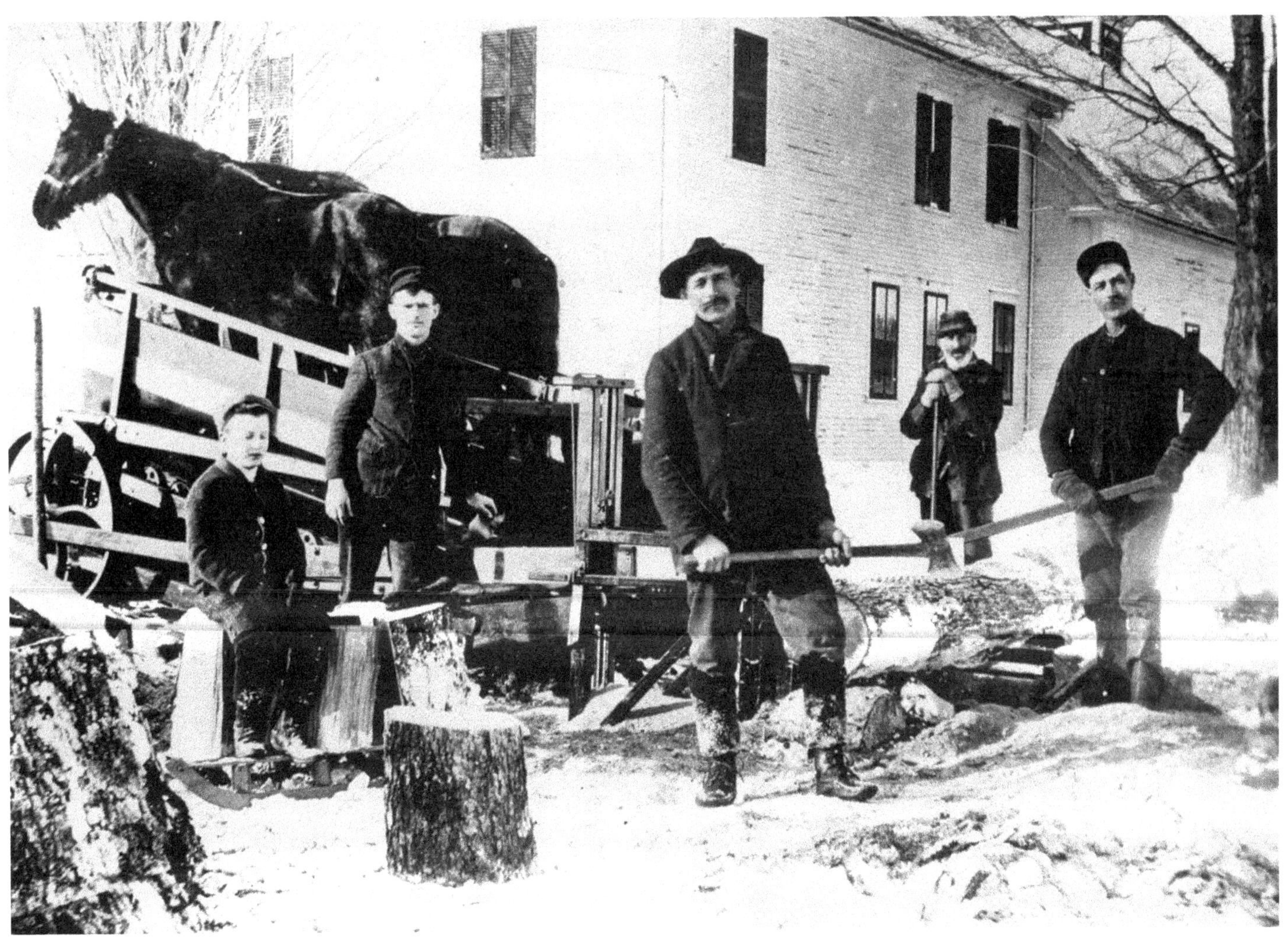

A horse-powered saw at the Webster farm in Danville. First invented in the 1830s, horse-powered treadmills were a great benefit to farmers, who attached these apparatuses to all sorts of tools, including butter churns, grain threshers, water pumps, and other devices. An eyewitness suggested that horses were less enthusiastic about the contraption than farmers were, observing how one horse "pulled right back and tried to lie down" when harnessed to the treads.

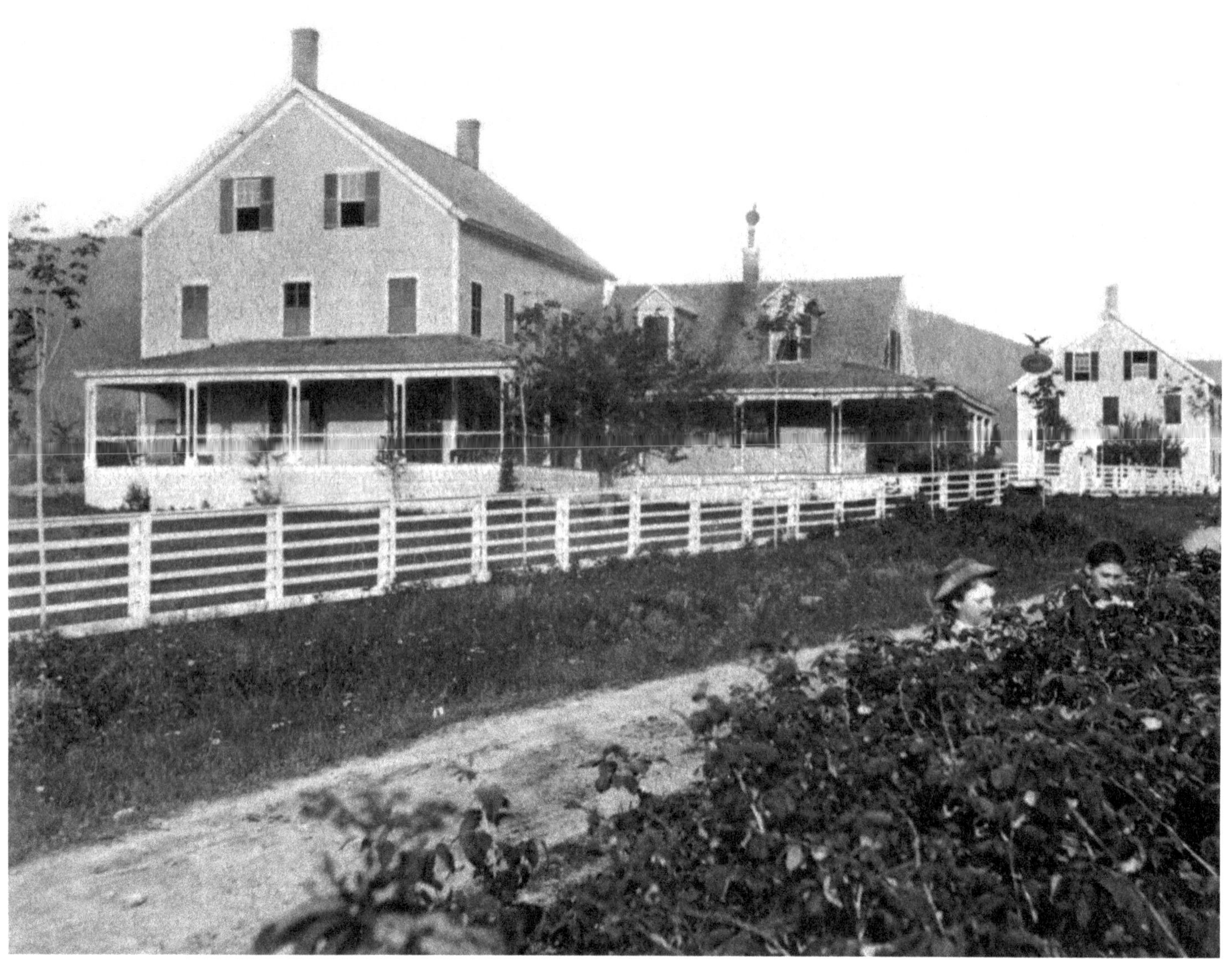

Joseph Battell's Breadloaf Inn in Ripton in 1880. An early advocate for land conservation, Battell urged the state to save forests from the lumber industry. He bought forested areas, including Camel's Hump, and donated them provided that the state would conserve them. Battell also rued the arrival of automobile traffic and was known to scatter sharp materials on the roadways near his home to puncture the tires of passing cars.

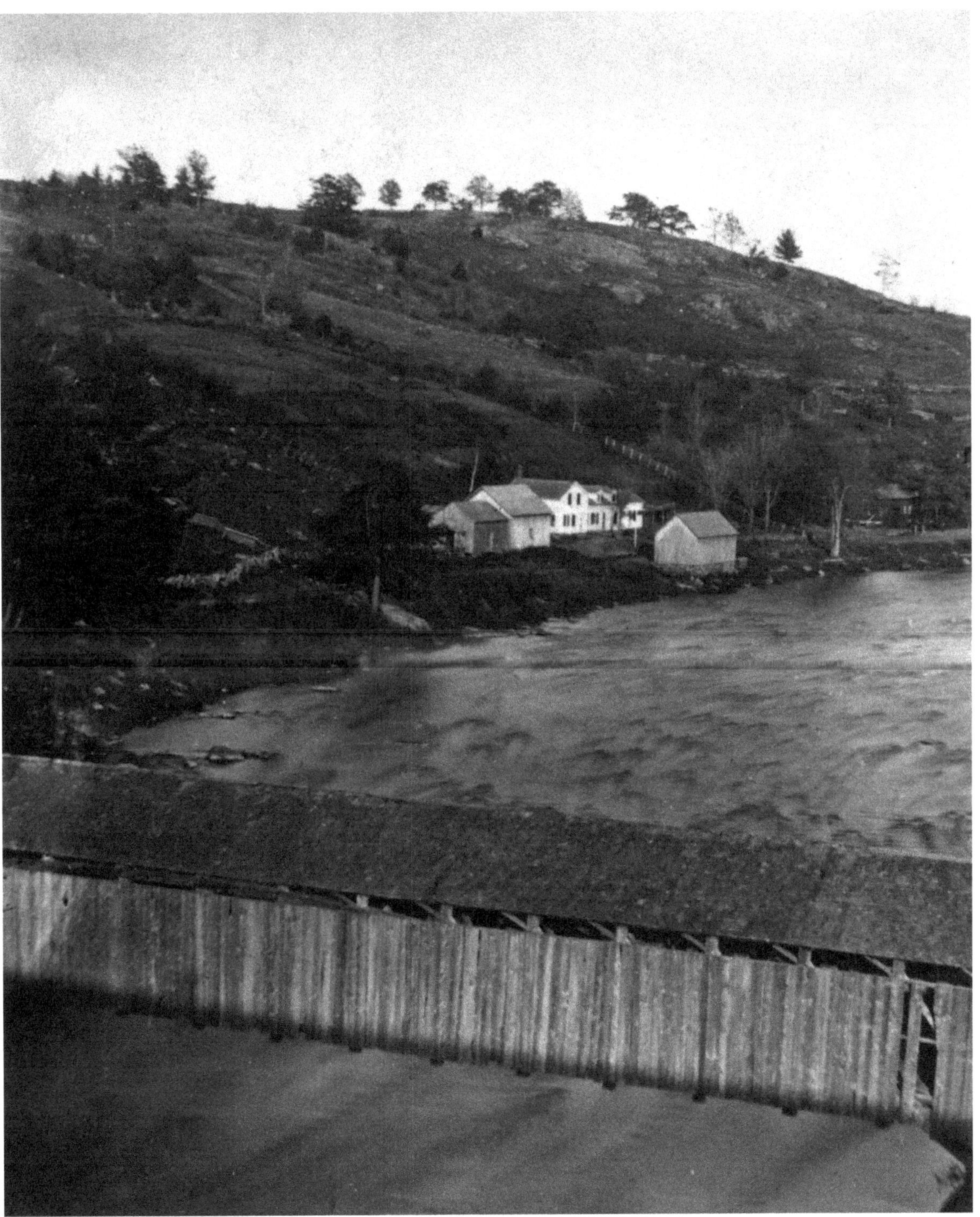

This covered bridge in Georgia was one of many in Vermont in the years before 1927. Vermonters built roofs over their bridges to add structural strength and protect them from the elements. In 1927, a massive flood washed away nearly 200 of the state's wooden bridges. Most of them were replaced with concrete-and-steel structures.

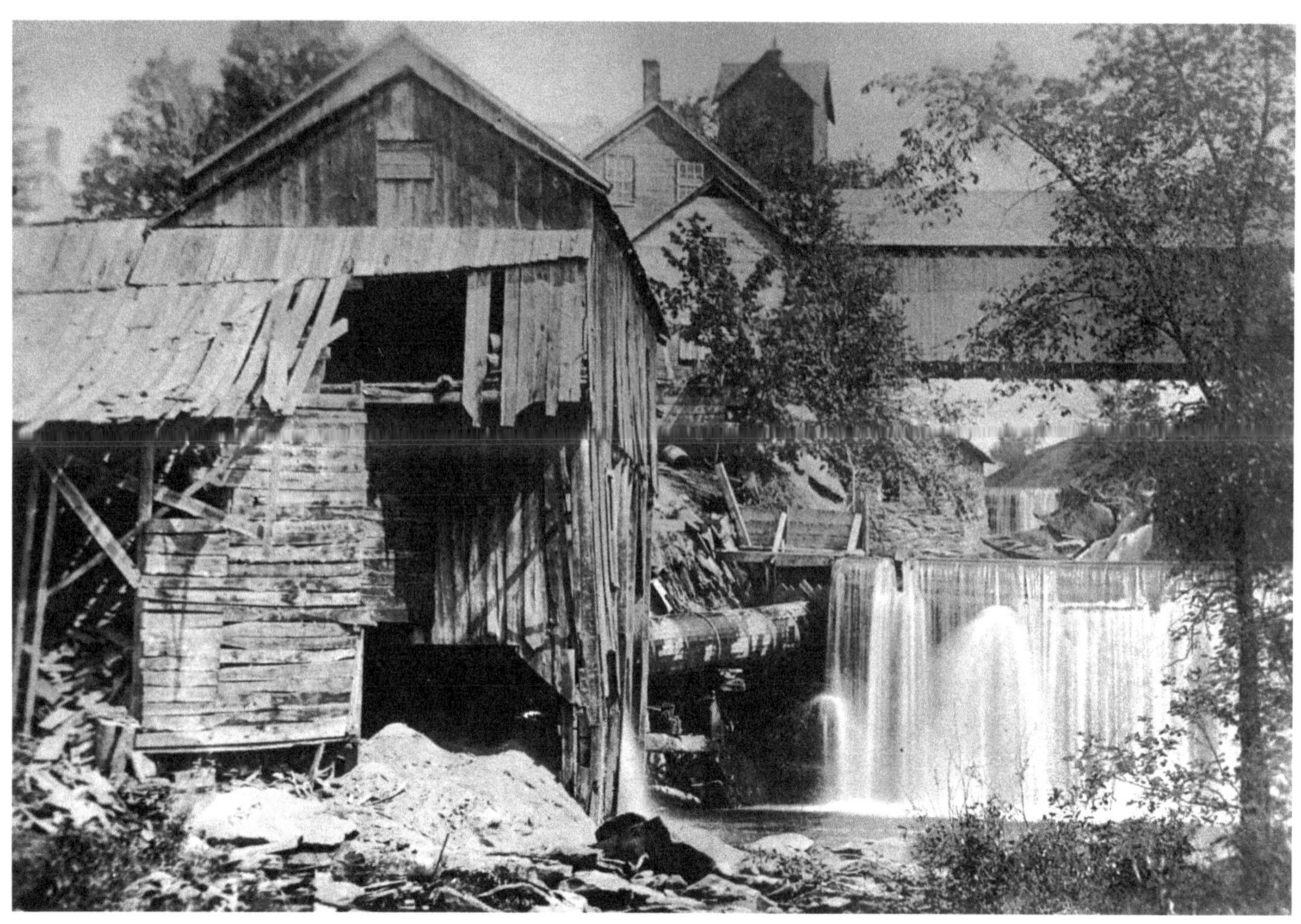

Jericho's Browns River was home to six mills before 1900, including the two in this photograph: the oft-photographed Chittenden Mill, with its cupola in the distance, and Joseph Sinclair's sawmill (foreground), built around 1830. The river was a place for both business and recreation. Referring to this image, a Jericho resident wrote in 1910, "This is the 'old hole' where I used to pull out brook trout big as whales when I was young and imaginative."

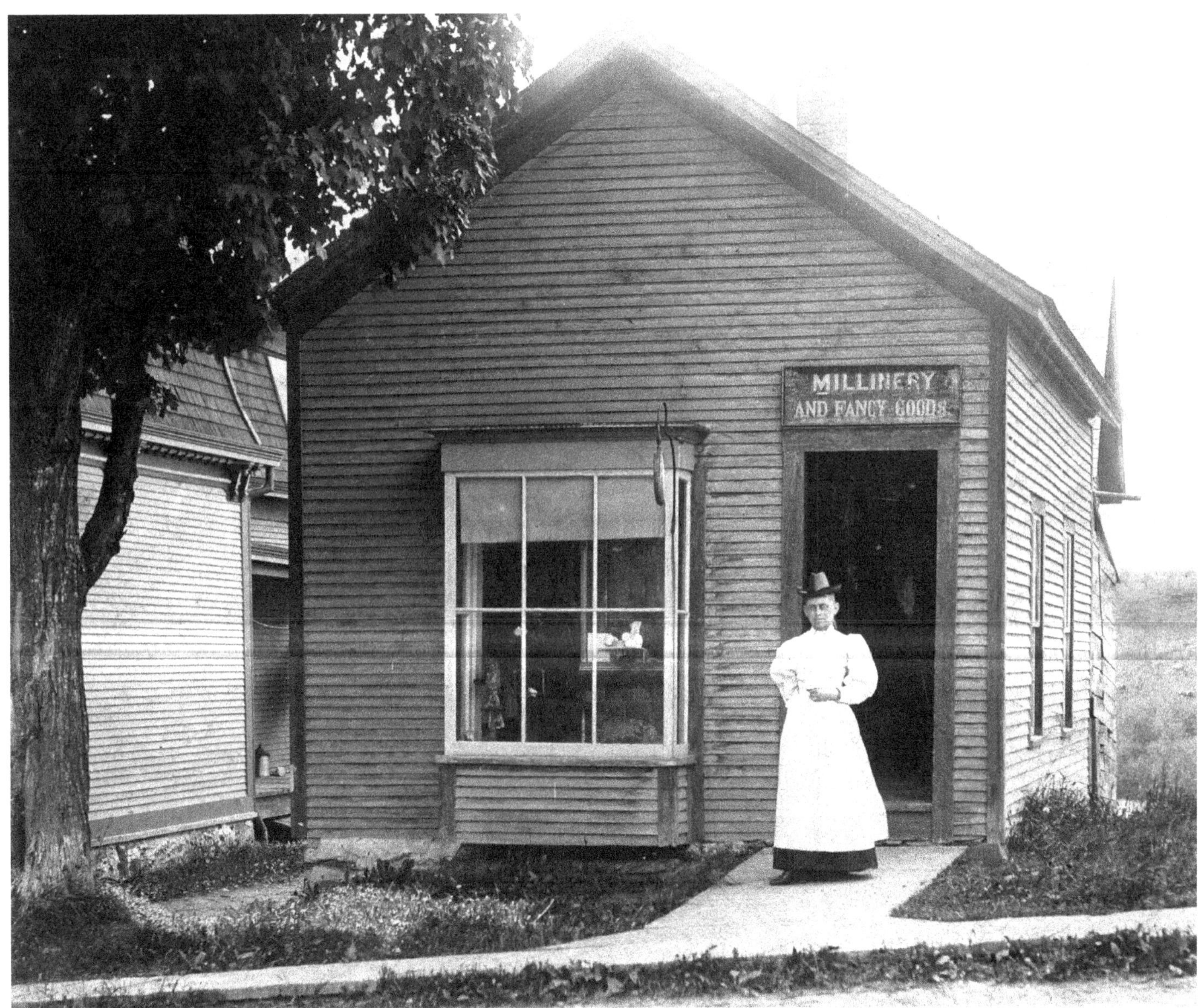

Mrs. Lucy A. Martin, in Jericho. Martin worked as a milliner on Church Street (now Route 15) for more than 30 years. Her husband, Buel, was a jeweler and clock dealer—his round "sign of the watch" hangs from the front of this building. Their house is to the left. Milliners like Lucy received their fine cloth and ribbons from the nation's larger port cities, either by rail or by post.

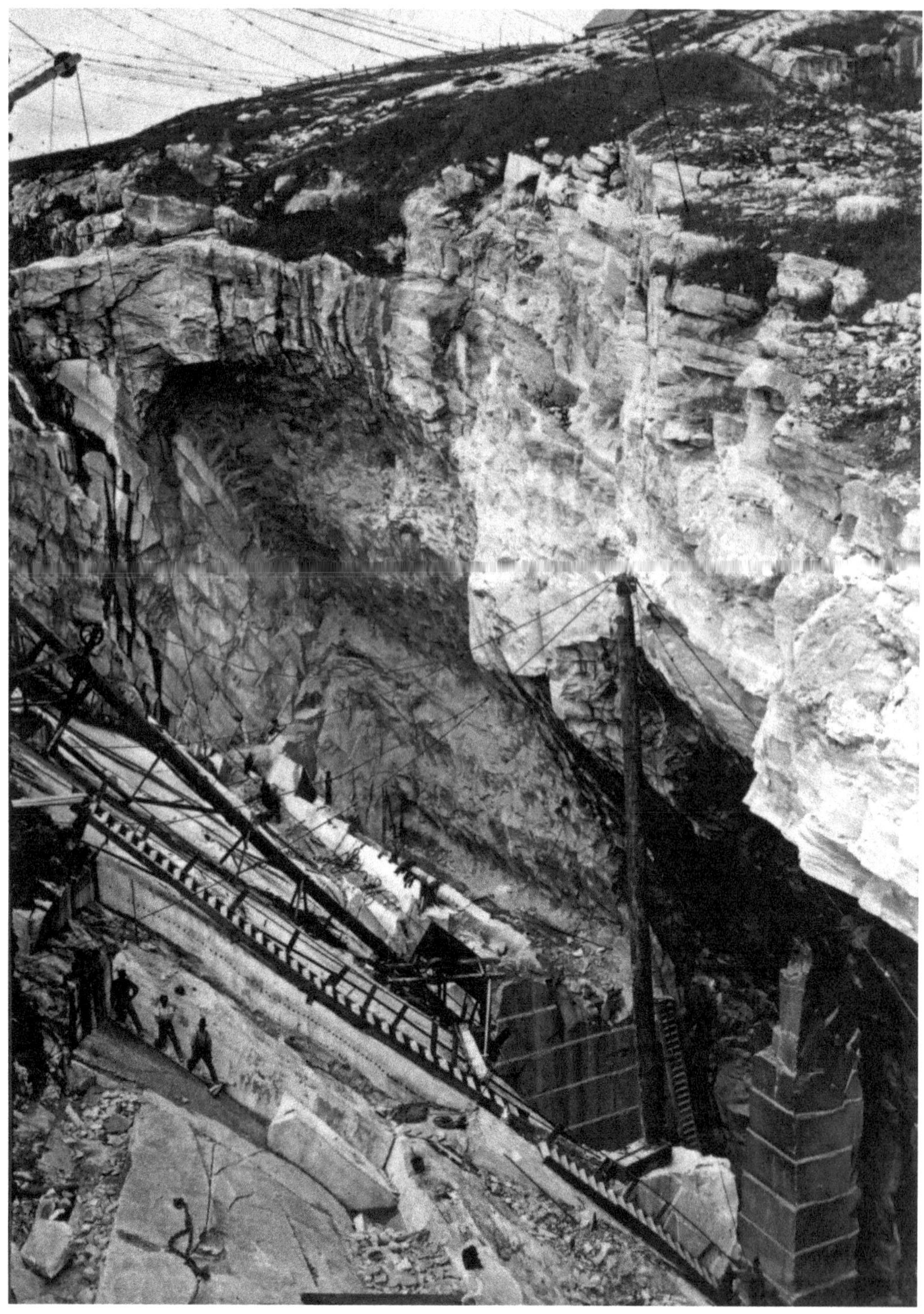

Hoisting marble in West Rutland. Before 1863, marble quarrying in Vermont was completed largely by hand. A quarryman earned between $1.40 and $2.80 on each of his 10-hour to 12-hour shifts, and he completed a good day's work if he could cut a one-foot by ten-foot channel into the solid marble. Beginning in the 1860s, most quarries converted from hand channeling to reliance on steam power.

From the 1830s forward, Rutland's marble deposits were the most mined marble quarries in the state. Redfield Proctor, owner of the Vermont Marble Company, enticed Italian stone carvers and Swedish immigrants to work in the region. Workers organized in the 1880s, demanding improvements such as a public library, evening school for workers, and a 10-hour workday. Proctor responded by persuading legislators to split the town into three, thereby diluting the unions' influence over town politics.

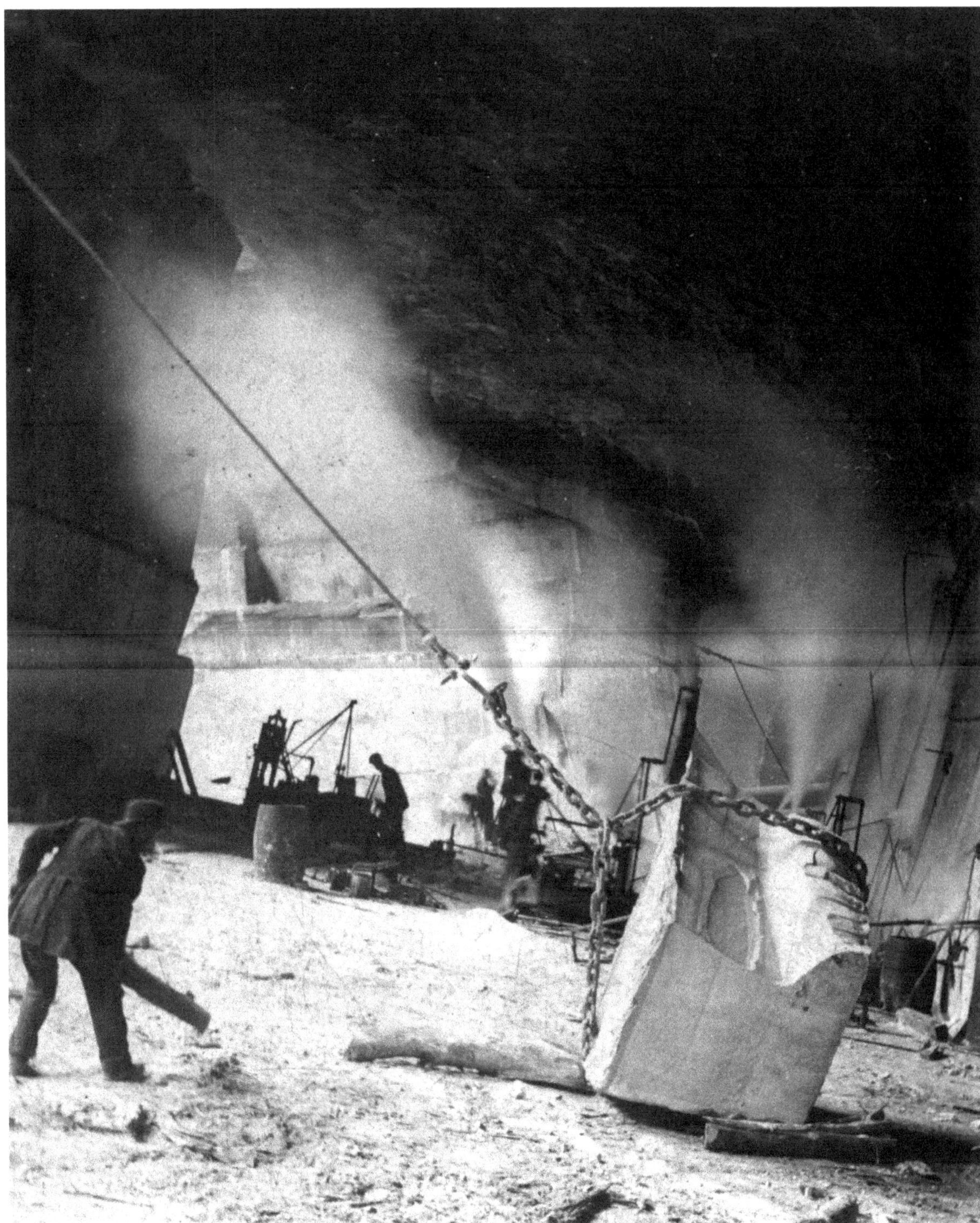

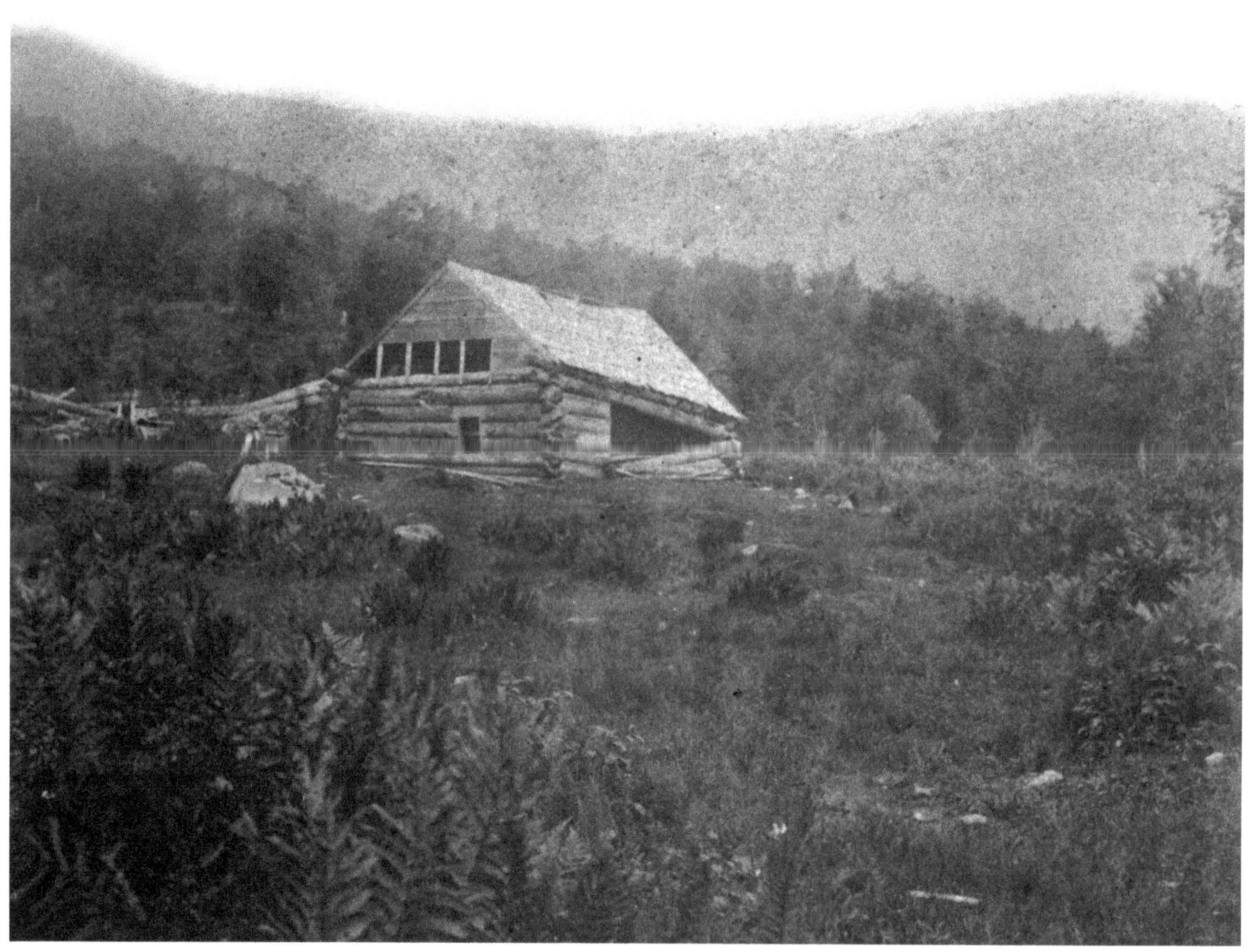

A logging house near Mount Mansfield. Logging communities cropped up everywhere during the nineteenth century—even on the side of this mountain. One community was equipped with its own boardinghouse, family cabins, blacksmith, and schoolteacher. Although highly lucrative and essential to building the nation, clear-cut logging for a time scraped Vermont's hills clear of trees. By season's end, neighbors in Underhill could see all of the Mansfield logging cabins initially obscured by the trees.

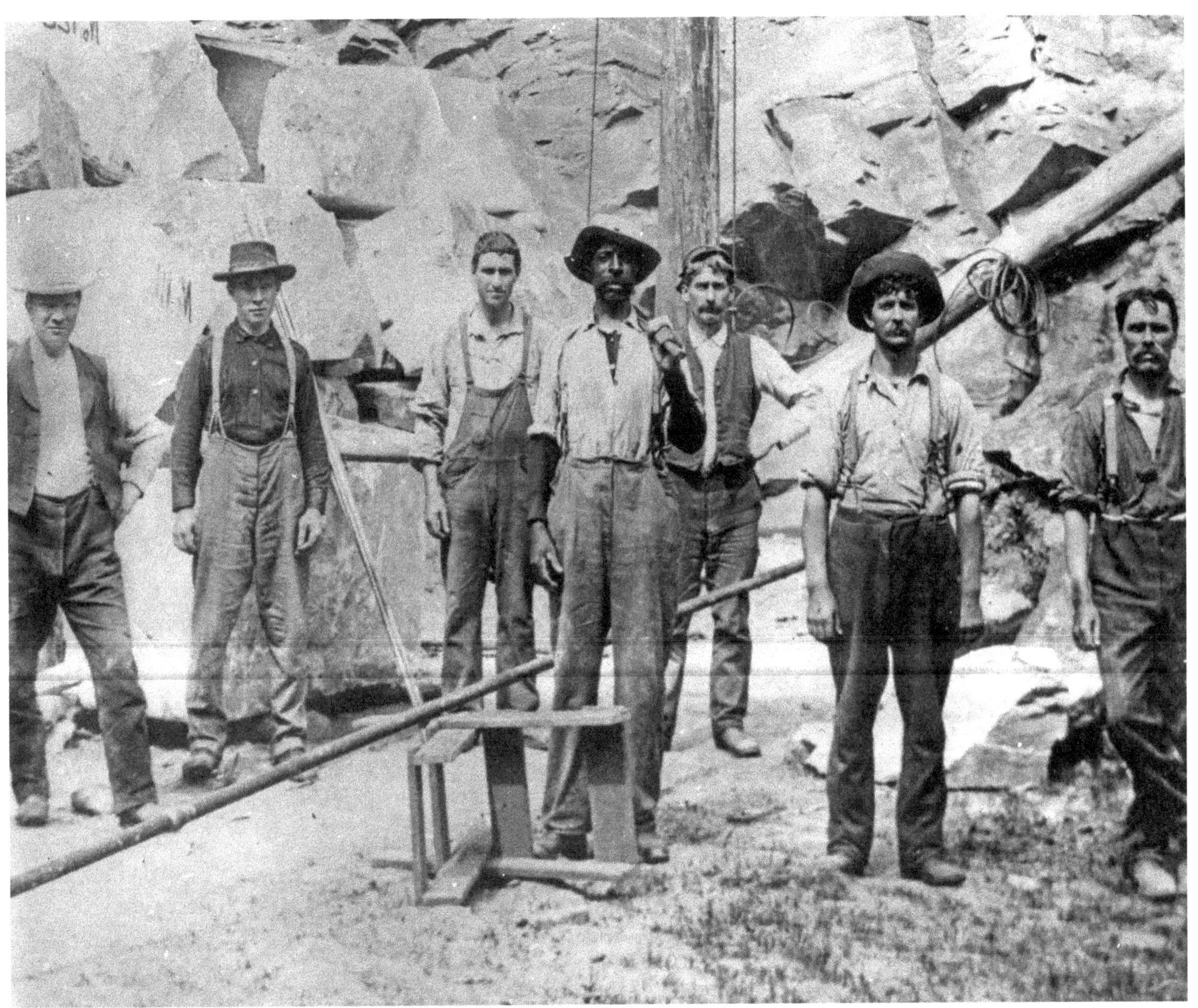

Soapstone quarrymen in Grafton. Opening in 1850, Butterfield & Smith employed 20 men in 13 soapstone quarries atop a hill in Grafton. Soapstone became popular because the slabs cut "like butter" into hearths, stoves, foot warmers, and griddles. Some mills also produced soapstone water pipes, which were posts with a long hole bored through, and sold them for a dollar each. The quarry closed in 1900 when more durable materials rendered soapstone a less attractive resource.

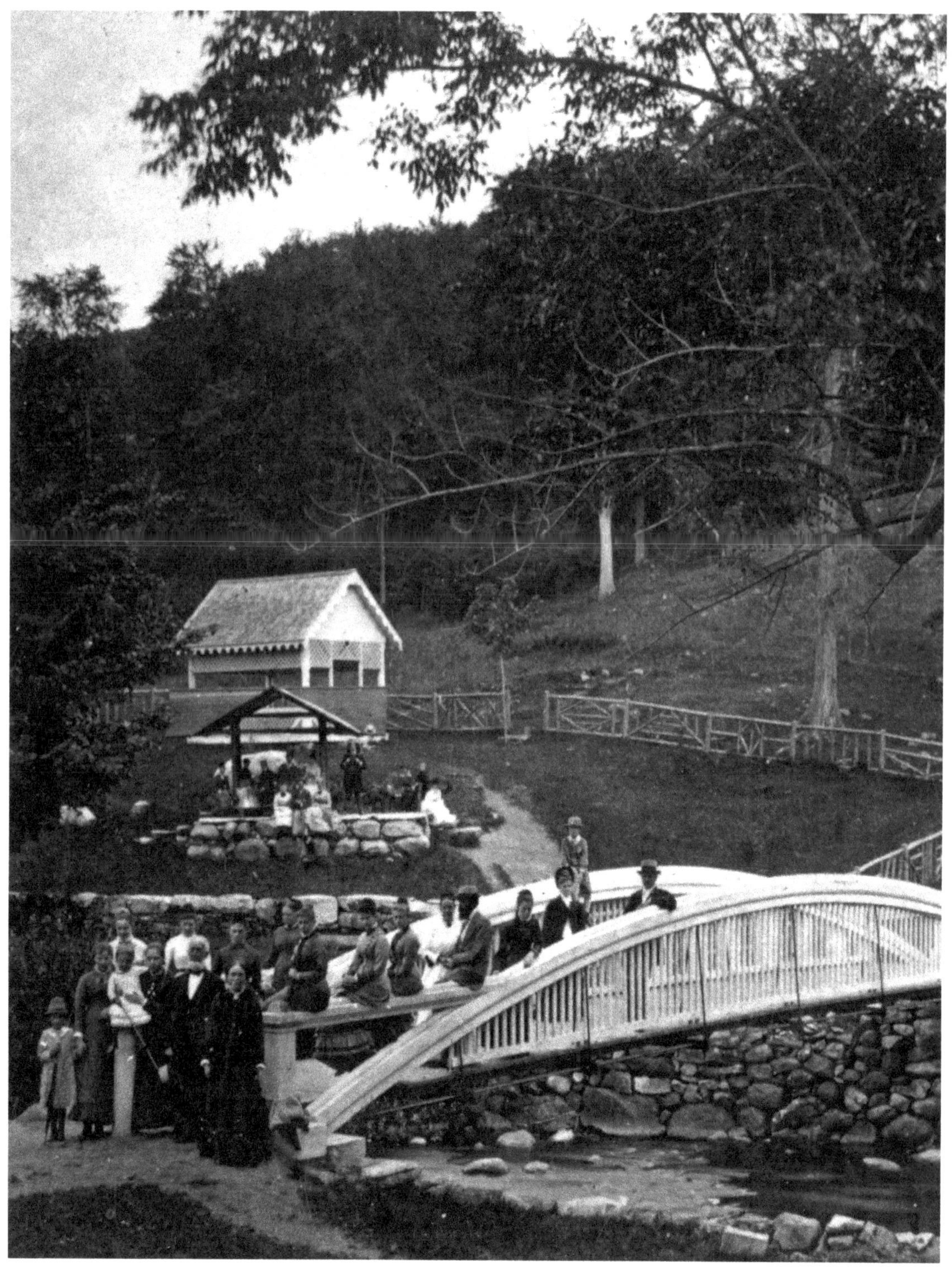

A party at Clarendon Springs in 1885. Vermont boasted more than 100 springs during the nineteenth century, some of which supported health resorts. Clarendon Springs offered diverse opportunities for recreation, including bowling alleys, croquet lawns, and stables. With a large number of clientele hailing from Virginia and the Carolinas, Clarendon's resort business declined after the Civil War. Other Vermont spas would also decline when resorts on the White and Adirondack mountains began to compete.

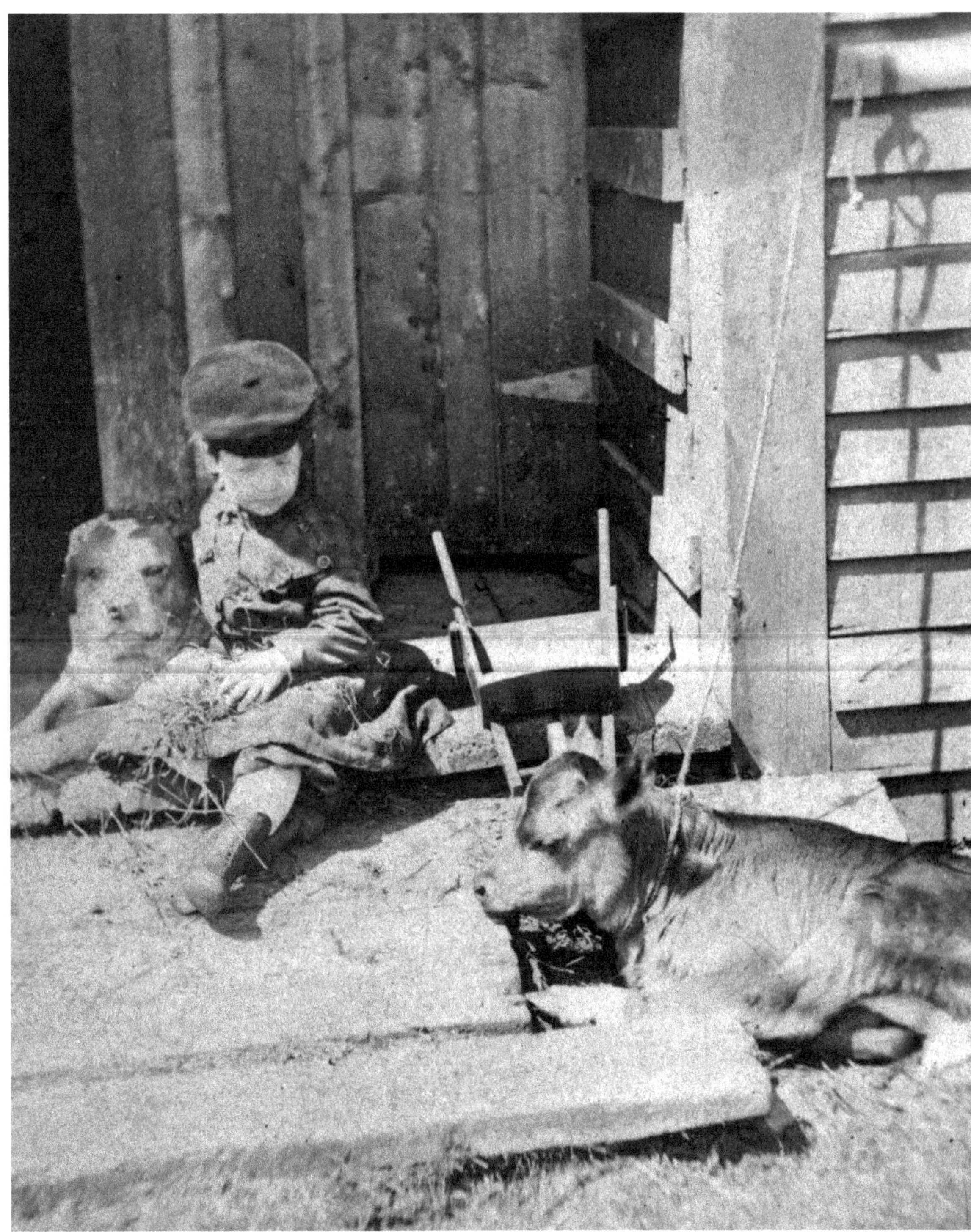

A child nestles with the family dog and a calf. With increased financial pressures and fewer people working in Vermont's rural areas, children became integral to keeping the family farm afloat. Even after dairy farming in Vermont succeeded, most rural areas experienced a marked population decline, with young people foremost among the emigrants.

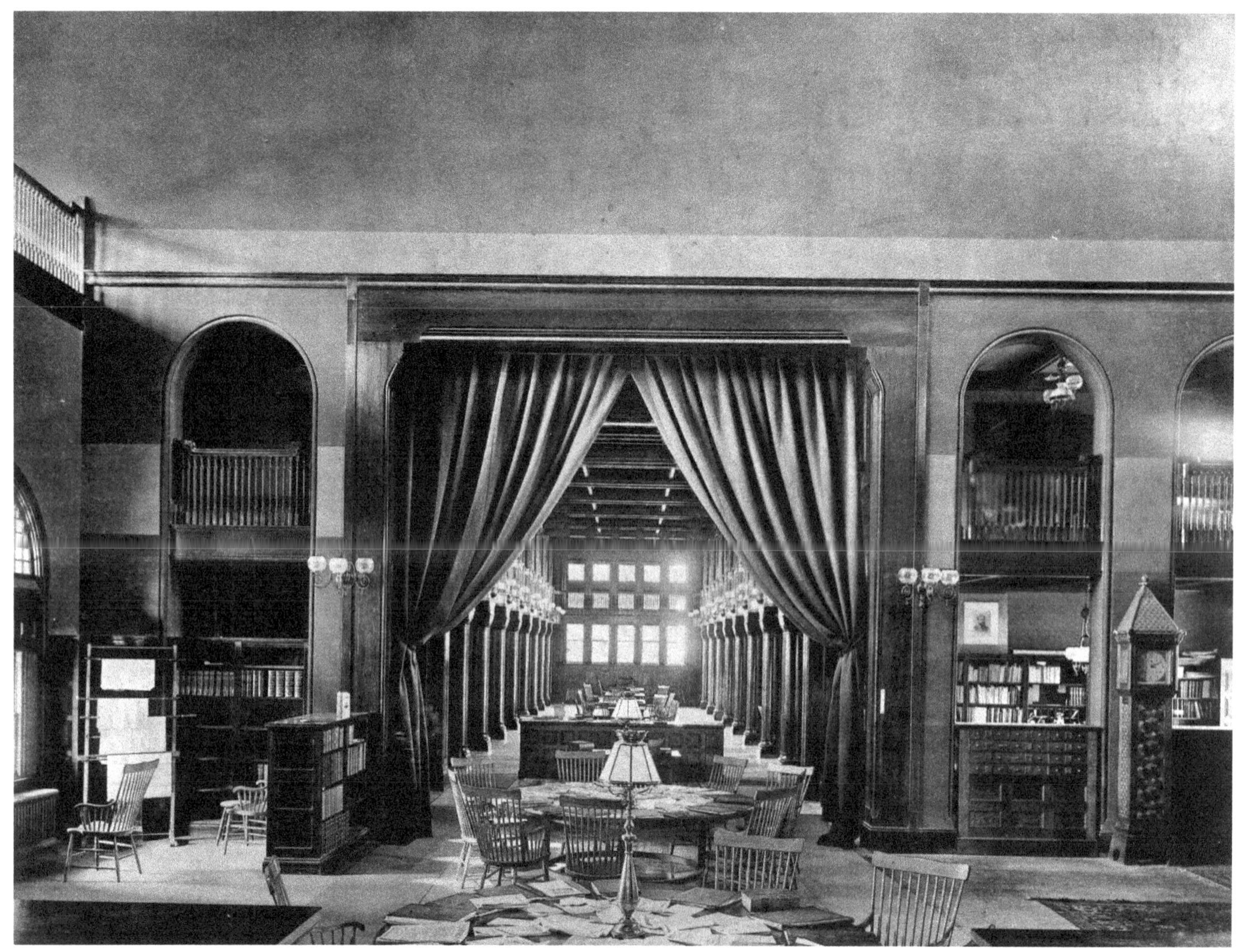

Billings Library, University of Vermont, around 1886. Starting with the few secondhand books of Abel Newell of Colchester in the 1790s, the university library grew to more than 7,000 volumes by the 1830s. The 1860s and 1870s brought significant growth to UVM, and in 1863 the university hired renowned American architect Henry Hobson Richardson to design the Billings Library. Richardson's Romanesque style has been called the first truly American architectural style.

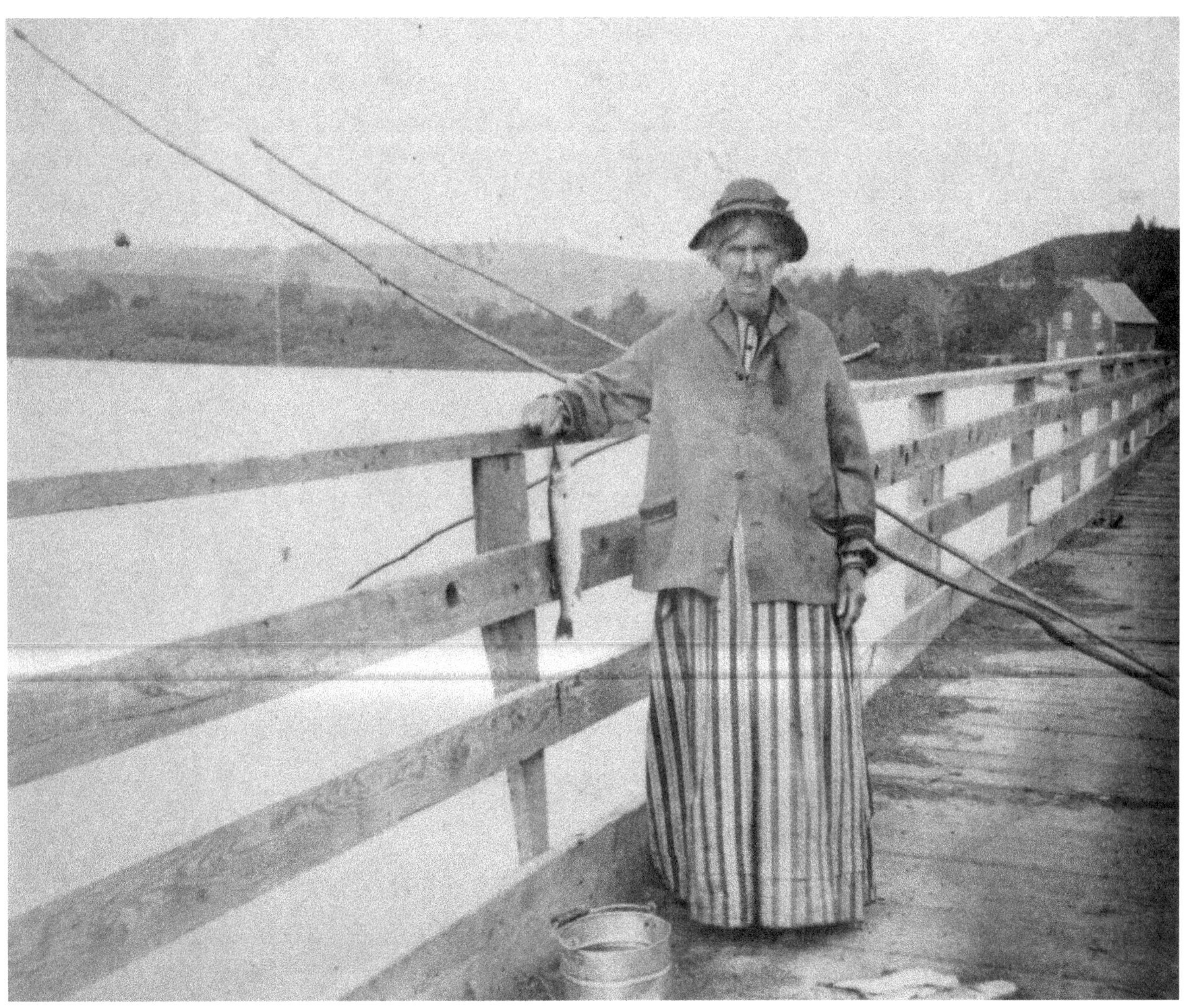

"Aunt" Sally Horton fishes from the Long Bridge at Lake Memphremagog, Newport. Known as the "fisherwoman of Lake Magog," Horton may have been one of many Western Abenaki who assimilated into the surrounding culture. Some Abenaki served as guides, farmers, laborers, and housekeepers, adopting the clothing and tools of the American majority. Abenaki and Mohican Indians inhabited parts of the land that would become Vermont before Iroquois invasion and European immigration diminished their presence.

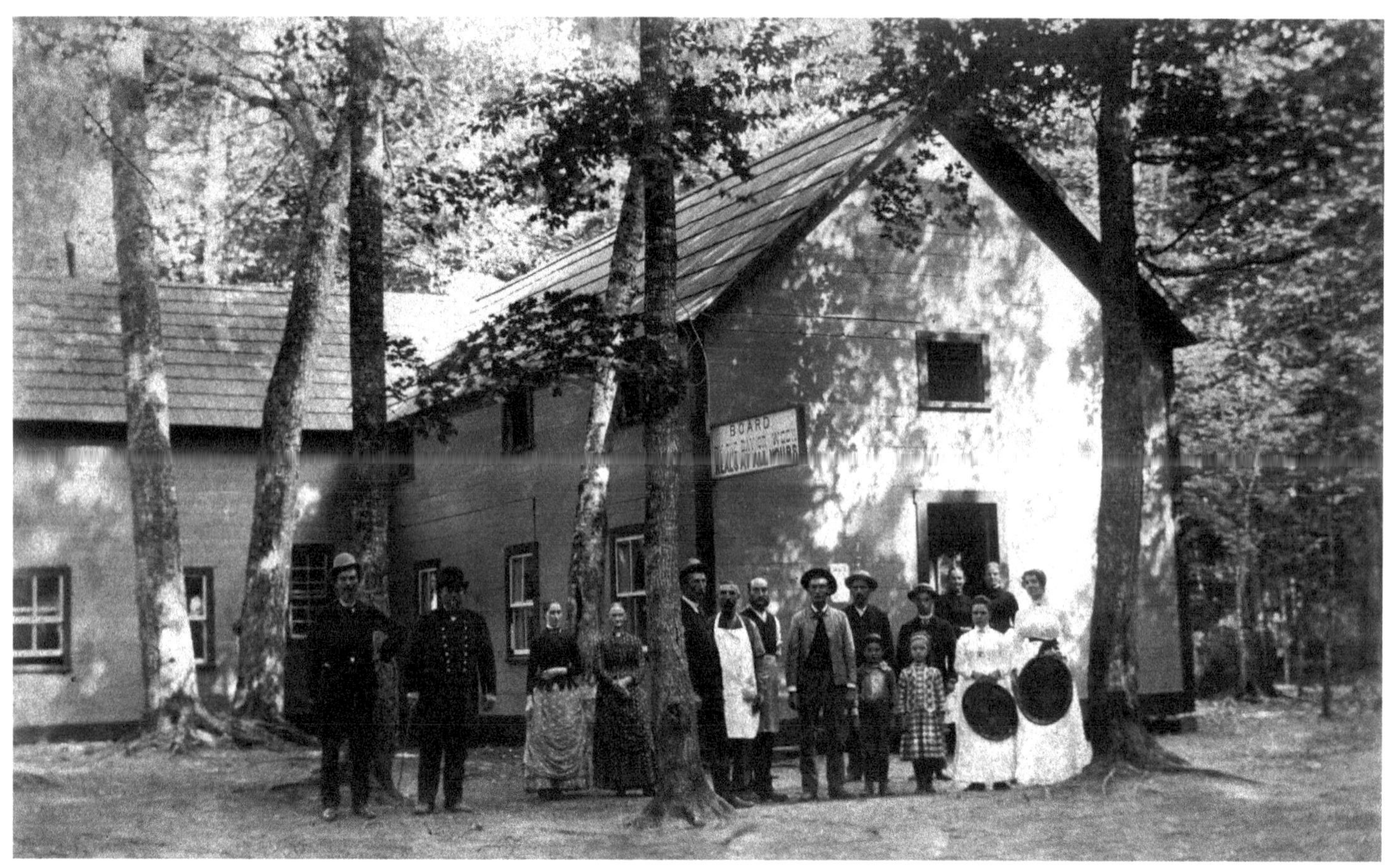

Campground Boardinghouse, 1890. Methodist camp meetings, an occasion for late summertime relaxation with a religious bent, moved to the Morristown area in the 1870s. Situated conveniently on the rail line, the campground seated 2,500 people, and in the 1890s served also as a setting for Republican speechmakers. Towns as far away as Essex and Sheldon built cottages to house visitors, and many pitched tents at the site. The campground closed in August 1902.

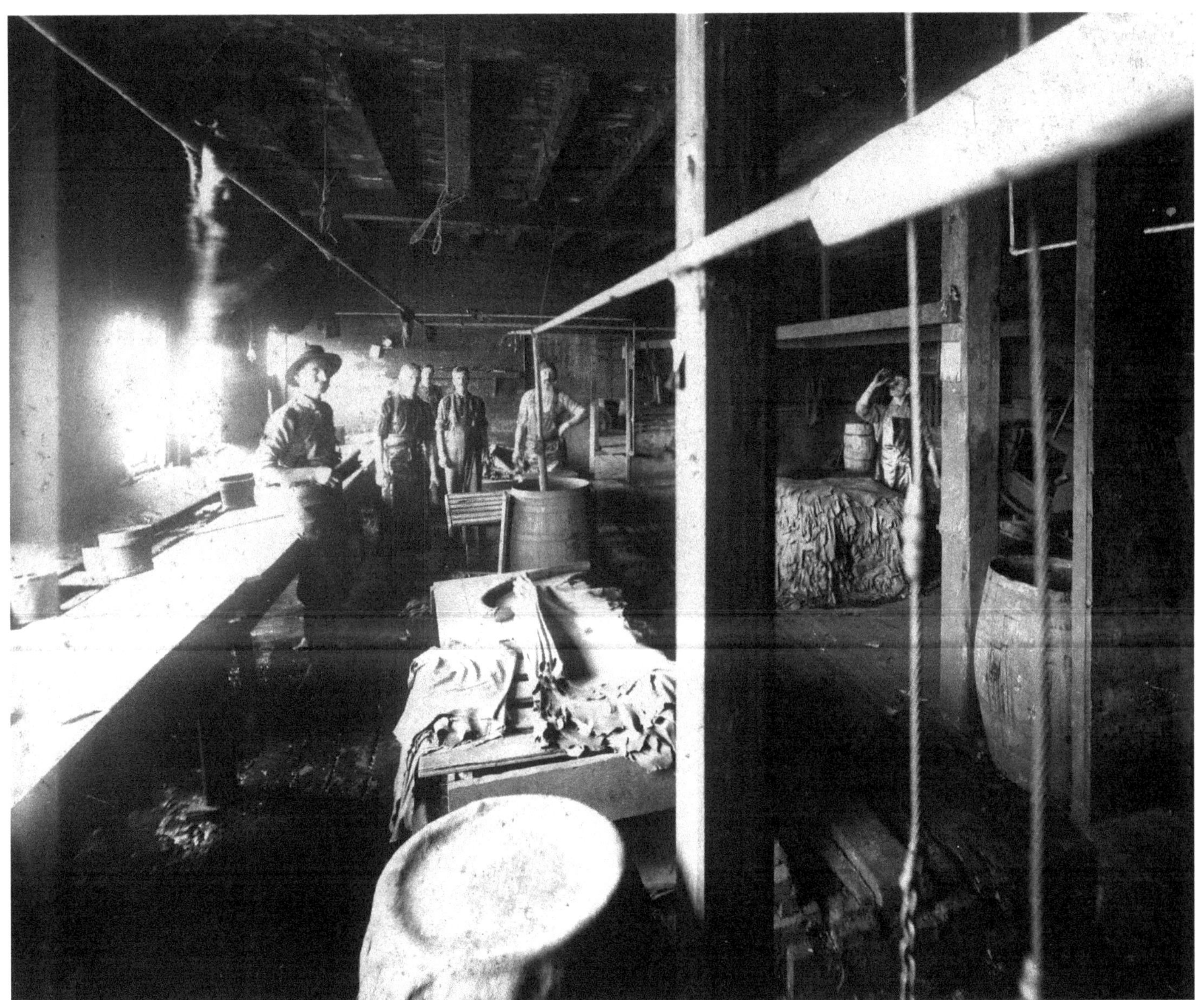

Opened in 1889, the Morrisville Tannery Company became one of the most stable businesses in town. Eventually the company's owners moved the business progressively farther from home—first to Waterbury, then to Massachusetts, and finally to New York. The tannery also saw the nature of its business change, first specializing in horse harnesses and then shifting to belt leather as horse travel became less popular.

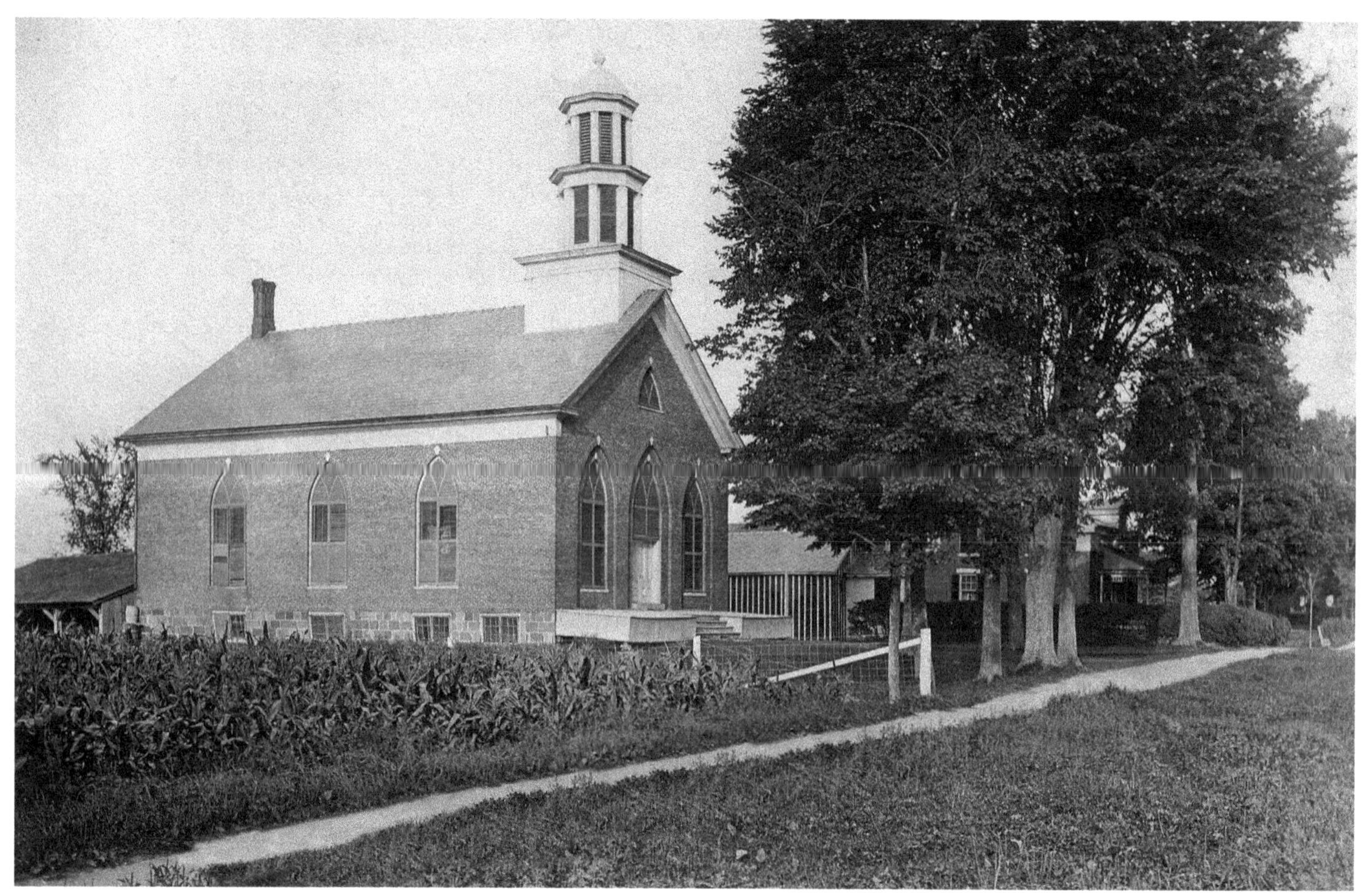

Williston's Old Brick Church, before 1900. Once the largest denomination in Williston, the Congregationalists built the Old Brick Church in 1832. Slowly, the congregation dwindled as splinter groups left to form their own denominations. Universalists built their own meeting place in 1860, and in 1869 the Methodists constructed a separate house. In 1899, the Congregationalists themselves left the Old Brick Church and merged with the Methodists down the road. The building remained largely vacant until the 1960s. It stands today as one of the town's landmark structures.

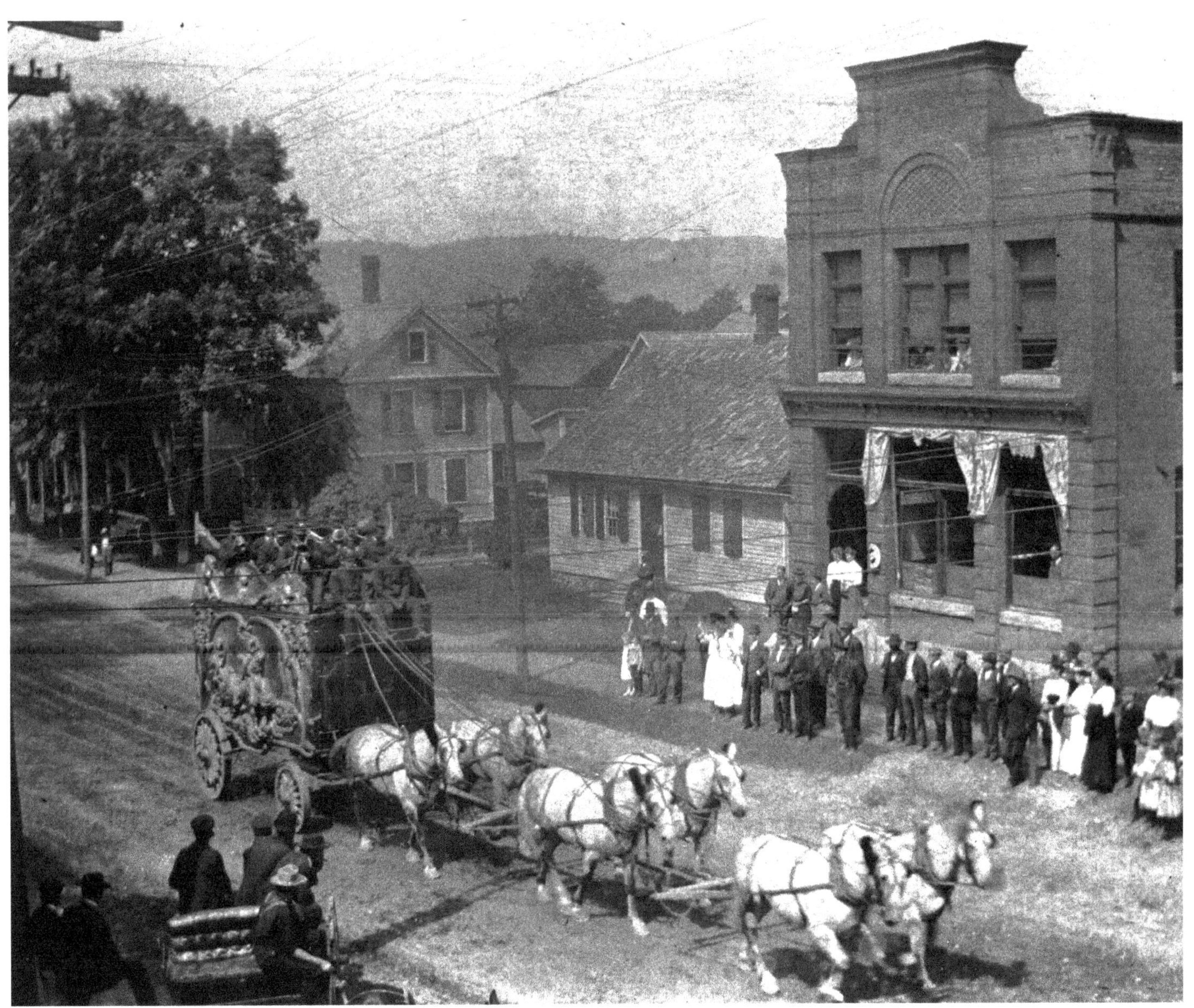

A parade in Morristown. The streets of Vermont's villages were long the meeting place for community gatherings. Morristown's main thoroughfares hosted various parades, animal races, military band concerts, and sporting events. In 1890, Morristown hosted a gala centennial, celebrating the town's anniversary with 10,000 attendees and a memorable procession down Congress Street.

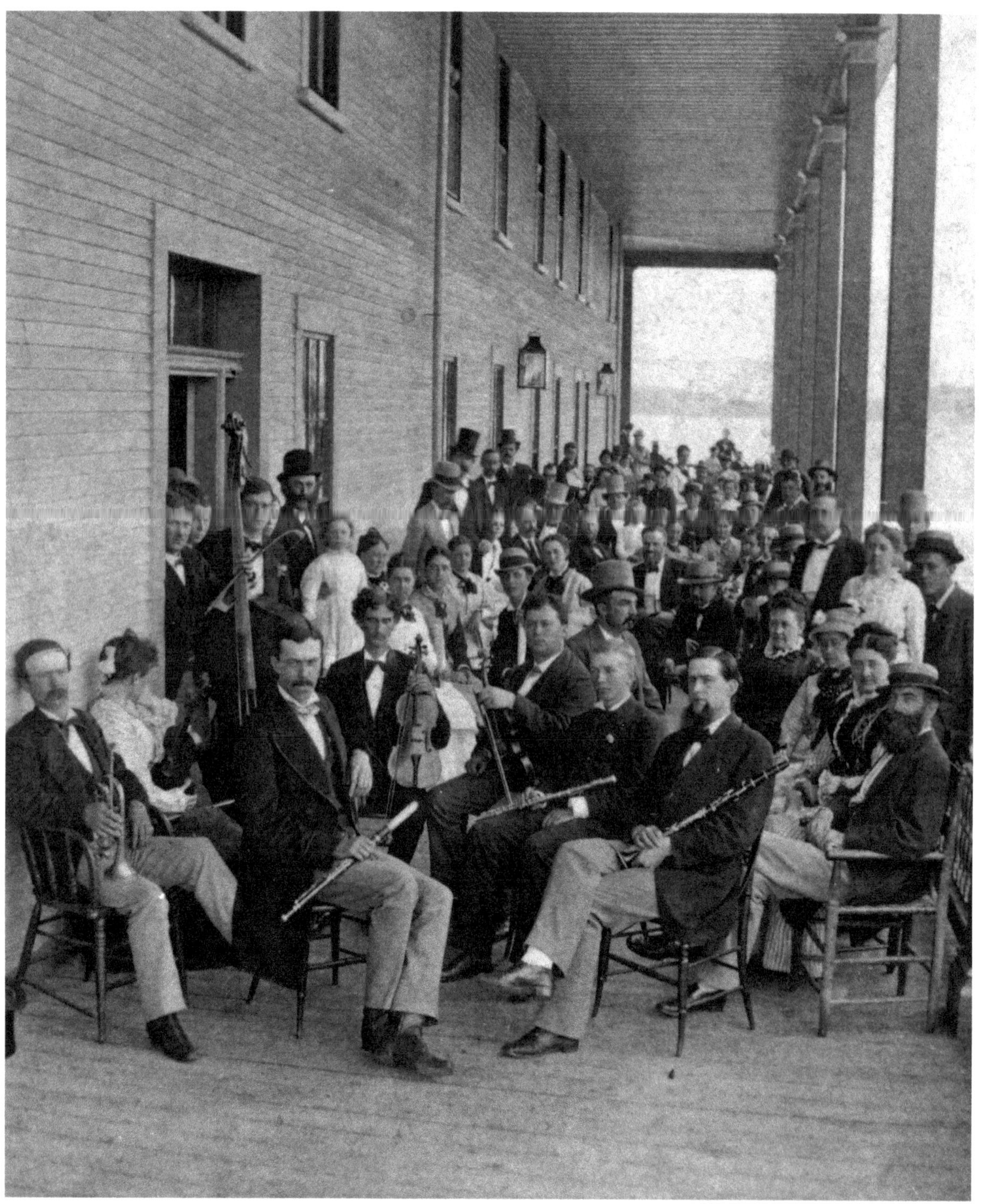

A balcony group plays at the Memphremagog House in Newport. The late nineteenth century brought an explosion of social and entertainment options to Vermonters, including professional associations, recreation clubs, and musical groups and gatherings. These activities and organizations helped to bolster community ties at a time when many towns were tackling the challenges of dwindling population.

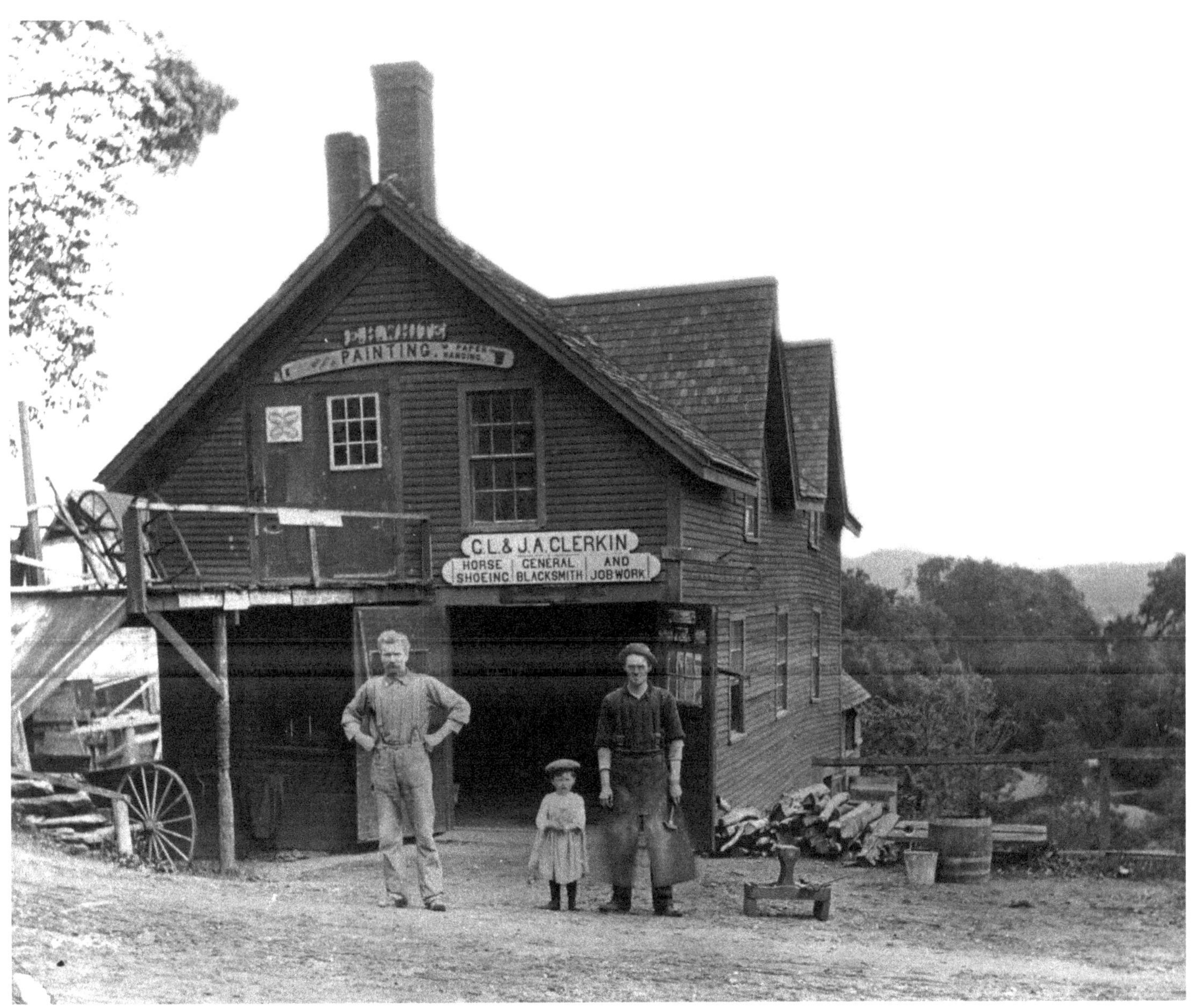

Jericho blacksmith J. Allan Clerkin (right), with his brother Ralph and father George. At the height of horse-and-buggy travel, blacksmiths enjoyed a robust trade shoeing horses and fabricating wagon wheels for the community. At least five of these artisans plied their trade in turn-of-the-century Jericho. When automobiles arrived some years later, a concrete bridge replaced the wooden one next to this shop and the resident blacksmith converted half his business into a service station.

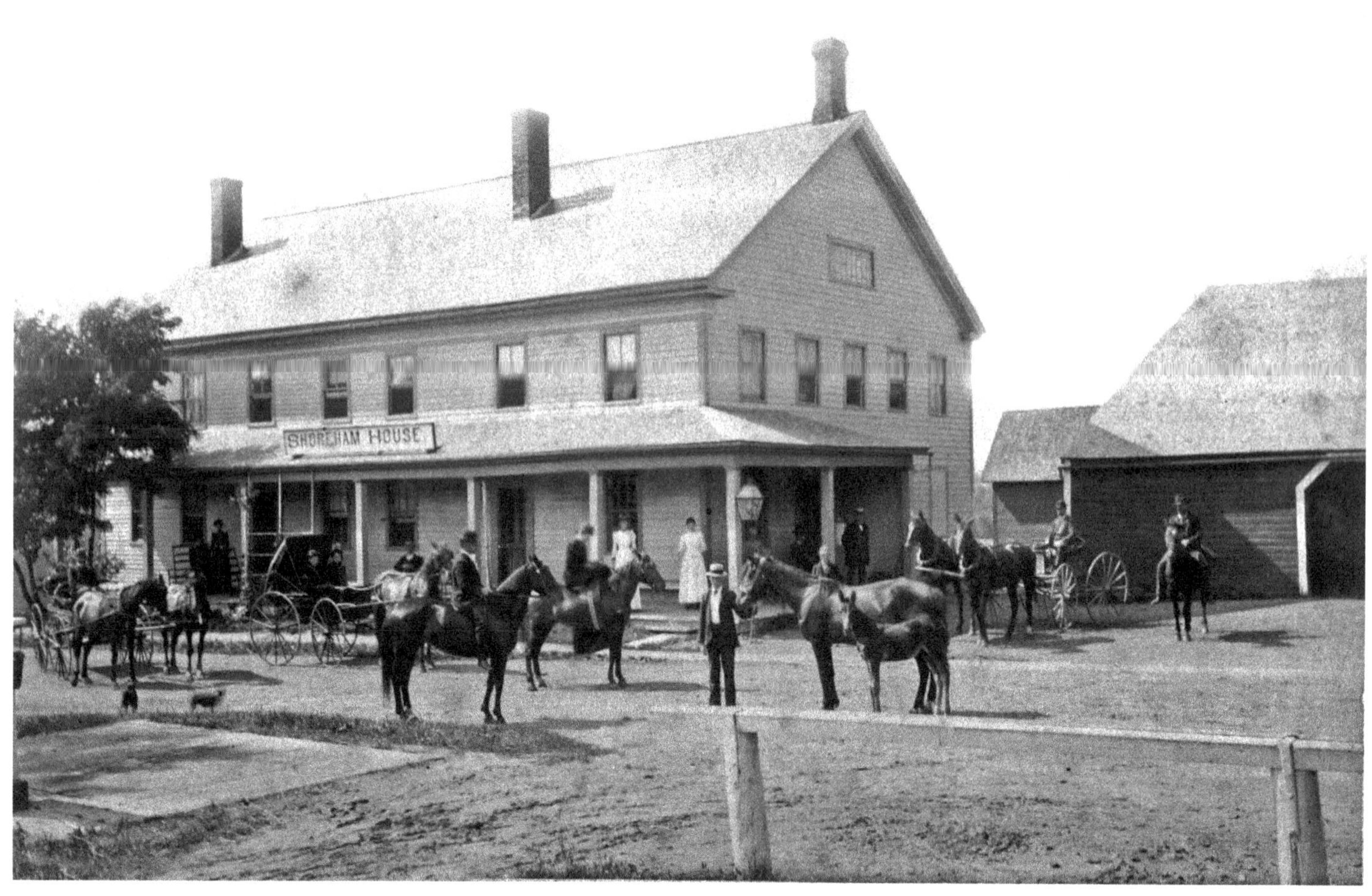

In the late nineteenth century, inns like the Shoreham House hosted travelers leaving Vermont for better situations. Novelist Nathaniel Hawthorne marveled at how this exodus made international junctions of Lake Champlain's port towns, describing the "continual succession of travelers who spent an idle quarter of an hour in waiting for the ferryboat, affording me just enough time to . . . penetrate their mysteries and be rid of them without the risk of tediousness on either side."

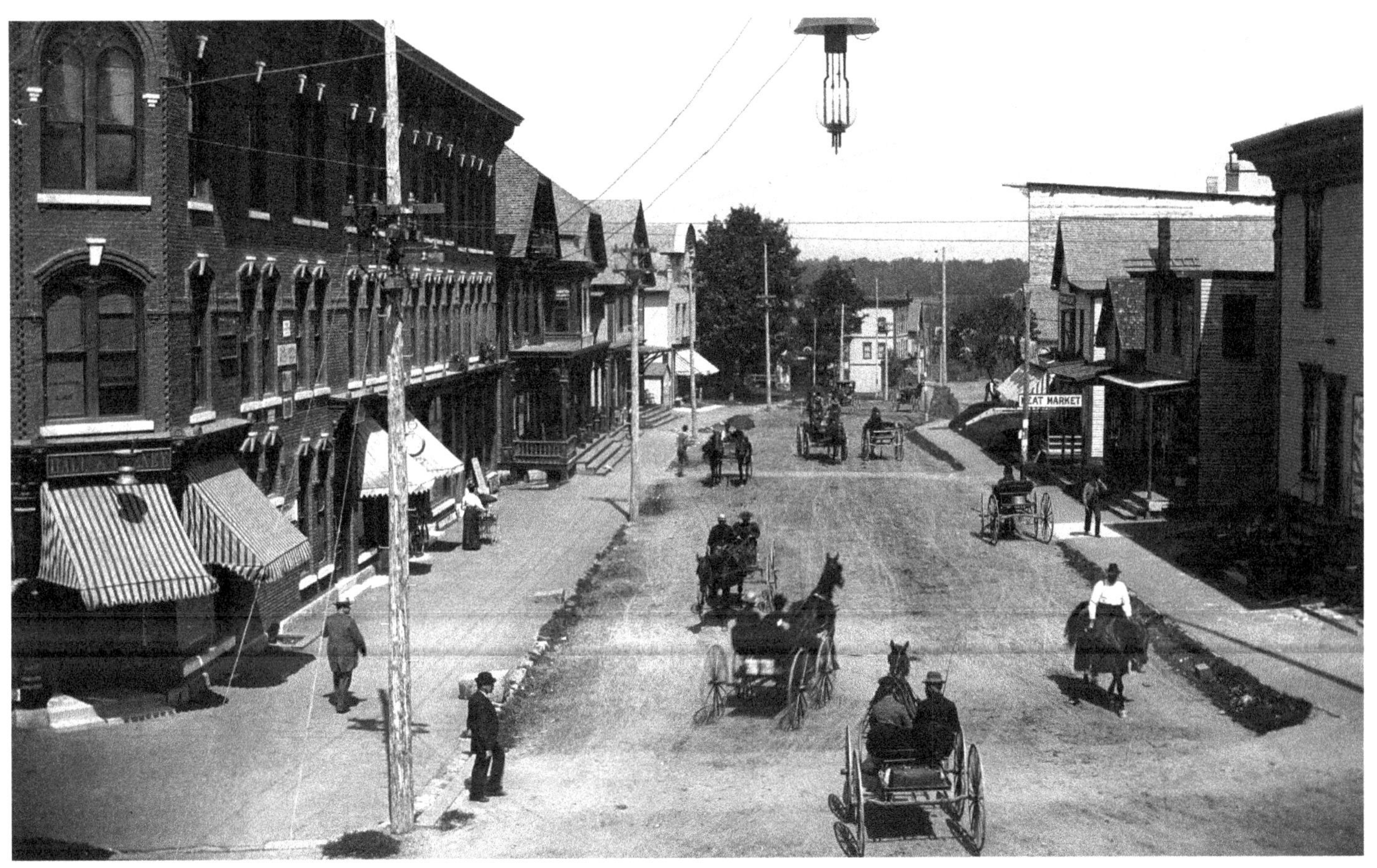

This photograph shows a streetlight on Morrisville's Portland Street, one of 21 arc lamps installed in 1895. The Lamoille River powered Morrisville's first electric plant, built in 1894. The plant manager started the plant at dusk and left it running until morning. If there was not enough water to power the lights through the night, the town's early risers woke up in the dark.

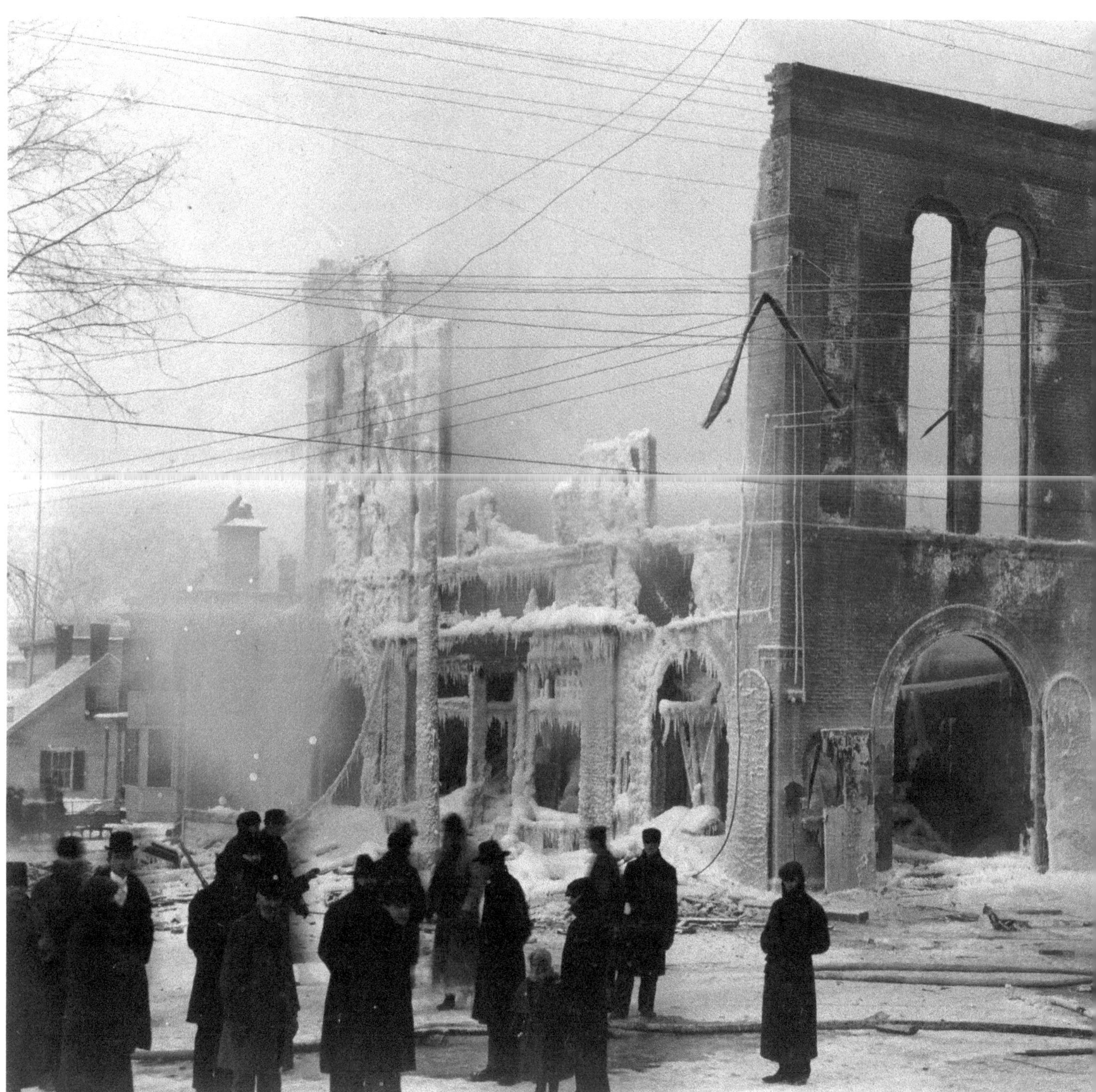

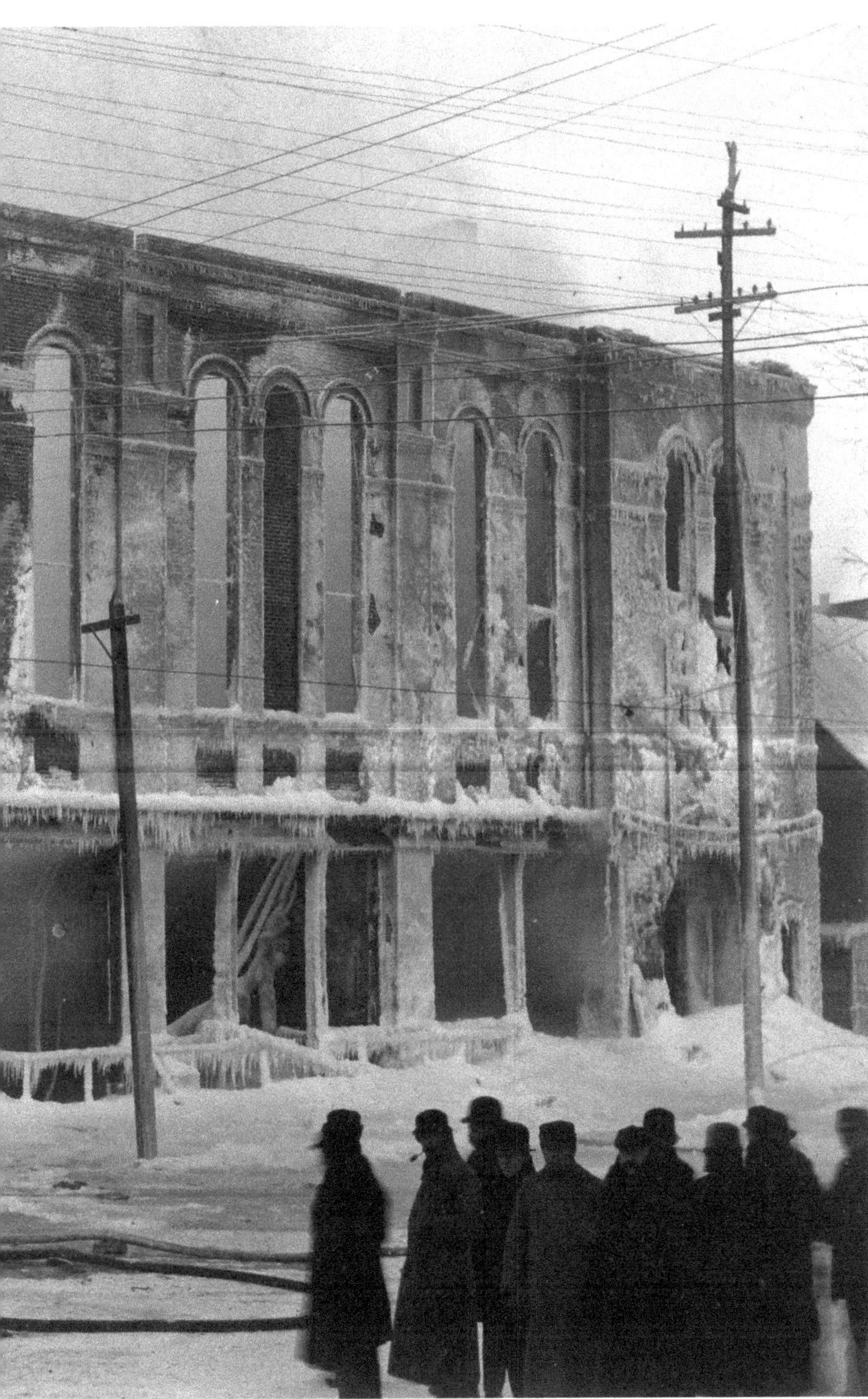

The Barre Opera House fire, 1898. Barre's Opera House attracted music, lectures, and theater that was heard the world around. When the theater caught fire one January night, firemen discovered that the two nearest hydrants had frozen. The roof soon collapsed in flames and the handsome edifice was gutted. In the following morning's paper, photographer H. E. Cutter announced that he would sell photographs of the fire for 25¢ apiece.

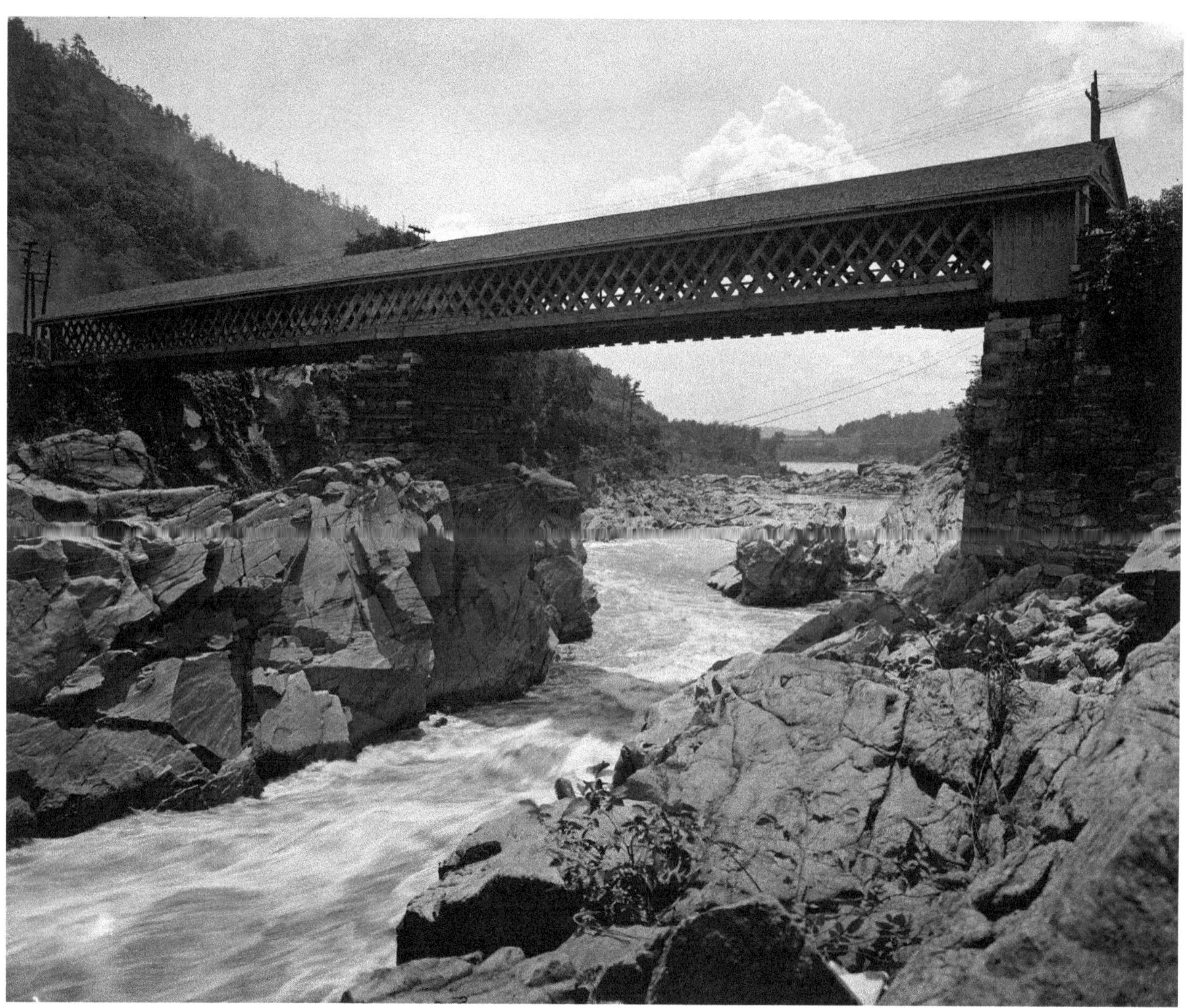

The Tucker Toll Bridge, shown here around the turn of the century. Nathaniel Tucker originally bought a toll bridge at Bellows Falls in 1826. It was the first bridge to cross the Connecticut River, and Tucker collected the tolls himself. One day he was surprised to look upriver and see another bridge about to crash over the falls. The intruder was the Cheshire Bridge, which had broken free and, fortunately for Tucker, happened to shatter before it hit his bridge. Within a year, Tucker chose to rebuild his bridge with this larger and higher structure, which endured through the remainder of the century.

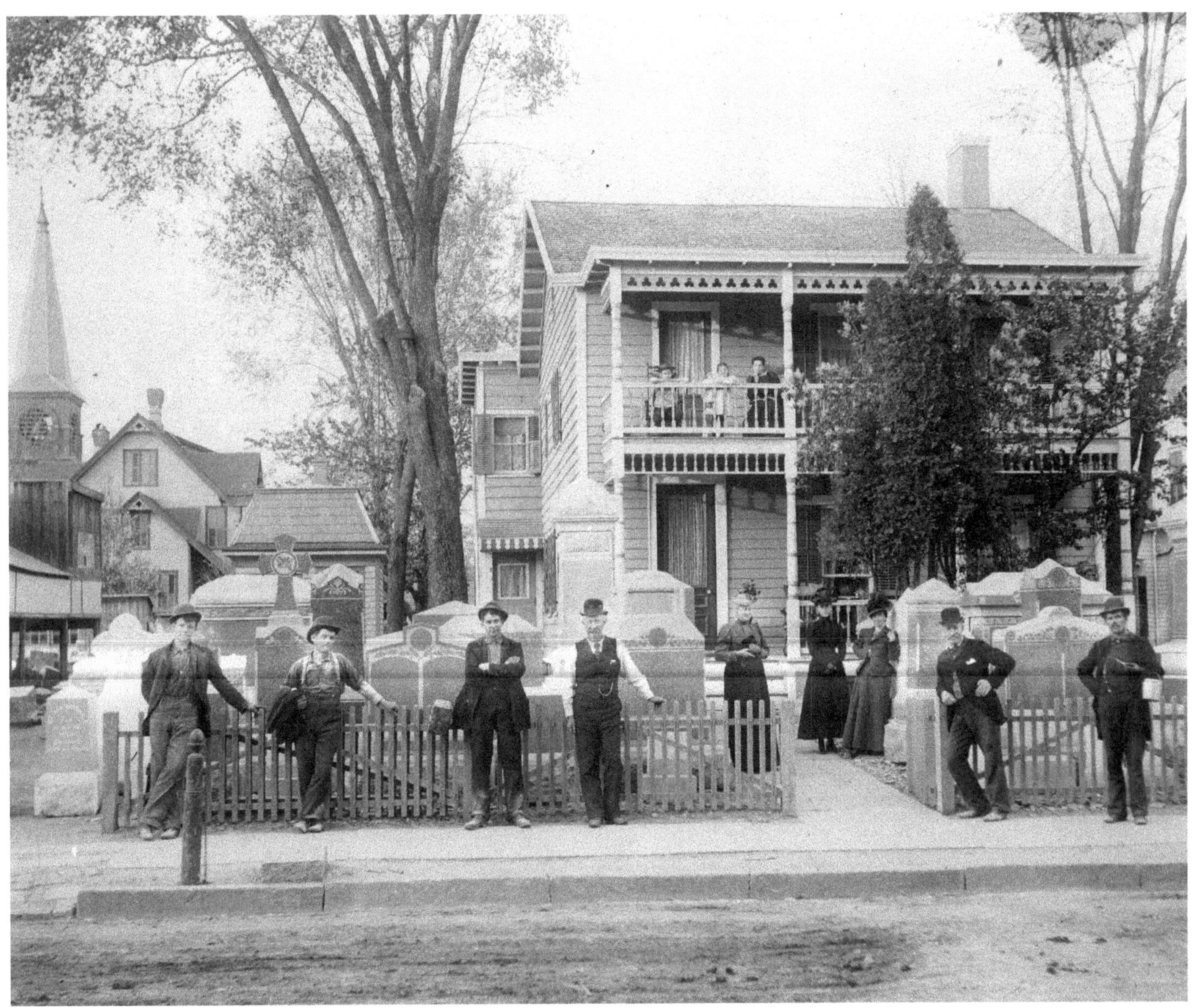

Vermont's early grave markers were made of limestone and marble, and sometimes slate or cast metal. Granite became the stone of choice in the 1880s because it resisted staining and erosion, and because it polished to a fine luster. Stone artisans from Italy and Scotland—along with Scandinavians, Spaniards, Lebanese, Greeks, and French Canadians—practiced their trade in Barre beginning in the 1880s.

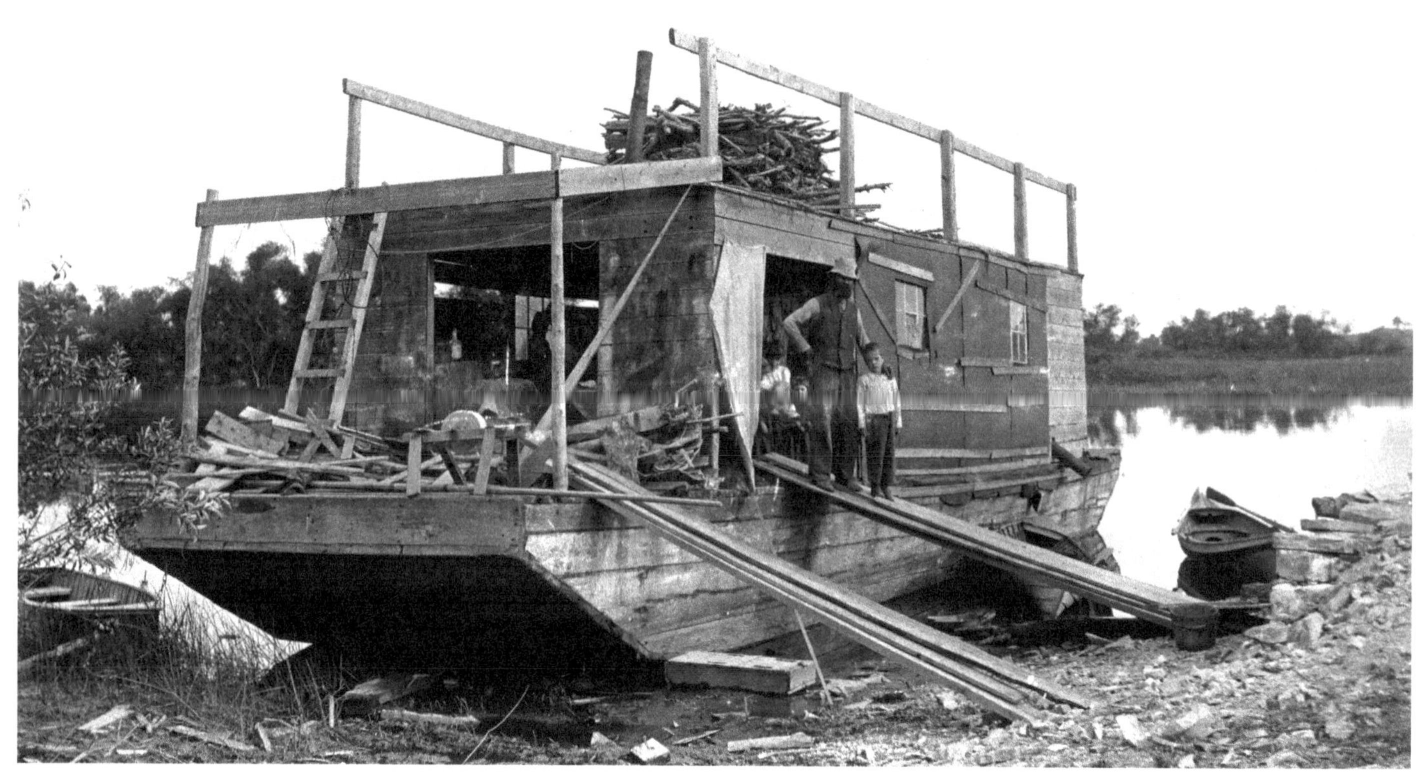

Thurlow Ploof and family on the Otter Creek, 1893. Nineteenth-century Lake Champlain hosted a vibrant maritime community of people living on the lake. They included "canalers," Vermonters who lived on boats that were towed through the waterways between New York and Canada, and families like the Ploofs, who served as day laborers in the lake's port communities. These laborers lived on their boats and squatted on nearby land when they needed to come ashore.

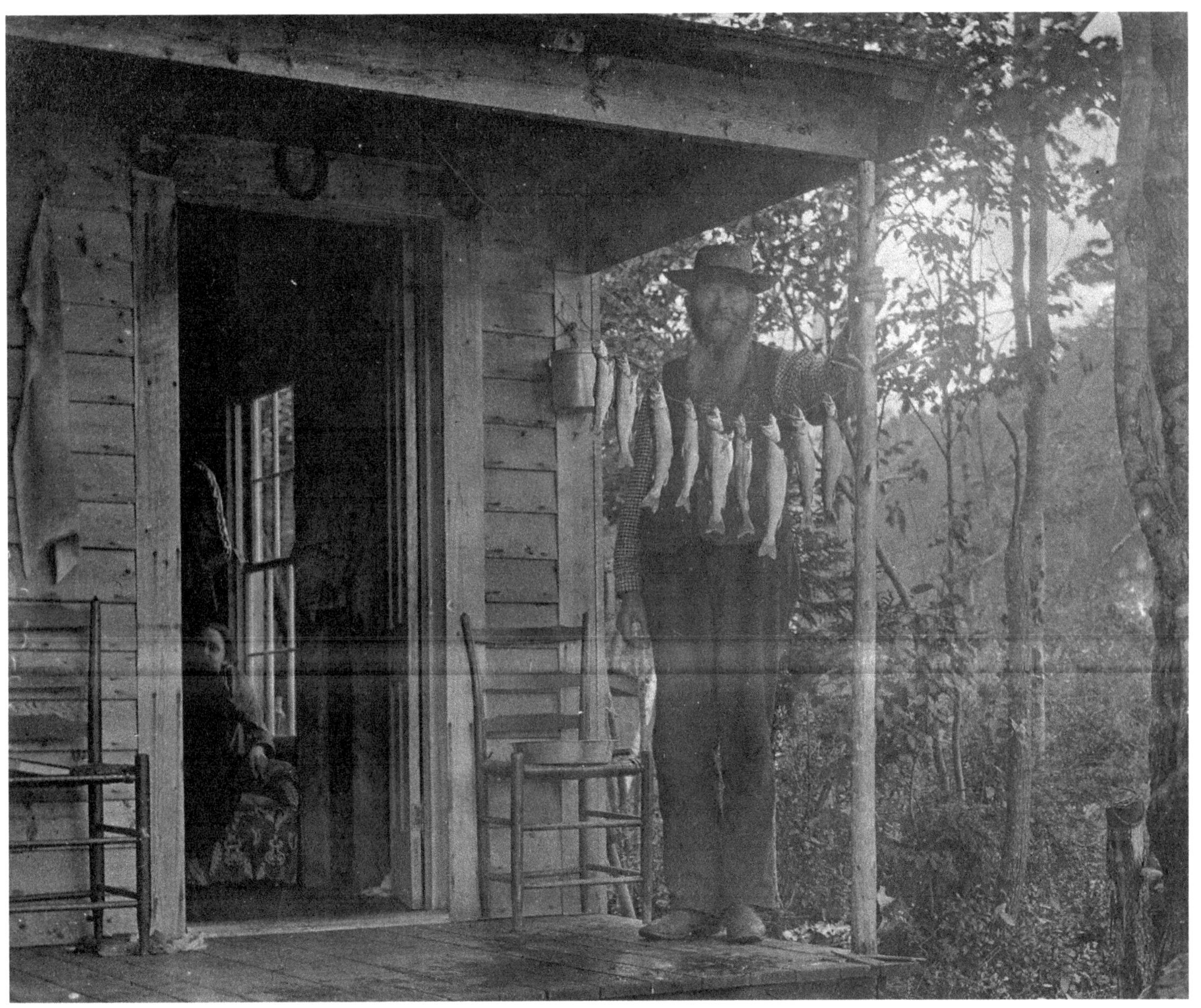

As early as the 1820s, some Vermont towns attempted to regulate fishing, but to little effect. The state became more involved when it enacted a statewide fishing code by midcentury, but the populace essentially ignored the law, viewing fish and game as their rightful means to self-sufficiency. State wardens began work in 1867. Here, Moses Pearson displays his trout catch from Shrewsbury Pond around the turn of the century.

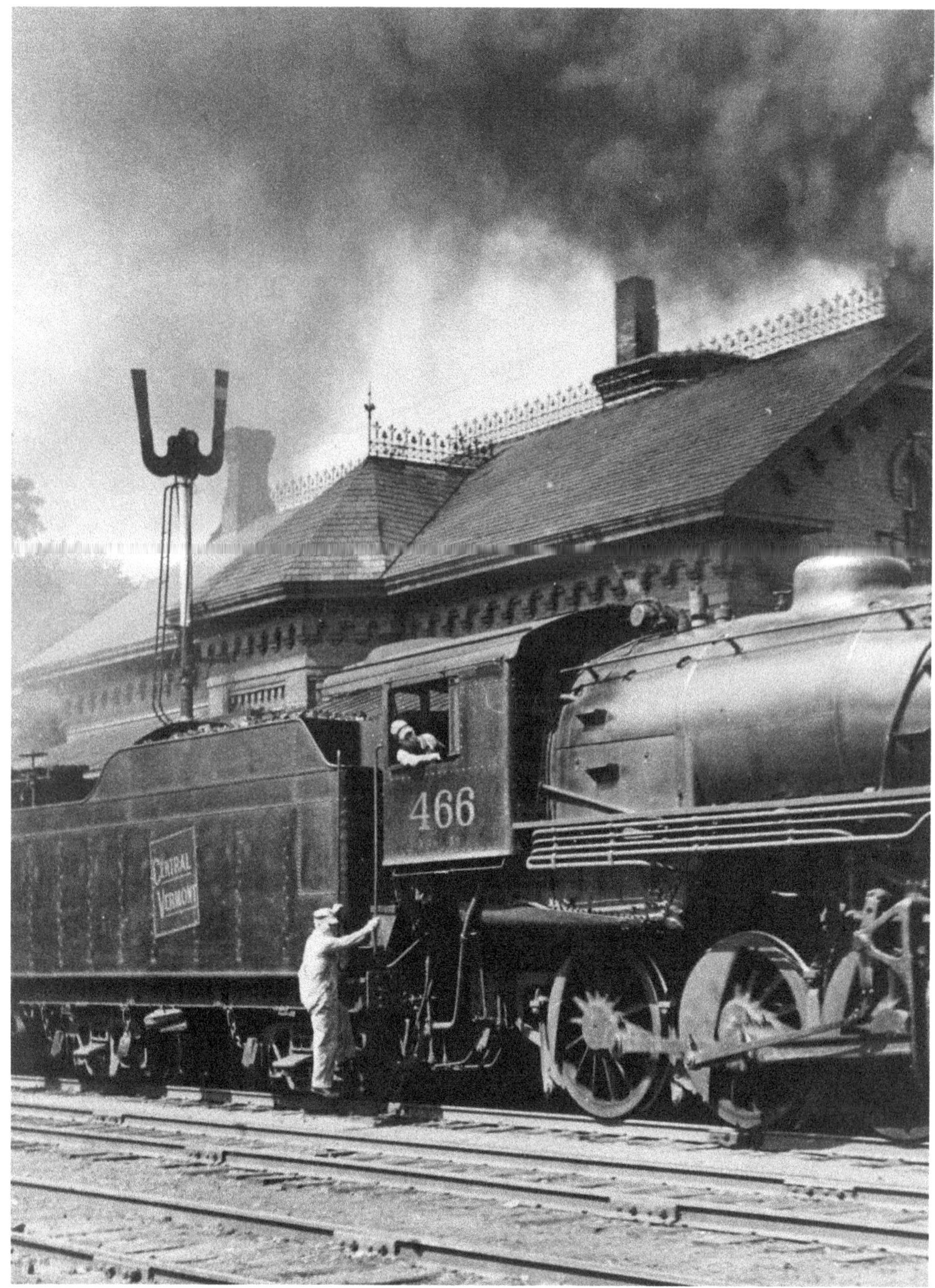

The 1881 Randolph Railroad station. In addition to hauling daily freight and passengers, the railroads promoted cultural activities. When Dubois and Gay's Hall hosted the Randolph Musical Association in 1899, the Central Vermont Railroad reduced its rates to help passengers attend the big day.

Two Worlds Collide

(1900–1926)

In 1891, the U.S. postmaster general administered a limited national test of rural postal delivery to some of the nation's outlying communities. Despite support from the nation's farmers and newspaper editors, both of whom stood to benefit from broader postal delivery, the Post Office Department dragged its heels in implementing the service. In 1896, a second national rural free delivery experiment incorporated Vermont's Grand Isle among the test sites. Within a decade, rural free delivery, began operating throughout much of Vermont. The new service benefited some, but threatened others. Some general store owners, for example, opposed RFD because it curbed the number of weekly visits residents must make to the village store. The service also added incentive for households to use mail order companies, obviating the need for residents to rely on town centers at all. Rural free delivery carried with it the potential to change the social and economic dynamic of many rural communities.

The dynamics of RFD illustrate what happens when old methods meet new practices, when favored traditions meet emerging technologies, when two worlds collide. Vermonters of the early twentieth century struggled to keep old ways working while accepting the progress, accessibility, and profits of a modern world. The result was that horse-drawn snow rollers existed alongside gas-powered snowplows, waterpower existed alongside electricity, bridge signs advised different speed limits for horse-drawn conveyances and automobiles, and women could tend the family farm or attend secretarial school.

The conflict between old and new played out most detectably in a growing division between Vermont's rural areas and its cities. Between 1860 and 1925, seven Vermont towns—Burlington, Barre, Montpelier, Rutland, Newport, St. Albans, and Winooski—made the leap into municipal incorporation. With their industrial, mercantile, and professional residents, these areas cultivated economic and political interests that differed significantly from those of farmers in less populated areas of the state. Cities also attracted large numbers of immigrants—Irish, French Canadian, Italian, Chinese, Swedish, Welsh—whose presence contributed to cultural diversity at best, and racial tensions at worst.

As Vermonters lived among these mounting divisions between rural and urban interests—between worlds old and new—they looked to the traditions of old Vermont, which would survive, widely romanticized, into today.

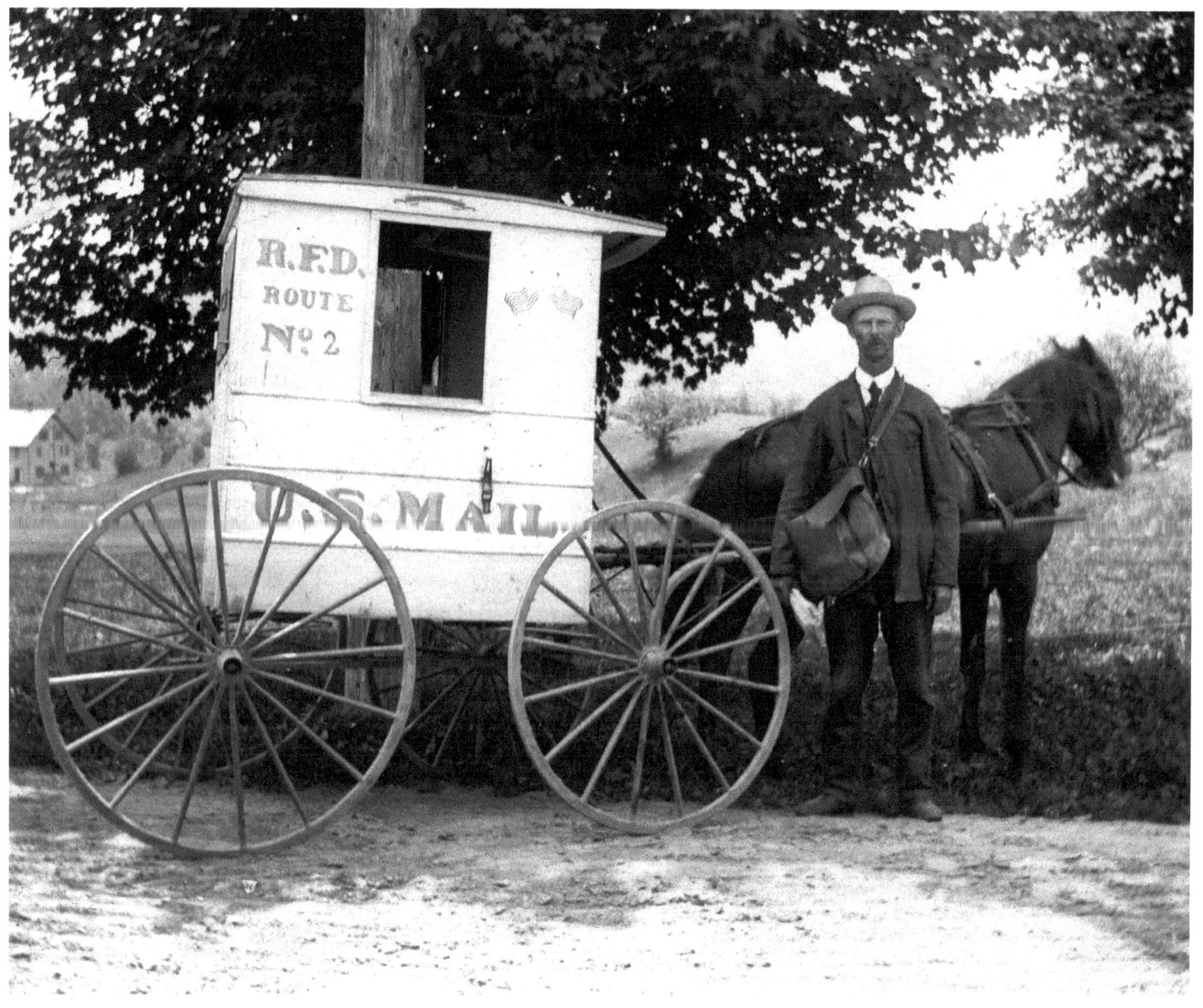

Charles E. Pitts, rural delivery carrier, travels from Shrewsbury toward Rutland. The town of Ludlow participated in a national rural free delivery experiment in 1891, and Grand Isle received RFD service in 1896. By 1904, there were 212 rural routes in Vermont, and the U.S. postmaster general declared that RFD appeared "to give great satisfaction to the community served." Rutland was the sixth town in the state to host the service.

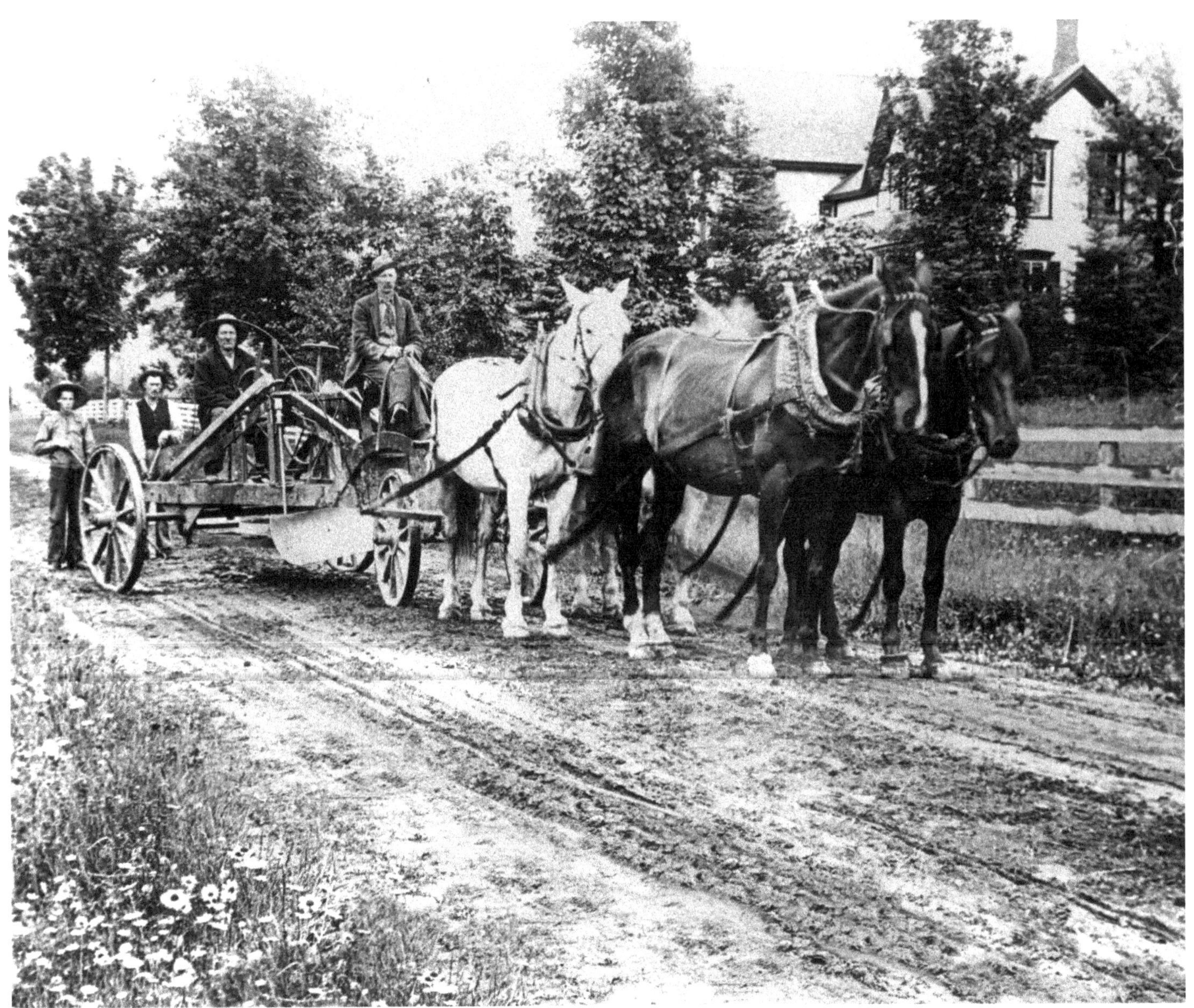

A road crew for the town of Jericho pauses for a photograph along the Nashville Road. This four-man operation included a driver, who managed the horses; the engineer, who lowered and raised the implement's blade; and two men on foot to spread out the dirt heaps. Vermont's reputation among travelers for its poor roads continued into the 1930s, with travel guides advising that visitors bring chains and mud hooks "to ensure a prompt getaway from the worst mud hole."

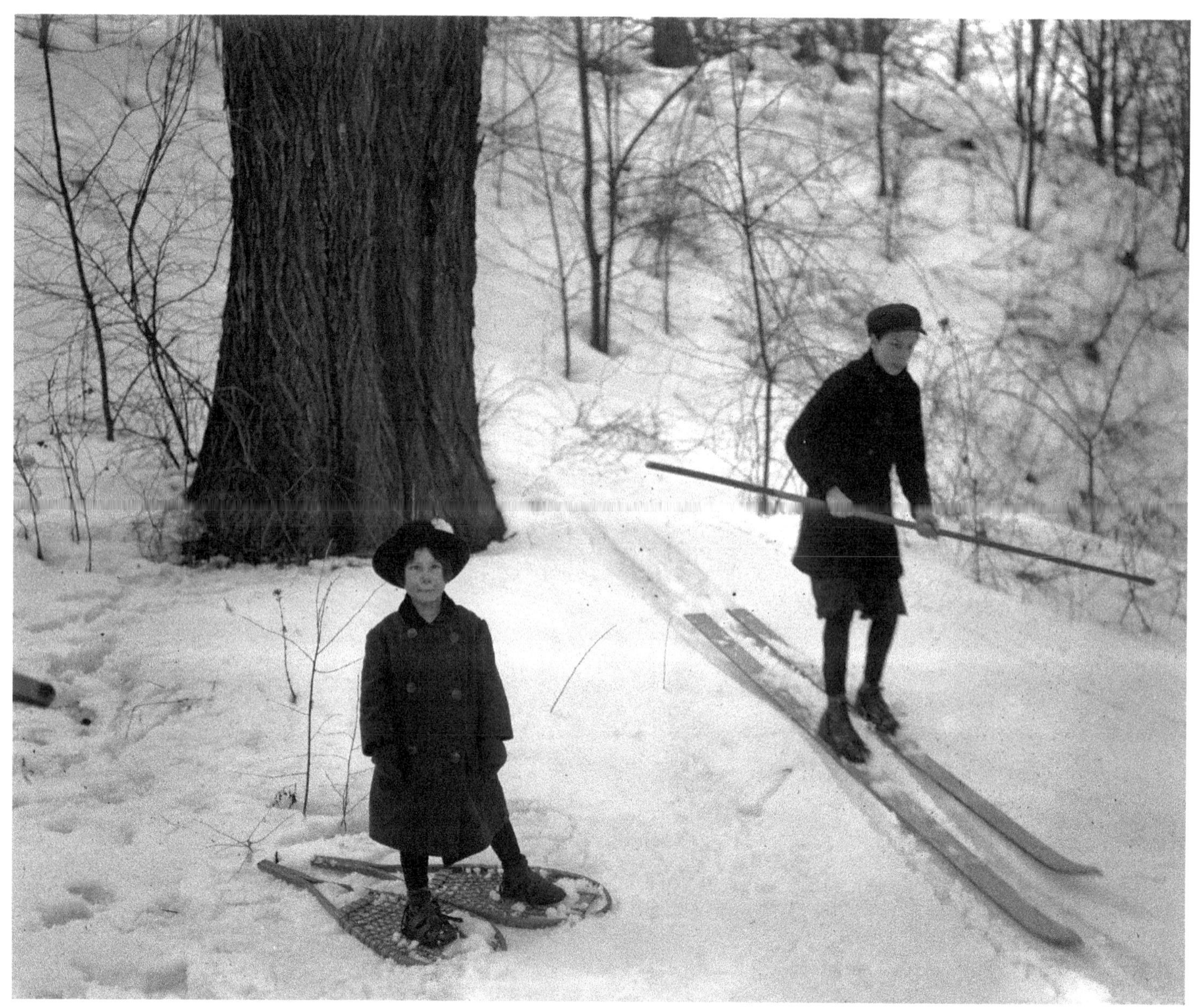

A young snowshoer and skier in Brattleboro. Lumber company proprietor Craig Burt experimented with handmade skis early in the twentieth century by soaking hardwood boards in hot sawdust and then turning up the front ends. While snowshoeing remained Vermonters' favorite sport through the 1920s, Burt advocated skiing since it would be "as good-business as any summer development we have, and much better than some."

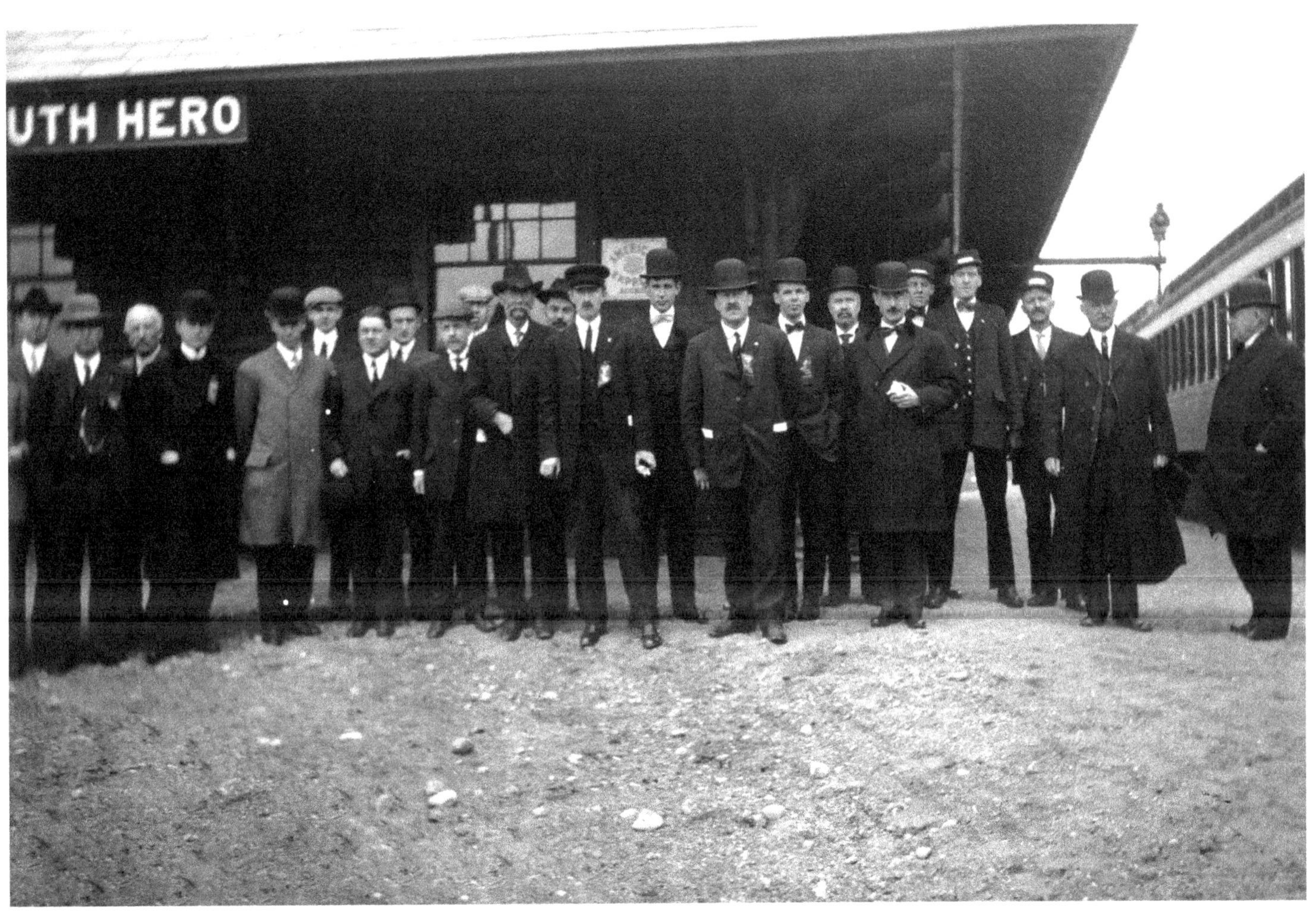

When competition from the country's western farms intensified, the state of Vermont experimented with a number of programs to help struggling local farmers. These included the Better Farming Special, a traveling railroad exhibit that traversed the state displaying modern machinery and horticultural methods. Farmers appreciated the assistance, but were skeptical of state involvement in agricultural programs, concerned that it might frustrate hands-on decision-making by those closest to the land.

George Clerkin at Chittenden Mills in Jericho. Built in 1856 by a Jericho resident who had amassed a fortune in the California gold rush, this five-story, cupola-topped mill operated for 90 years grinding grain. Clerkin learned the milling trade in Minnesota and worked at Chittenden Mills for 22 years. The mill ceased flour production when Clerkin died, but continued to grind grain for livestock through the early 1940s, using waterpower.

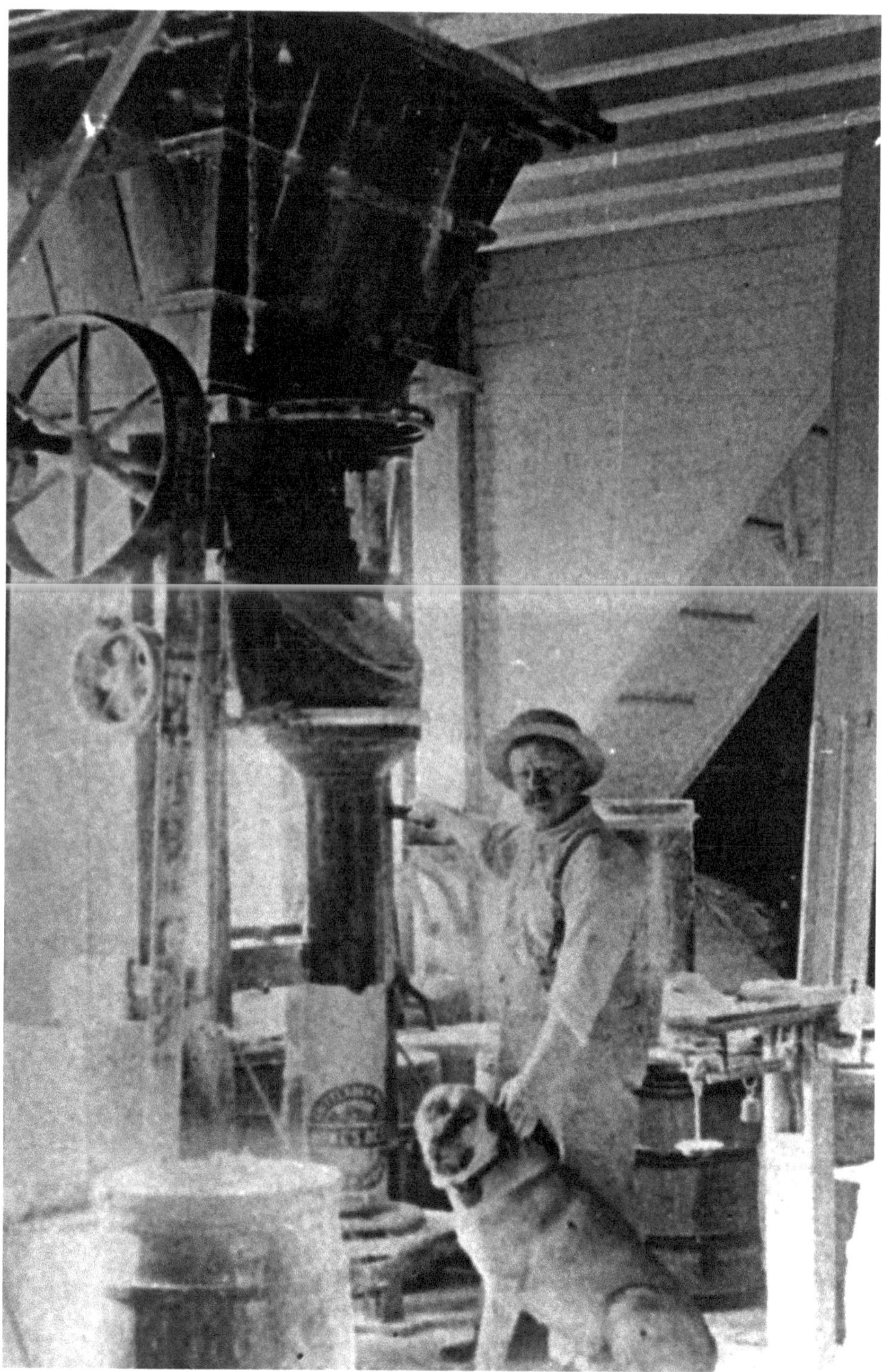

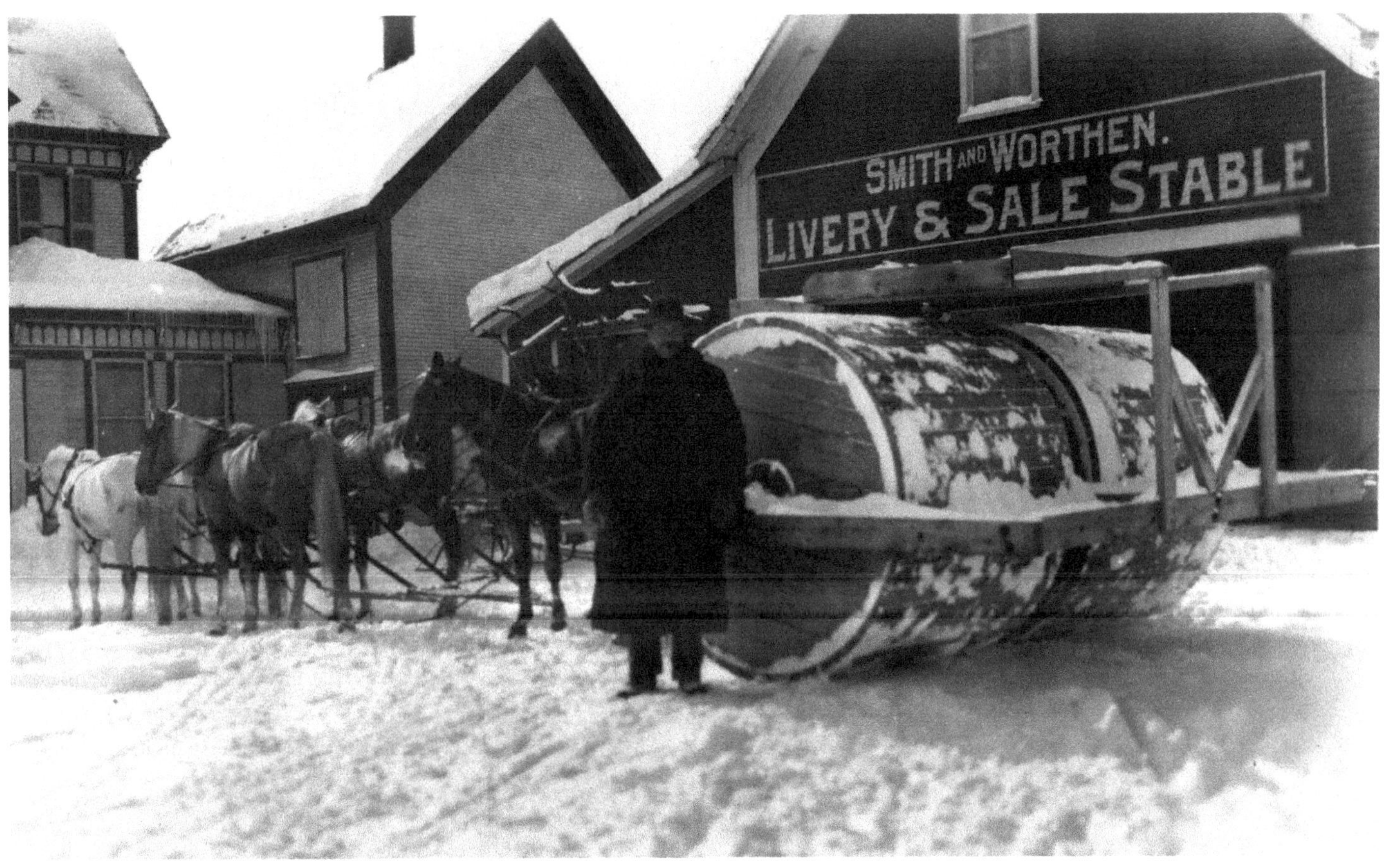

Andrew Smith drove this snow roller for the village of Morrisville during the early 1900s. He was an obvious choice for the job, since he owned the livery stable pictured in this photograph. During the winter months, Vermonters found compressing the snow easier than plowing it, for at least one practical reason—many residents used horse-drawn sleighs instead of wagons during the snowy season.

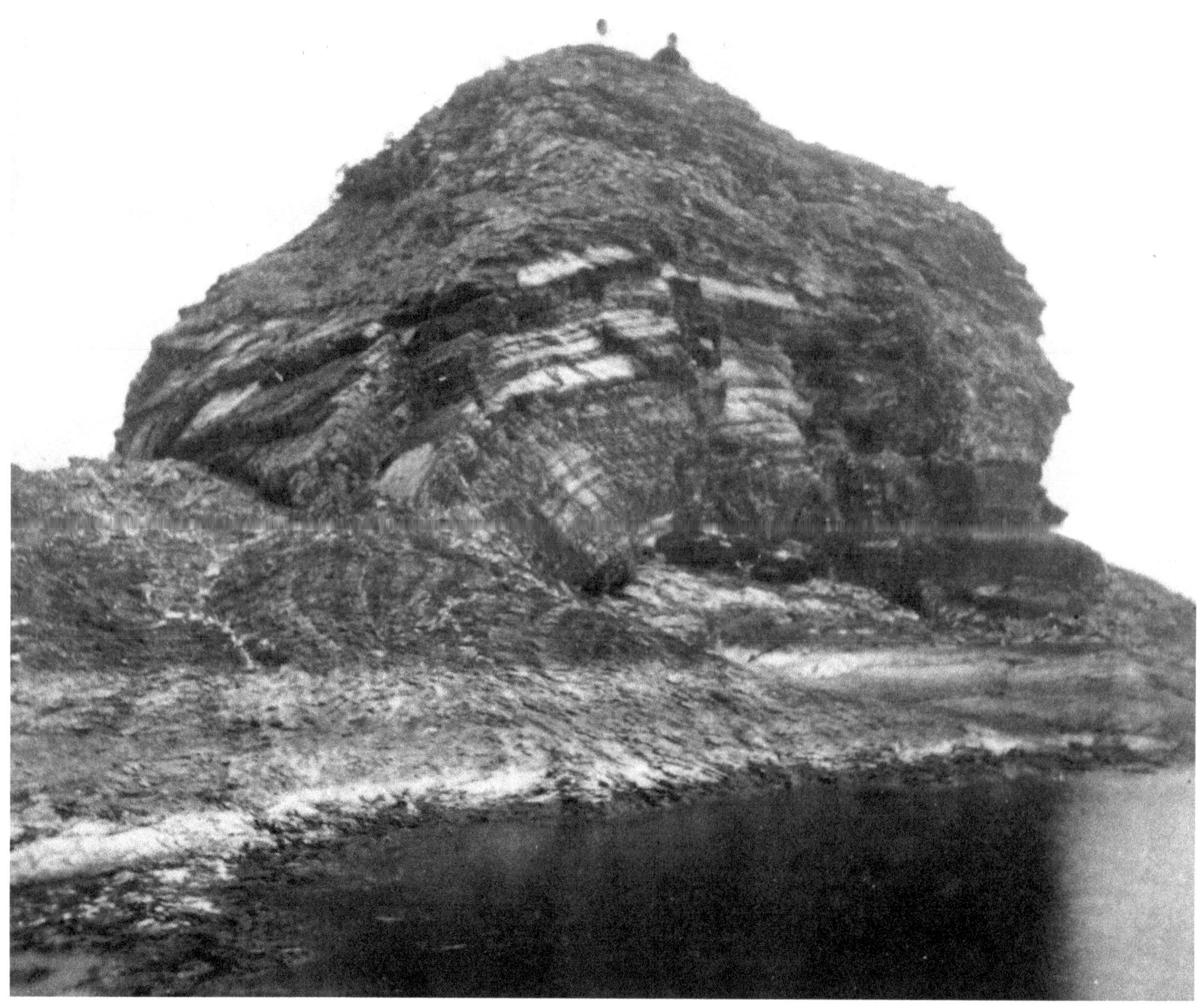

Odzihozo, or Rock Dunder, around 1910. Abenaki mythology tells of Odzihozo, a quasi-human figure who shaped the region's rivers and mountains. Odzihozo's last project was Lake Champlain, which he liked so much he perched himself on a rock in Burlington Bay and transformed himself into stone so that he could continue to enjoy it. Traditionally, Abenakis left offerings of tobacco when they passed the rock by canoe. Barely visible at the summit in this image, several visitors enjoy the view.

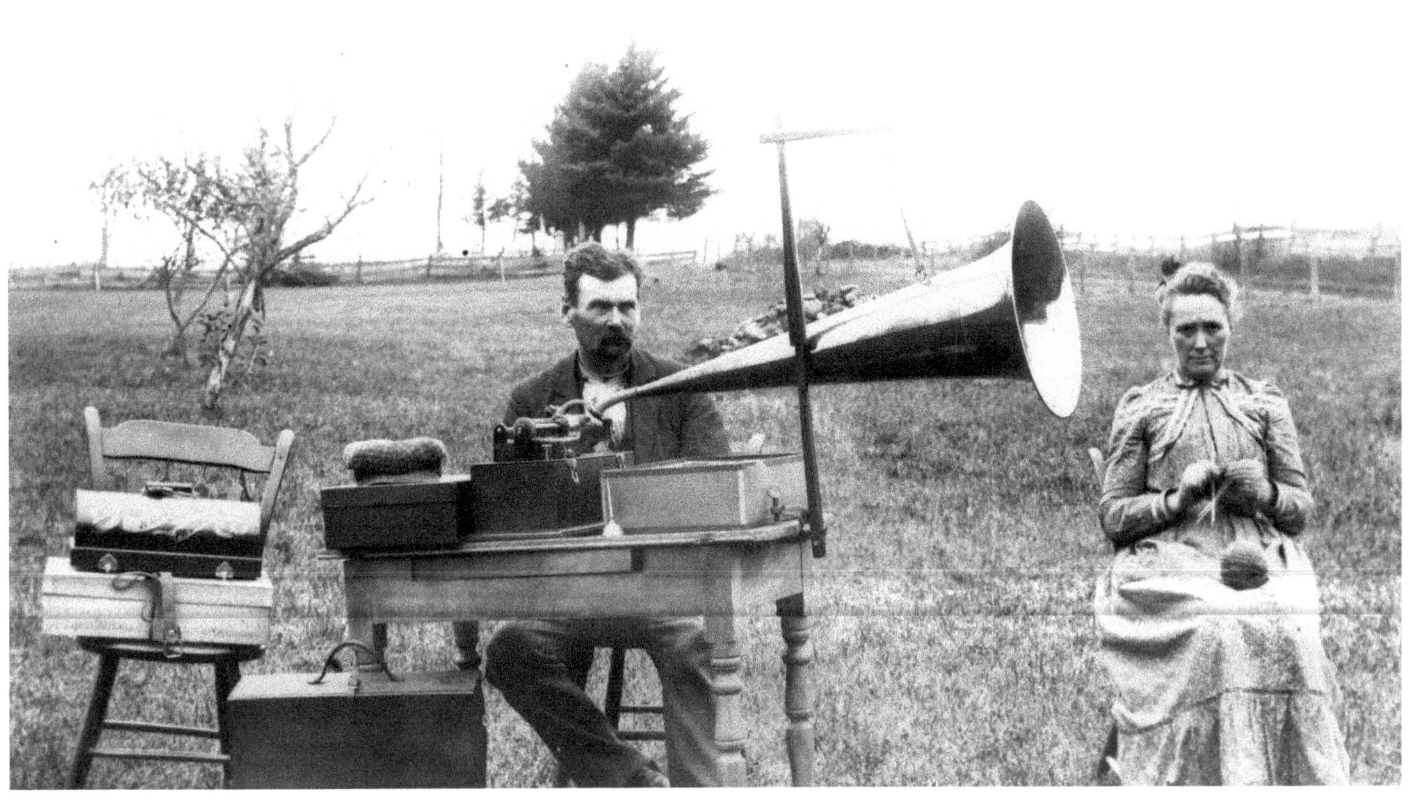

Dick and Nett Langmaid pose with their phonograph, table, and chairs near their home around West Danville in 1900. Traveling photographers of the day offered residents the opportunity to record themselves and their most-prized belongings—furniture, livestock, and the family home—for relatives afar. No doubt the Langmaids particularly cherished their phonograph. Invented by Thomas Edison in 1877, these instruments were just becoming affordable at the turn of the century.

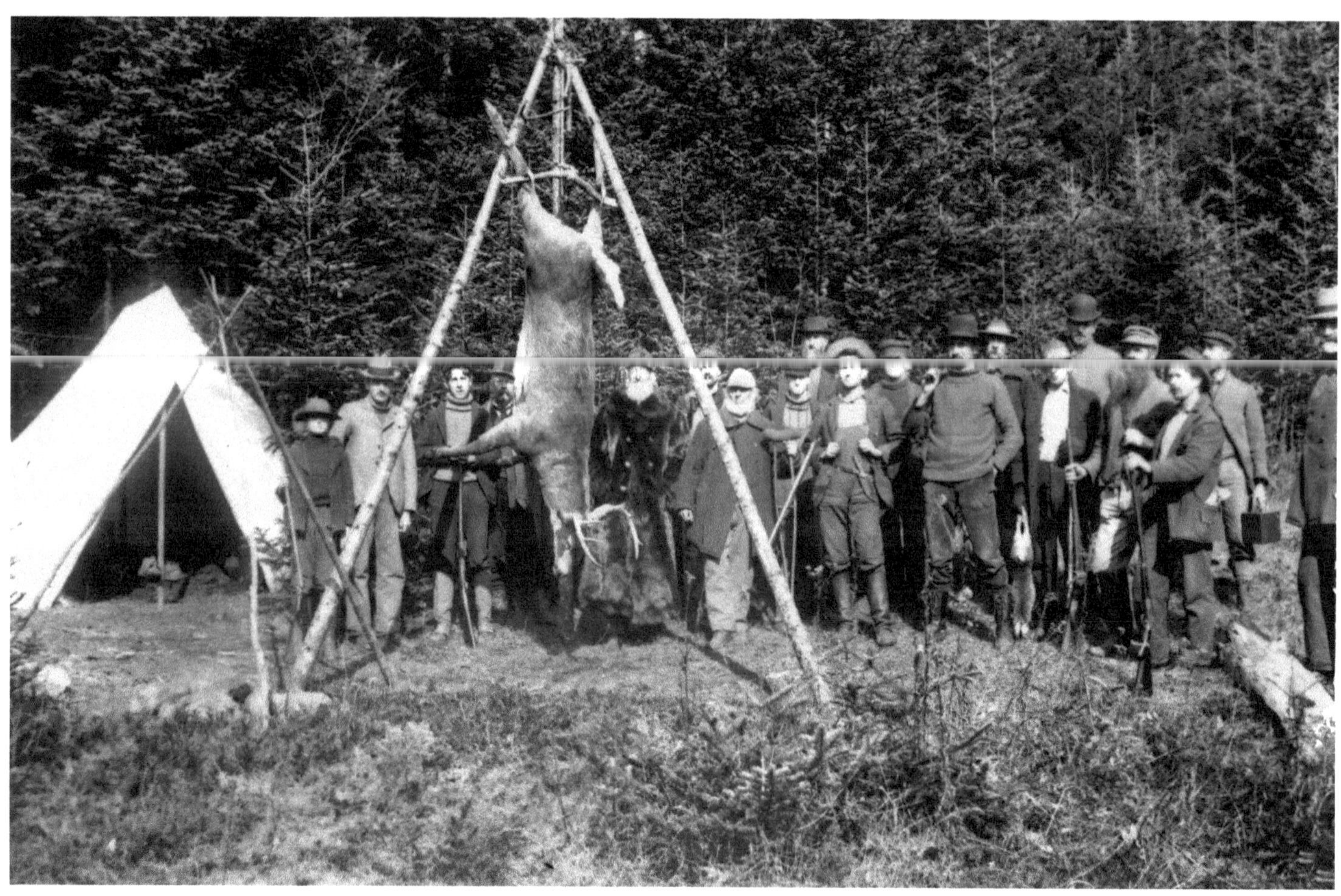

A deer camp in northeast Vermont. Hunting deer in Vermont was prohibited from 1865 to 1897, the result of overhunting during the early nineteenth century. The state reintroduced the animals by importing 17 deer from New York in the late 1870s. In the 1890s, the state broadened the jurisdiction of the Fish Commission to include game and reopened the sport. Hunting licenses were required of out-of-staters at first, and then of in-state residents as well.

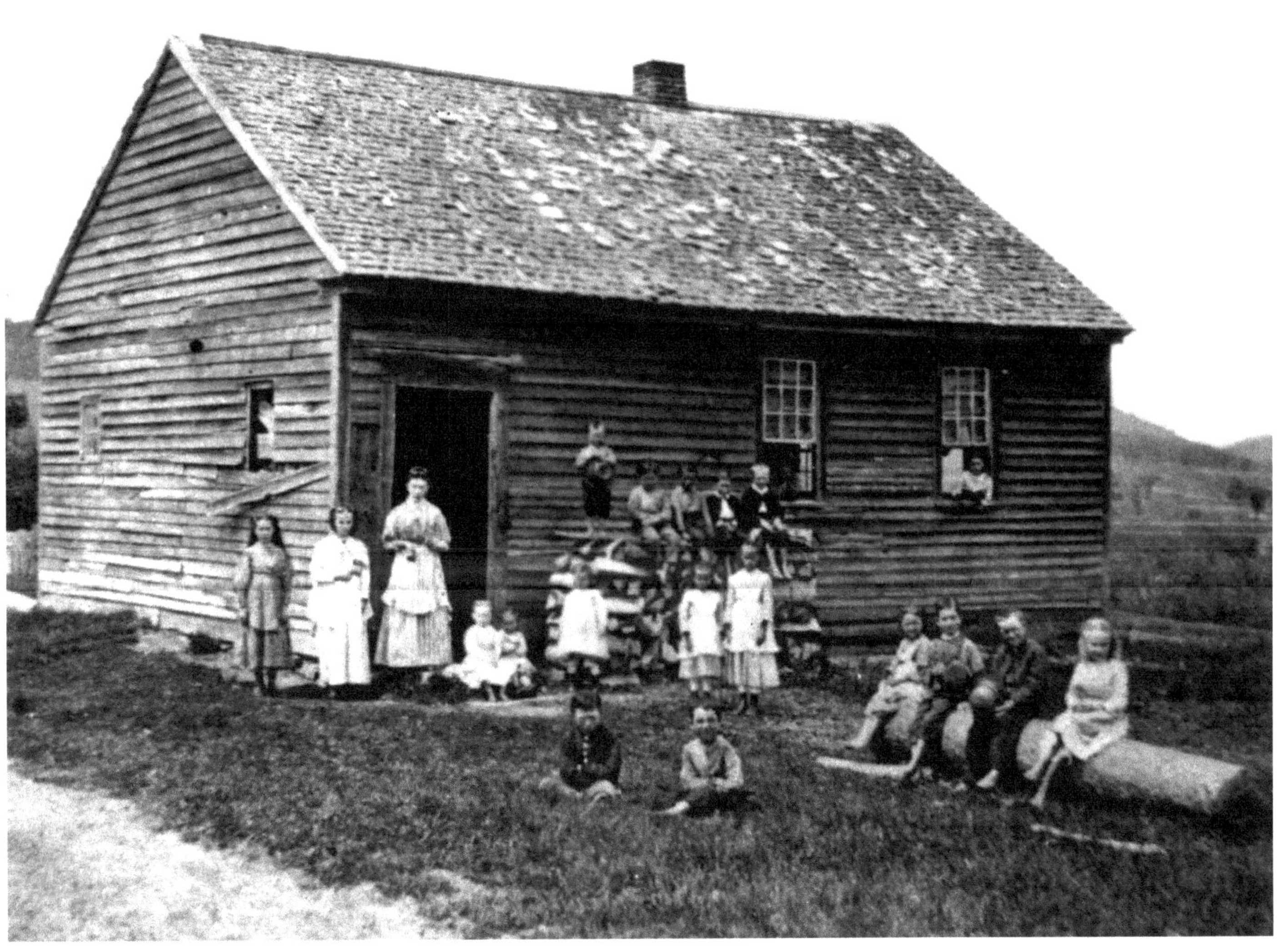

Church Street School, Jericho. Educational reformers long complained about the one-room schoolhouse, advocating instead for standardized textbooks, state-supervised teacher preparation, and a grade-based system not possible in a one-room school managed by a lone teacher. Many Vermonters, however, viewed state-level reforms as impositions on town control and vehemently resisted the changes. It was not until the turn of the century that most towns willingly gave up local control and formed larger administrative districts, or unions.

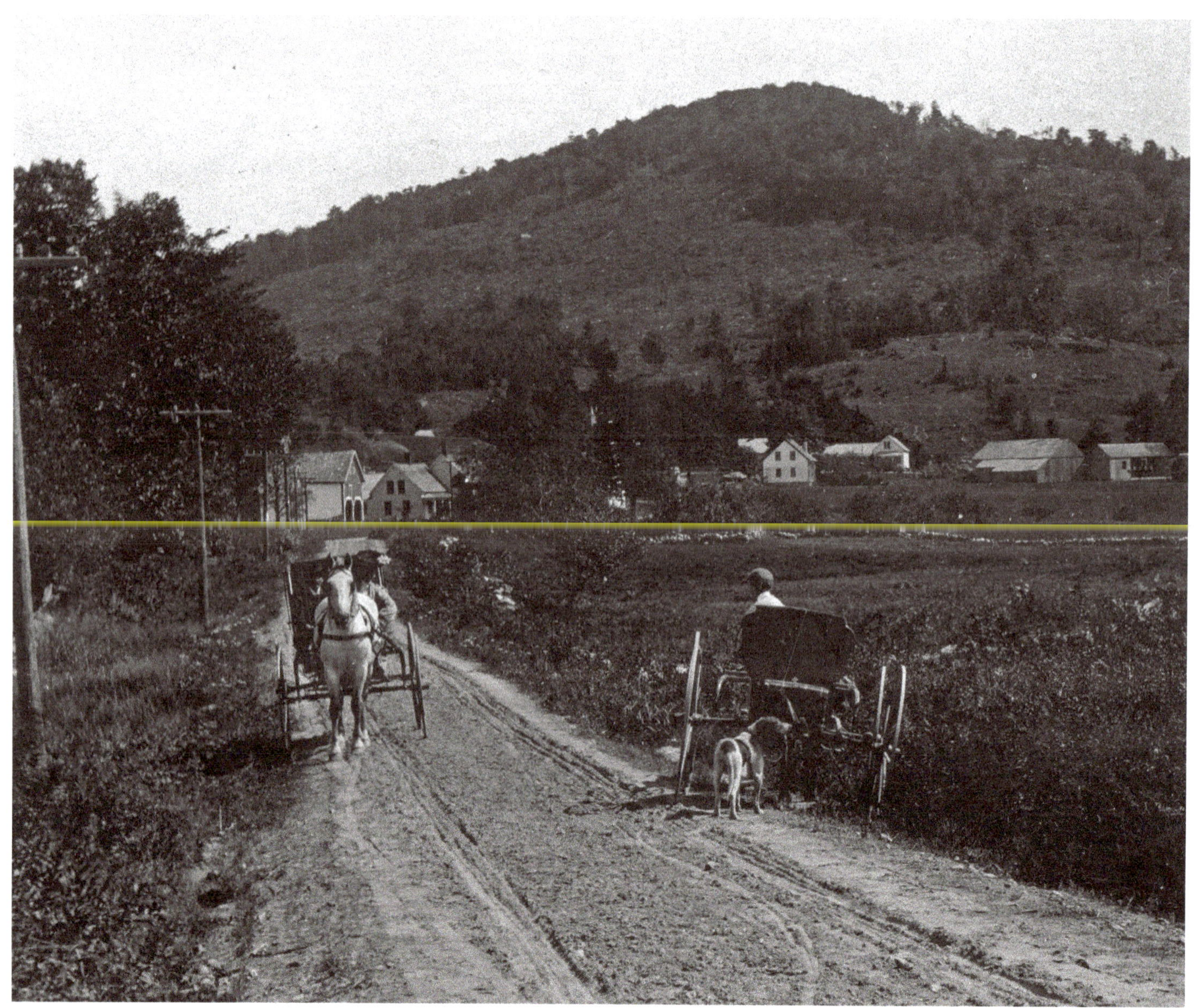

Yielding the right-of-way in Shrewsbury. As early as 1805, state laws prohibited coaches from turning off the road "with an intent to evade the toll," and by 1900, with 14,825 miles of road in Vermont, more regulation was clearly needed. In 1933, the state took full control of the highways. Vermont roads were also notoriously sloppy, which led to the Vermont League for Good Roads, organized by citizens in the 1890s.

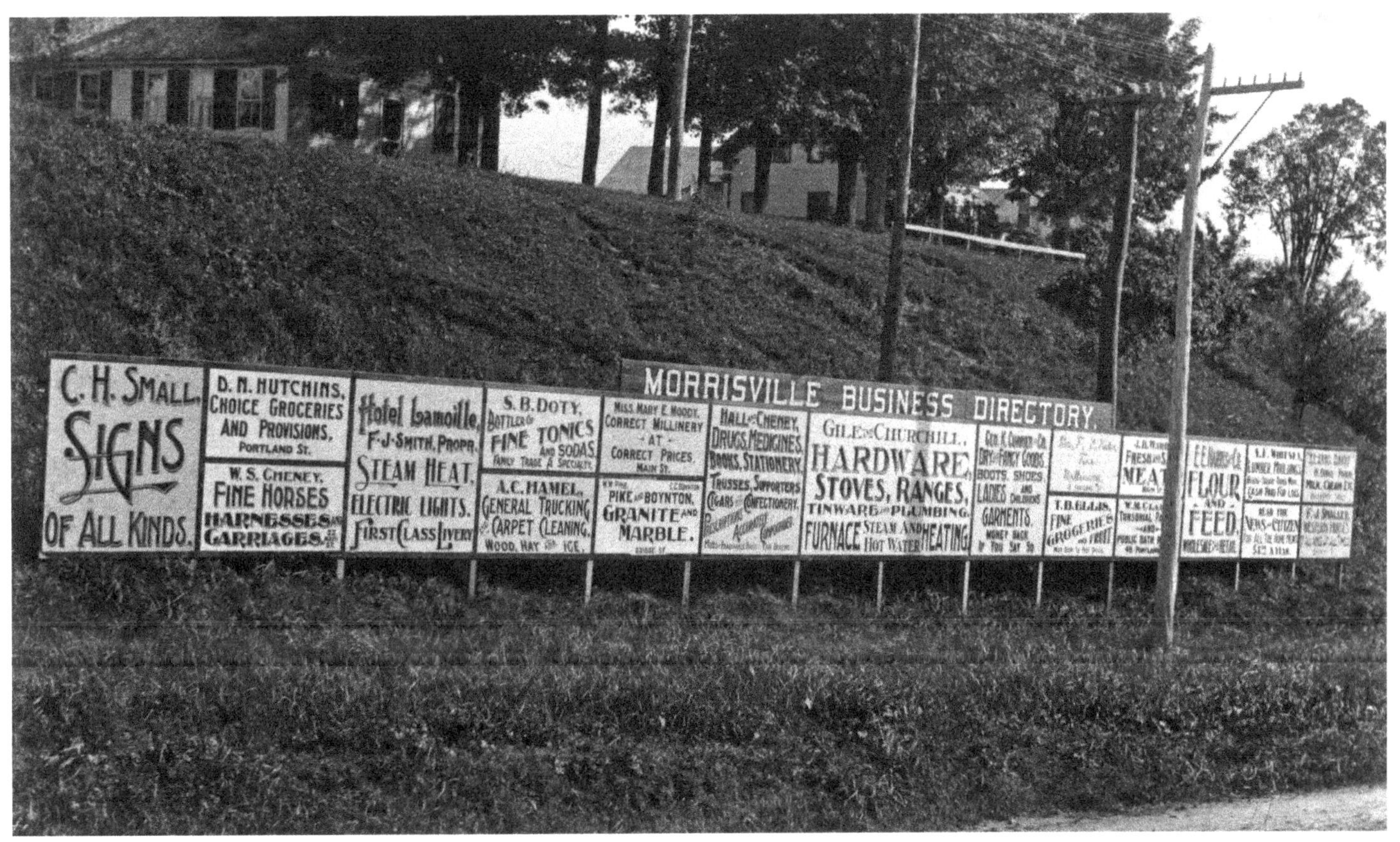

Around 1900, this hand-lettered business directory below East High Street greeted travelers from Stowe as they entered Morrisville. In 1937, the town of Springfield became the first to introduce highway billboards. The signs created consternation among some. Well-known writer, publicist, and founder of Weston's Vermont Country Store, Vrest Orton once called billboards "un-Vermonterish." In 1967, the state banned billboards altogether—but only after a fight with lobbyists, who argued for their benefit to tourists.

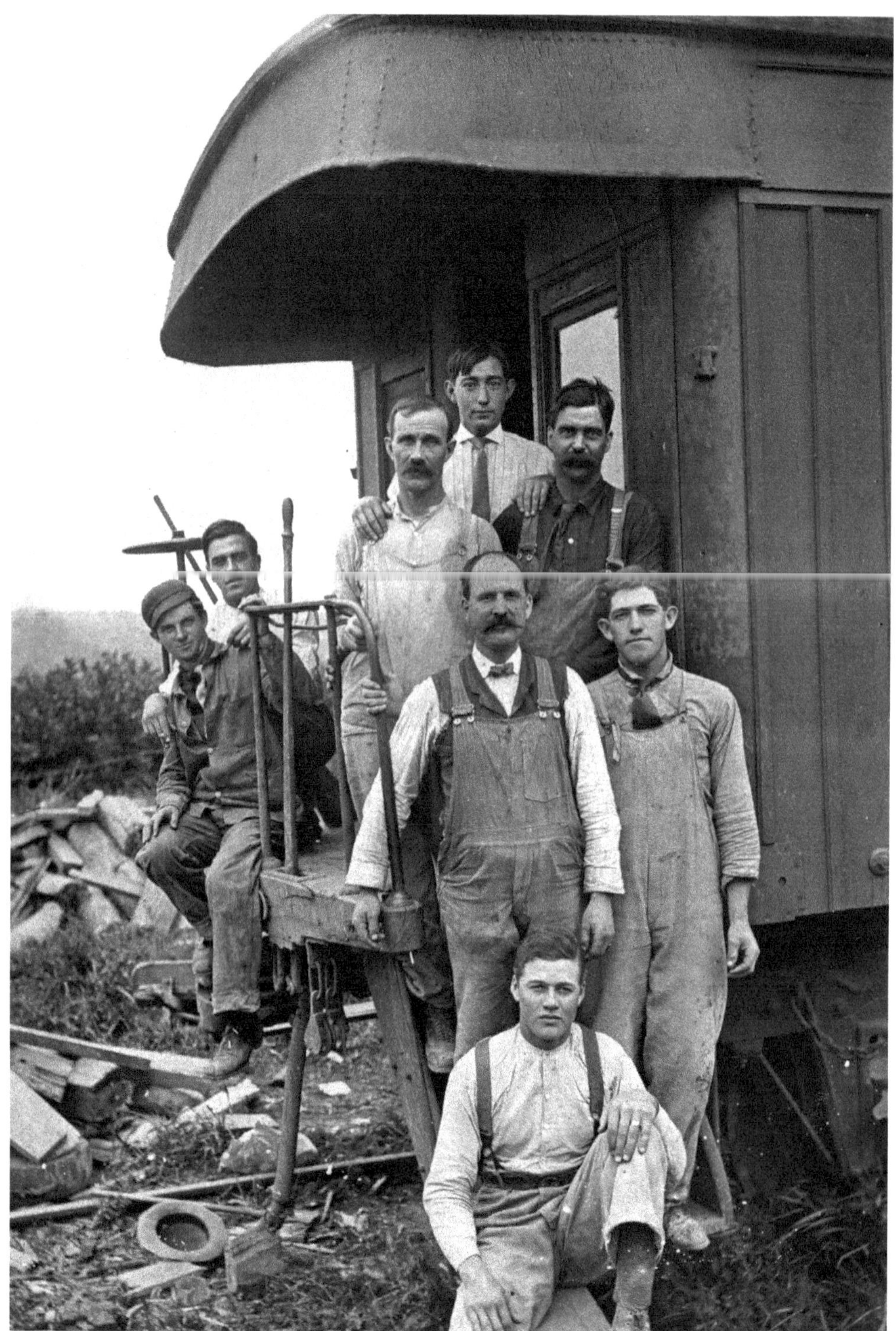

The Rutland Railroad quickly laid track from Rutland to the Burlington area, but like many of Vermont's railroad ventures, the company struggled to complete its route as far as the state's border. In 1907, the Rutland employed no fewer than 35 engineers, 13 conductors, 40 clerks, and 12 firemen to stoke the trains' fires. Railroad companies and their allied industries provided employment for many people in depot towns.

A dressmaker in Barre. In 1900, Barre's employed women worked most commonly as dressmakers or milliners, teachers, "sales ladies," or servants. The city also boasted a female hotel proprietor, bakery owner, china painter and artist, two restaurant owners, and a postmistress. With 114 granite dealers and 27 granite quarries in the area, many women also contributed to household incomes by taking in stonecutters as boarders.

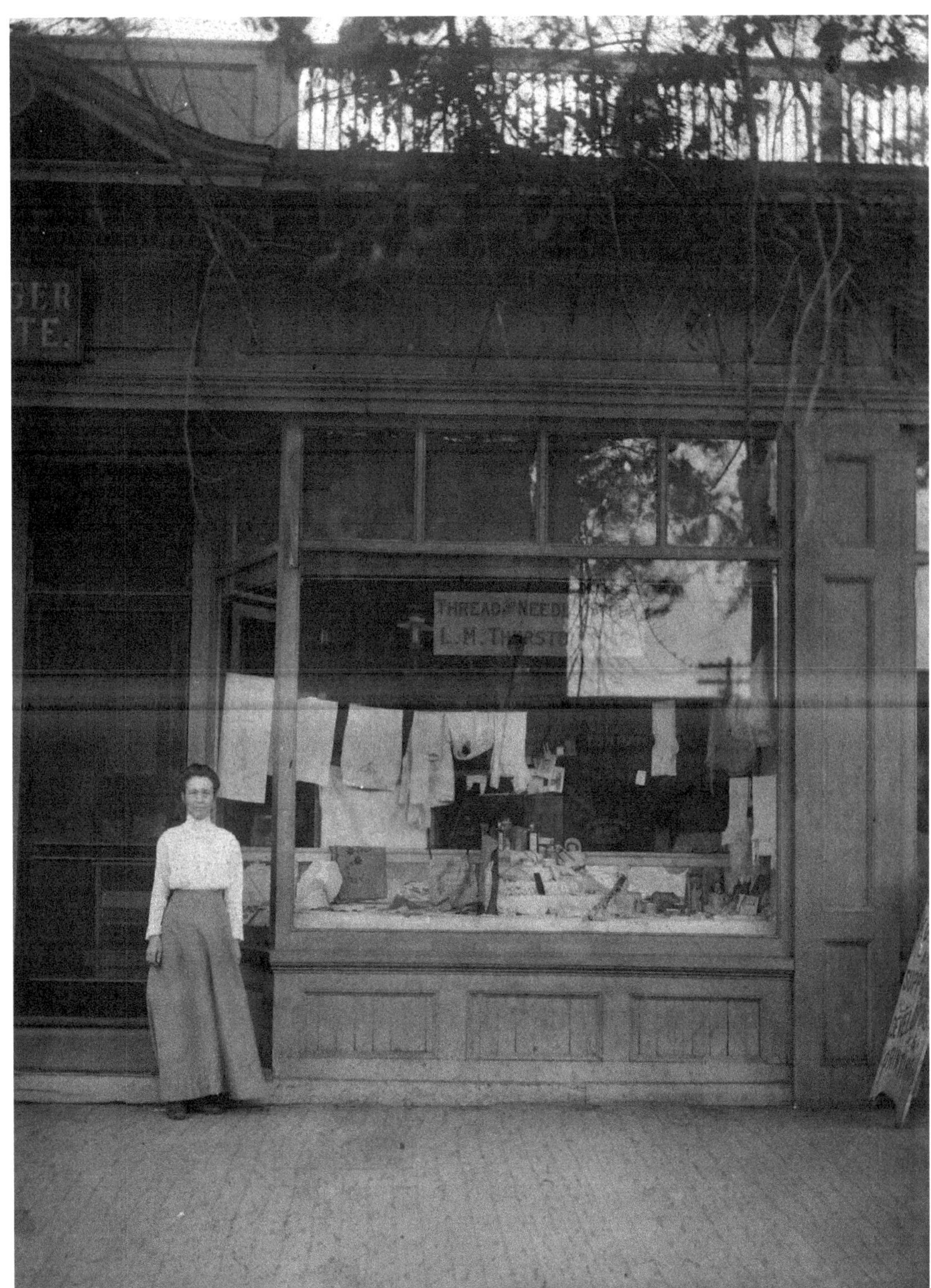

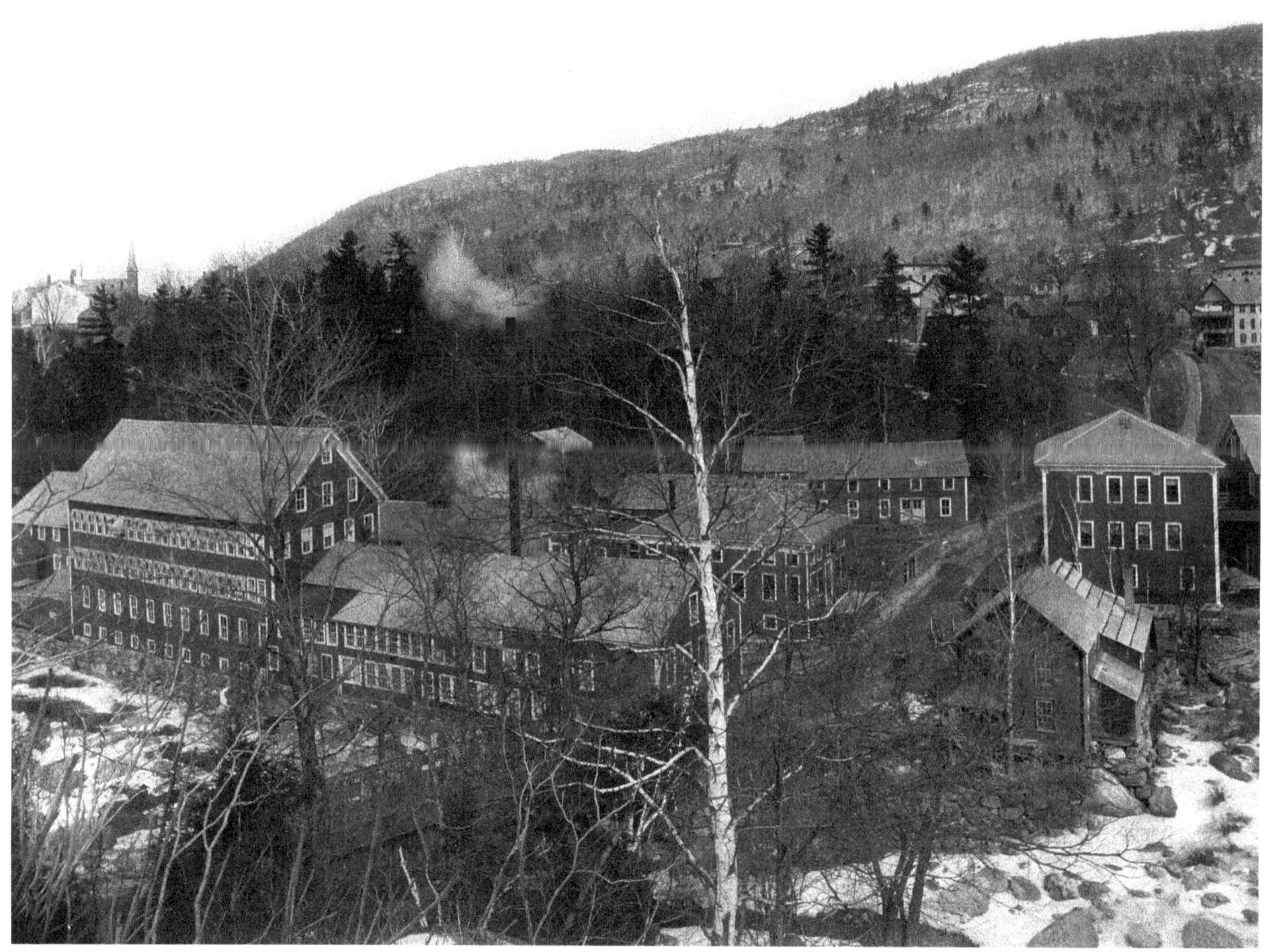

The Bristol Manufacturing Company was once one of the largest casket manufacturers in the United States. The company's lavish catalog boasted highly crafted designs using pleated silk linings, selections of hardwoods, and elaborate construction methods—quite a change from the simple pine boxes that preceded the Civil War. The company profited alongside a bustling national funeral industry, which benefited from a Victorian-era taste for the ornate.

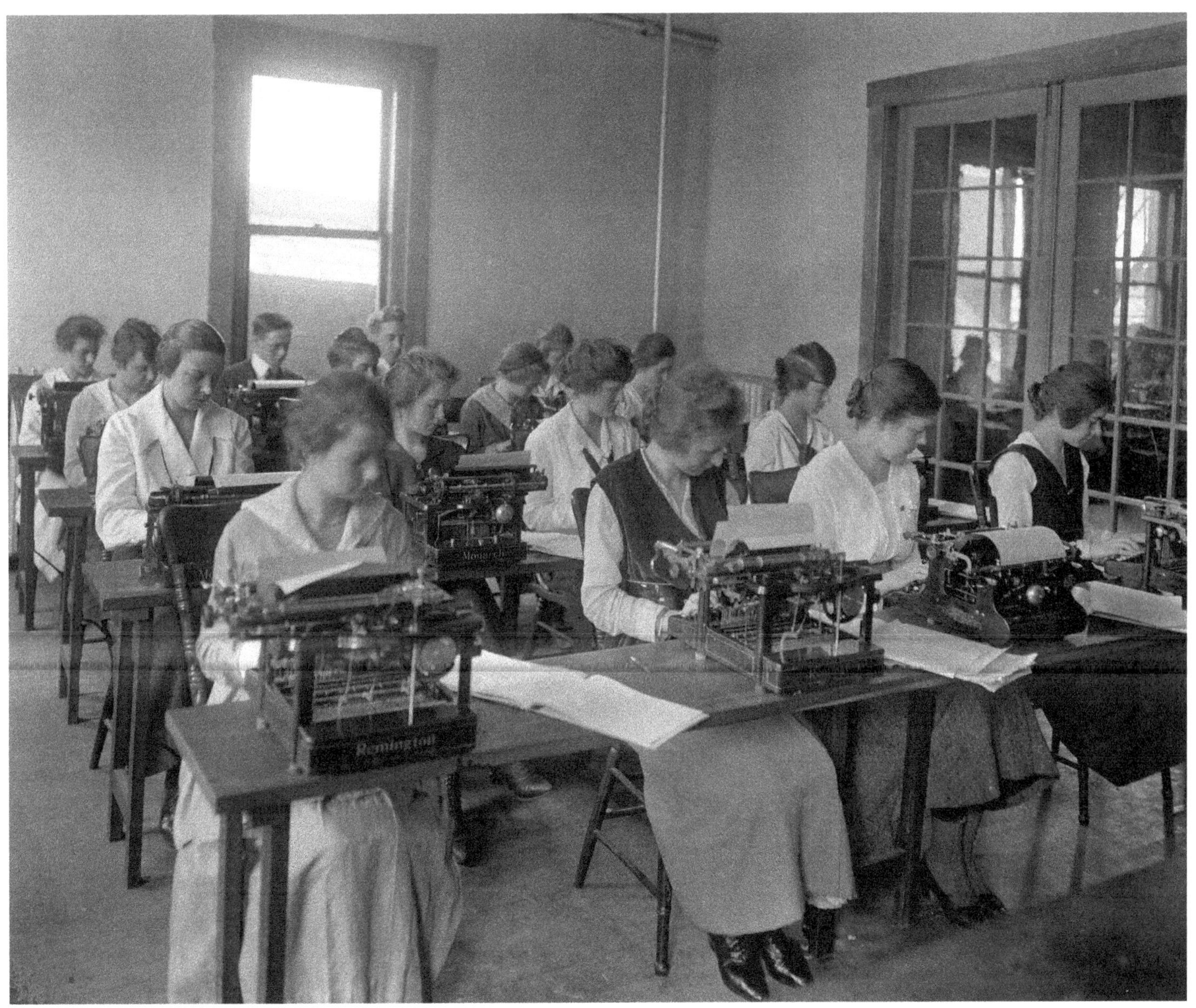

Clawson-Hamilton Commercial College, Brattleboro. Around 1908, Neil Clawson's Clawson-Hamilton College supplied "experienced or inexperienced" bookkeepers, clerks, and stenographers at no charge to nearby businesses in Brattleboro. The school also bought, sold, rented, and repaired typewriters. In 1918, Clawson-Hamilton joined the Bay Path Institute of Springfield, Massachusetts, and renamed itself the Brattleboro Business Institute.

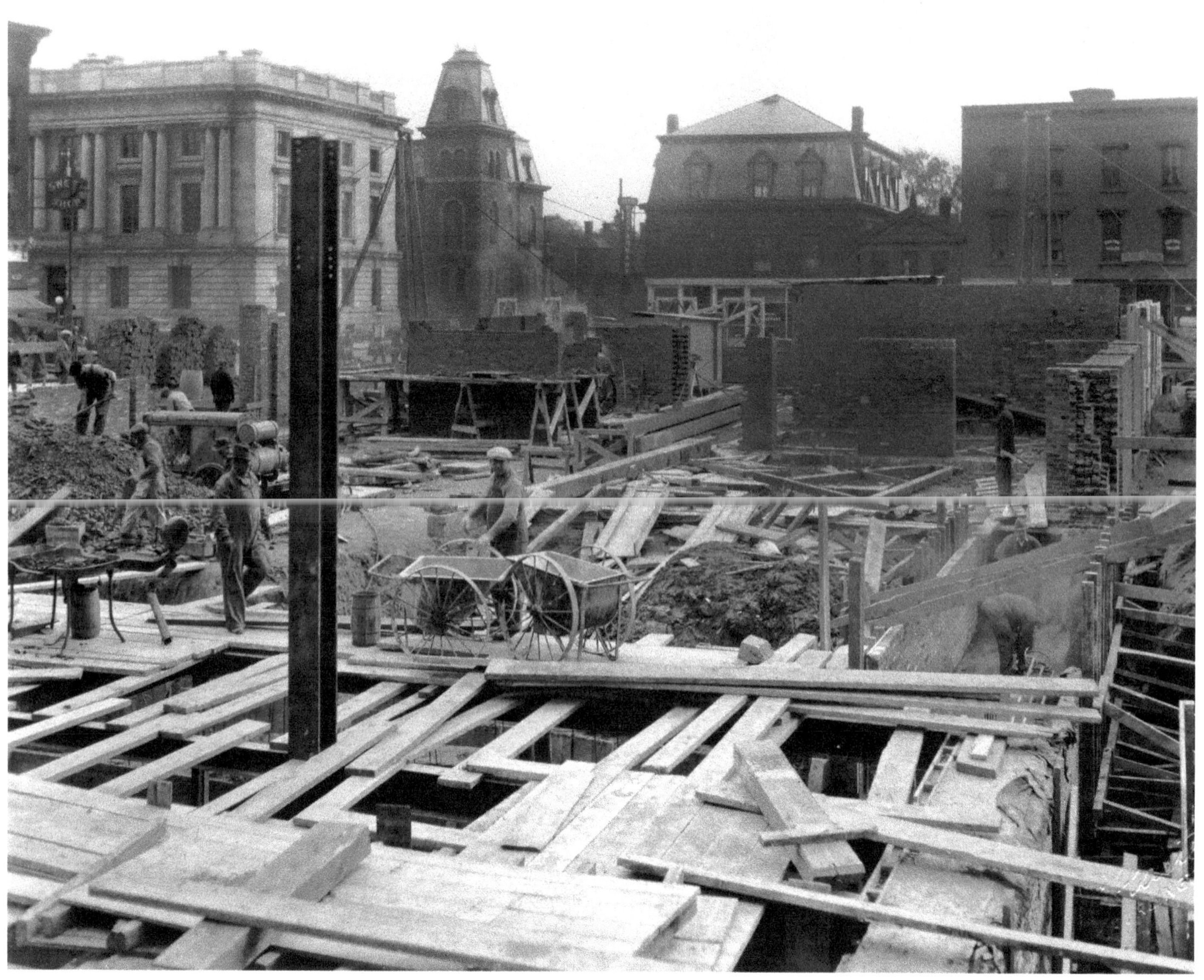

Built in classical revival style, Burlington's City Hall featured marble from Proctor, granite from Barre, slate from West Pawlet, and bricks from Essex Junction. City residents paid out nearly $500,000 to complete the new structure—including more than $23,000 to McKim, Mead, and White, a premier New York architecture firm of the era. The 1926 project, one of many large-scale Burlington construction projects in the 1920s, earned Mayor Clarence Beecher the nickname "Beecher the Builder."

The history of traveling ministers in Vermont begins early, and with the church consolidations and railroad accessibility of the mid–nineteenth century, ministers found even more opportunities to move around. In this 1910 photograph, incoming minister Walter Baker bids farewell to outgoing preacher Christopher C. St. Clare at the Morristown depot.

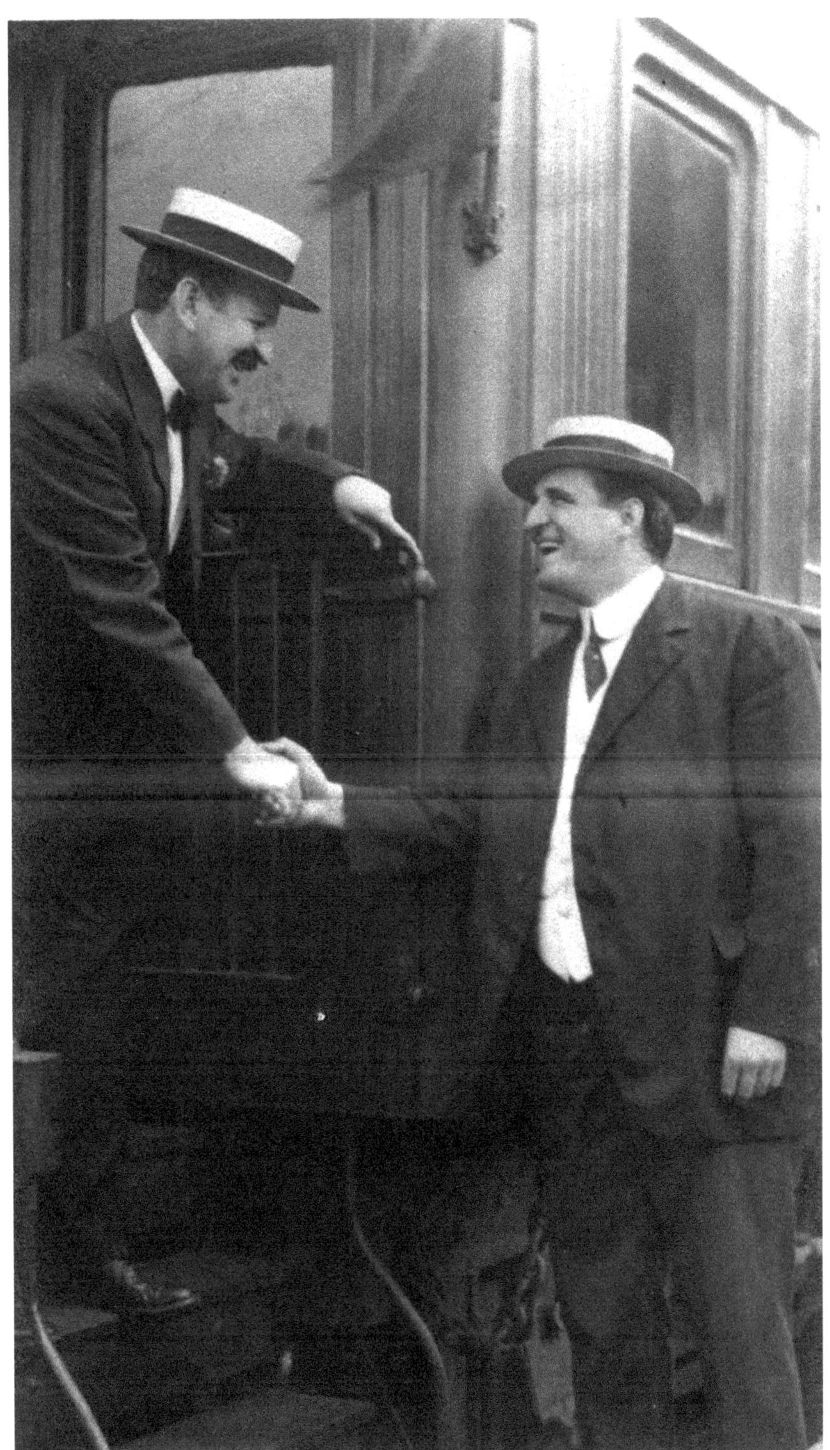

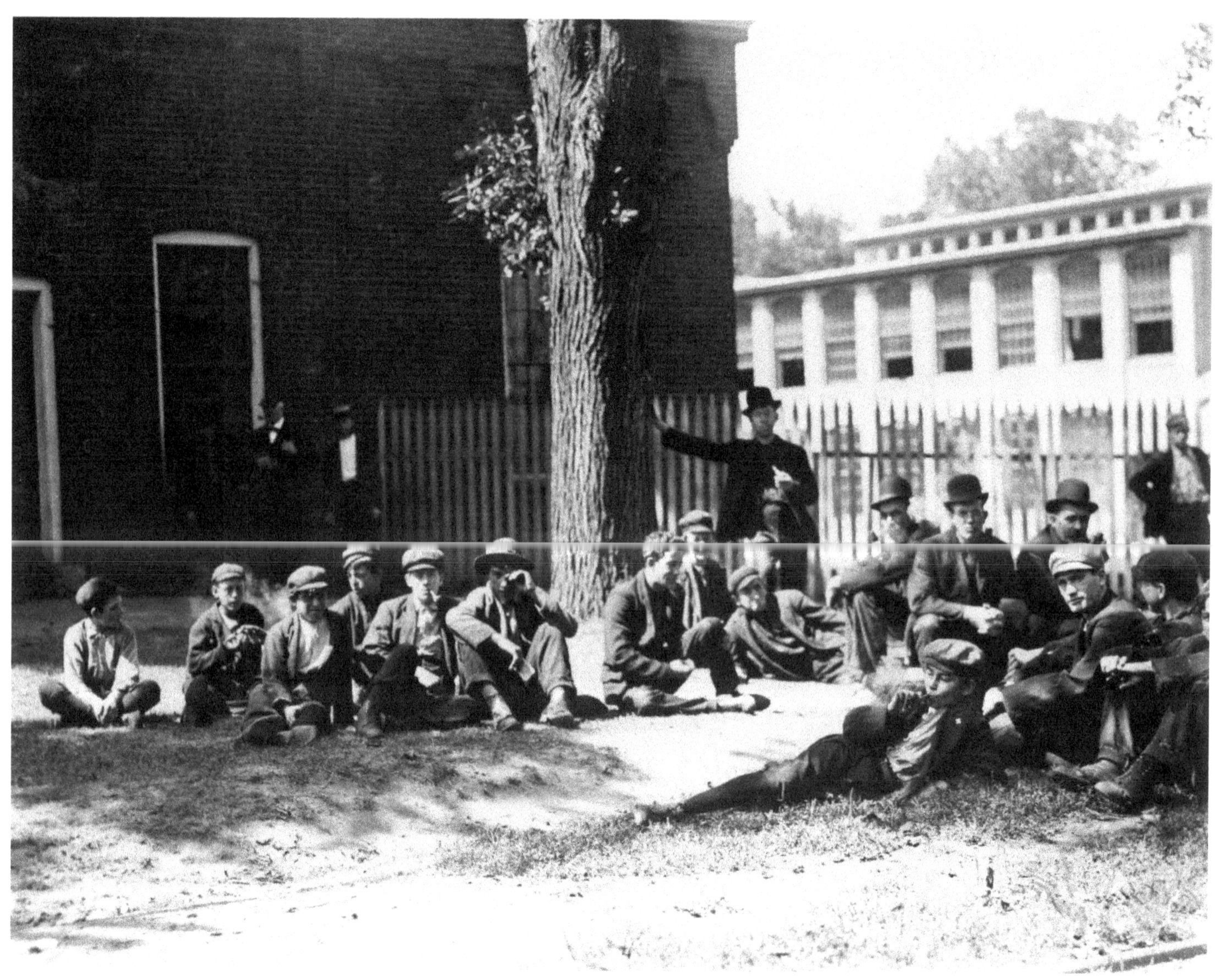

Youngsters take their lunch break at Bennington's Holden-Leonard Company in 1910. While Vermont's rural areas struggled with population losses through much of the nineteenth century, the state's 12 largest towns grew in population. In addition to immigration from places like Canada, Ireland, Sweden, and Italy, much of this population increase resulted from the influx of young people moving from their parents' farms to work in the mills and factories of the industrial towns.

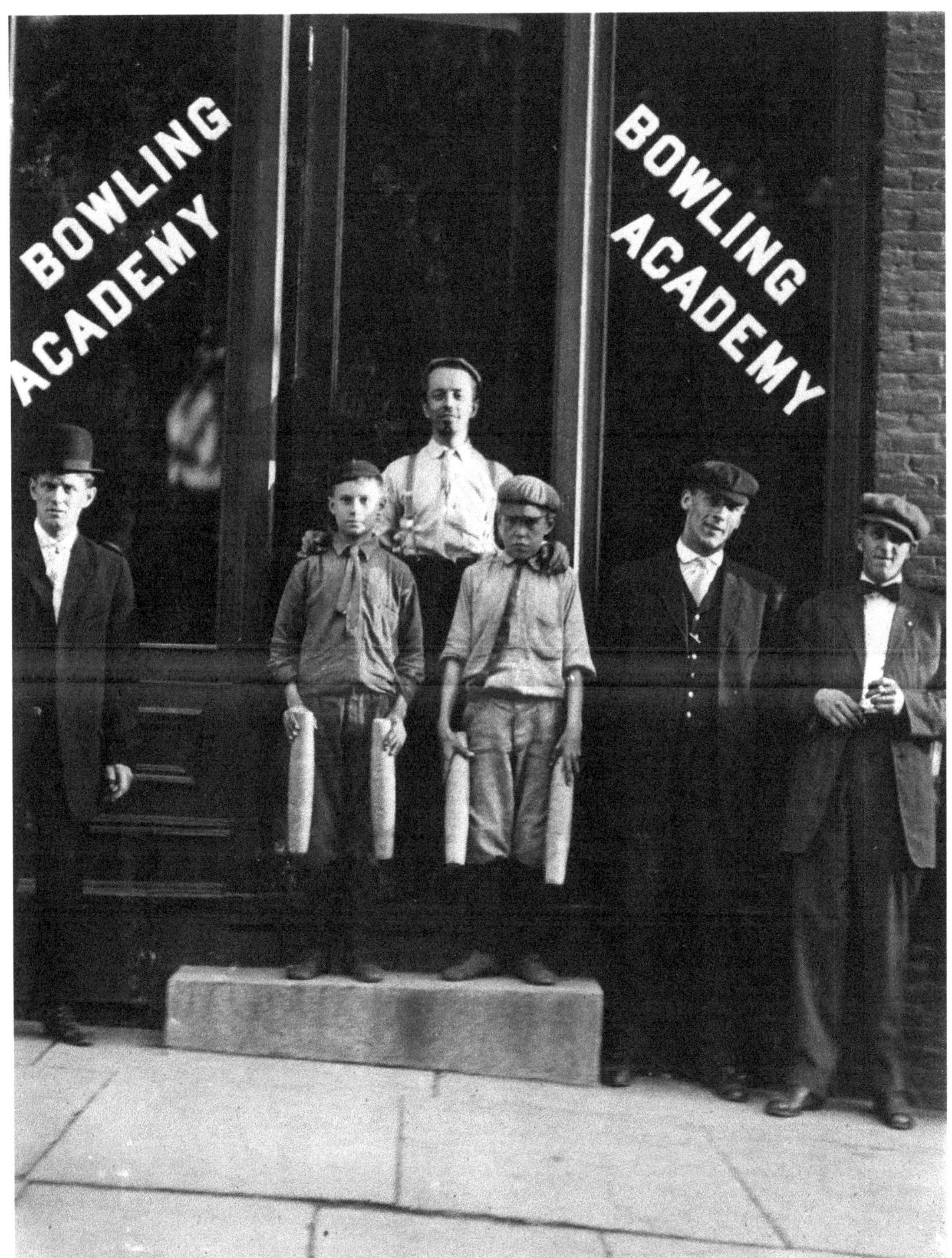

Two "pin boys" and associates at the Bowling Academy in Burlington around 1910. Although bowling became much more mainstream after World War II, in its early years the game was associated with immigrants and saloons, places that most women avoided. Burlington's 1910 city directory lists one bowling establishment: Herbert Pitcher's restaurant and arcade at 165 Main Street.

A young worker at Burlington's Hickok Lumber Company, around 1910. Horatio Hickok's Pine Street manufacturing company sold lumber, packaging boxes, cloth boards, and shooks. Hickok contracted with lumber harvesters in Underhill, and like many nineteenth-century manufacturers, employed young people who had come from the rural areas seeking work. Lewis Hine, who took many photographs on behalf of the National Child Labor Committee's efforts to eliminate child labor, took this photograph.

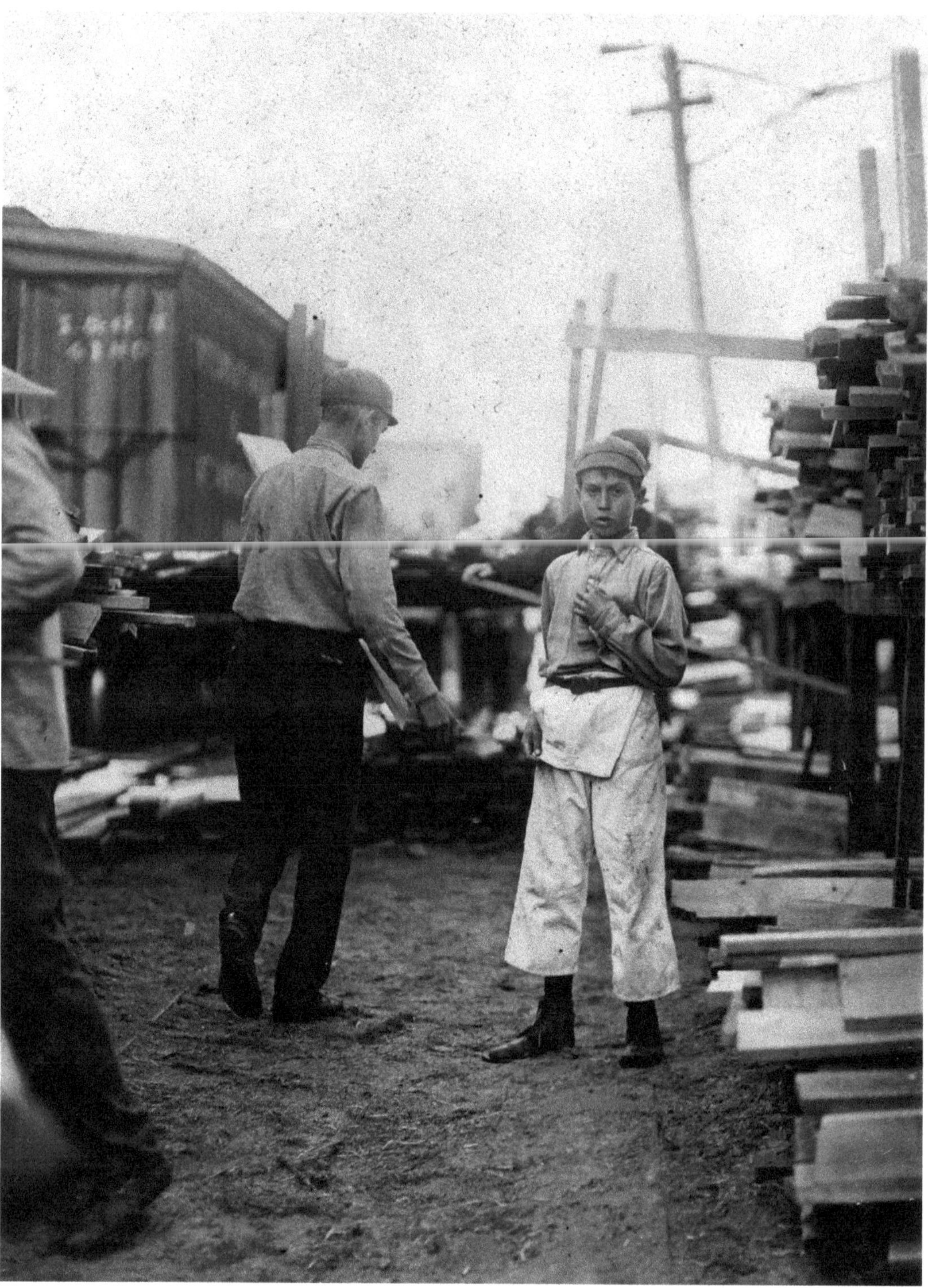

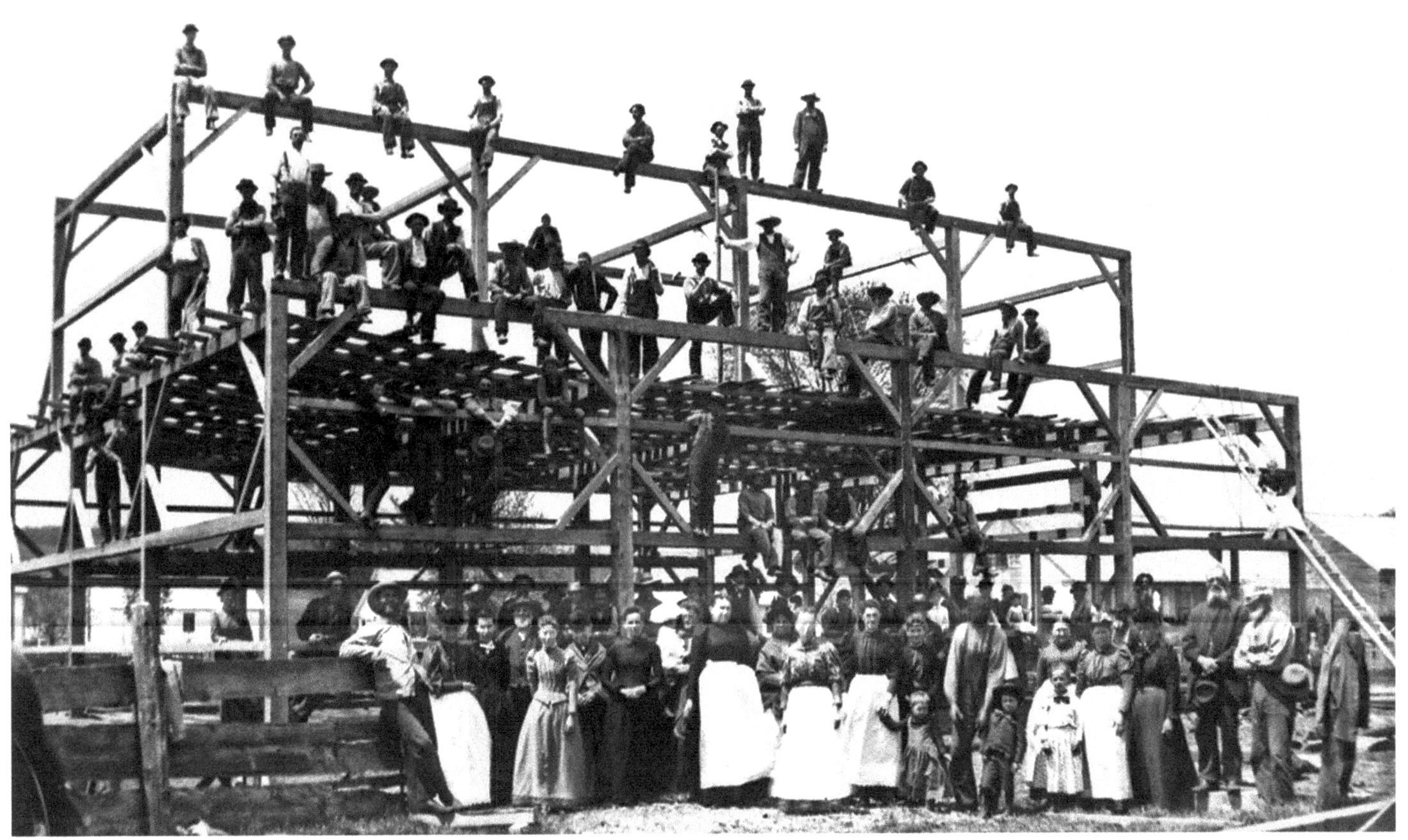

A barn raising in North Danville around 1910. The success of the nineteenth-century lumber industry left few large trees to furnish long timbers for barns such as this one. Farmers often harvested the trees for their barns from their own property. Balloon or plank framing became more common in the twentieth century, in part because it required less lumber and labor than post-and-beam timber-framing, shown here.

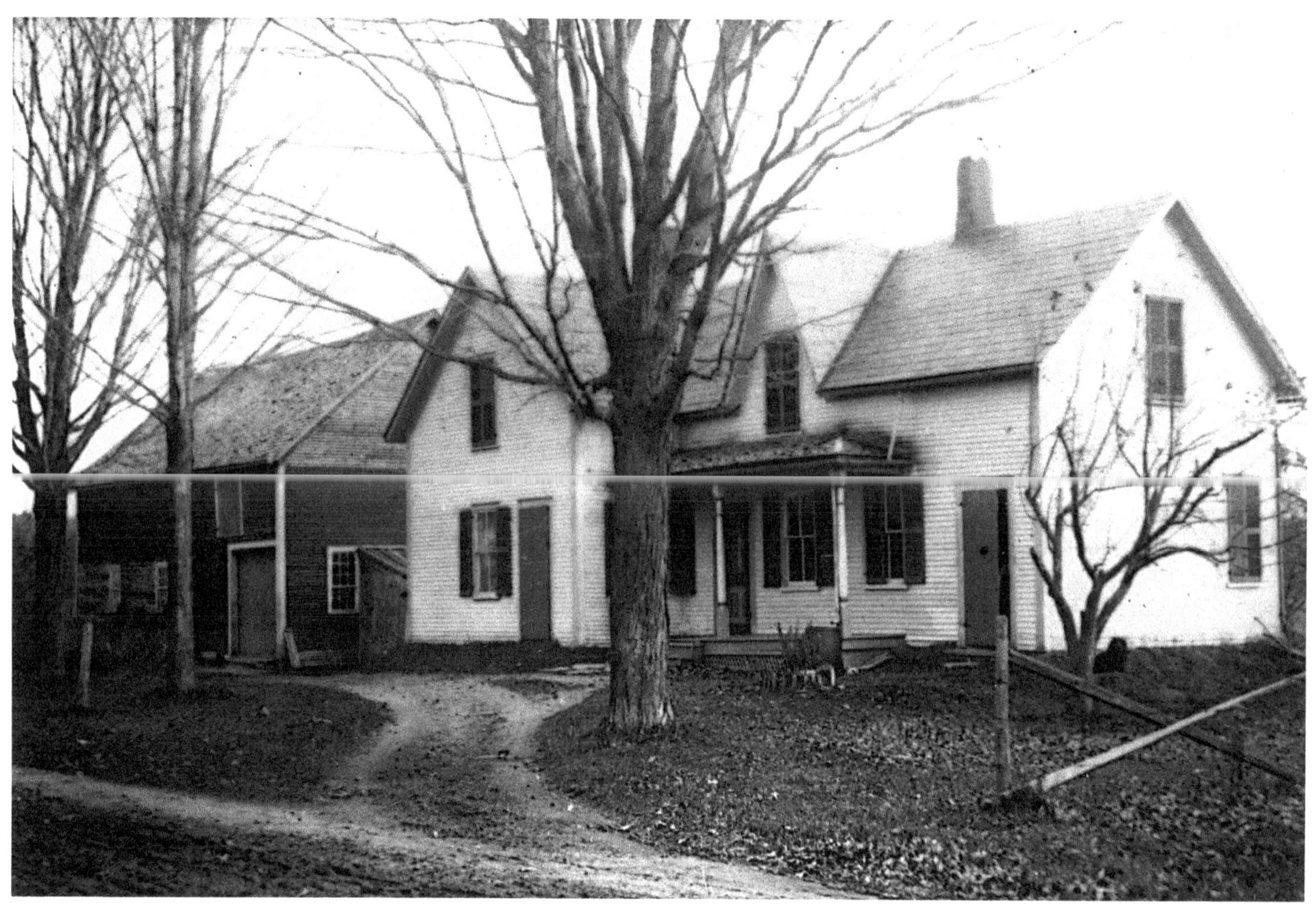

A farmhouse on Lee River Road in Jericho. A popular form of New England architecture, the "big house, little house, back house, barn" was a nineteenth-century design. The string of connected buildings progressed from a formal parlor (big house) to a kitchen (little house), storage area (back house), and animal shelter (barn). Some suggest that the layout protected farmers from weather, but the arrangement may simply represent an efficient use of workspace.

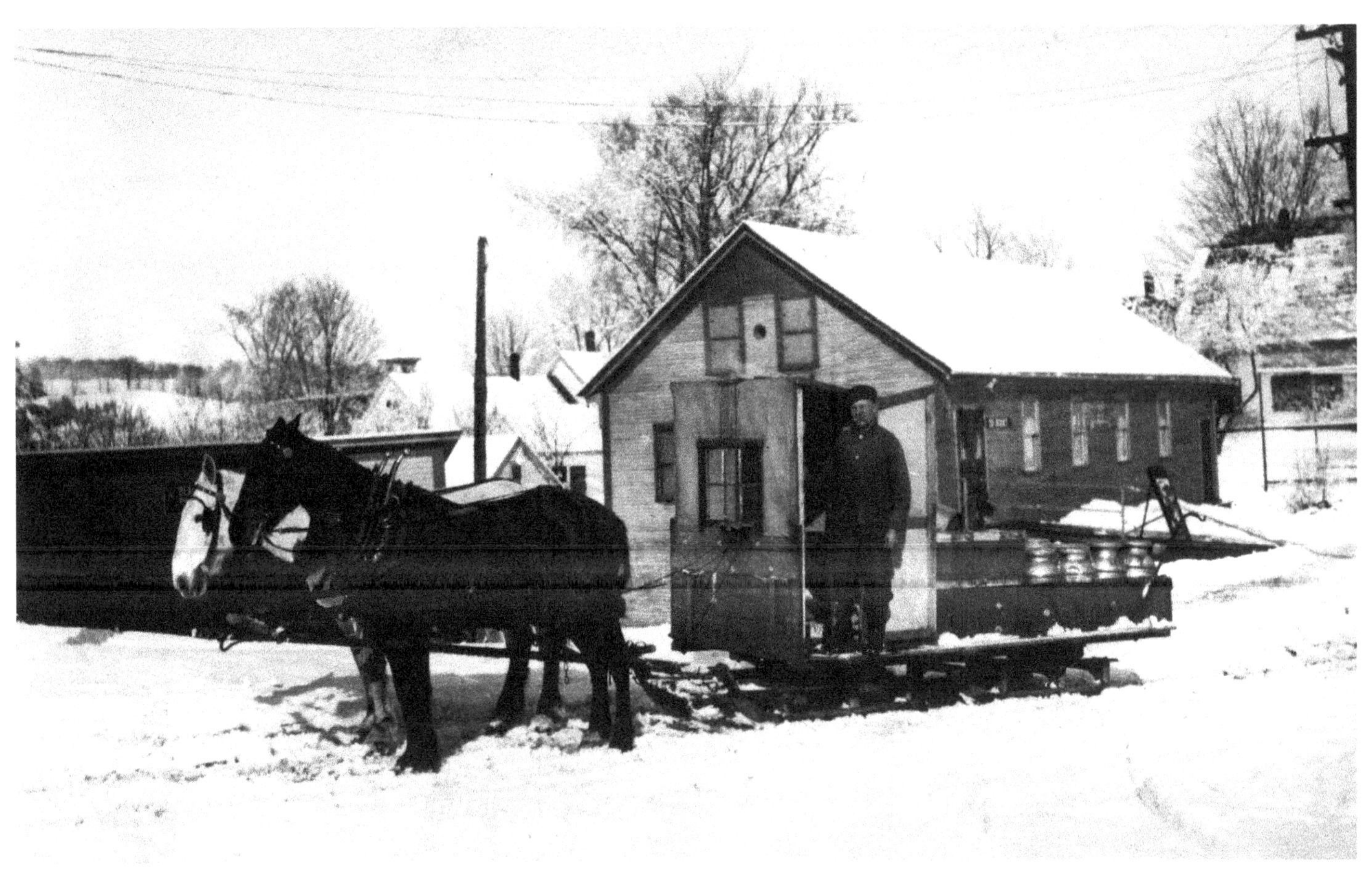

A man transports milk in Jericho by horse-drawn sleigh, complete with an enclosed cab and windshield to keep out the sharp winter air. New modes of transportation greatly affected dairy farmers in Vermont. Refrigerated railcars allowed Vermont cheese, butter, and especially milk to travel to more distant markets like Boston. By the early twentieth century, most farms located near railroad hubs had significantly increased the size of their herds to capitalize on rail transport.

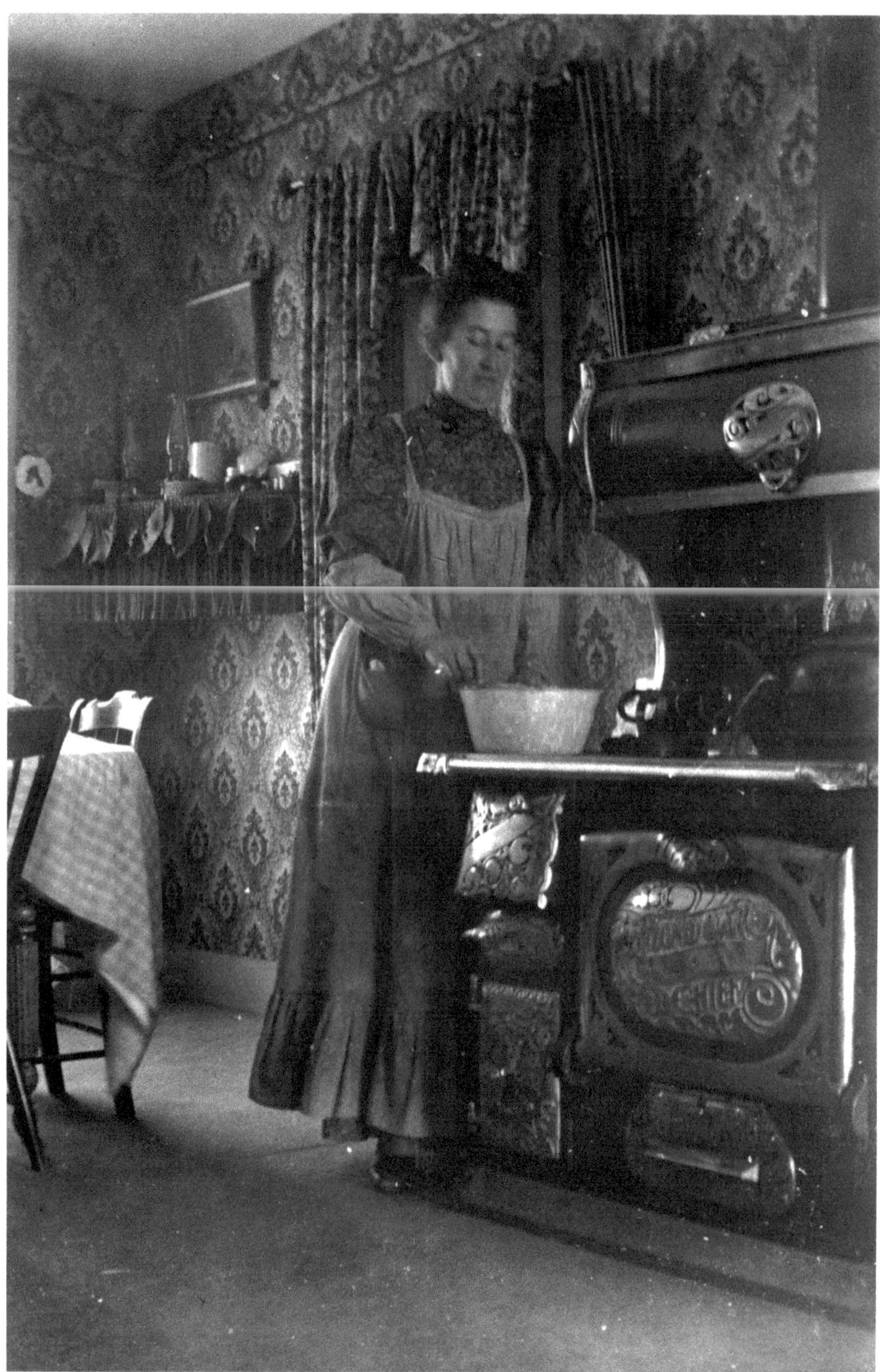

Bertha McLaughlin in her Snipe Island Road farmhouse in Jericho. Bertha's husband, Albert, was a farmer and a cook on the Rutland Railroad. When he was away on the rails, Bertha and their four children tended the family farm. Bertha's Adirondack Chief cook range was well equipped for her daily household tasks of making meals, canning produce from their garden, and heating large quantities of water for laundry, bathing, and household cleaning.

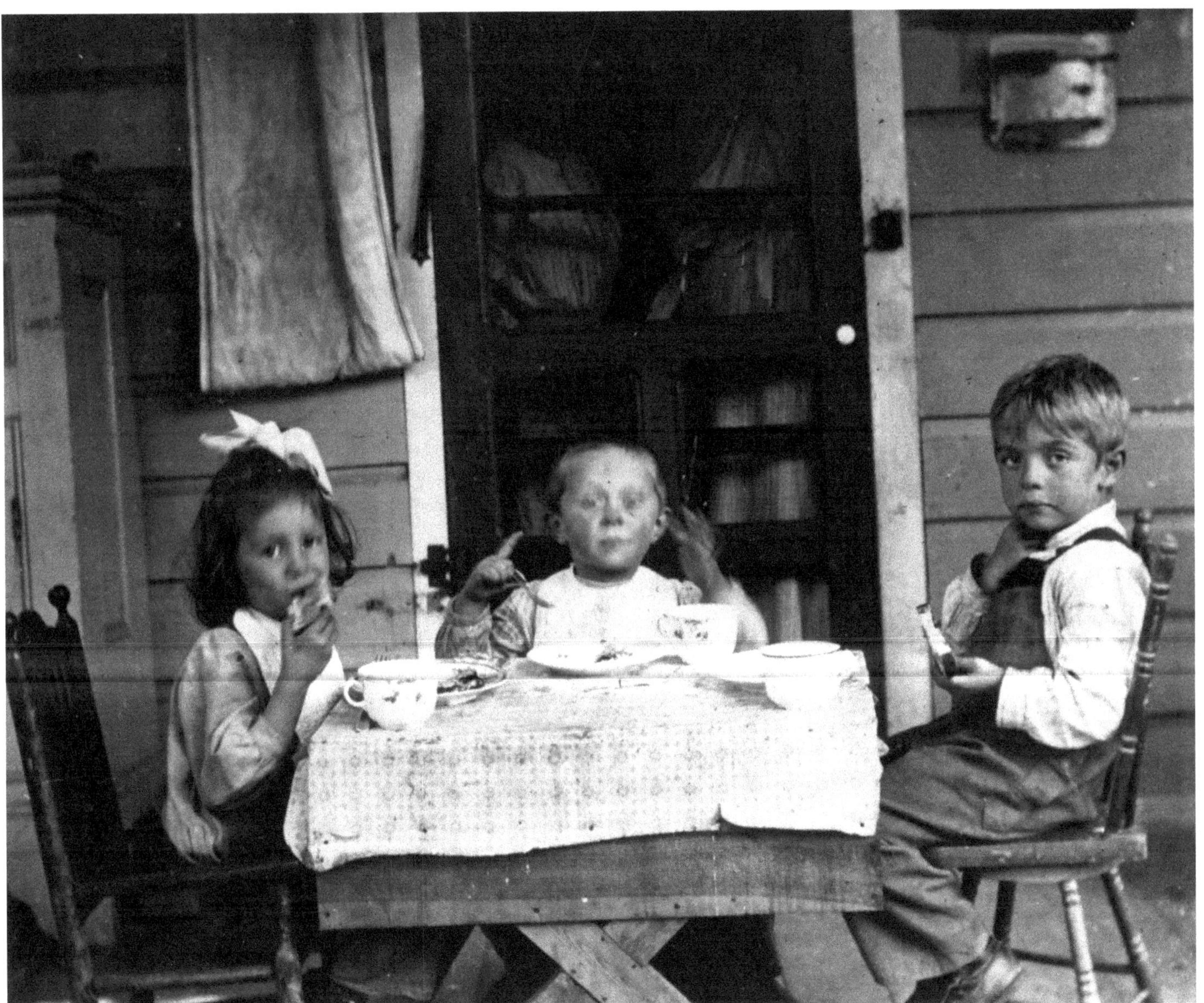

Starting in the 1820s, many of Vermont's young people left the state to follow better opportunities to the west or in southern New England. By 1895, "Vermonters abroad" had organized networking associations in Boston, Lowell, Providence, Brooklyn, Chicago, Denver, San Francisco, and other cities. In turn, towns in Vermont, New Hampshire, and Maine organized "Old Home" Weeks—festivities designed to draw native-born progeny back to spend their fortunes at home.

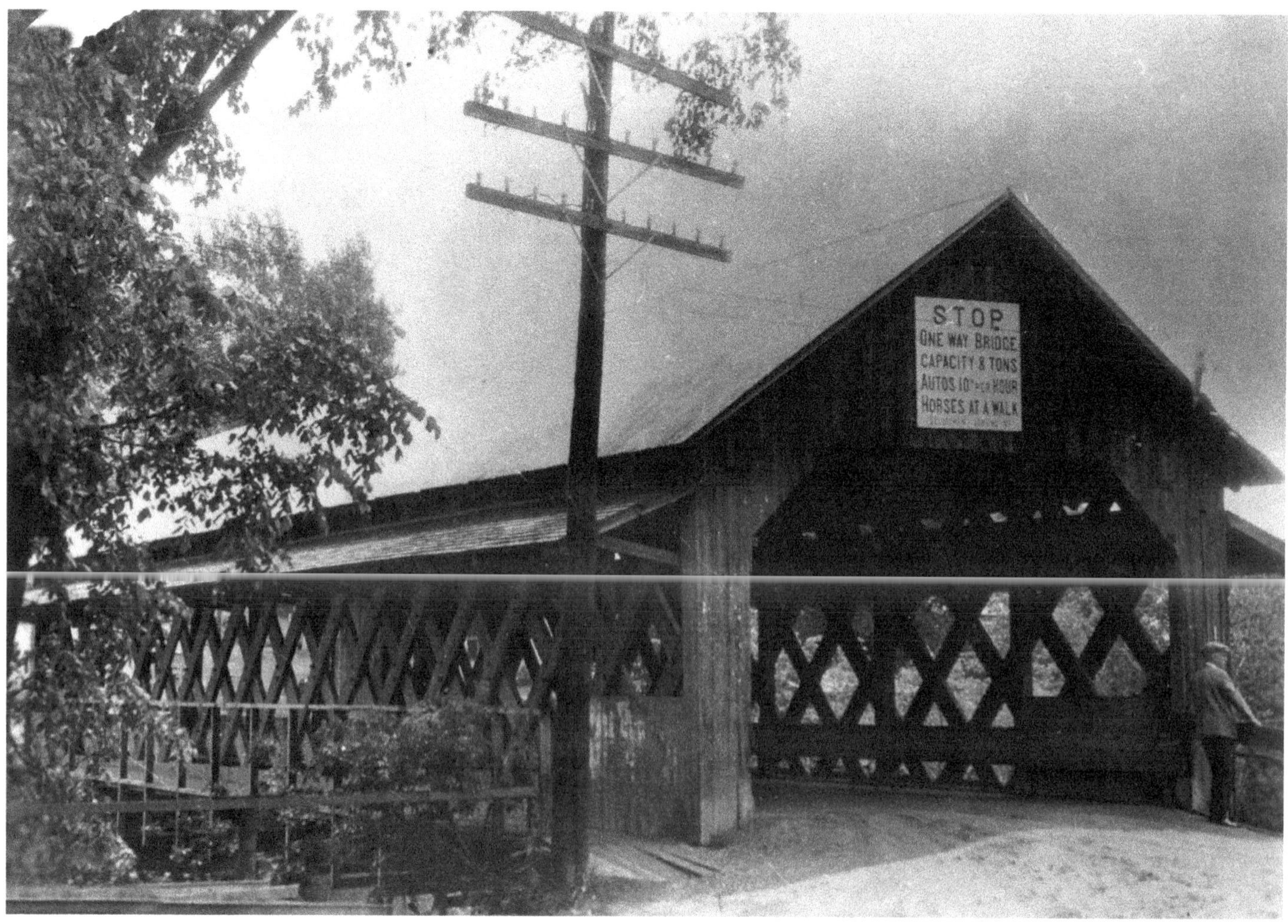

Covered bridge at Jericho. This bridge suggests the many transportation modes of the early twentieth century, including automobiles, horses, and walking. Jericho resident Earl Cross recalled that children used the road for sledding: he and his friends would zip toward the bridge, hoping to make the sharp turn just before the entrance. When Cross missed his turn one year, he crashed into the old Home Market—much to the surprise of the clerk inside.

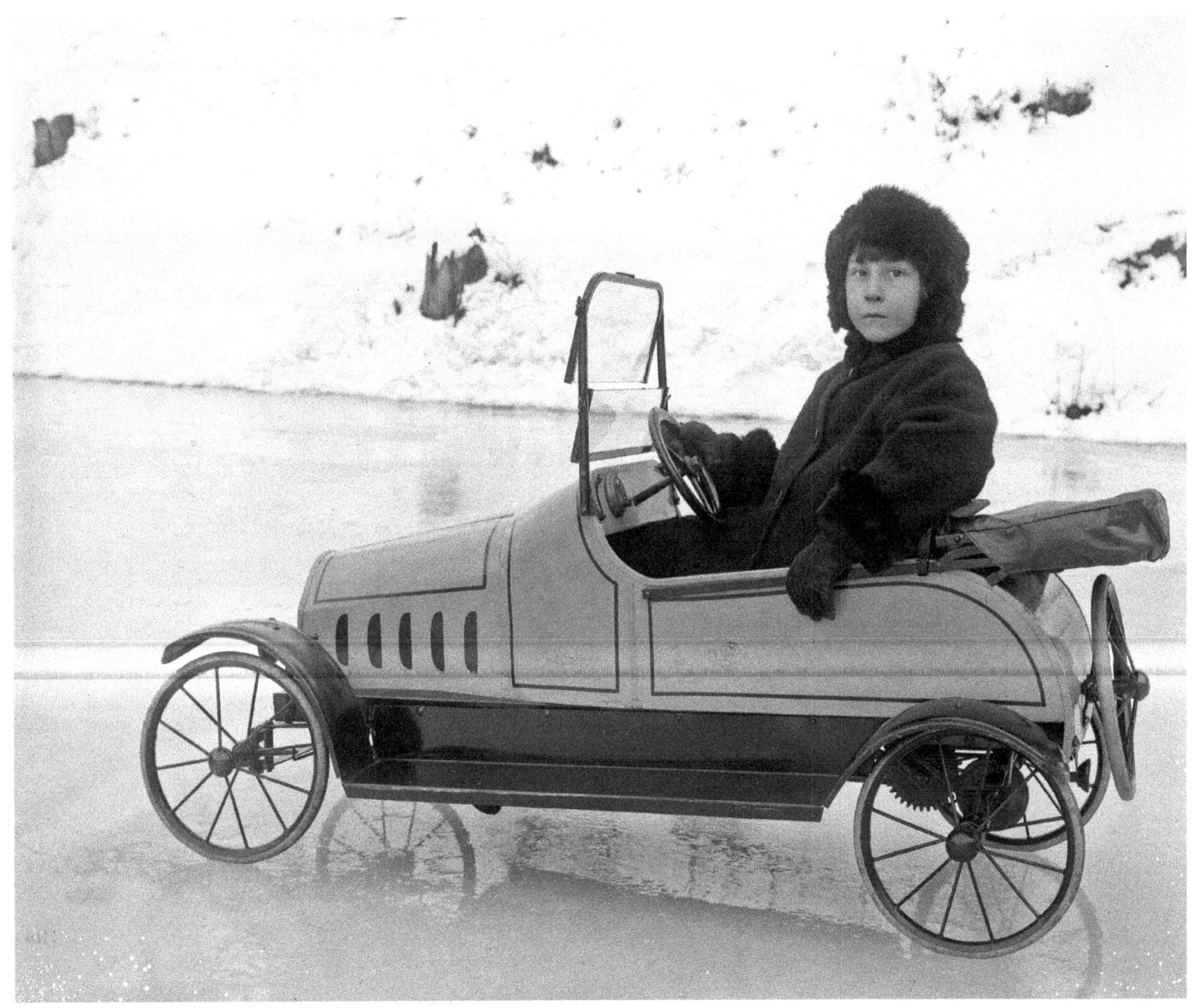

A young Paul Crown drives his toy car across the ice. Crown was the son of Brattleboro-based photographer Benjamin Crown and his wife, Clara. By the time Paul was ten, his three older brothers—Harold, Raymond, and Richard—all worked while still living at home. Raymond worked in a toyshop and may have provided this mechanized car—complete with gears and a spare tire.

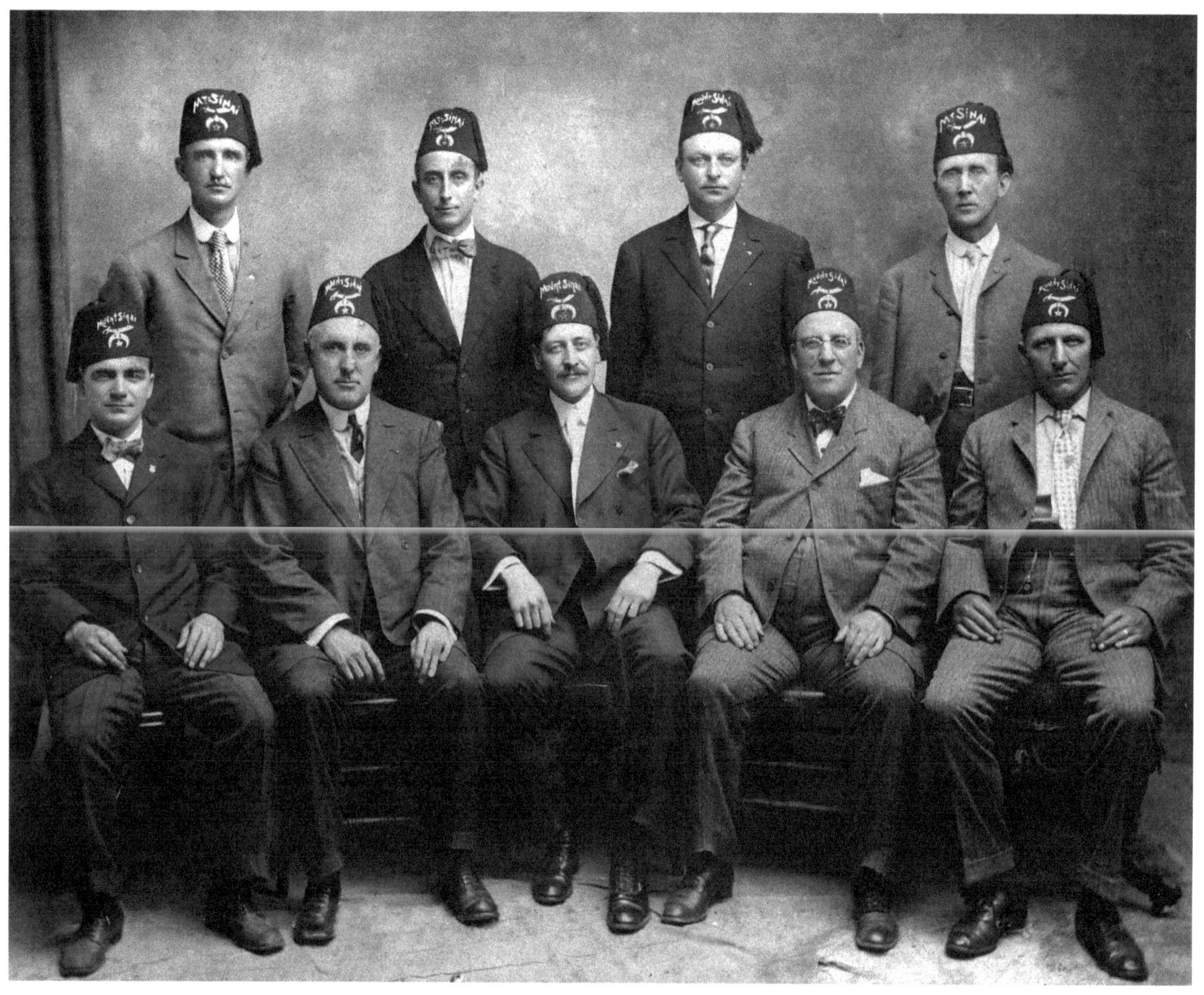

Nobles of the Mystic Shrine, Mount Sinai Chapter. Conjured up in New York City as a new outlet for the Masons' fraternity, the "Shriners" stressed fun and fellowship by combining socializing, philanthropy, and the romantic exoticism of foreign lands. In 1876, Montpelier (Mount Sinai) followed New York City (Mecca) and Rochester (Damascus) as the third temple in the organization.

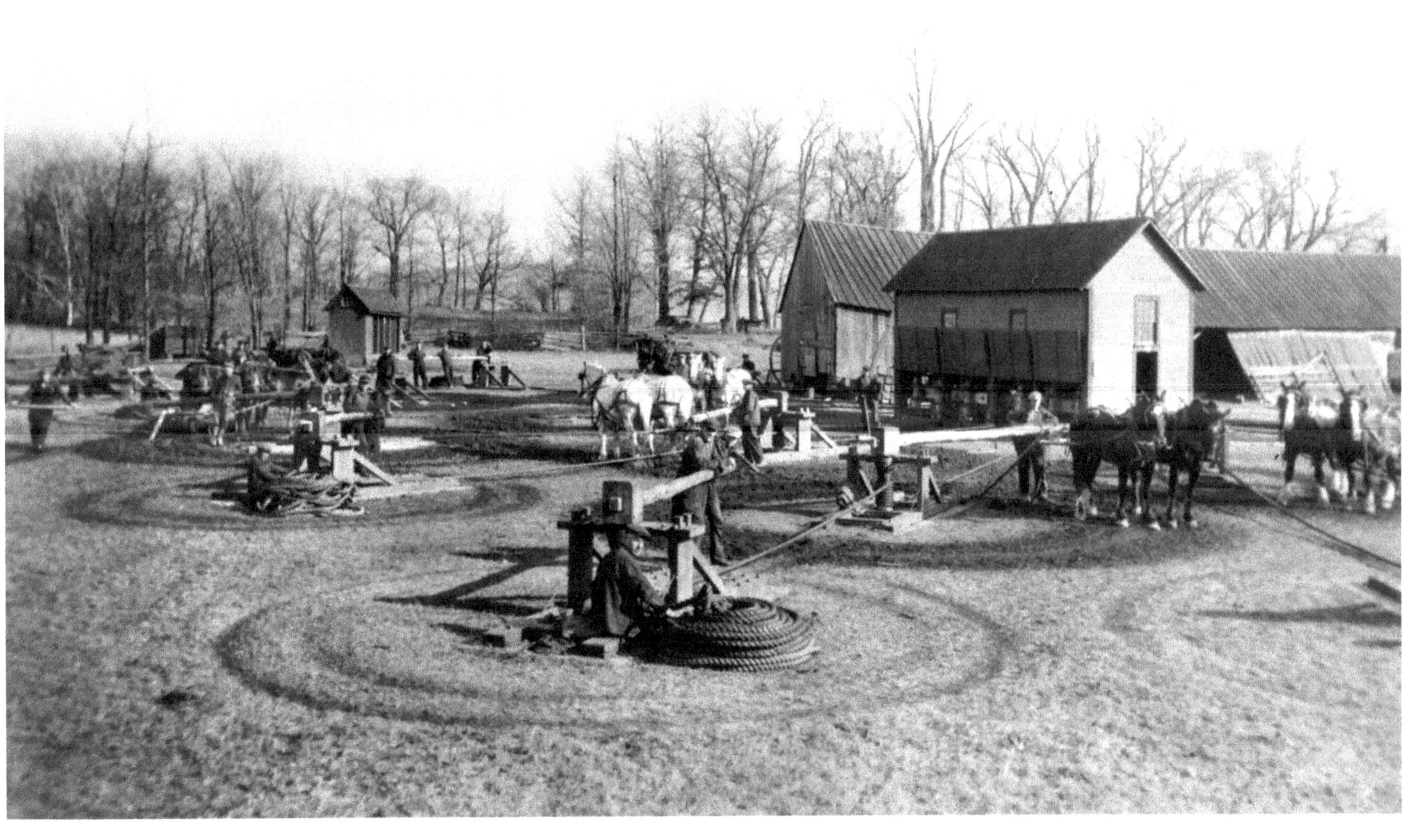

The Shelburne Shipyard's marine railway operated by horse power before 1929. The railway consisted of two tracks that stretched into the water at Shelburne Bay. Boats steered onto a cradle riding on rails and were hoisted out of the water by 14 horses. Vessels as large as *Vermont III* and *Ticonderoga,* both sidewheel steamers more than 200 feet long, were pulled aground with this horse-driven mechanism.

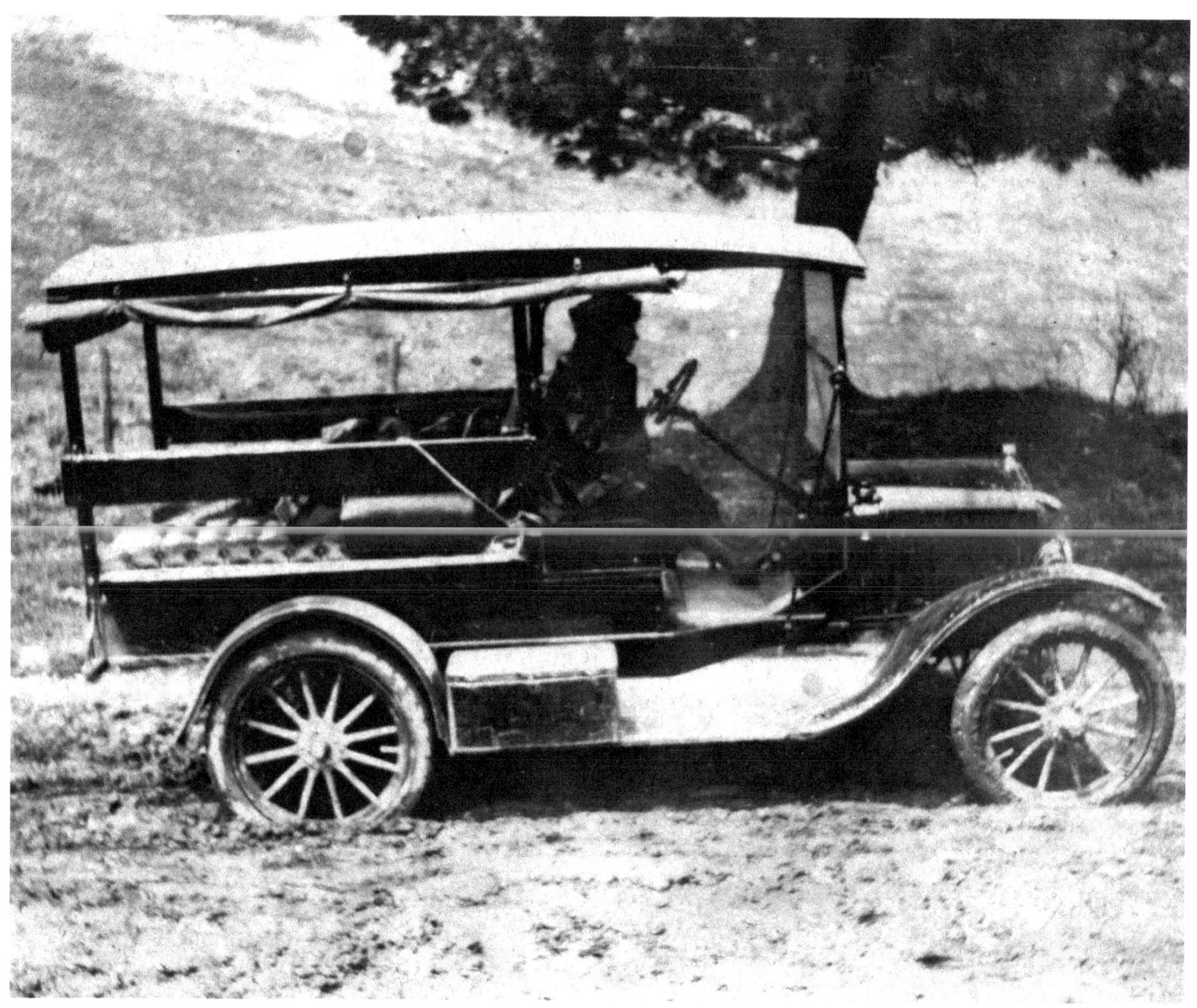

School buses, like this one in Jericho, facilitated school consolidation. From the early 1800s forward, most Vermont towns had numerous school districts, to keep short the distances children must walk to attend. By the 1860s, however, some legislators were complaining that this multi-district system had resulted in "two thousand little educational republics" and a lack of resources for rural schools. Beginning in the 1870s, many communities closed some schools and consolidated the system into a smaller number of districts.

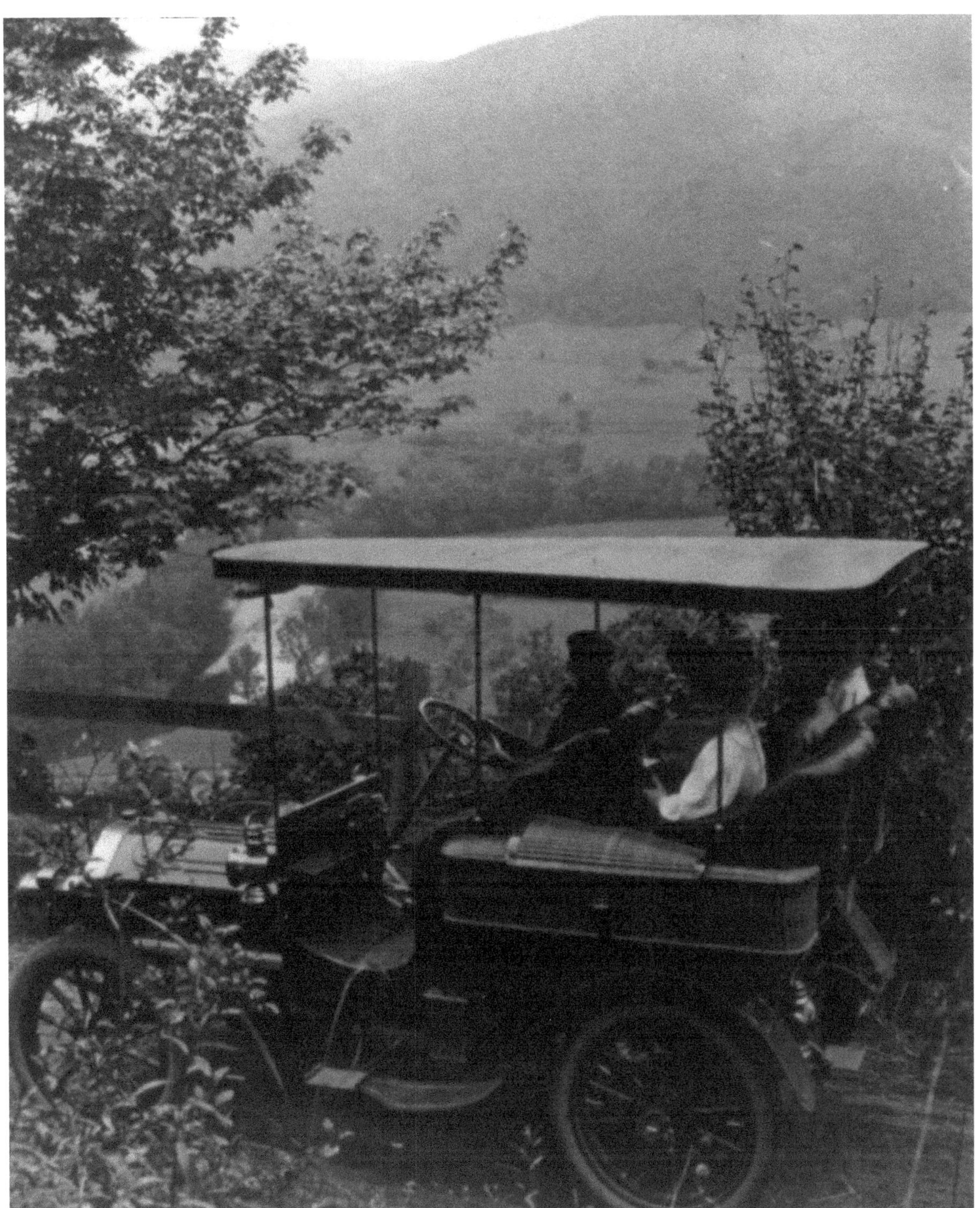

With the advent of the automobile, Vermont hosted more tourists from elsewhere. The state created a Bureau of Publicity in 1911, and many farmers started to offer "farm vacations" for travelers itching to escape the bustle of the nation's cities. Vacationers worked on local farms during their summer visits, to the extent that many farmers came to rely on tourist season for essential labor.

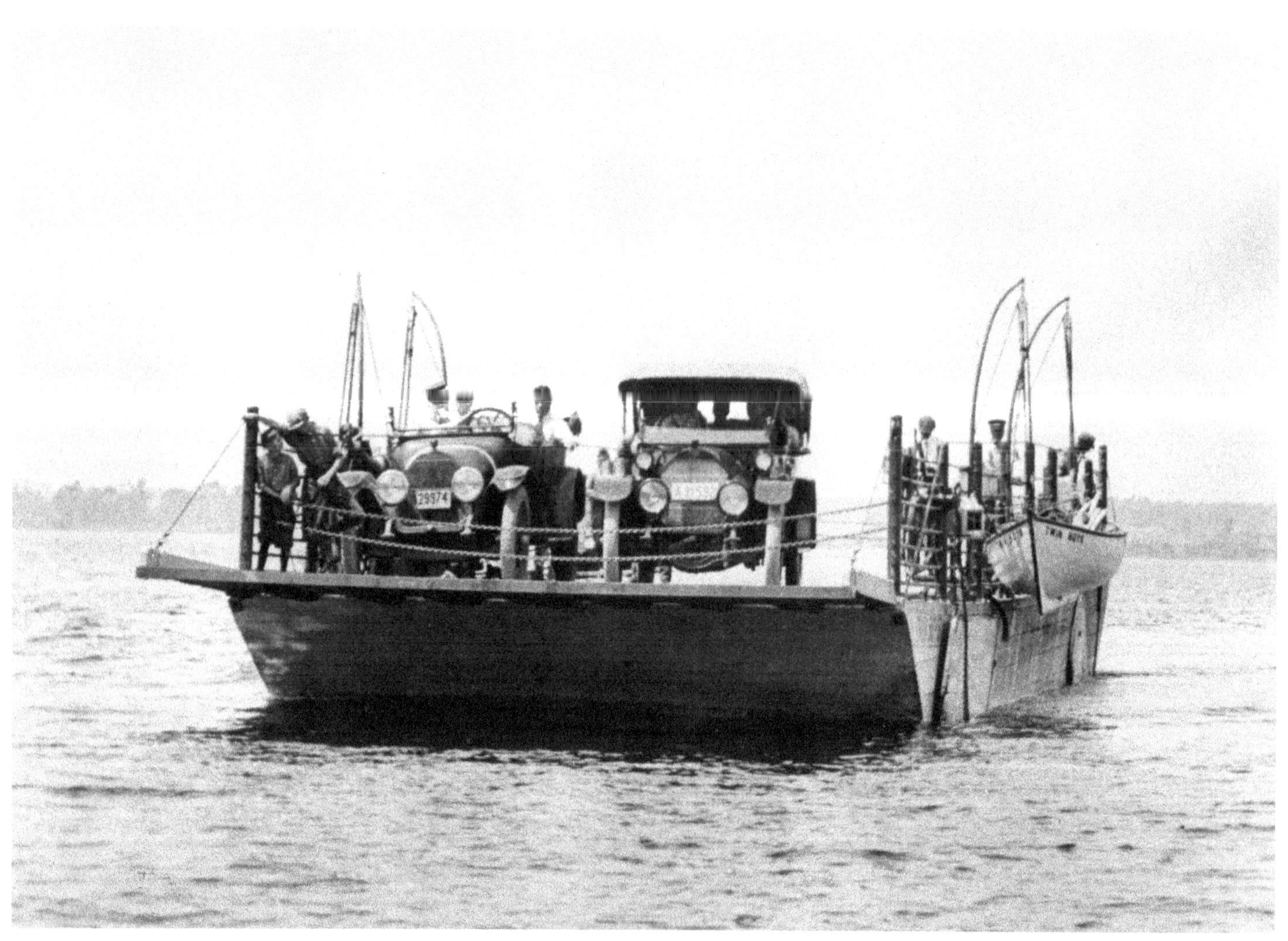

Twin Boys started operating in 1916, carrying up to 15 cars between Rouses Point, New York, and Alburgh. The gasoline-powered ferry was named by reference to the sons of the owner, William Sweet. Travelers recalled their early trips on Lake Champlain's numerous small automobile ferries as a worrisome experience—alluding to the deckhands, who carefully assessed the weight of vehicles and the ferry's available space. The frequency of strong winds on the lake also ensured passengers an exciting ride.

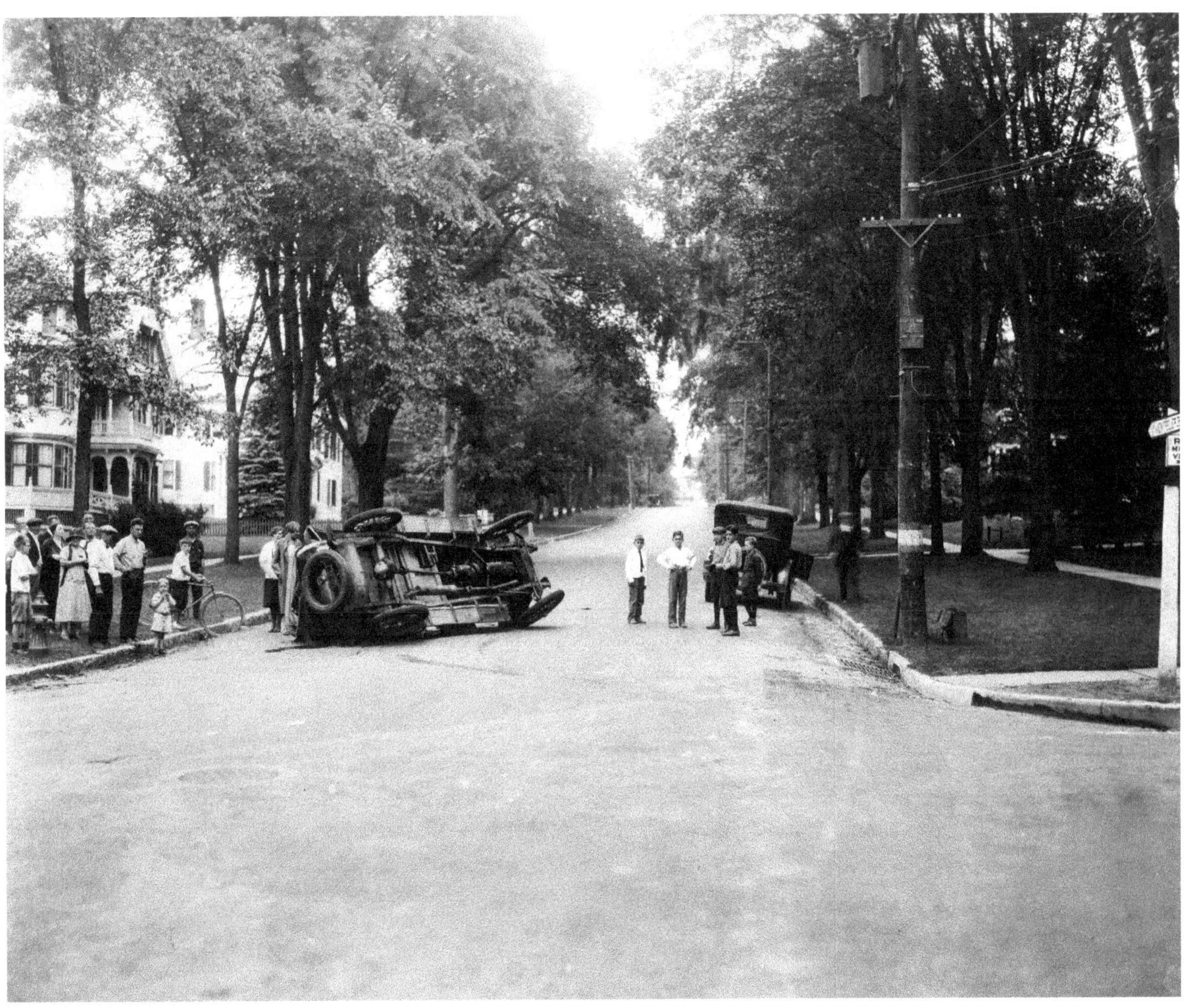

The architect of one of Vermont's first automobiles, bicycle mechanic John J. Williams of Montpelier, told his son that a car was "easier to handle than a bicycle. You don't have to balance it." Williams, who later owned a car dealership, often assigned his son the task of teaching customers how to drive their first vehicle—a process he called "breaking them in." Driving automobiles didn't come easy to all Vermonters—this accident in Burlington has attracted quite a bit of attention.

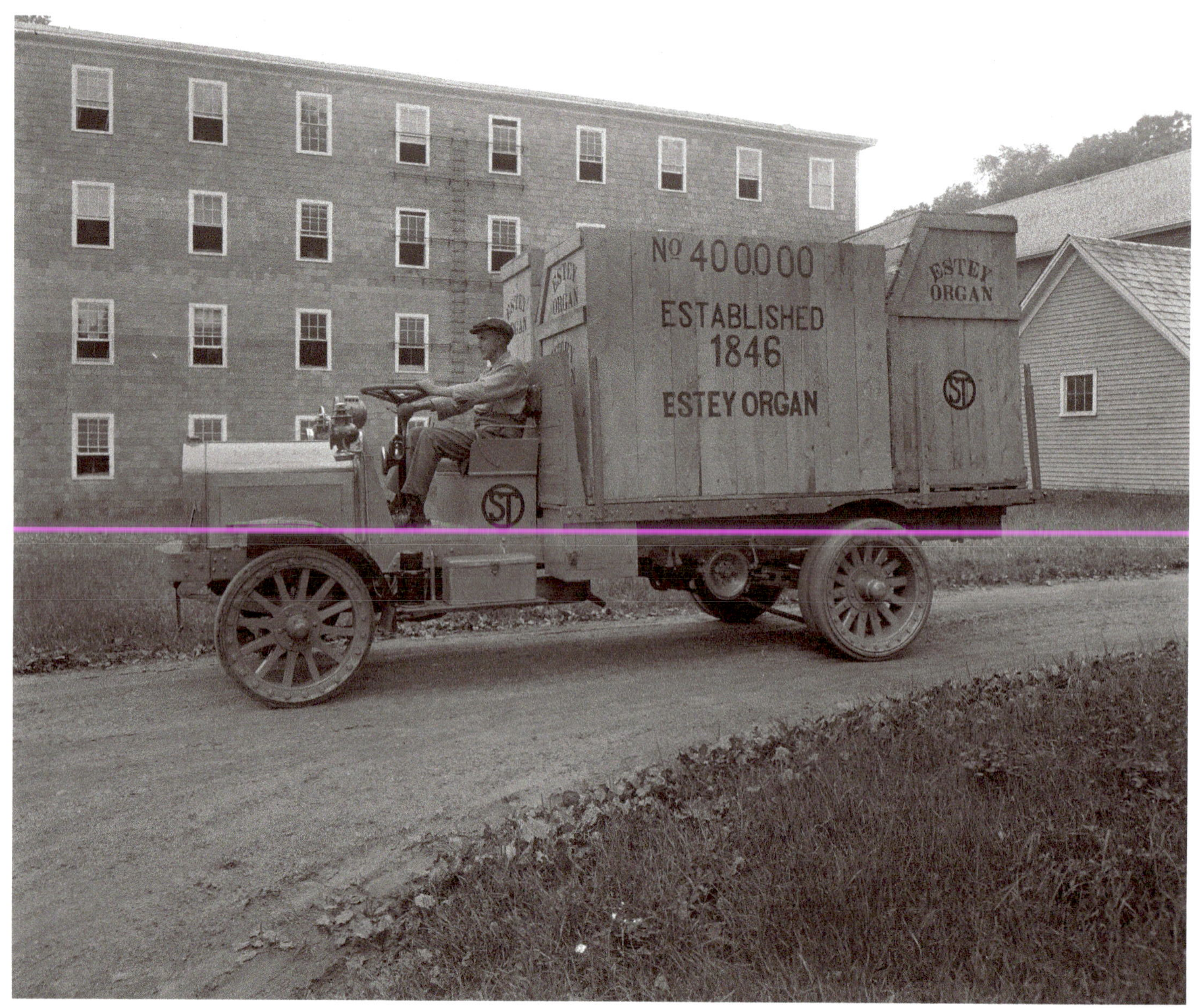

Plumber Jacob Estey built a highly successful organ business in Brattleboro. More affordable than the piano and easier to keep tuned, the reed organ became the quintessential Victorian-era instrument in American homes. Brattleboro hosted a long list of music stores and instrument makers, including one whose organ was deemed, dubiously, "better adapted to accompany the scraping hum of a wood sawyer."

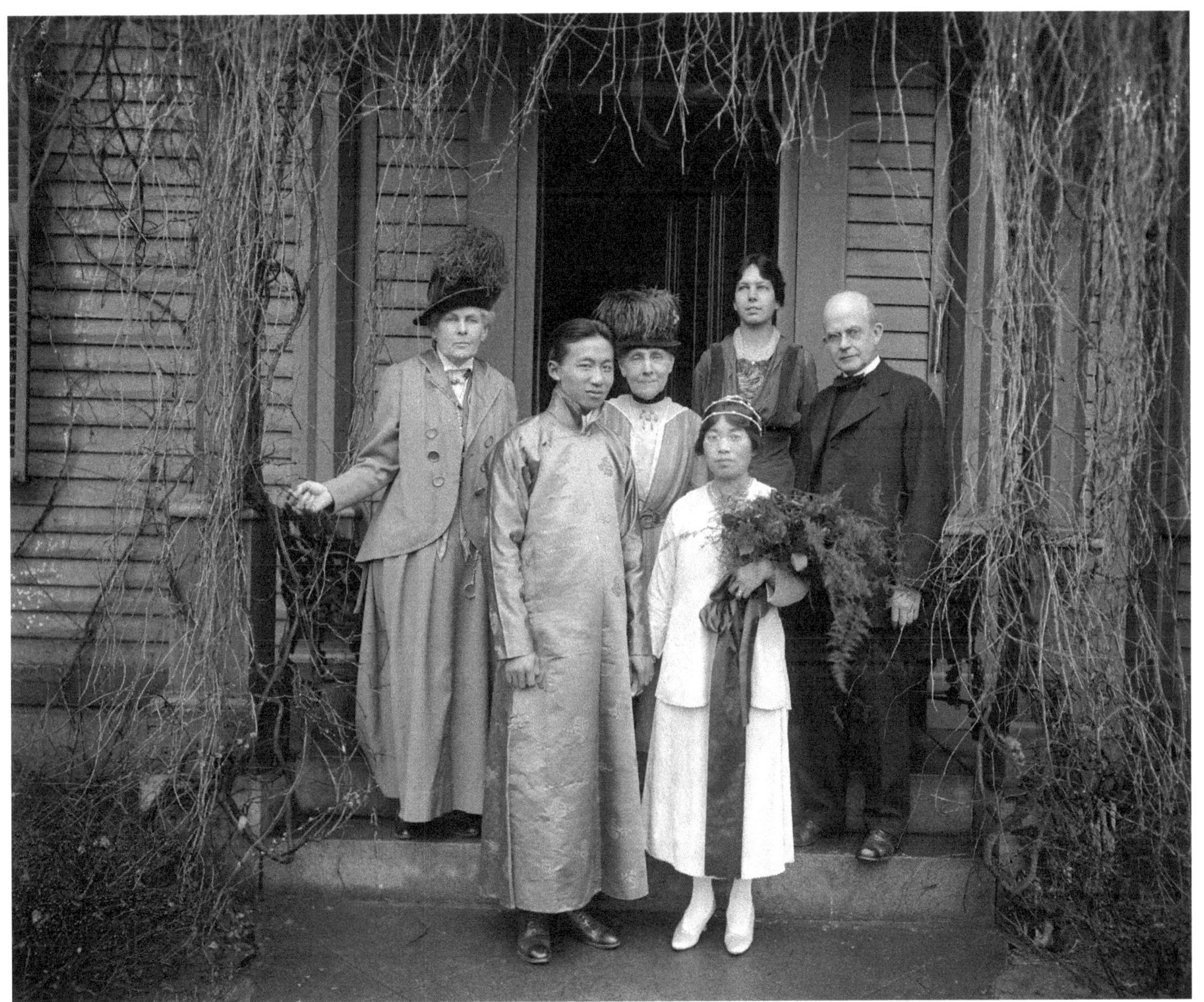

Brattleboro photographer Benjamin Crown took this wedding photograph of Yangma Kno and Mai Tsu in 1918. Census takers recorded fewer Asian immigrants living in Vermont during these years: the number dropped from 42 persons in 1900 to just 10 in 1920. The 1920 census lists three Asian immigrants living in Brattleboro: Edward Uchida, a golf club manager; F. Moy Fing, who ran a laundry; and Masser Itagaki, private chef for organ company president Jacob Gray Estey.

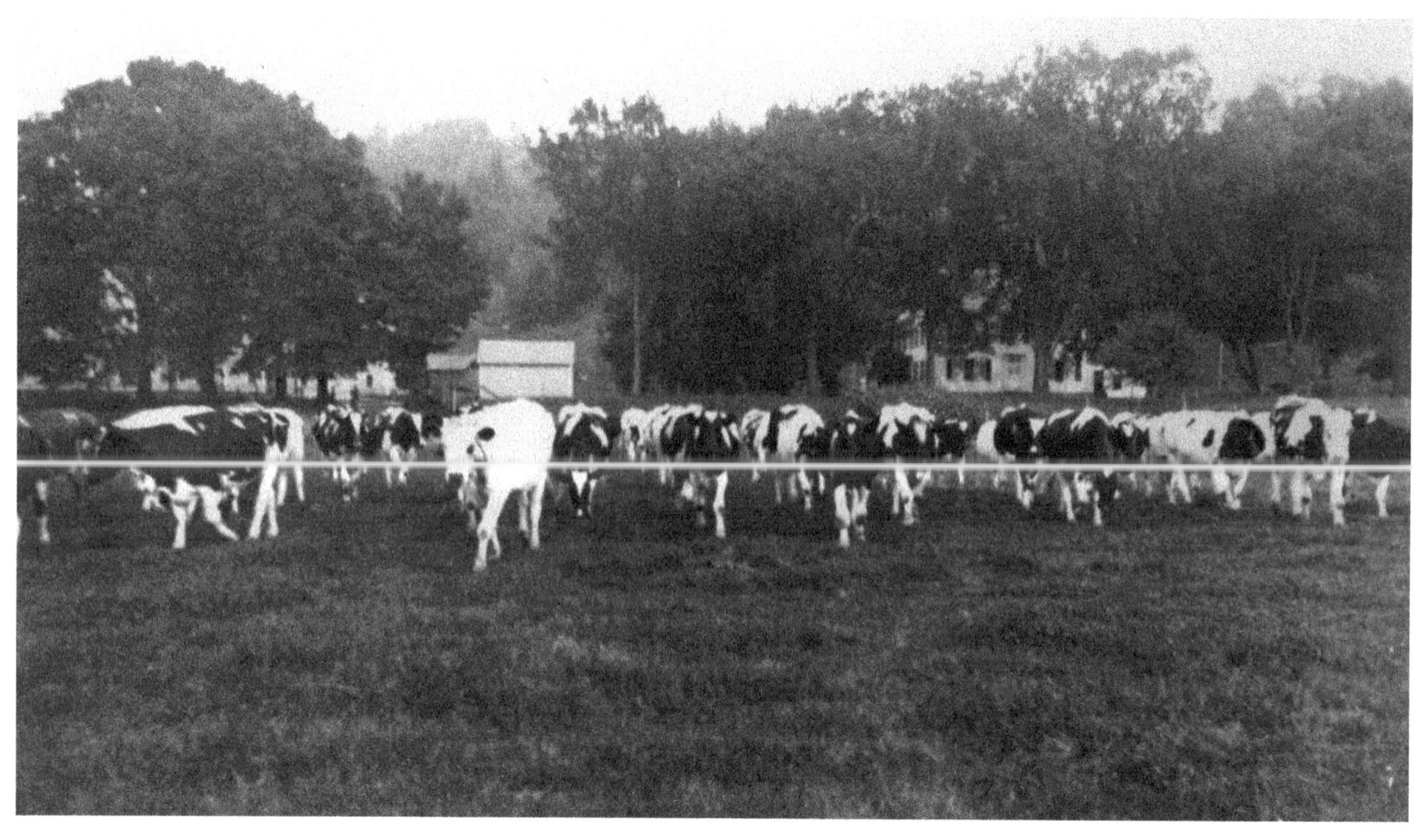

Vermont's early agricultural economy focused first on wheat and then on wool, but by 1900 most Vermont farmers had turned to dairy production. They also diversified their products to protect themselves from competition from western states. Wilson A. Bentley, Jericho's "Snowflake Man," famous for his thousands of photographs of snow crystals, recorded this image in the pasture next to his home.

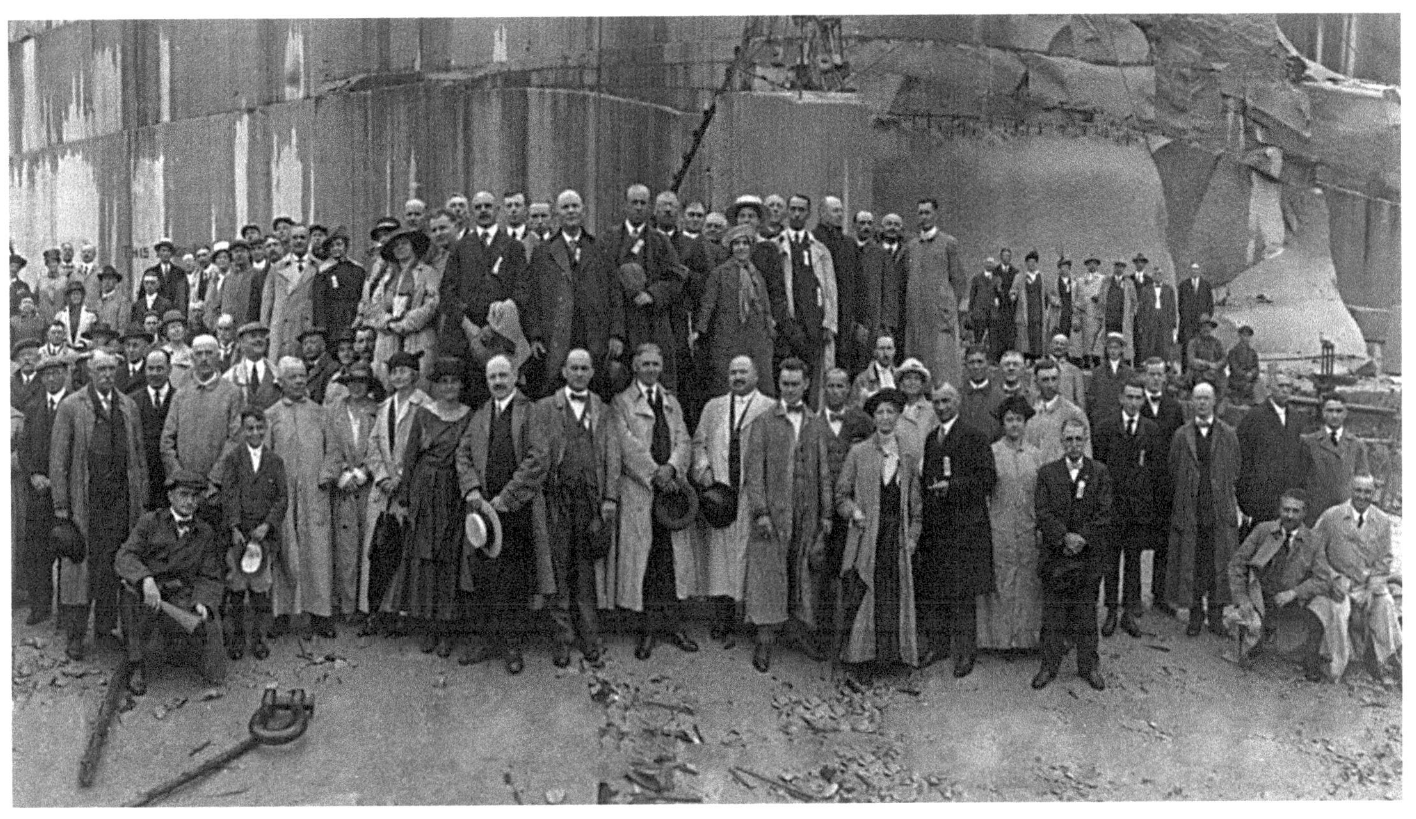

The Association of American Cemetery Superintendents held this convention at Barre, recognized as the premier source of granite in America. Many of the nation's cemeteries had allowed plot holders to select their own plantings and to care for their own plots, the result being that many cemeteries quickly became unkempt. This prompted a more active involvement from cemetery superintendents, who began selecting plantings and defining acceptable monument styles for their patrons.

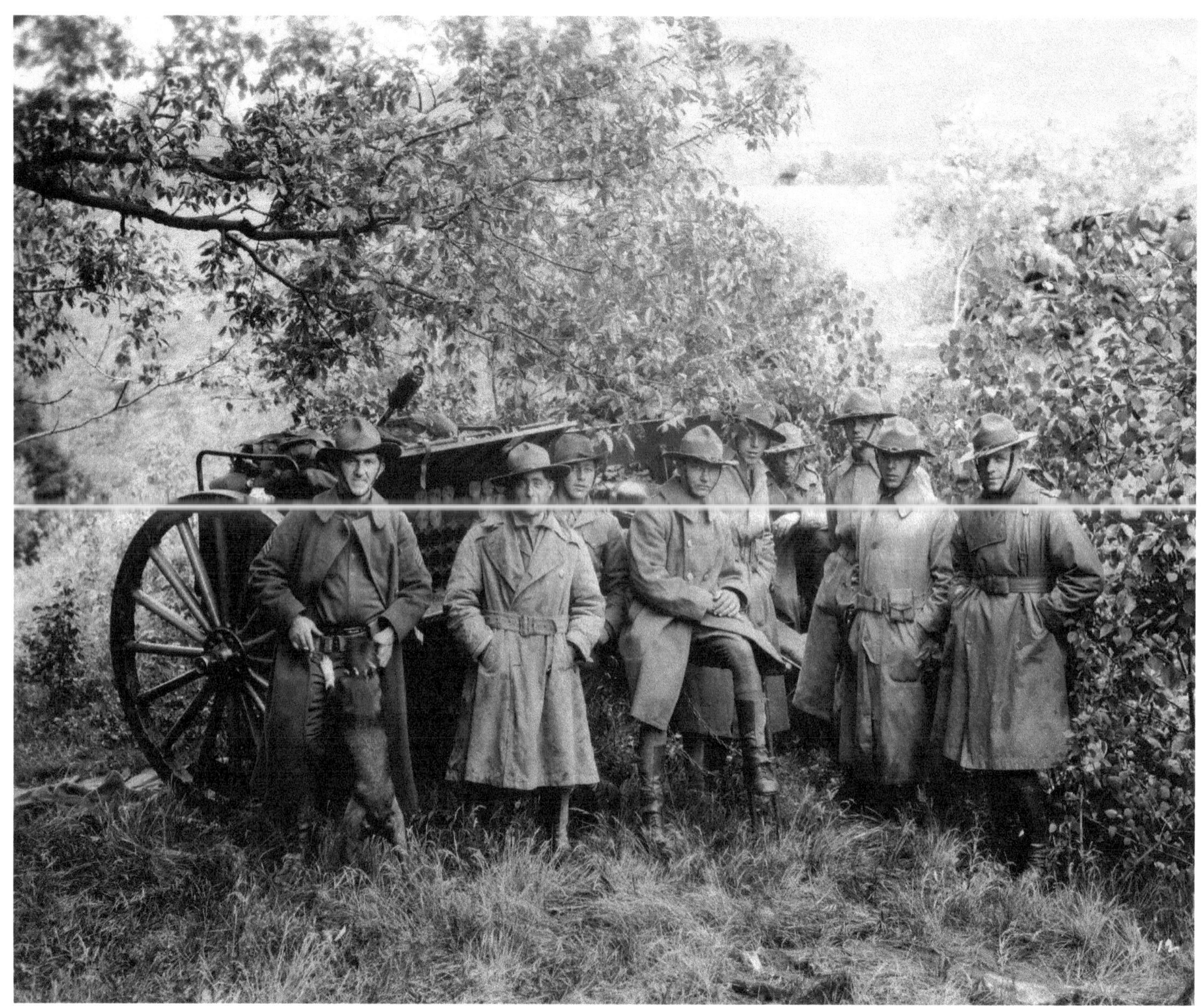

Built in 1893, Fort Ethan Allen boosted the cultural offerings of the region. The parade grounds hosted townspeople for baseball games, band concerts, training camps, and horse shows. This exchange between the fort and the surrounding communities also posed challenges: in 1935 the fort's marshal reported that "a number of women" in Burlington had become "a menace." The city's matron of police quickly apprehended them.

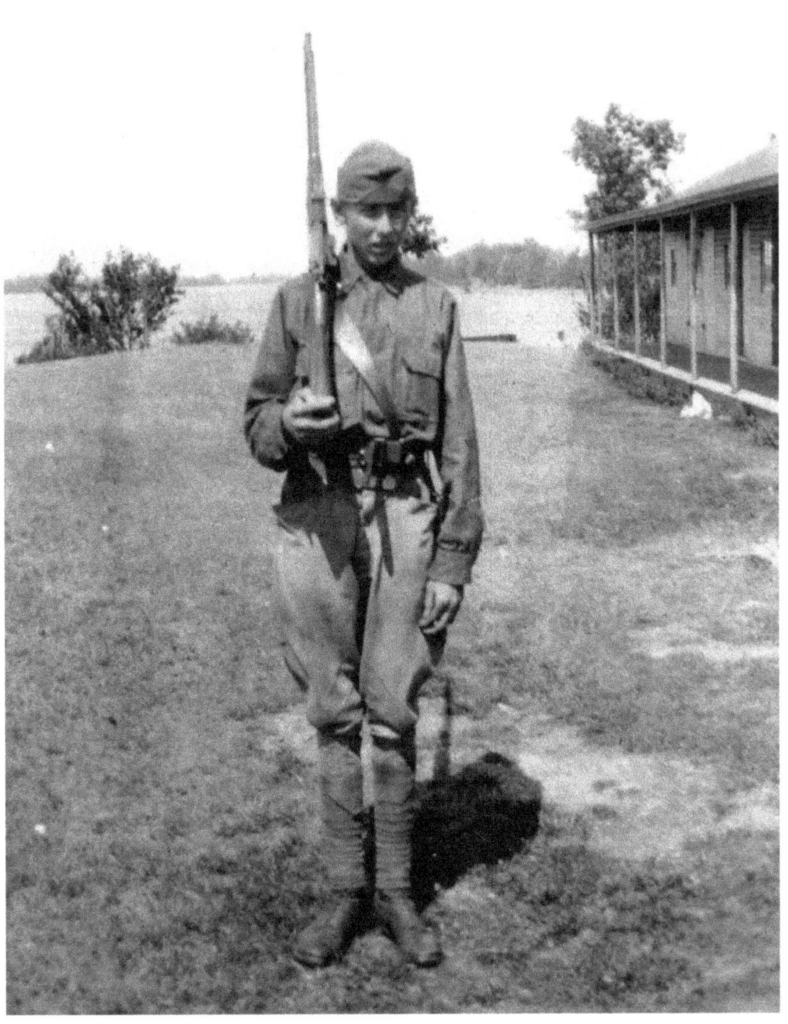

Fort Ethan Allen Training Camp, 1919. When Vermont's Redfield Proctor became President Benjamin Harrison's secretary of war in 1892, he advocated establishing a military outpost near either Swanton or Essex Junction. Some Vermonters supported the idea, others did not. The St. Johnsbury newspaper editor, among the latter, suggested that "Vermont wants a military post as much as a toad wants a tail." Proctor, a Vermont native, was a graduate of Dartmouth College. His storied life included service in the Civil War, a career in law, and another in business, in which he served as president of the Vermont Marble Company. Proctor became governor of Vermont in 1878, later the 37th U.S. secretary of war, and finally a United States senator.

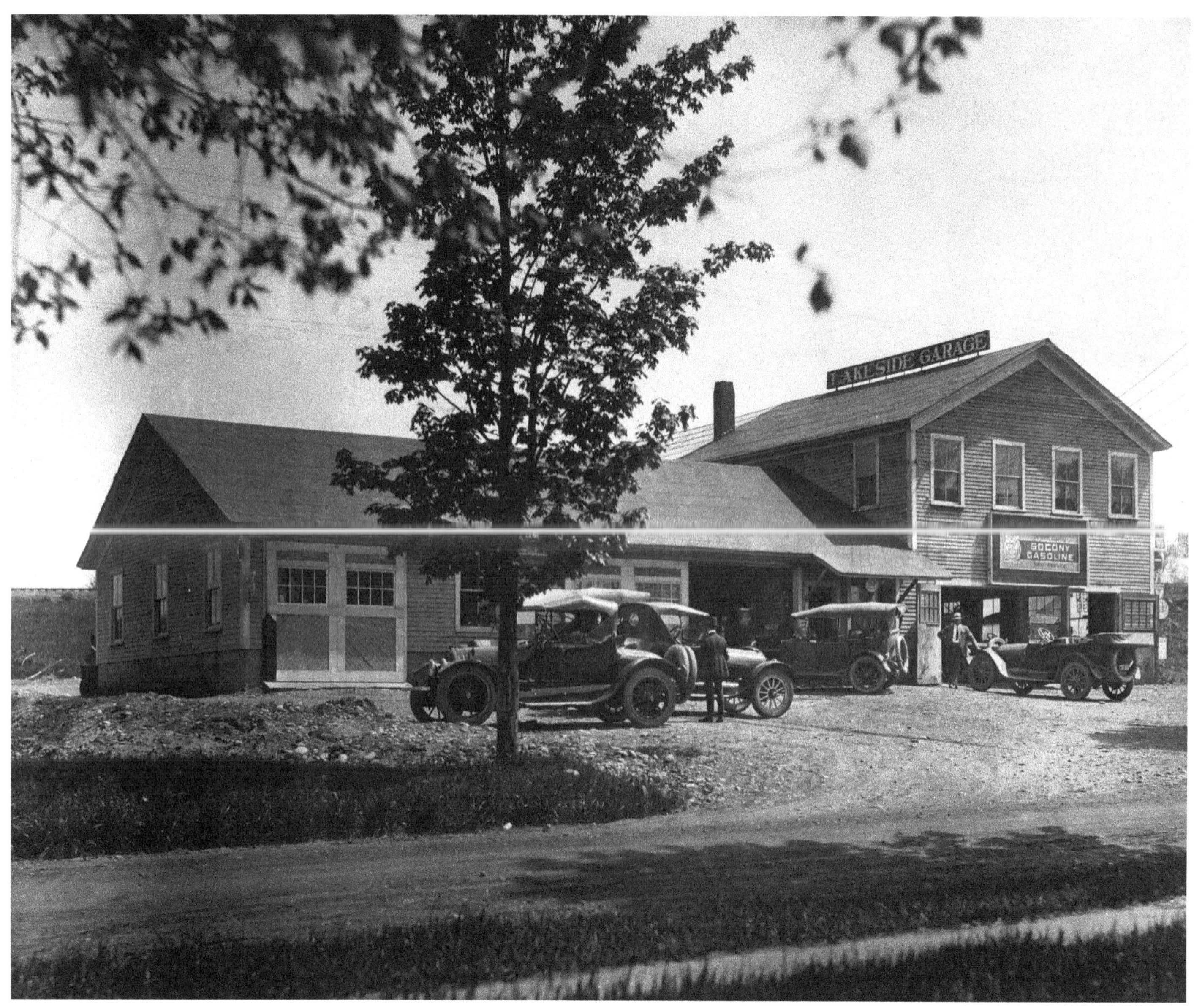

Lakeside Garage in Morrisville, about 1919. Taking its name from a resort area on the Lamoille River called "Lake Lamoille," the Lakeside Garage opened in 1916 under the proprietorship of James Reed and Fred Peck. Reed, a machinist by trade, bought out Peck within two years, and Peck entered the lumber business. The garage operated as a service and repair station for 25 years, becoming a Ford dealership in the 1950s.

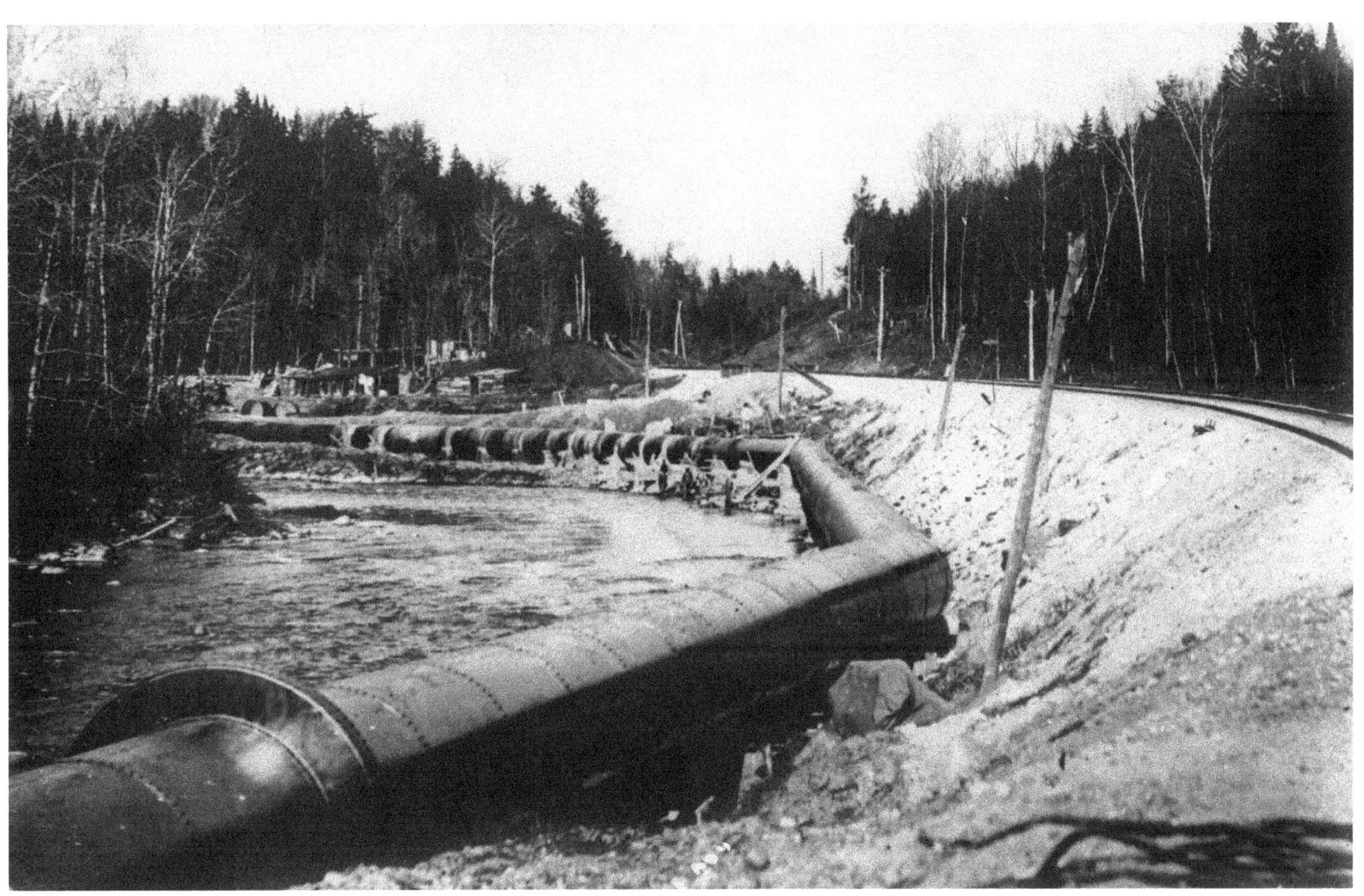

A pipe laid for the new hydroelectric plant in East Montpelier in the early twentieth century. Electricity reached many of Vermont's largest towns by 1890, but no more than a handful of rural communities until after 1900, and even then technology crept slowly into Vermont's farming communities. In 1920, only a tenth of Vermont farmers had electricity. Driven by hydroelectric power companies that often resided outside Vermont, rural electrification gave rise to debates over in-state versus out-of-state control that persisted into the 1960s.

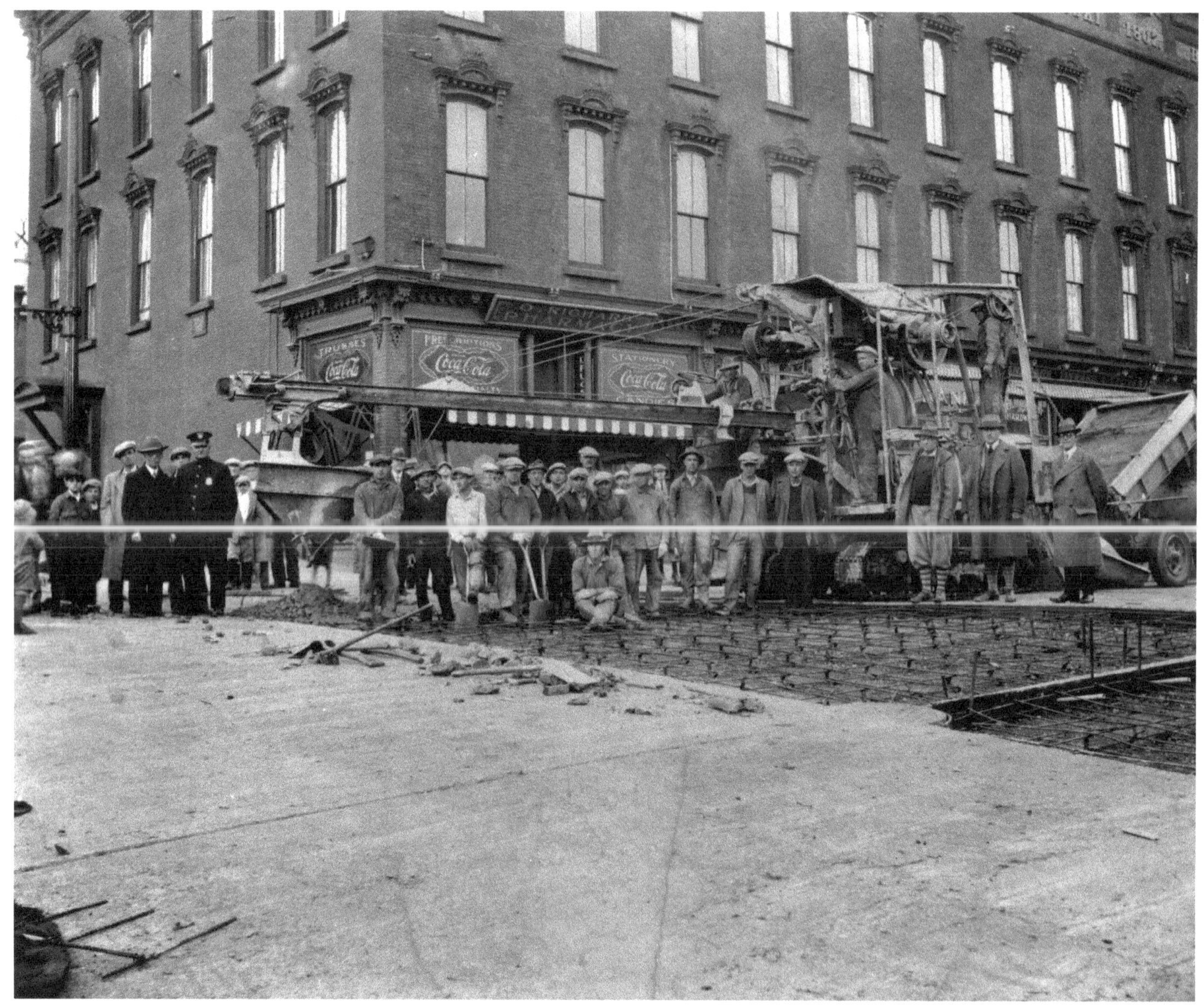

Paving at West Allen and Main Street, Winooski. Part of Colchester since its charter in the 1760s, the mill-driven, multi-ethnic area of Winooski was home to more people than rural Colchester. In 1921, Winooski split completely from Colchester, making it nearly the last city to incorporate in Vermont. Winooski residents quickly embraced a number of urban improvements—including creating police and fire departments and paving the streets.

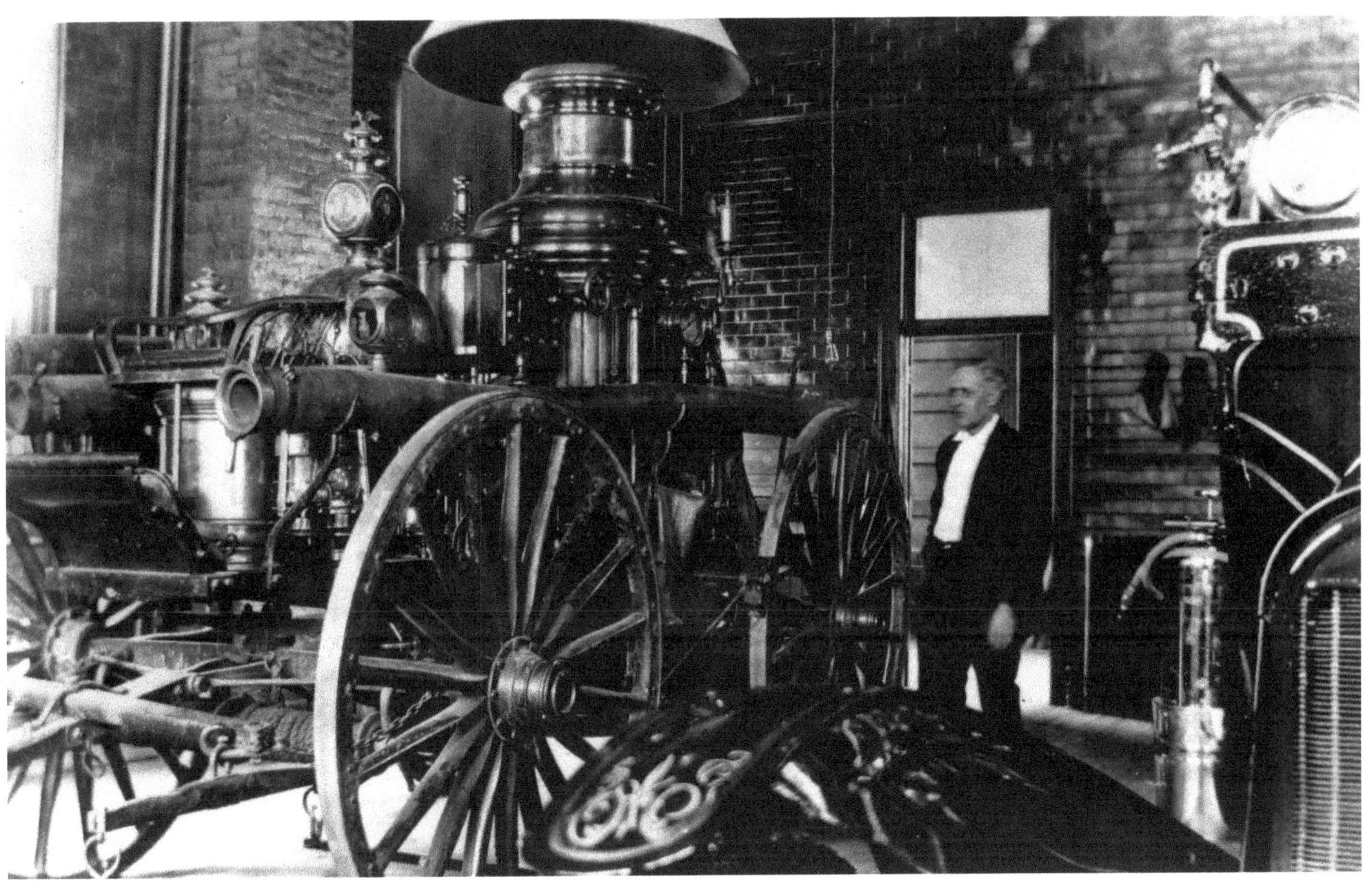

Steam pumper at the Old Fire Station in Winooski. When Winooski was incorporated in 1921, residents quickly built an infrastructure that included a municipal fire department. It was during these years that cities around the nation benefited from the prevention efforts driven by national insurance organizations. These efforts included formalized building and zoning codes, advocacy for sprinkler systems, and rules to govern modern—and sometimes dangerous—conveniences like electricity and fuel.

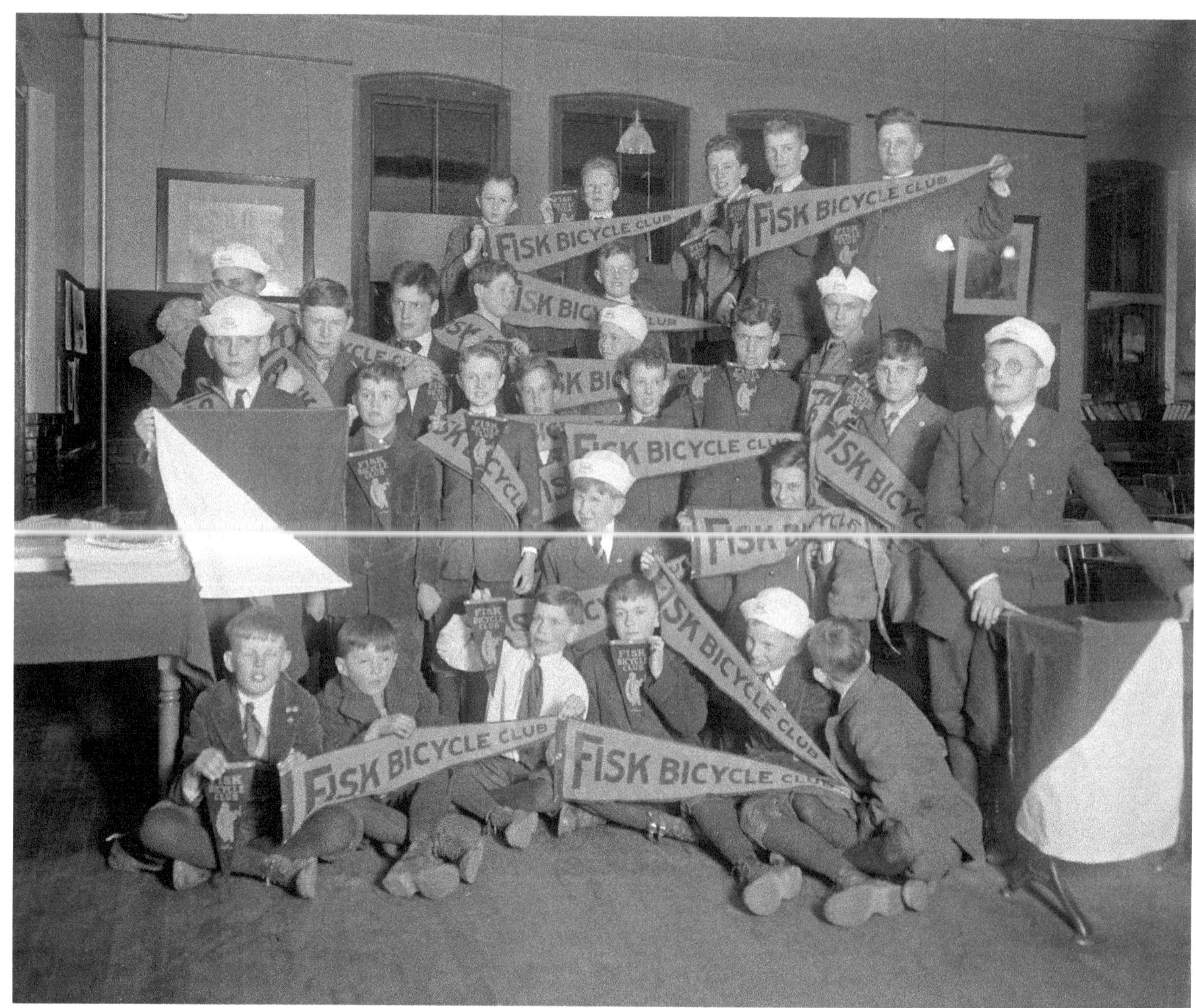

The Fisk Tire Company opened around 1900 near Springfield, Massachusetts. The company was a motivated marketer, enlisting Norman Rockwell to illustrate advertisements. It also initiated a bicycle club that became popular among boys. The Fisk Tire boy, a company mascot, appears on the banners in this photograph: a pajama-clad youth sporting a tire on one shoulder and a candle in the hand opposite, with the slogan "Time to Re-Tire" written underneath.

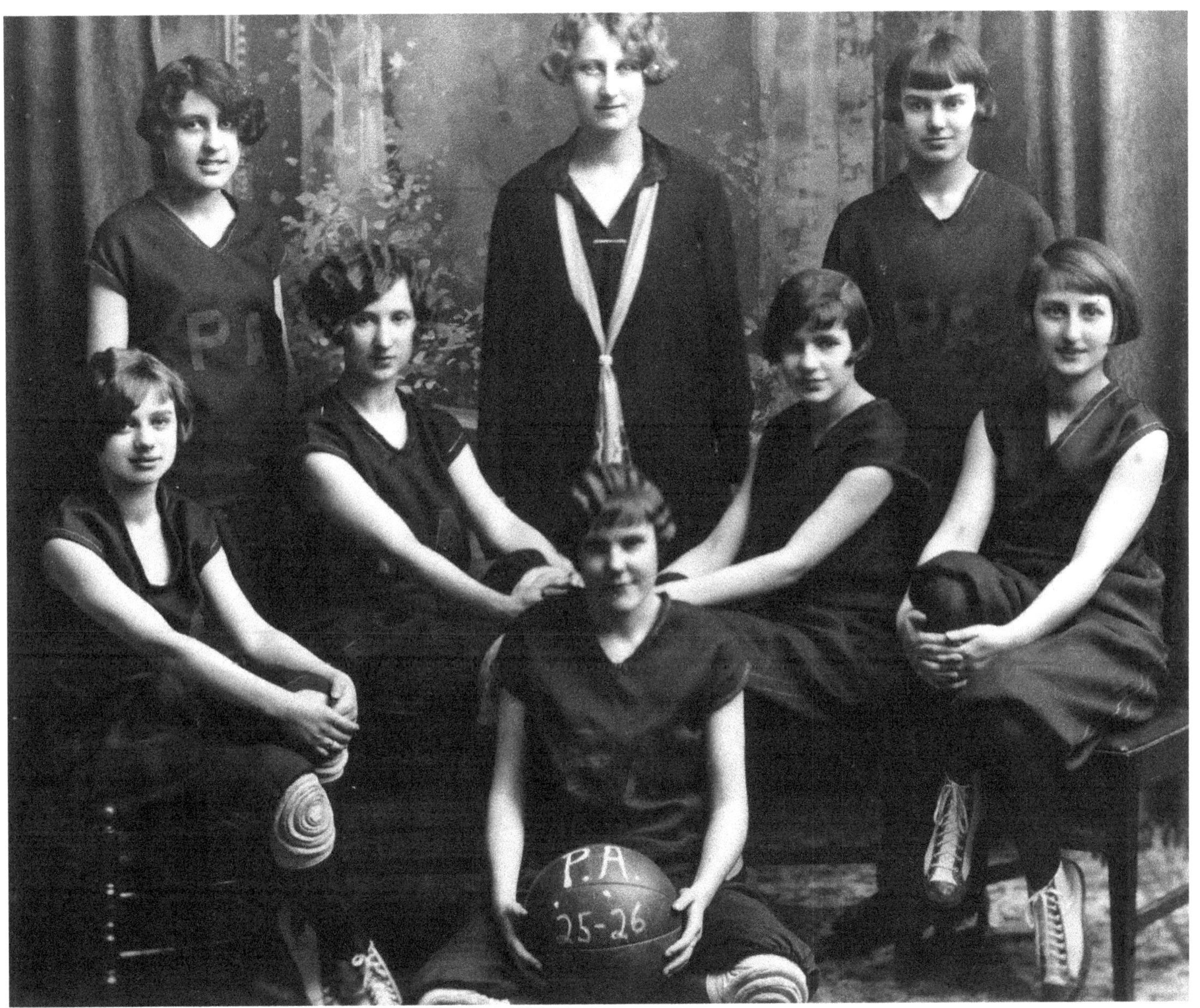

Girls' basketball at Morrisville's People's Academy, 1925. Invented in 1891 (originally using a soccer ball) by James Naismith, basketball was the stomping ground for nineteenth-century discussions of morality and decorum. One advocate urged that basketball remedied the woman's "inability to leave the personal element out of thought or action," because "it is impossible to pose in basketball."

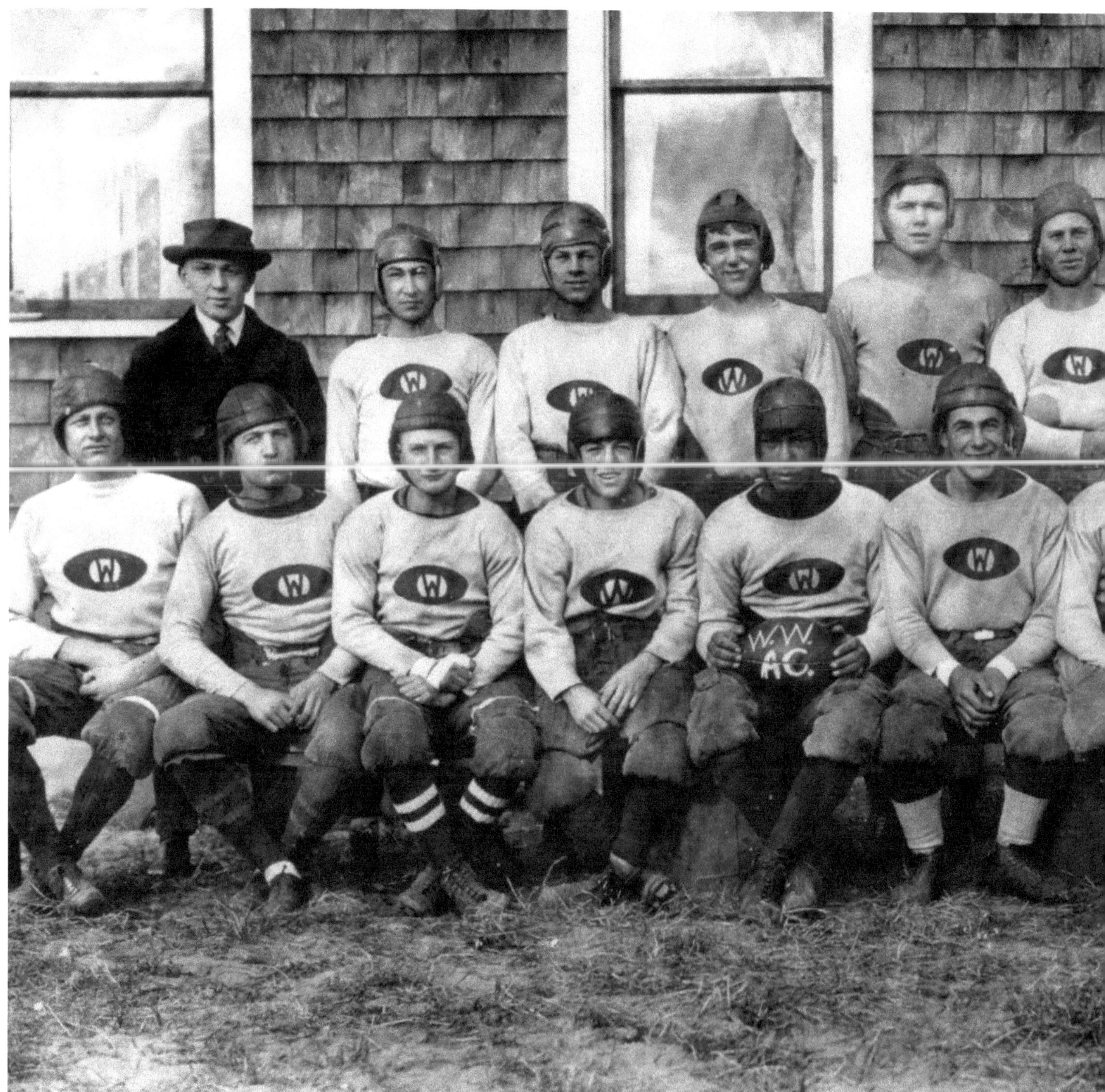
W.W.
A.C.

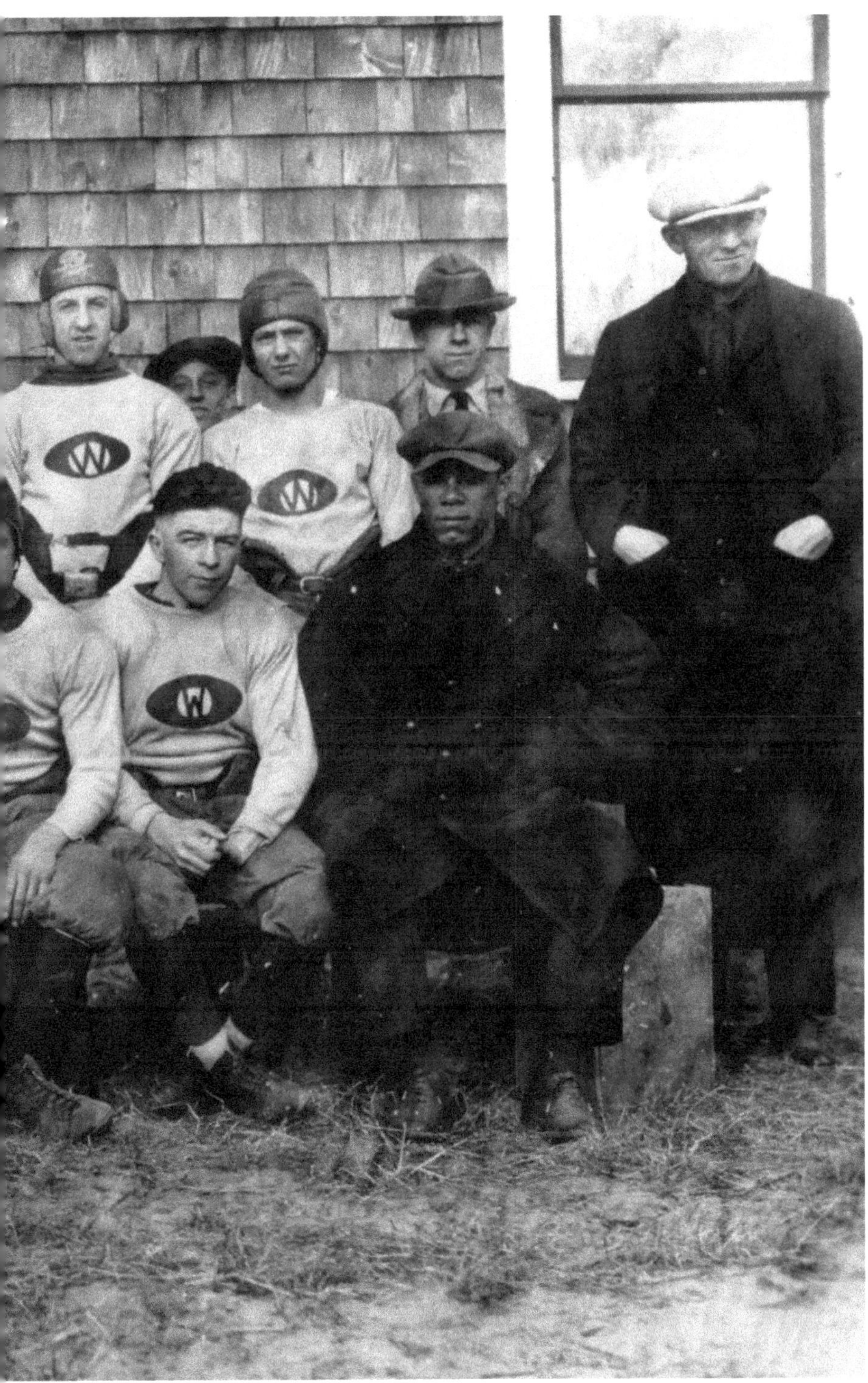

The Winooski Whirlwinds around 1924. Winooski did not have its own football team until 1931. Before that year, city residents and high school students joined forces to play for teams like the Whirlwinds. This photograph also suggests Winooski's cultural diversity, which by this time was home to Americans of varying descent, including Polish, Irish, African, and especially French Canadian.

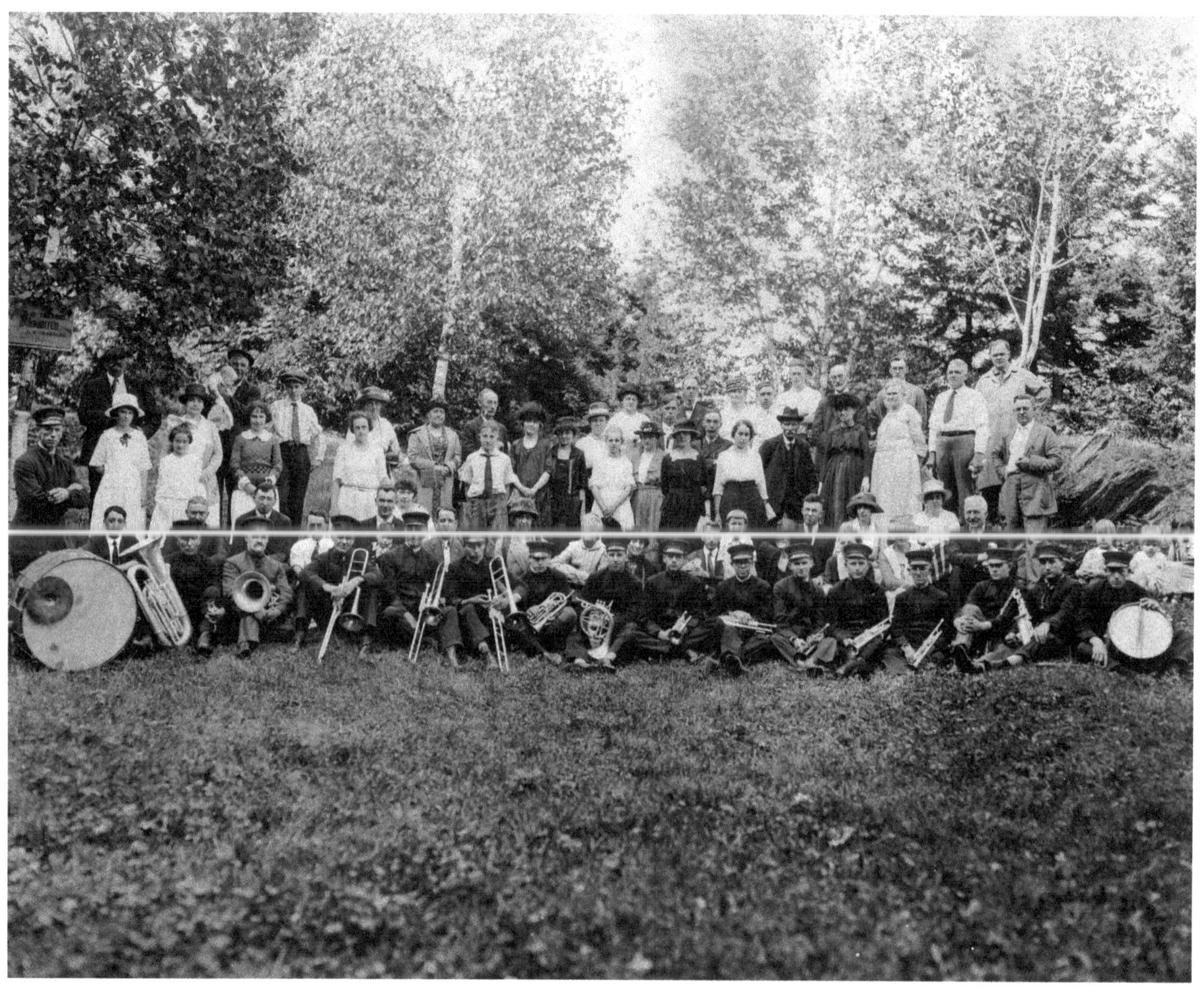

Randolph's Green Mountain Band, around 1923. Between 1900 and 1910, the number of town and touring bands in the United States peaked. Town bands grew less popular once other diversions—automobiling, the phonograph, motion pictures, and radio broadcasts—became available. After 1920, the number of these bands dwindled, many consolidating into regional groups.

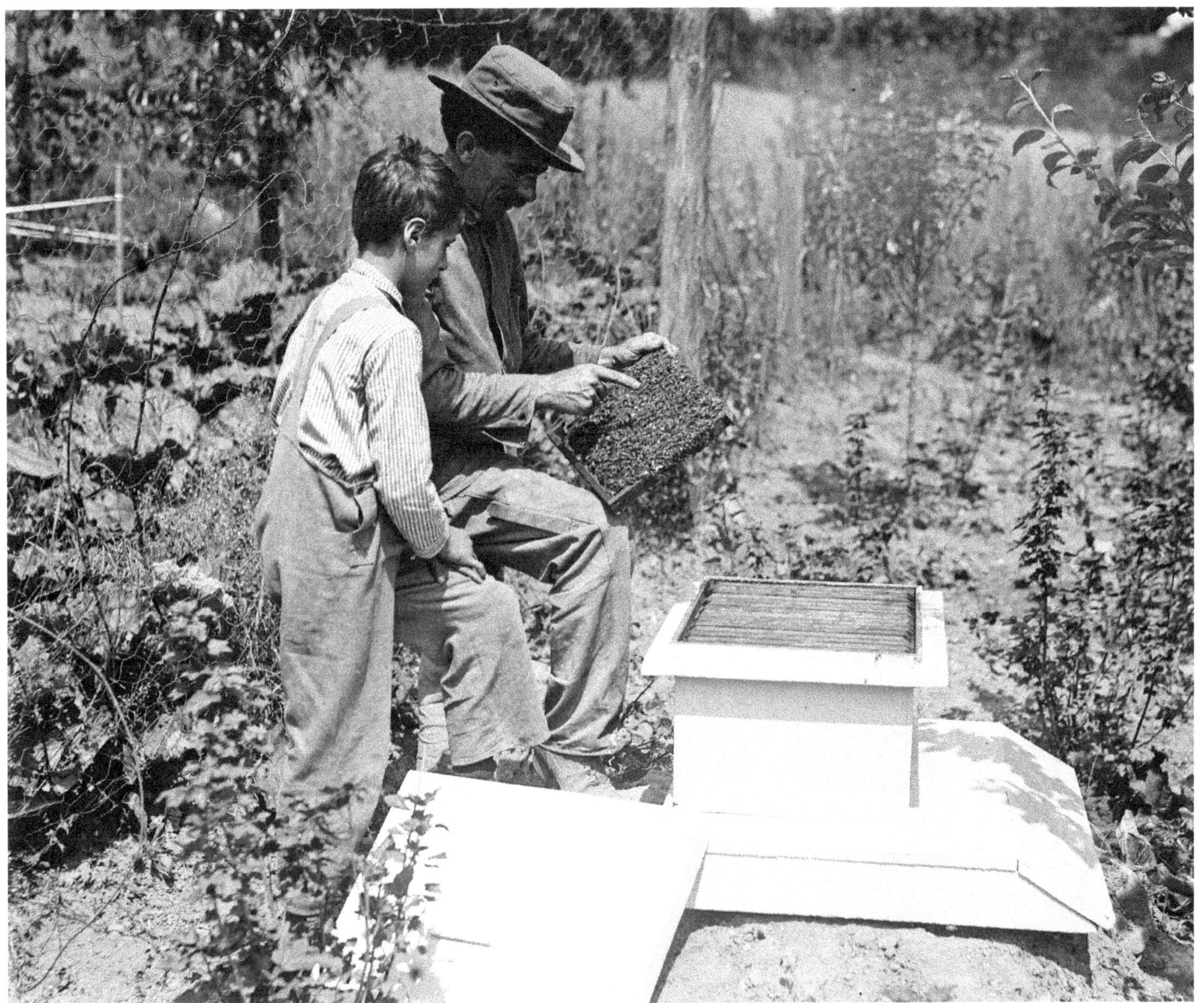

A farmer and his son keep bees in Bennington. Starting in the late nineteenth century, many Vermont farmers adopted a more scientific approach to agriculture. They gleaned advanced methods from the Vermont State Agricultural Society, agricultural fairs, grange organizations, and the University of Vermont. More than just competitive advantage, one pamphlet suggested that the new scientific farming offered an added benefit: a "mental culture" for young people who sought more than "mere physical drudgery." These two brave apiarists appear to be handling a slat of live bees without wearing protective gear and without having annoyed even one of the stinging creatures. Must be the scientific approach.

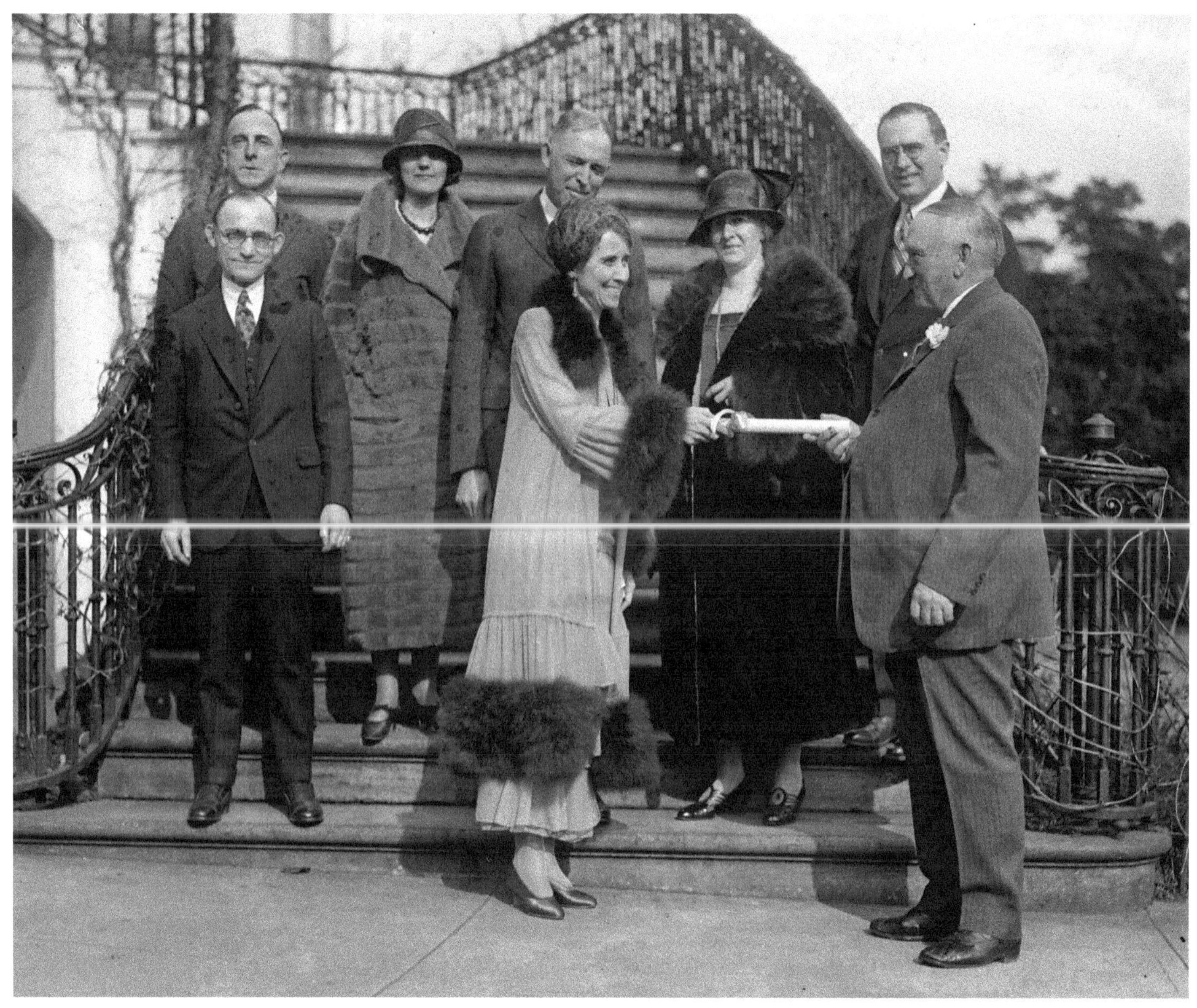

During the early twentieth century, some resourceful Vermonters raised mink and fox for their valuable furs. One mink ranch in Jericho started with two female minks and one male, and within five years had 500 animals. This trend toward farm-raised animals contrasted with that of earlier decades, when most traders hunted animals in the wild. In this photograph, Vermont fur dealers present First Lady Grace Goodhue Coolidge with a coat in 1925.

A Flood of Change

(1927–1949)

In what some have called a "forty-five-hour cloudburst," Vermont experienced the greatest flood in its recorded history on November 3 and 4, 1927. It came quickly and unexpectedly. In Montpelier, one family headed with their infant toward high ground in a nearby cemetery. Travelers at the Central Vermont Railroad station retreated hastily to the attic and spiritedly rang the station's bell for help. A family in Middlesex camped out on the second floor of their home, fortunate to have taken a handful of crackers to tide them over.

Harrowing and heroic flood stories are many, and the details are astonishing: train tracks dangling from cliffs, bridges snapping in half, livestock washing away, lumber mills being crushed, and houses floating off their foundations and running aground some distance downstream. Eighty-four Vermonters died and a conservative estimate of losses exceeded twenty million 1927 dollars. The Winooski Valley was particularly hard hit, with deaths concentrated in the communities of Bolton and Waterbury. Governor John Weeks signed legislation to help recovery efforts, and President Coolidge, a Vermont native, authorized federal funds to aid the rebuilding.

The Flood of 1927 significantly altered the role of Vermont state government in local affairs. Since the nineteenth century, local town governments had repeatedly blocked state efforts to regulate fishing and hunting, to structure schools, and to build state highways. Go-it-alone Vermonters, accustomed to simple lives, had staunchly defended the idea of self-sufficiency. But with roads washed away and bridges missing, they were in no state of mind to reject external aid on the grounds of traditional local independence. The flood put Vermonters in a mood to accept government aid, and this mood led towns finally to cede control to state and federal agencies. Nevertheless, battles over local control continued for many decades: would Vermonters allow the federal government to relocate Vermont farms in order to build flood reservoirs? Would the state cede "sub-marginal" farmlands to the federal government in exchange for relocation packages to struggling farmers? Moreover, would Vermonters accept a state-sponsored police force?

In response to many issues, the answer was a resounding *no!* But to others—libraries and bookwagons, dairy farming programs, parent education, and support for labor unions—many Vermonters had capitulated and would acquiesce.

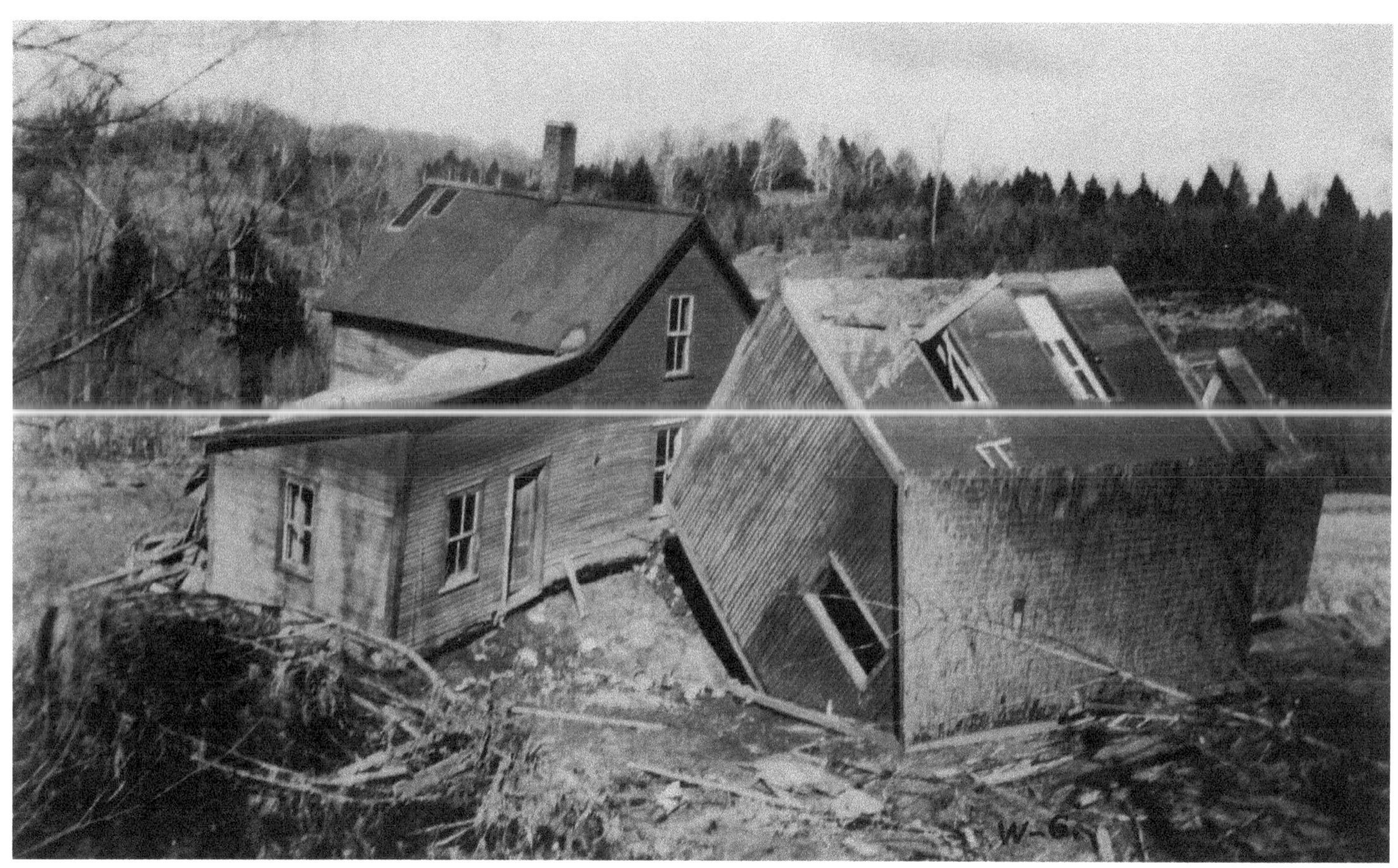

A flood-ravaged home in Waterbury. The Flood of 1927 took seven lives in Waterbury. These included the Sargent family, whose house pulled from its moorings and hastened into the floodwaters, and Gladys Cutting and her three children, who drowned when their makeshift raft of hammered-together doors capsized. Gladys's husband, Harry, who began swimming when the raft could not support his weight, survived. Neighbors found him 12 hours later in a treetop.

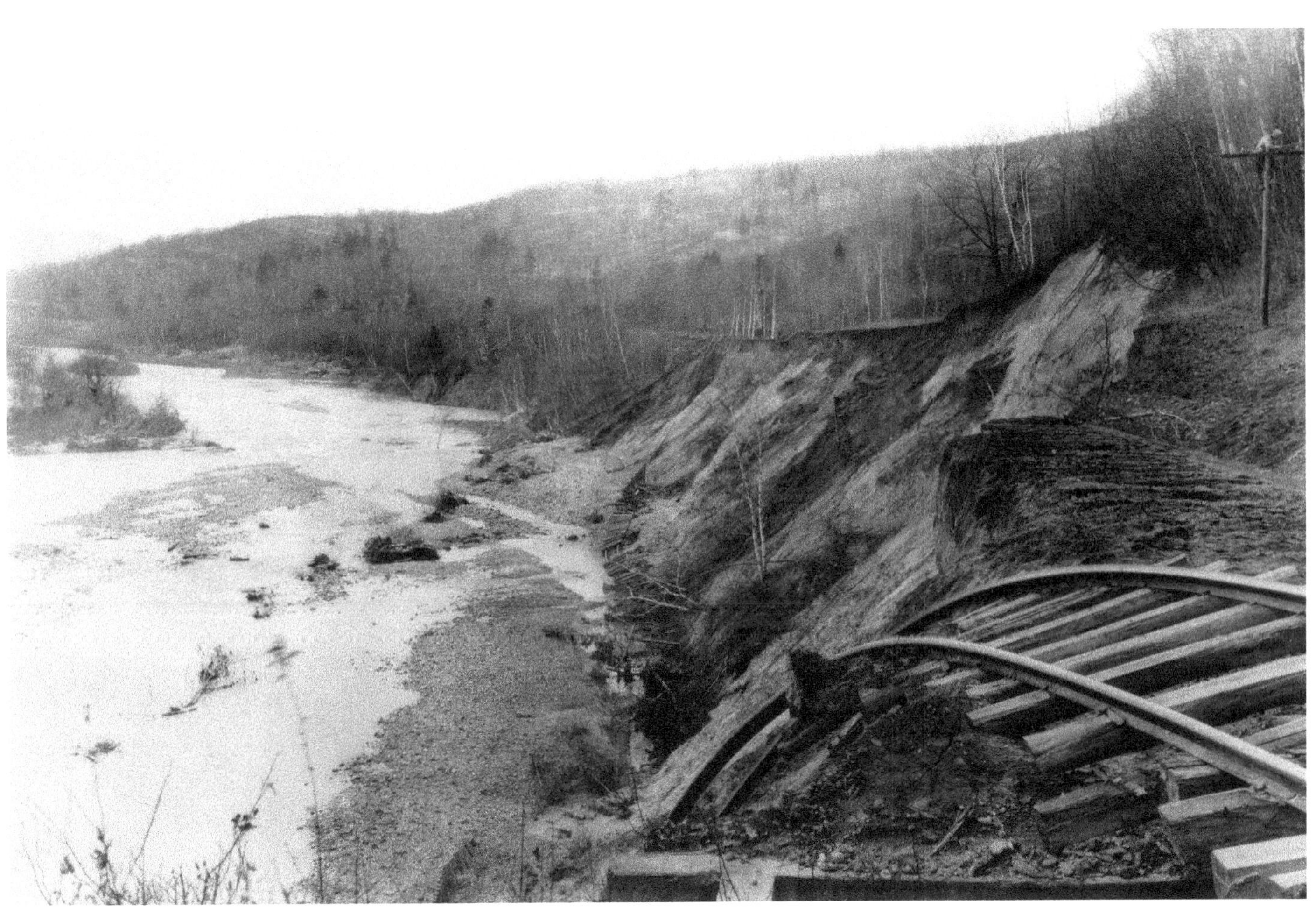

Slip Hill near Middlesex, 1927. Even before the great flood, the Central Vermont Railroad's construction department had long denounced the stretch at Slip Hill. Engines inched up the 400-foot embankment, which gave way when floodwaters blasted through. In this view, the railroad tracks linger, hanging in a garland from the eroded precipice and lying mangled along the gravel bar below. All told, the Central Vermont Railroad sustained three million 1927 dollars in flood damages.

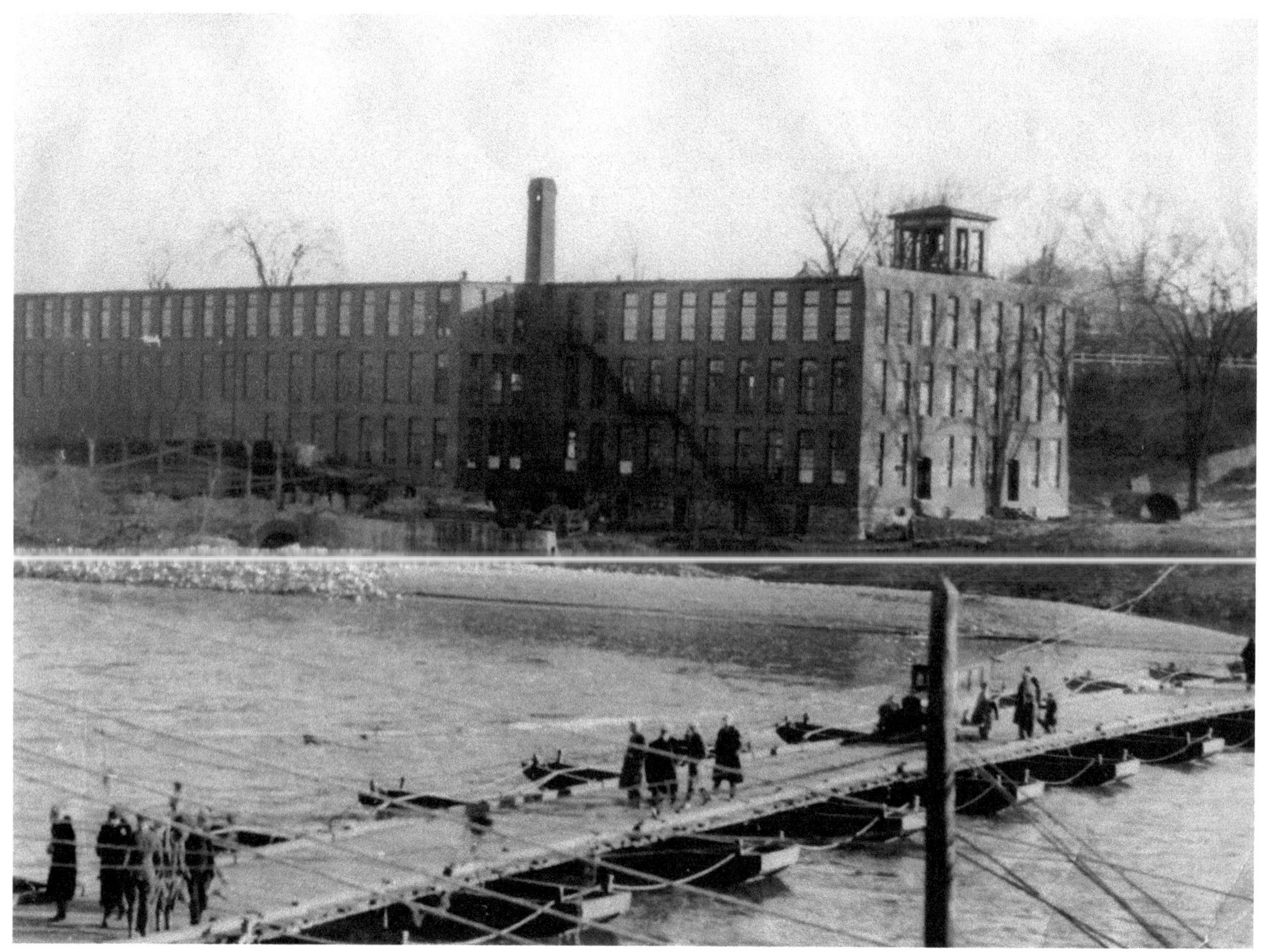

The Army Corps of Engineers constructed this pontoon bridge in Winooski days after the old bridge washed away in the 1927 flood. Town residents heard their bridge rupture with a "loud cracking noise, snapping wires, splintering poles." Some also remembered a terrified mare that floated over the dam with her colt's mane in her teeth. Dubbed the greatest natural disaster to hit Vermont, the flood killed 84 Vermonters, 55 of whom lived in the Winooski Valley.

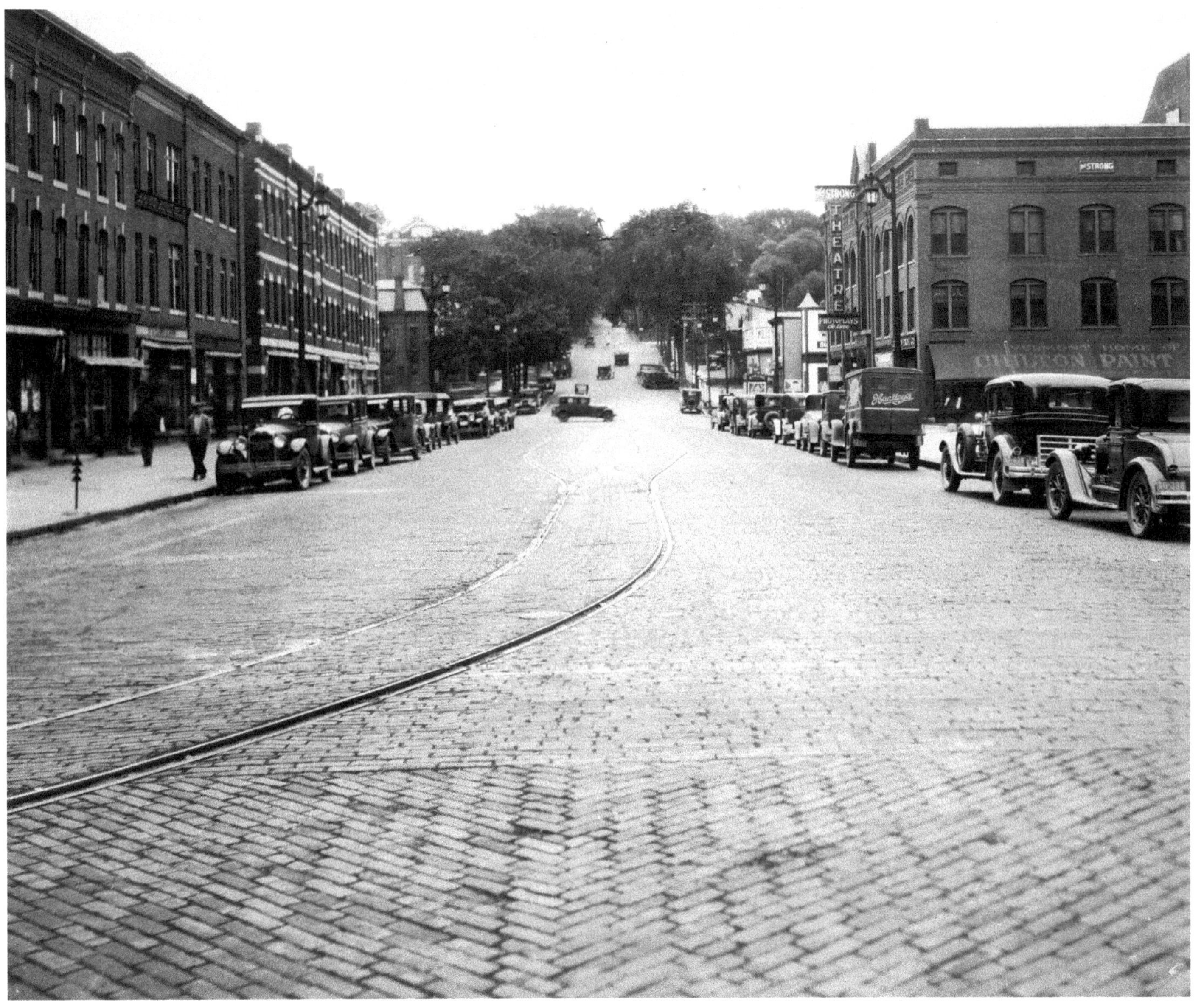

Burlington's Main Street was originally paved in 1912, with brick pavers laid over a sand-and-concrete base. In 1929, the street department replaced some of the bricks with asphalt laid over the old trolley tracks. Unlike the uneven pavers, the asphalt provided a "smooth, dustless, noiseless pavement" which was "satisfactory in every respect." The city peeled up the trolley tracks in 1943 to provide scrap metal for the war effort during World War II.

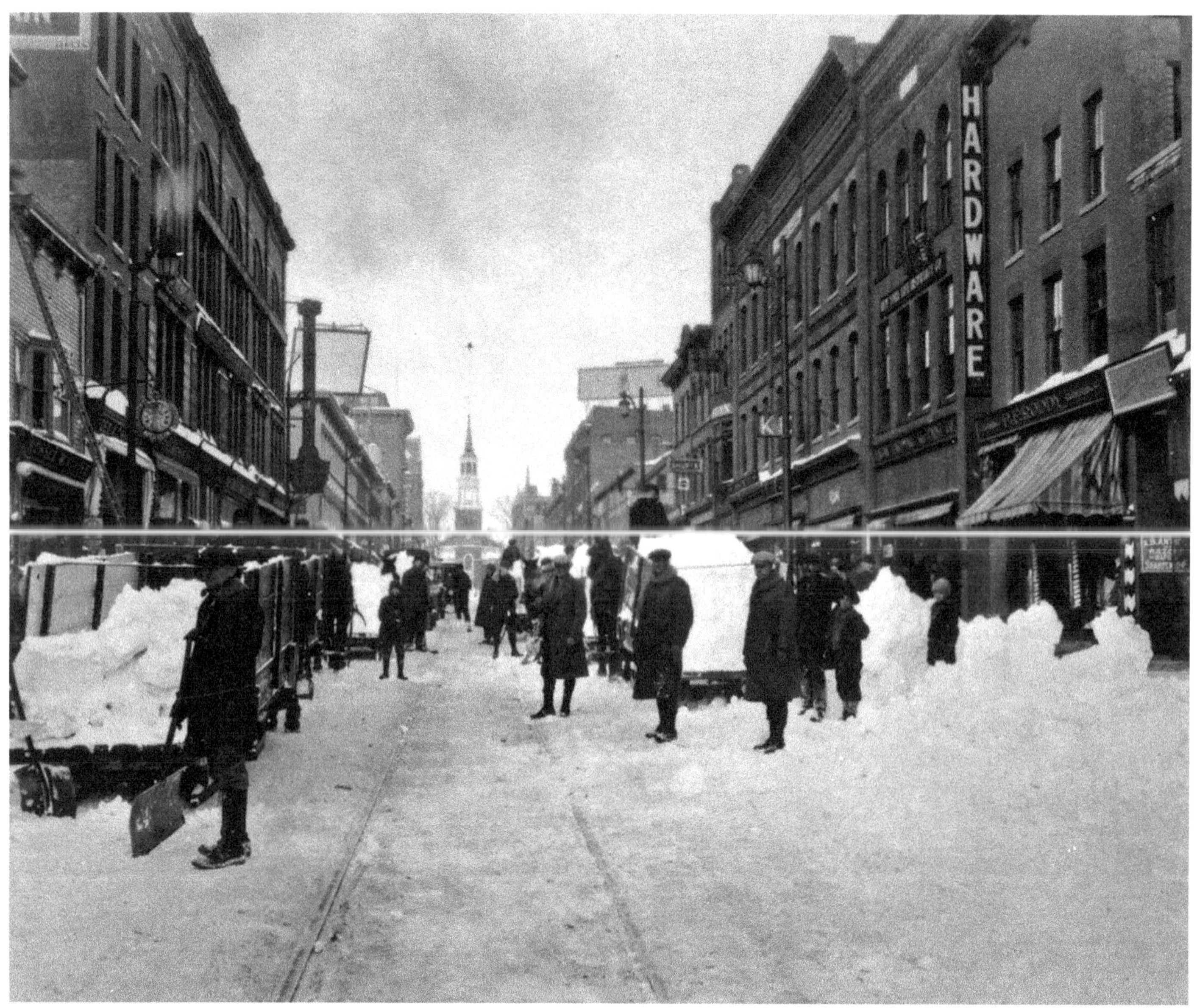

Shops on snow-covered Church Street. Shoppers from surrounding towns and states visited Burlington, and the city endeavored to be a good host. The early twentieth century brought marked growth of the downtown area, including shops and eventually paved streets, sewers, and sidewalks. In 1914, Burlington City Hall even included a staffed "Rest Room," managed by the Rest Room Association, which provided a stopping place for weary travelers and shoppers to relax before they returned home.

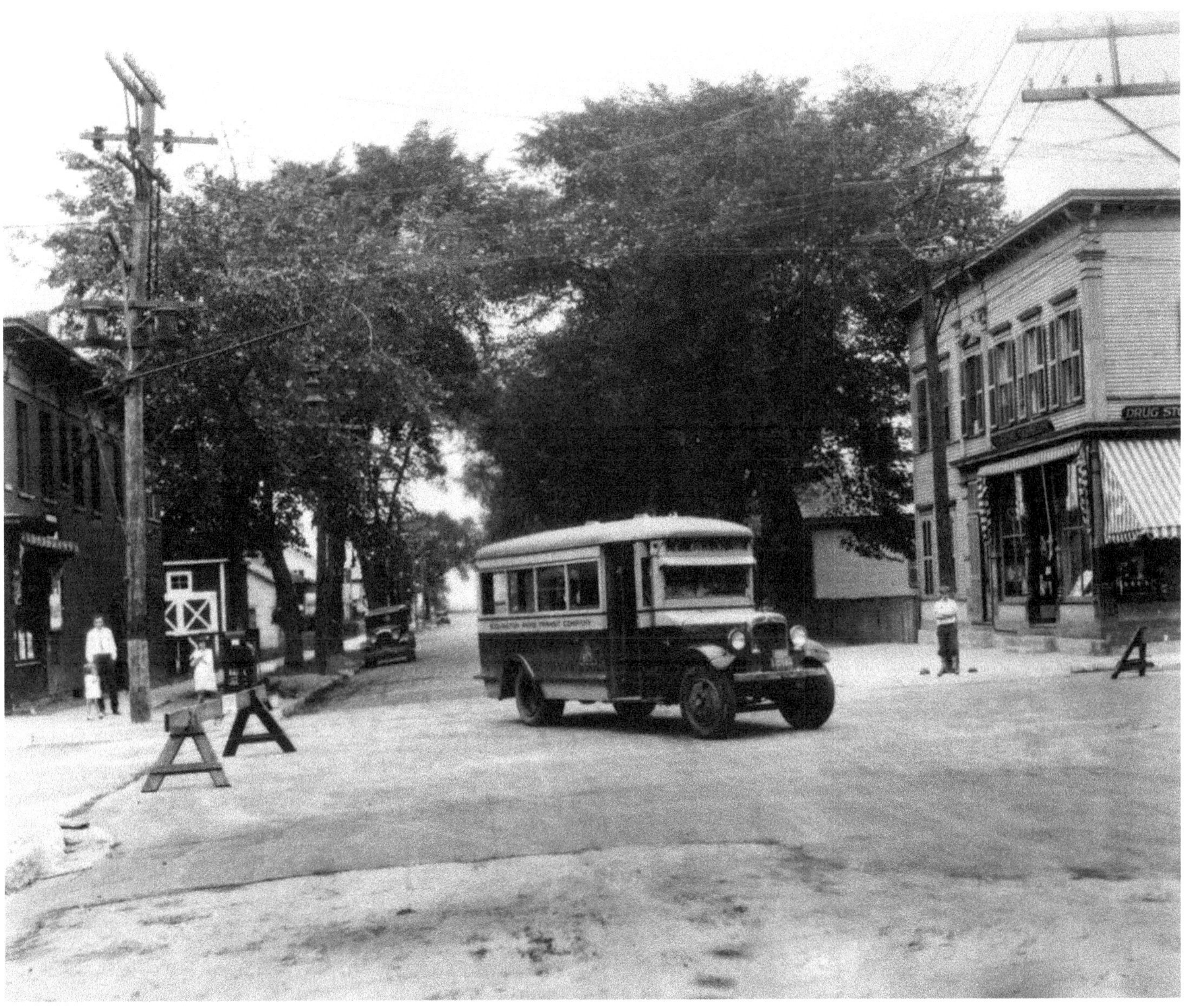

A Burlington Rapid Transit Company bus pursues its North End Loop route at North and Champlain streets. The company was born of the Appleyard Motor Company, a car dealership on South Winooski Avenue, and offered service to Burlington, Winooski, and Essex Junction. All lines ended at City Hall Park.

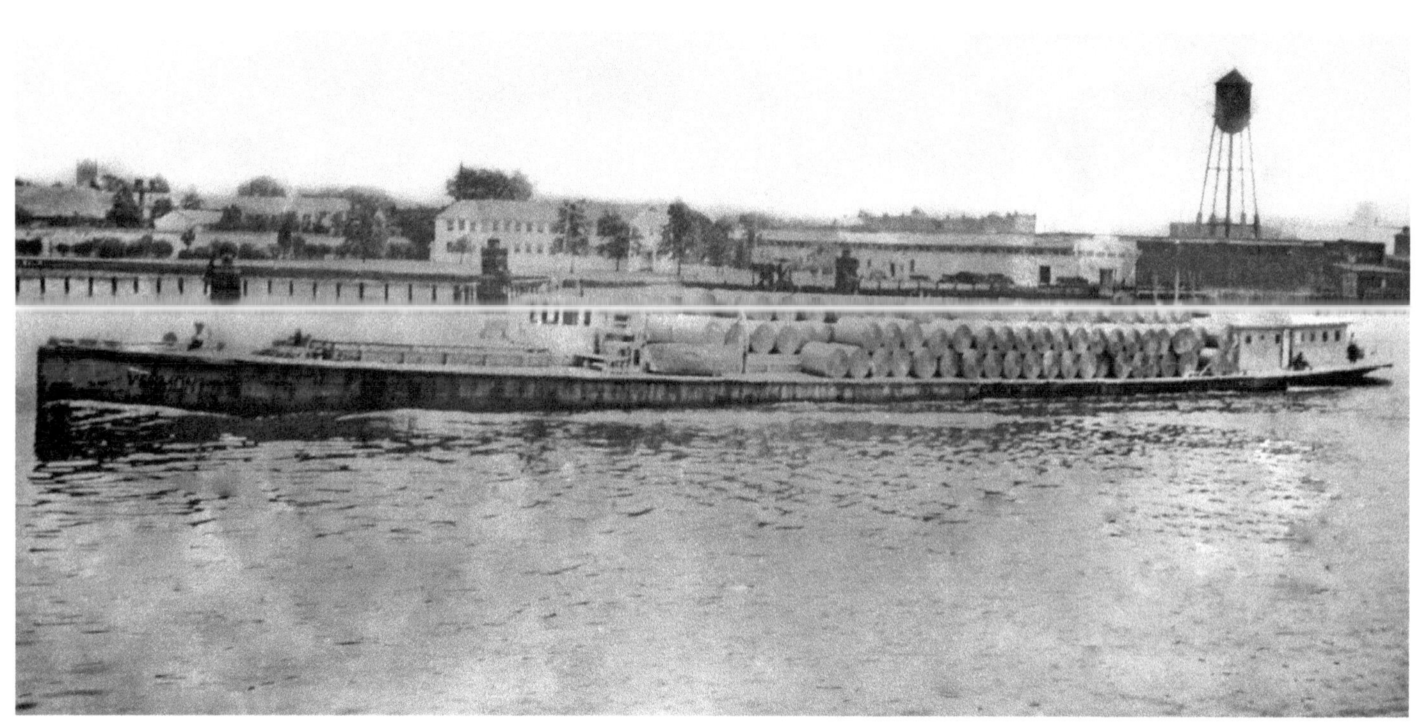

Vermont III, formerly a sidewheel steamer, was built at the Shelburne Shipyard in 1903. The palatial steamer boasted 56 crew members, including dozens of waiters, two stewardesses, a cook, pastry chef, barber, newsstand operator, and six firemen. When steamer traffic dropped off with the rising popularity of the automobile, the top decks were removed to convert the vessel into a freighter for coastal use. Here, the *Vermont III* carries rolls of newsprint.

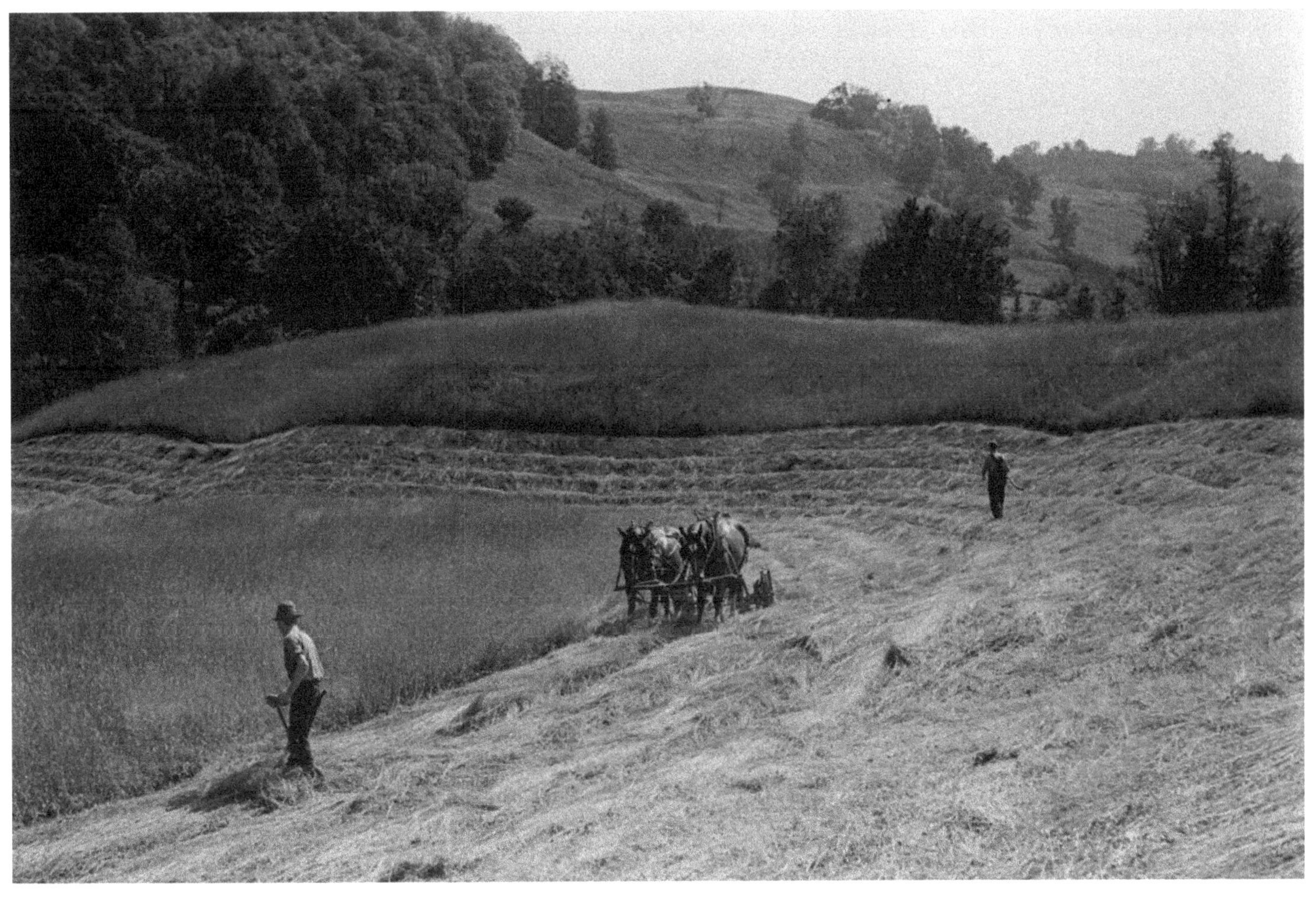

Cutting hay in Windsor County. Before mechanization, cutting hay was generally a group effort among neighboring farmers. Families enlisted their neighbors' help to finish the chore before a rainy day molded and spoiled the drying hay. For some children, the season offered a rare opportunity to visit other parts of the community.

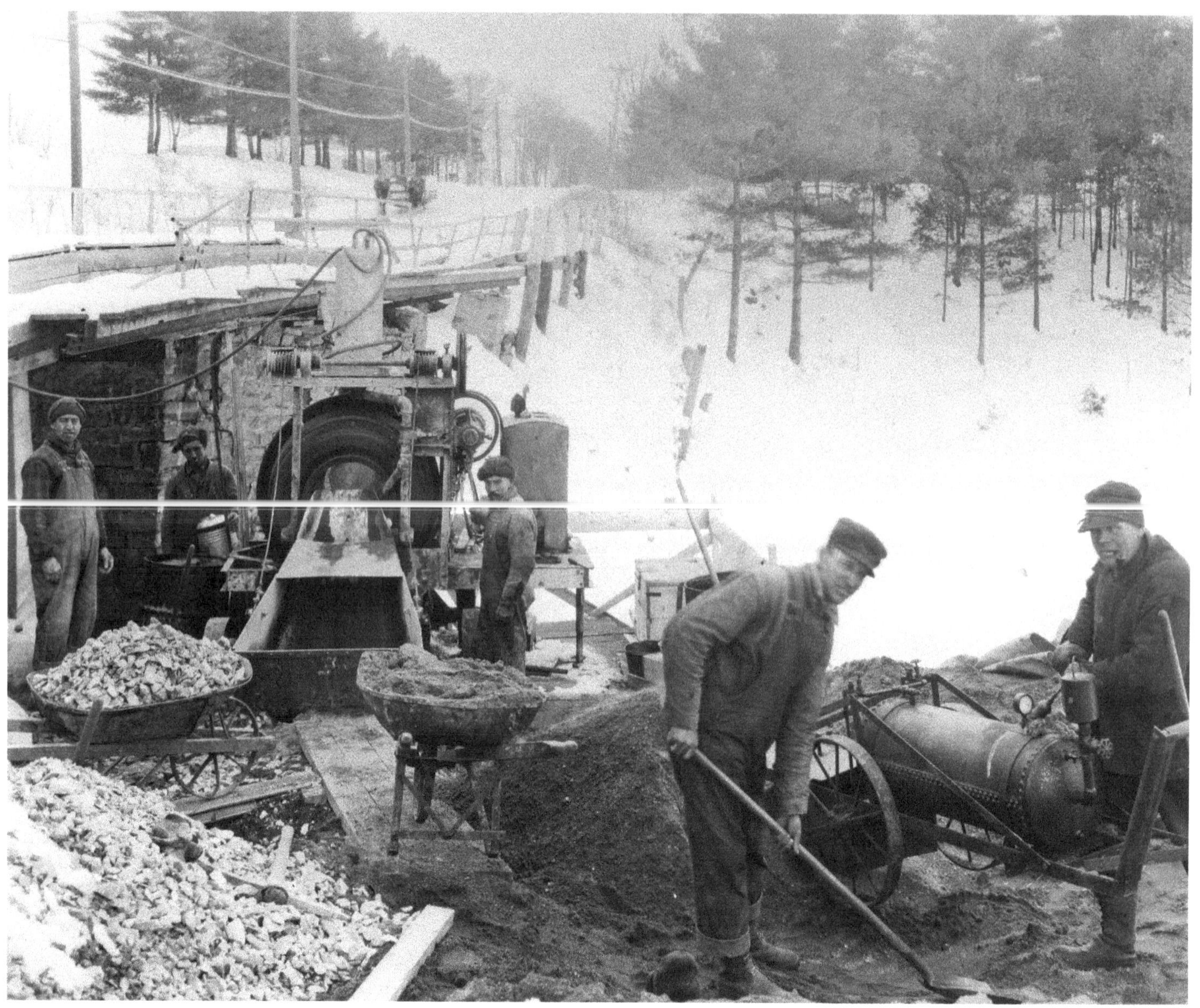

Improvements to Potash Brook Bridge on Shelburne Road, South Burlington. The street department had been paving Shelburne Road since 1921, and final improvements to this bridge helped complete the project after the 1927 flood. The crew added reinforced concrete, and the town made plans to reseed and plant small willows on the shoulders to prevent further erosion.

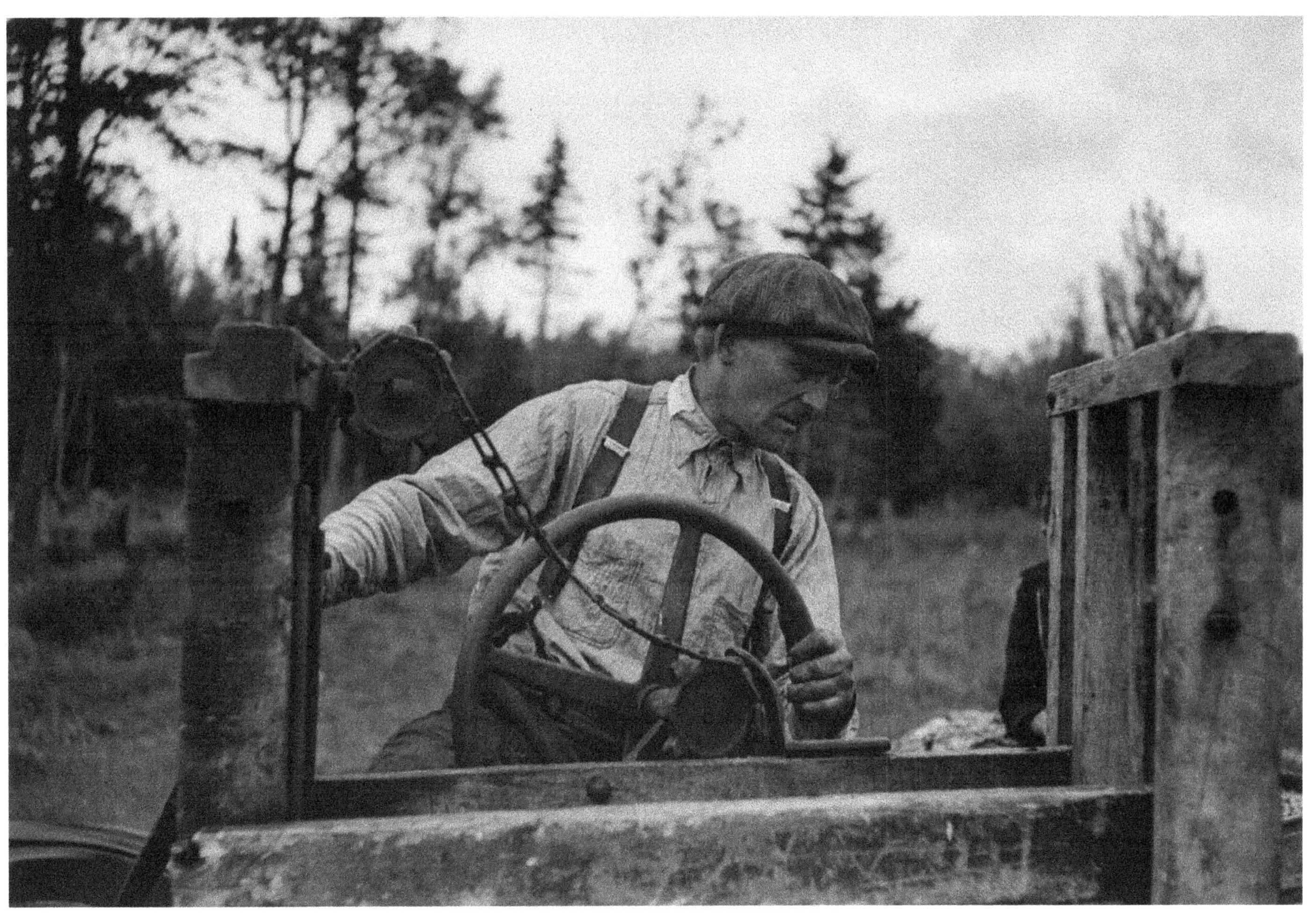

A gasoline-powered farm implement in operation near Hyde Park. Continued refinement of the automobile's internal combustion engine brought a new tool to Vermont's small-scale farmers: gasoline-powered machinery. Like the horse-powered equipment and steam-powered machinery of the nineteenth and early twentieth centuries, the gasoline-powered engine, an inexpensive and portable source of power, offered farmers an affordable way to improve productivity.

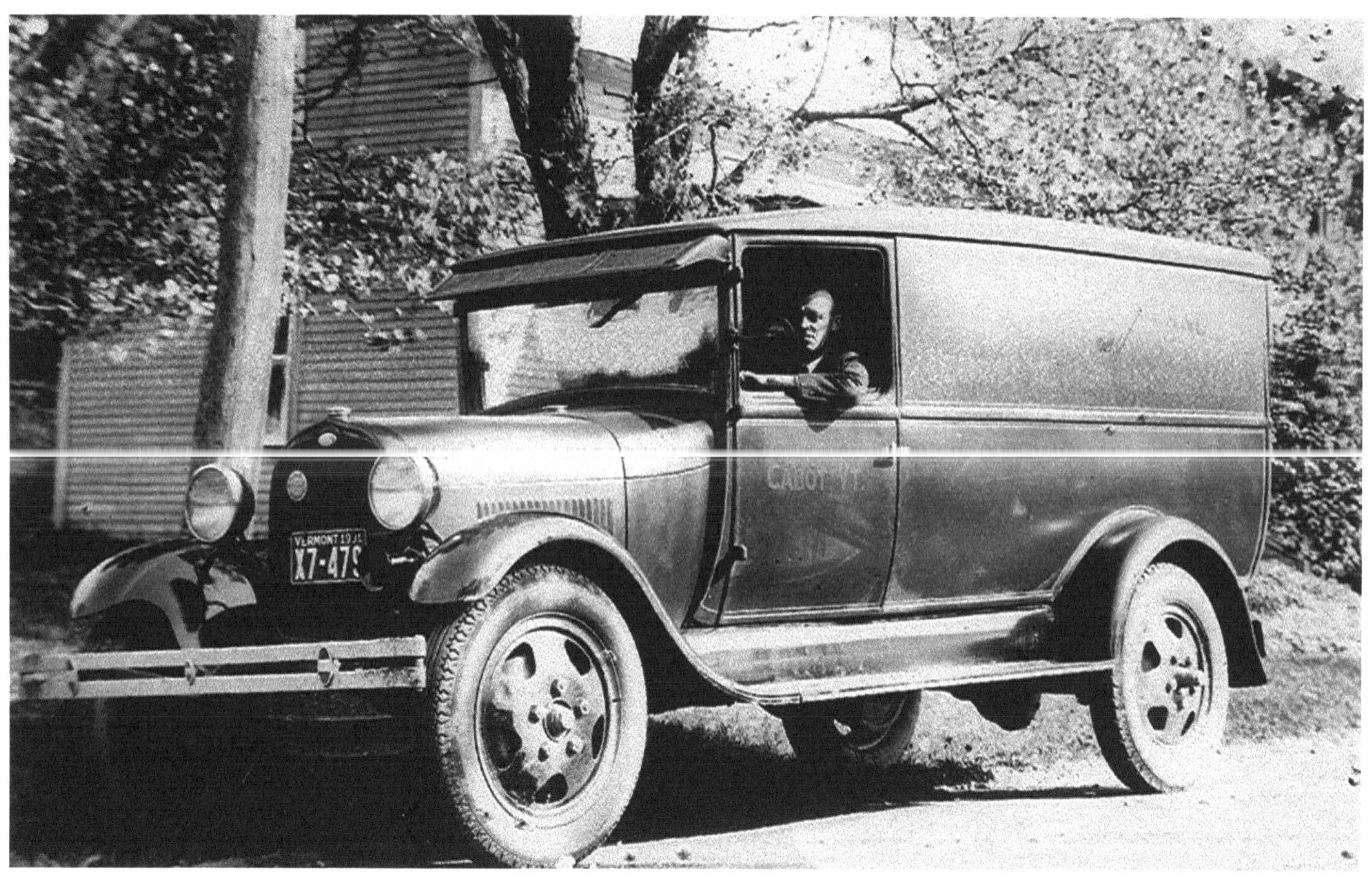

A Cabot Creamery delivery truck makes the rounds in 1931. In 1919, 94 farmers combined forces to purchase what would become the Cabot Creamery plant. Early on, the creamery produced butter for sale under the Rosedale brand. In 1930, the cooperative began making cheese.

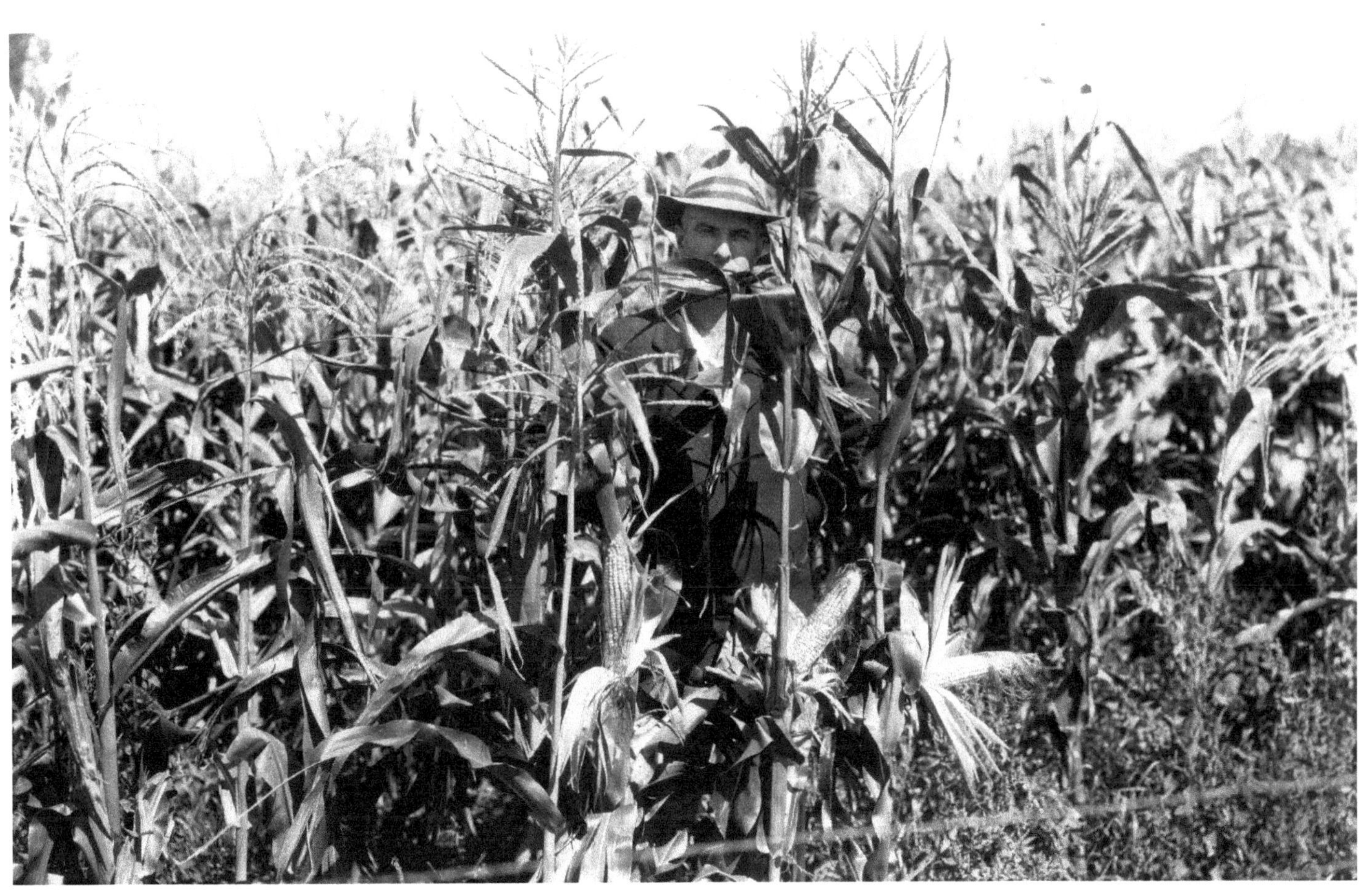

In addition to milking, Vermont's dairy farmers found much of their time occupied with another task: feeding their herds. Although sheep, the earlier mainstay of Vermont husbandry, could be left to graze, cows needed both grass and grain. Hay and corn became commonplace on any Vermont farm, and silos to store corn silage rose up across the state. This farmer poses among his silage corn at St. Albans Bay in 1932.

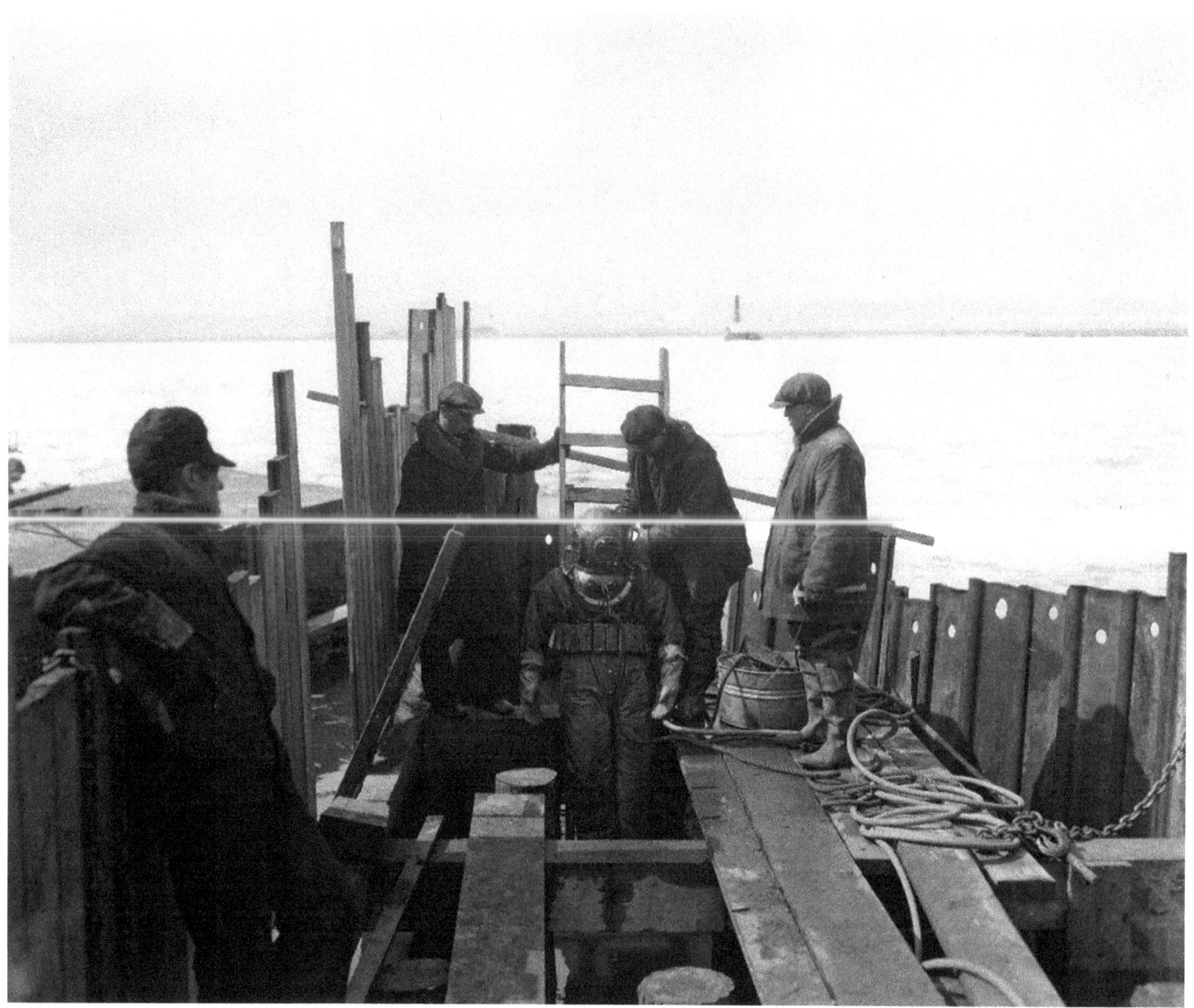

A diver works on the Burlington sewer. In 1932, Burlington undertook what city officials proudly touted as "without a doubt the largest project ever to be constructed" in the state at that time. The trunk line sewer ran down Maple Street to Lake Champlain and could reportedly handle storms equivalent to the heaviest on record—no doubt a reference to the 1927 flood. The project used 38,000 bags of cement, 24,000 bricks, and 5,000 tons of crushed stone.

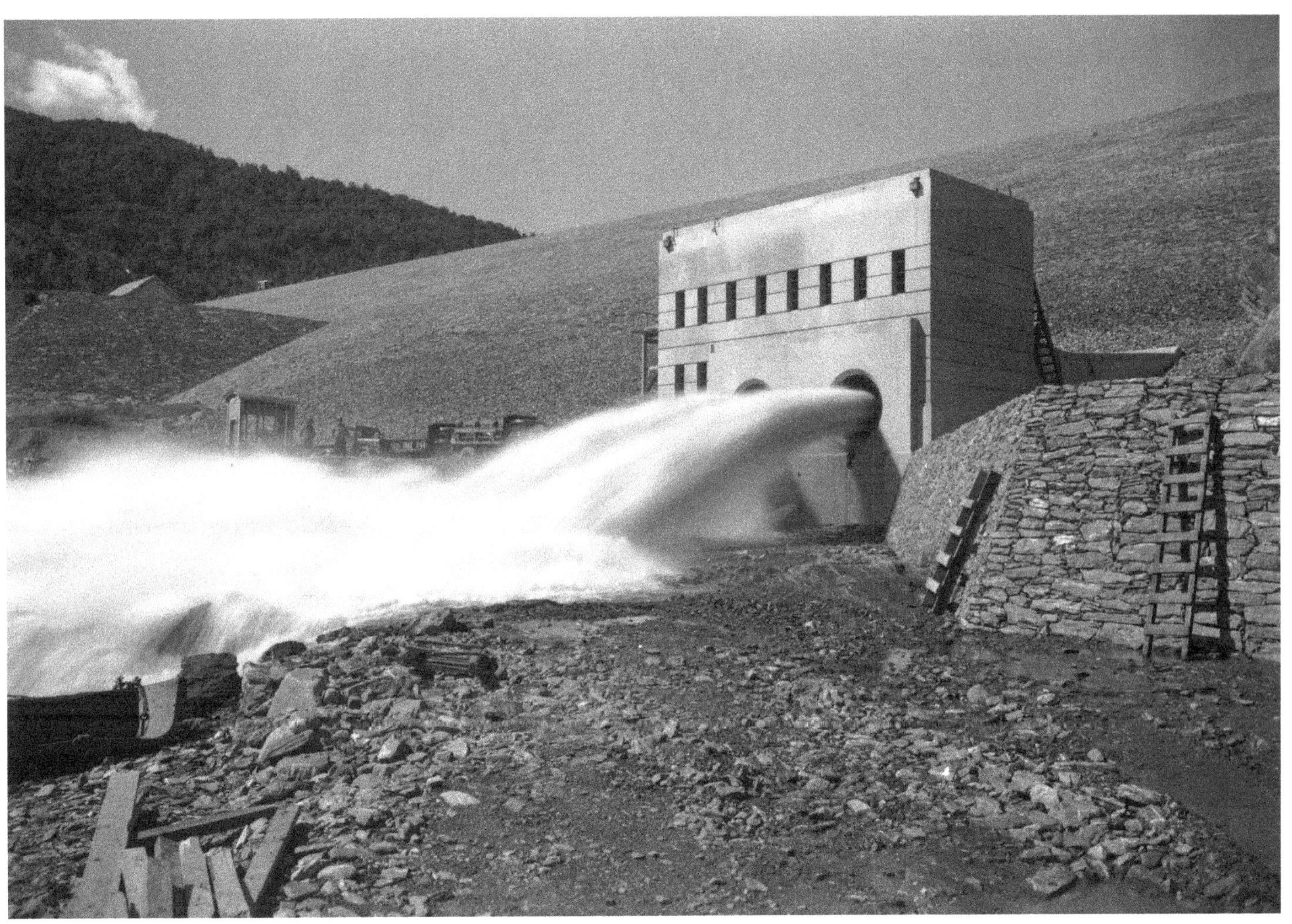

The Little River Dam at Waterbury. One of seven dams proposed to help control the Winooski River after the 1927 flood, Little River was built by the New Deal's Civilian Conservation Corps in the late 1930s. Two thousand men worked day and night in three shifts to complete the project. Eerie night scenes of men working under the lights attracted nighttime visitors to a nearby observation terrace, including President Franklin Roosevelt in August 1936.

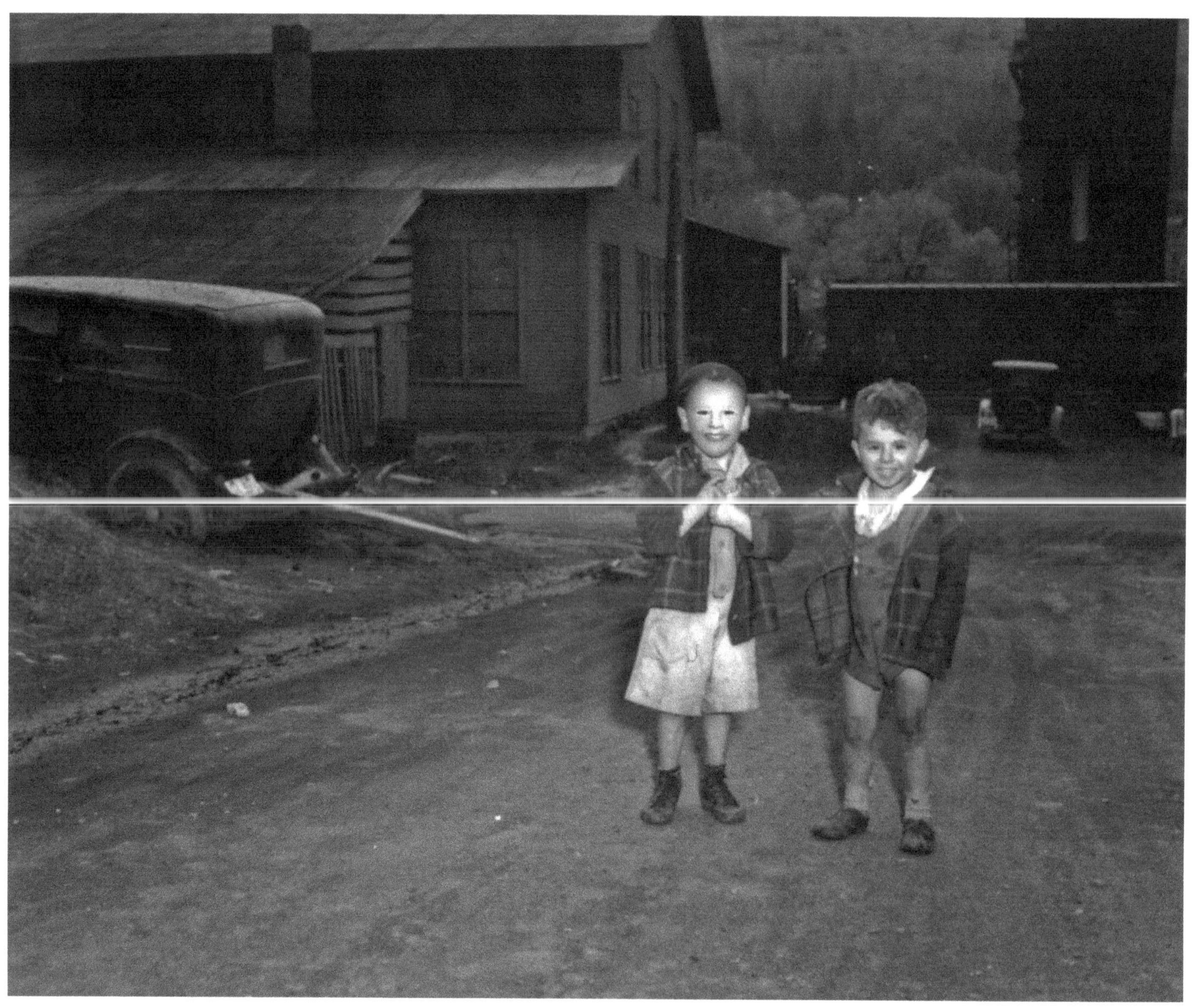

Franklin Roosevelt's Works Progress Administration, a New Deal program that came to Vermont in the 1930s, provided parent and adult education programs in the state. The WPA built 15 parks and 30 playgrounds, served more than two million school lunches, and provided nurses and music teachers to rural communities. While Vermonters welcomed many of the New Deal programs, they also resented federal intervention in local affairs.

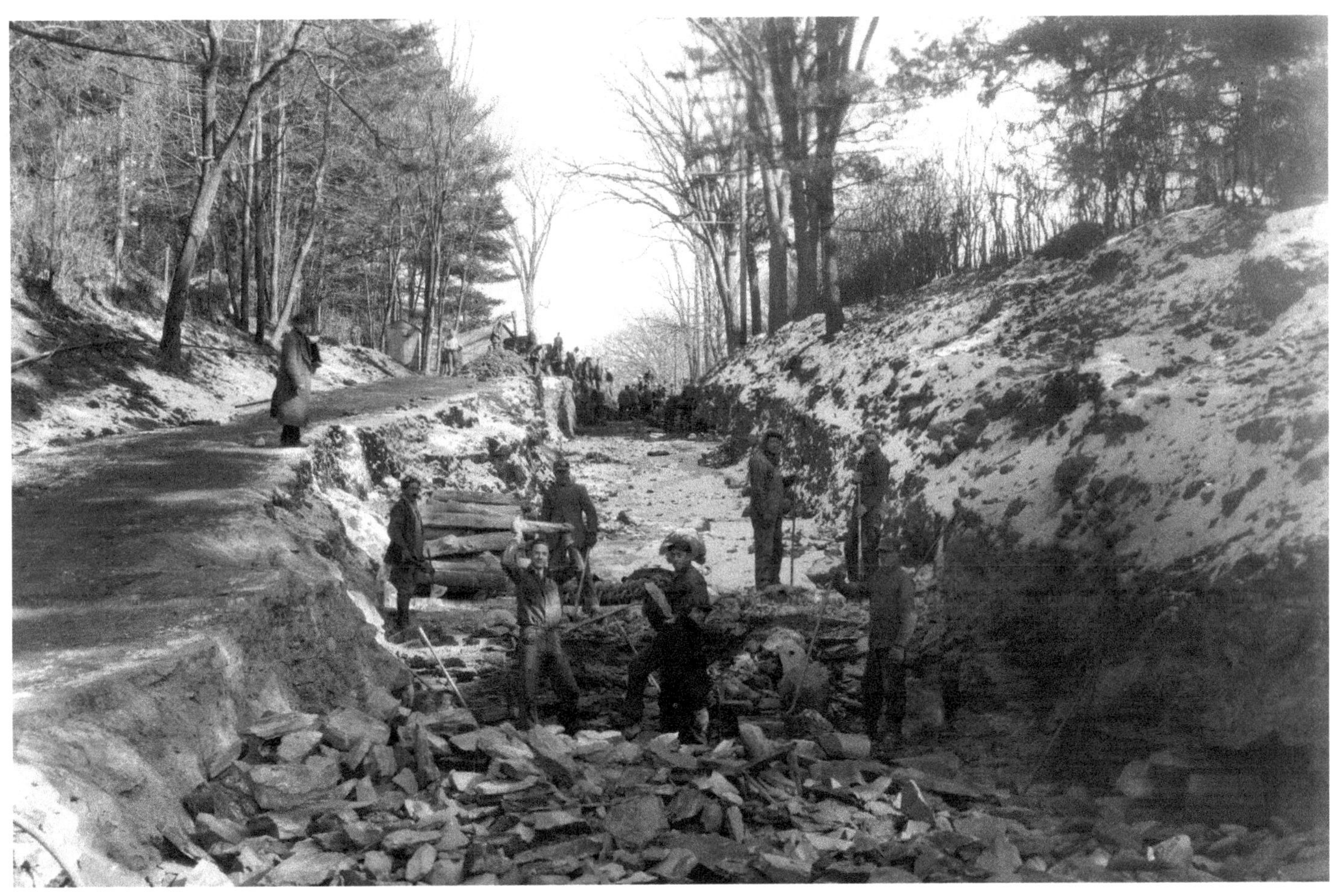

During the 1930s, Burlington took up a number of street-building projects, many of which were funded by the Works Progress Administration (later known as the Work Projects Administration). Here, the Street Department digs down seven feet during construction of Cliff Street. The workers blasted through solid rock and dug into ground frozen by the winter weather.

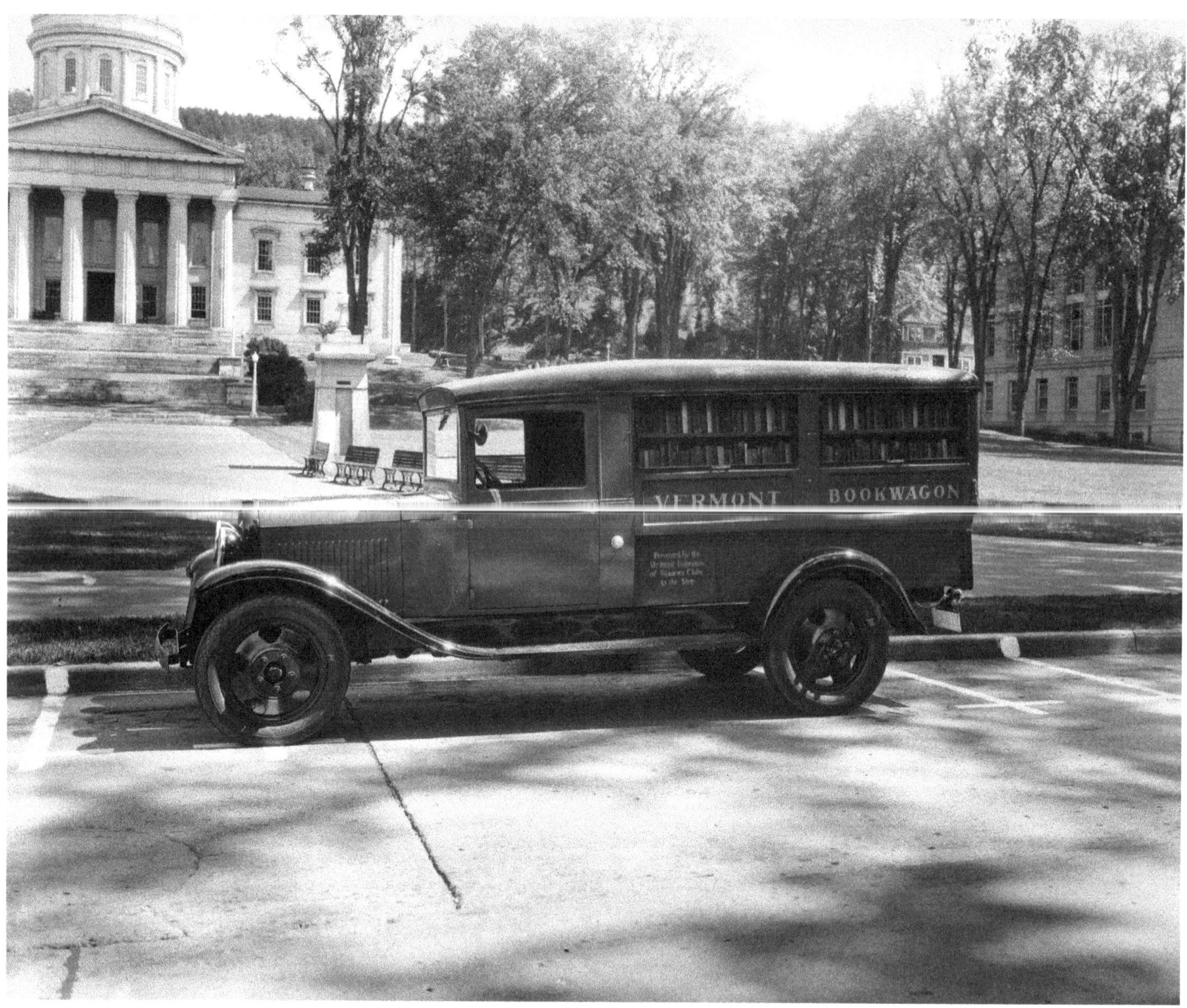

A bookwagon in Montpelier in 1932. Before 1915, four Vermont towns (Burlington, Rockingham, Fairhaven, and Morristown) received $80,000 in grants from Andrew Carnegie to construct new library buildings. Seven years later, the Federation of Women's Clubs donated the first state bookwagon. The vehicle brought books to smaller libraries and residents whose towns lacked library services. The service peaked with ten vehicles in the 1960s and was discontinued in 1974—only to be reinvigorated in the late 1990s.

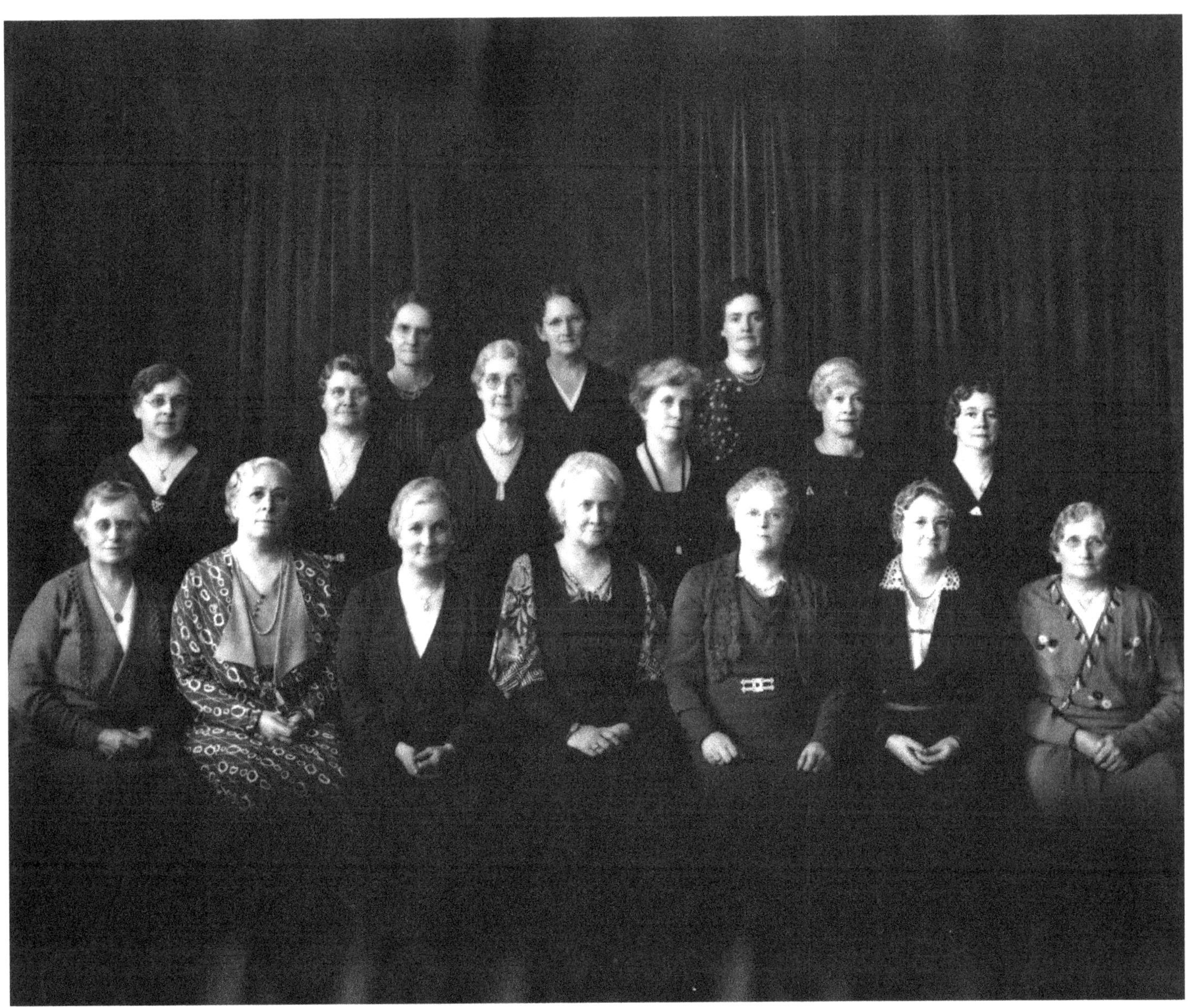

Vermont legislators in 1935. Between 1921 and 1940, women occupied 100 seats in the Vermont House and 8 seats in the Senate. The state's female legislators favored legislation relating to home and family, including investigation of adoptive families, child support for women whose husbands were injured or deceased, liability insurance for school transportation, and an allowance for sheriffs to select women as deputies.

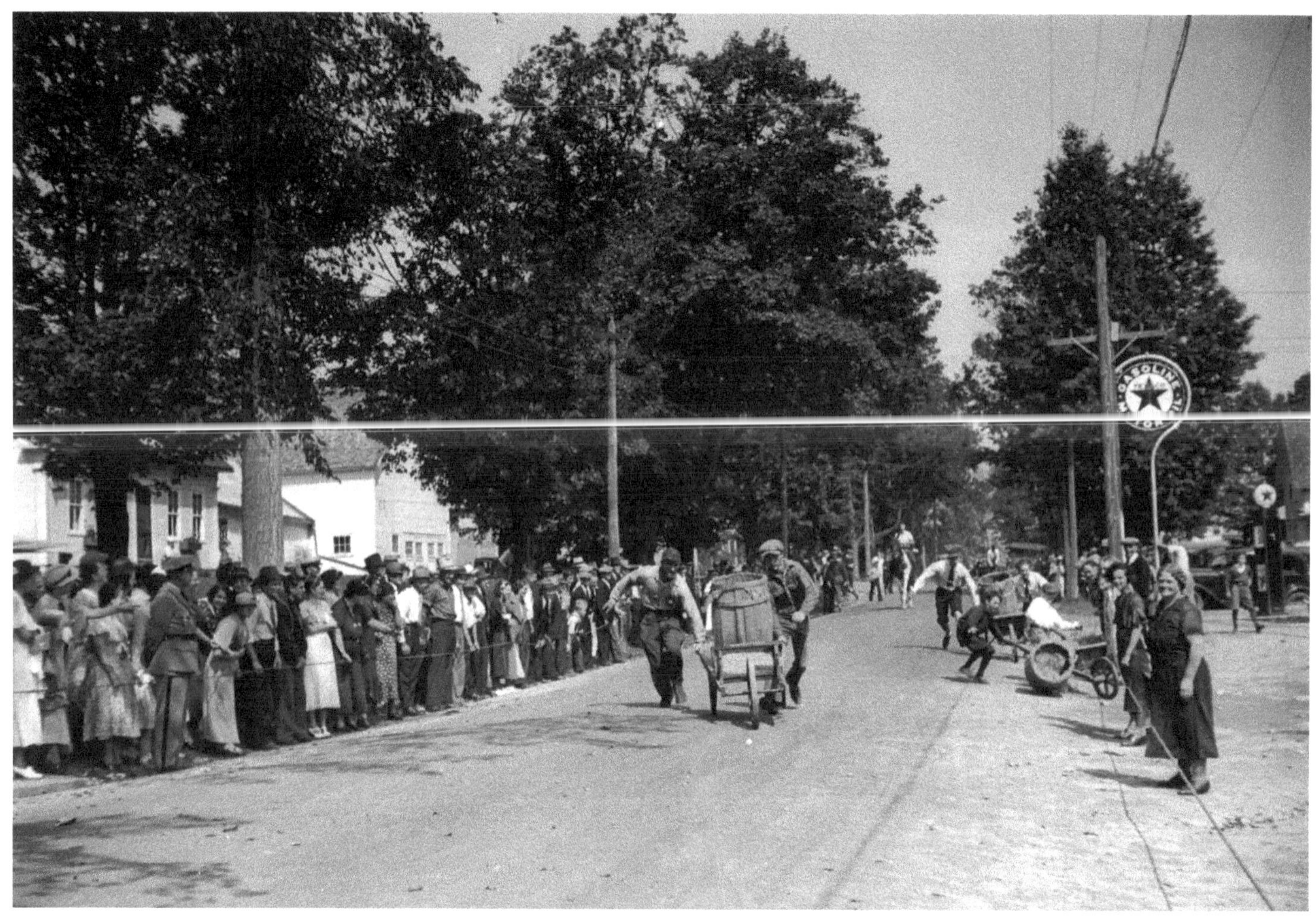

A wheelbarrow race at the Albany Fair in 1936. Late summer and early fall in Vermont mean it's time for the fair. County fairs have always been local events, complete with homegrown farm products and entertainment for and by the locals. From horseshoe-throwing competitions to peg races, the county fair is an important piece of small-town America history. The peg race required participants to tie up their horses, move off a distance, run back, harness the animal, and zip to the finish line.

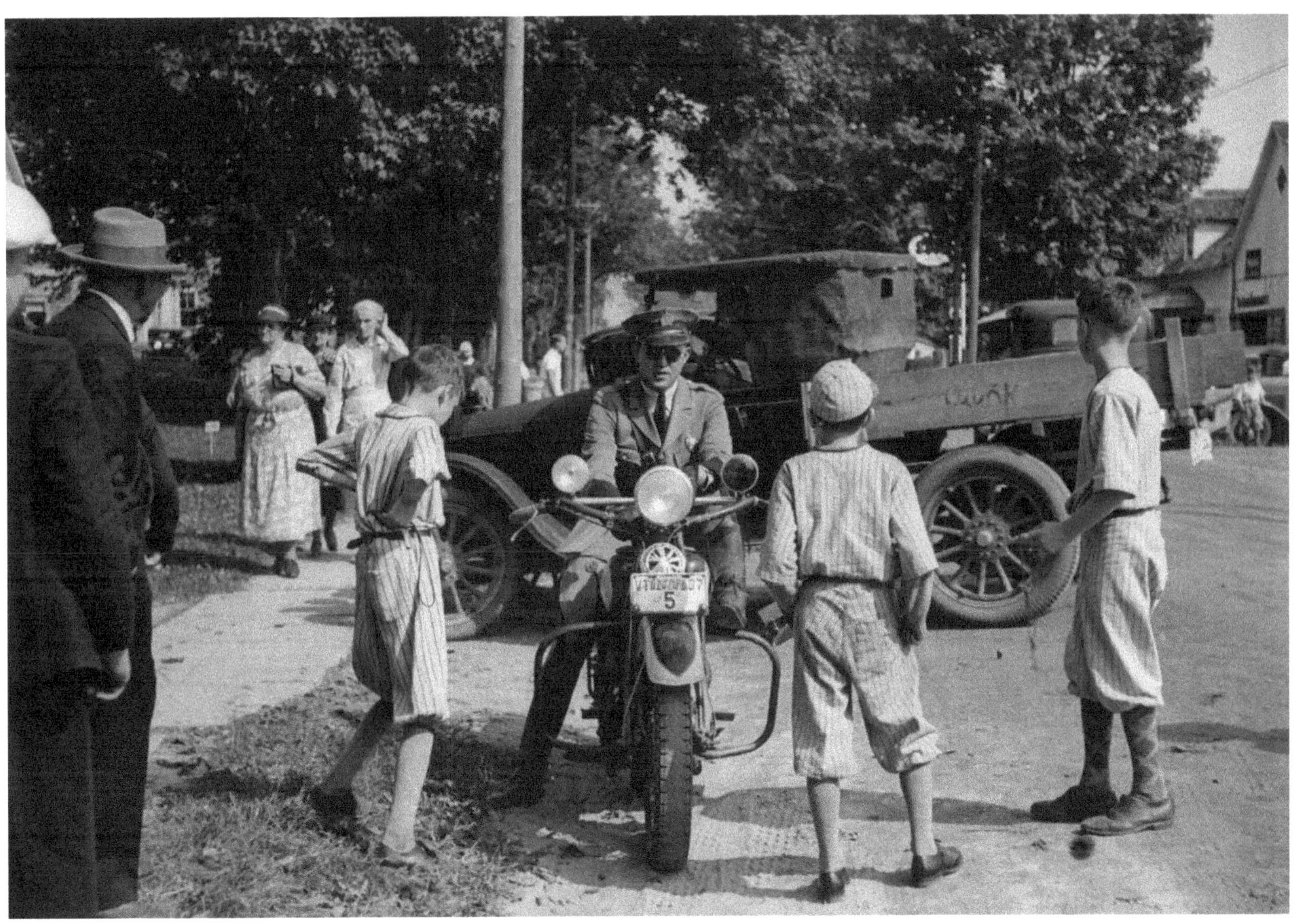

A police officer at the Albany Fair in 1936 is surrounded by young admirers. In 1918, a lone inspector, Ara Griggs, was assigned the task of enforcing laws on 15,000 miles of state highway. In 1925, the state created the Vermont Highway Patrol. Officers purchased their own motorcycles and worked only in summer, a time when out-of-state tourist vehicles represented nearly half the traffic on the road.

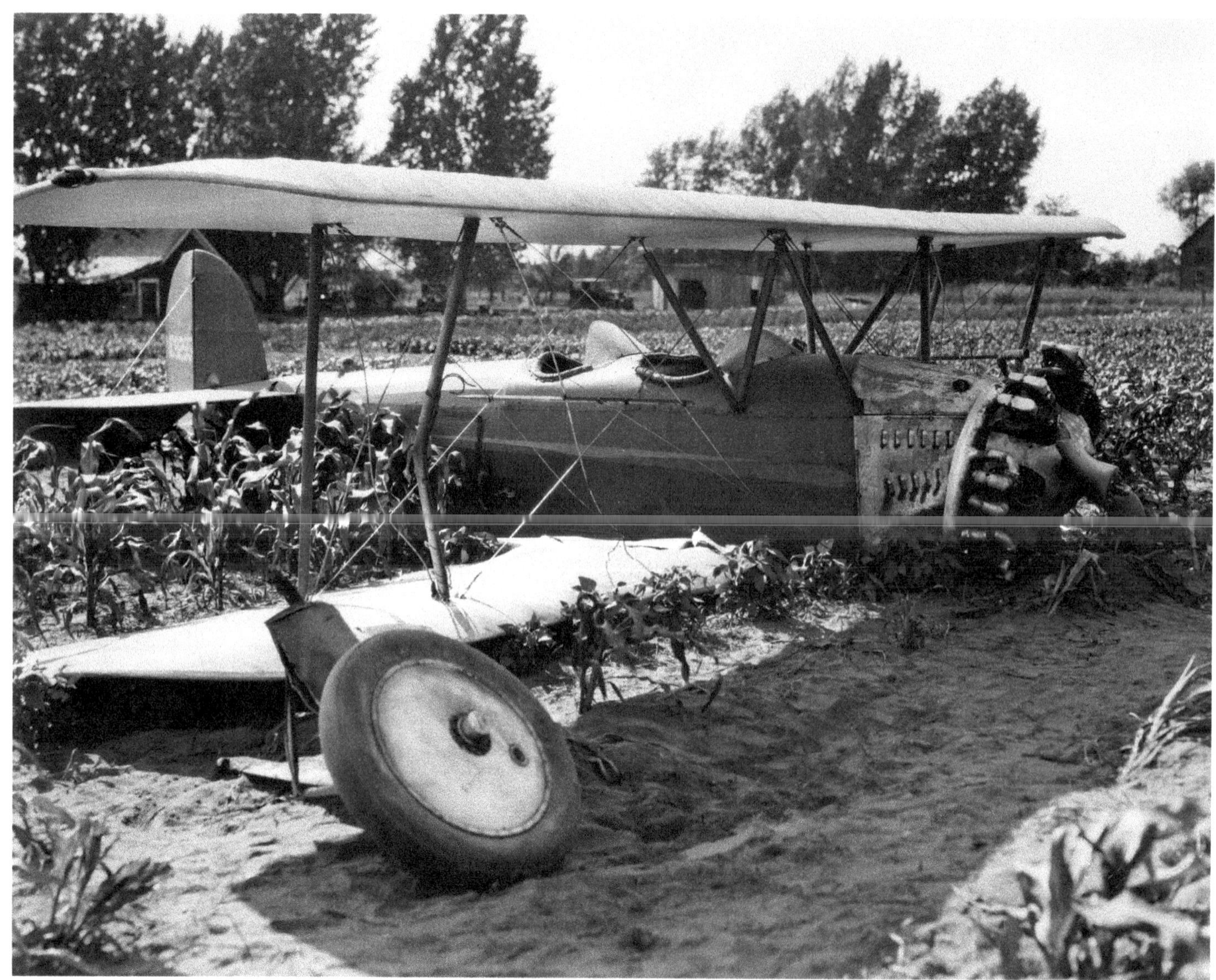

Biplane crash, Burlington. In 1919, the city of Burlington leased a cornfield near Williston Road for use as an airport, and the street department cleared a runway with a horse-drawn road grader. Grace Pugh, who in 1938 became the first woman licensed to fly in Vermont, recalled that she received her pilot's license from the Department of Motor Vehicles. At that time, no department existed for managing air transportation.

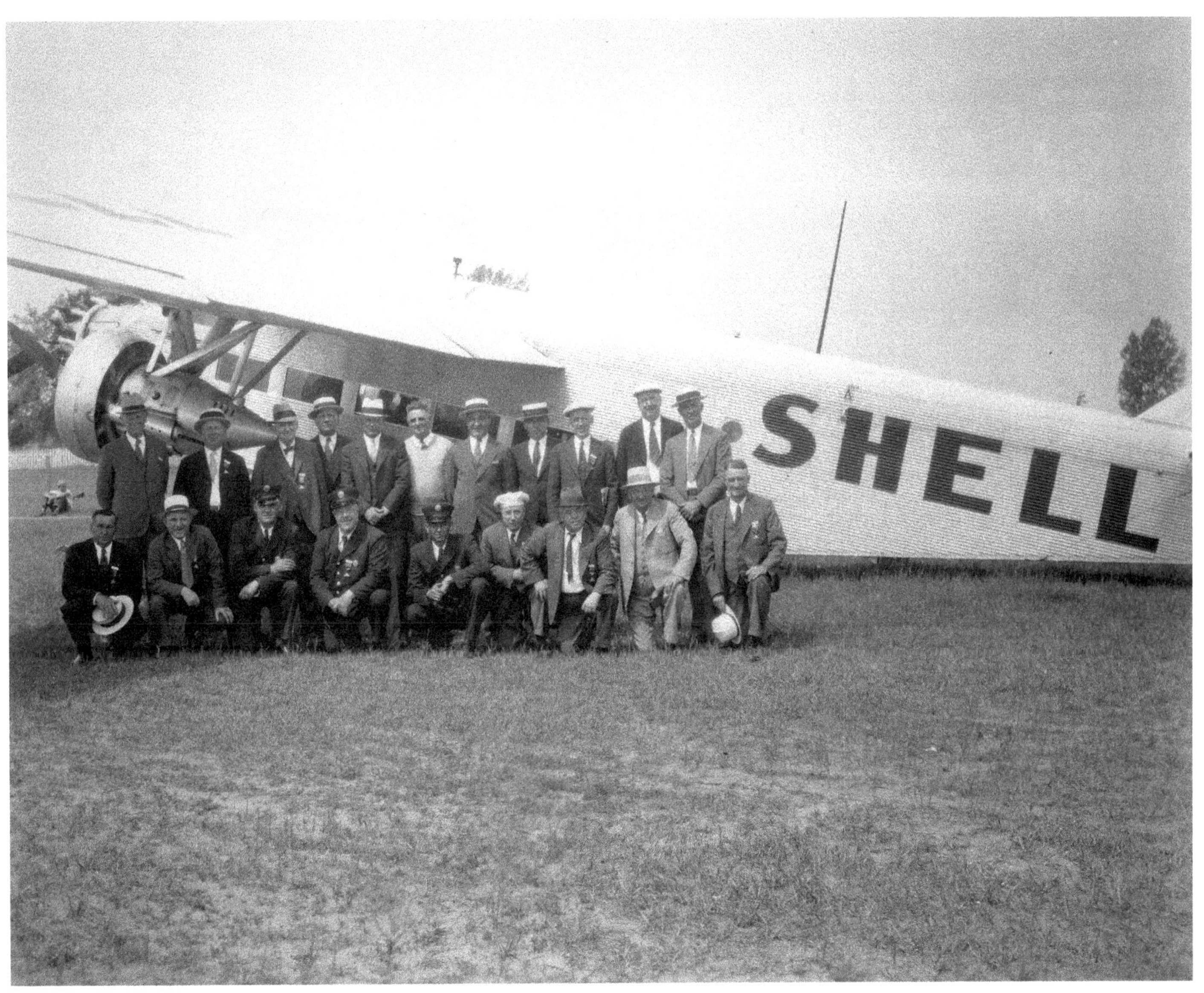

In 1931, the Burlington Municipal Airport was officially approved for commercial traffic. Arrival and departure announcements came via the railroad, and weather reports came by way of Western Union or the telephone. Often, reports turned up after planes had already taken off. In 1942, the airport adopted an air traffic control system: controllers stood on the open roof and directed incoming planes with a light in one hand and a microphone in the other.

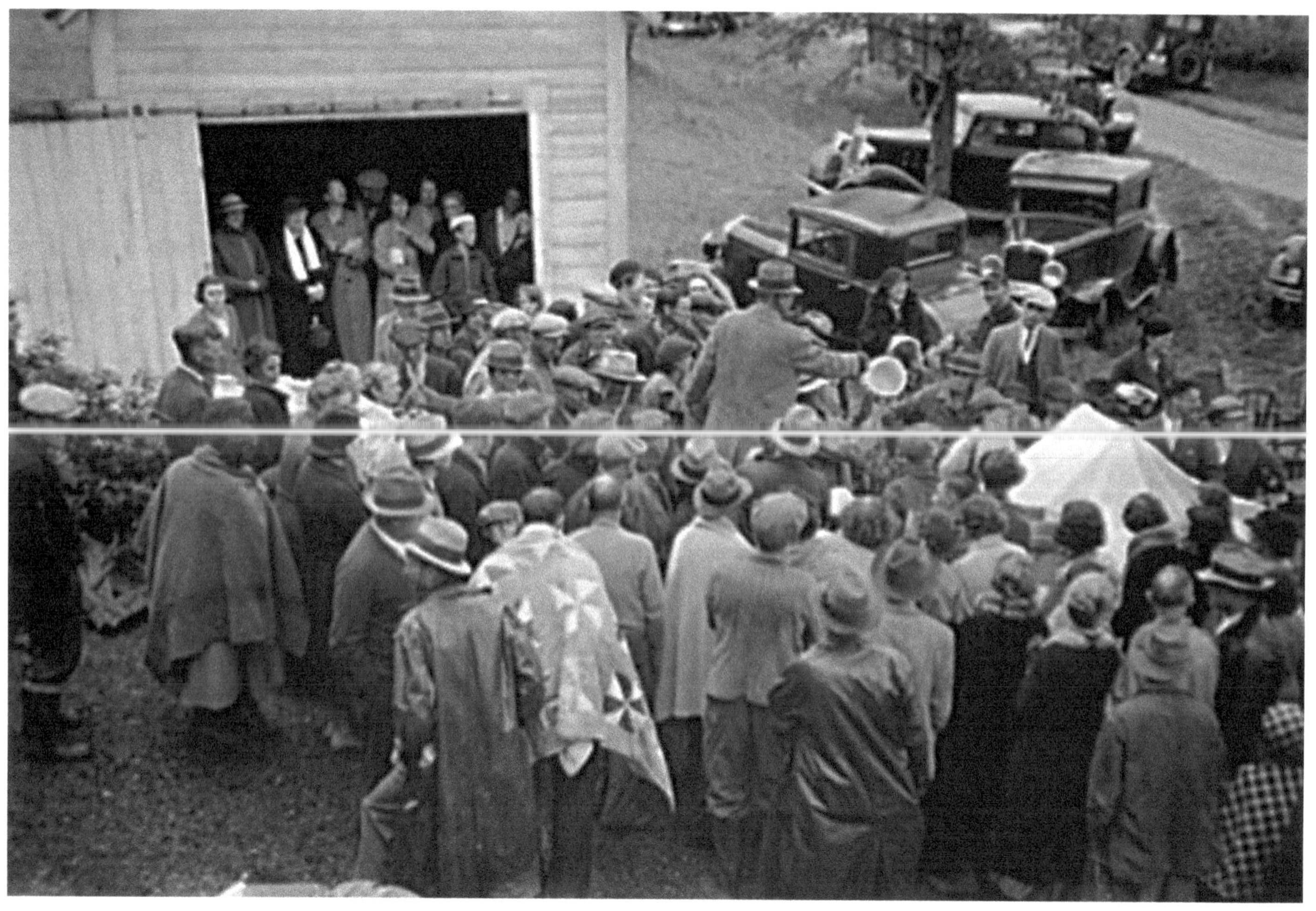

An auction near Hyde Park, 1936. One New England auctioneer recalled how "carefully dressed city businessmen and farmers in overalls" typically became friends at an auction "at least for the day." Regulars arrived seeking bargains but enjoyed the socializing, whatever the outcome. Estate sales were also a reminder of dispersed families and hard times, with children too far from home to help care for family property. In her will, Ferrisburg's Elizabeth Robinson instructed that there would be no auction, deeding her home instead to become Rokeby Museum.

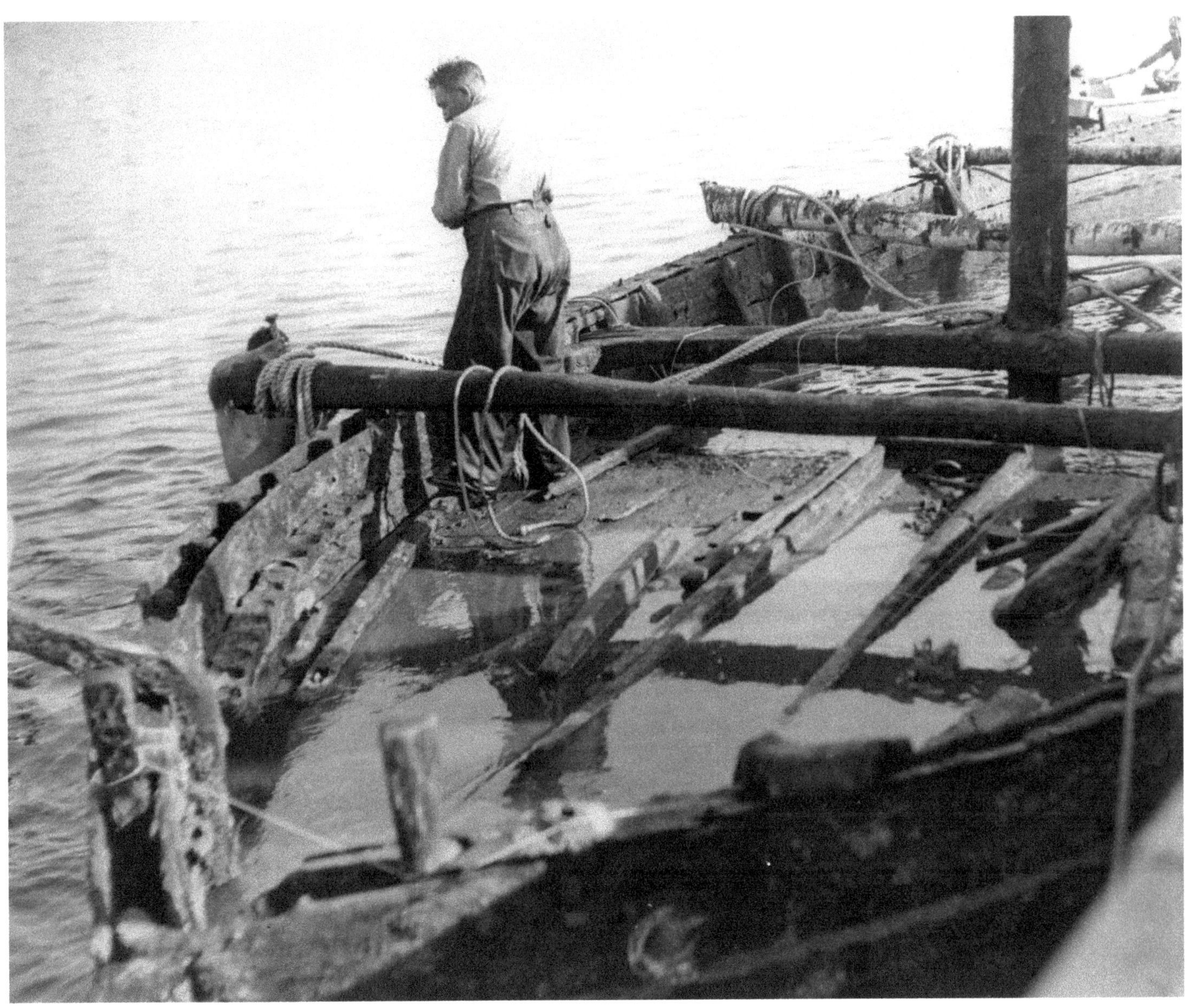

In October 1776, *Philadelphia* sank to the bottom of Lake Champlain during a battle near Valcour Island. In 1935, a salvage team found the vessel with its mast still standing and a cannonball lodged in its hull. Spectators watched the recovery operation, and the *Burlington Free Press* asked a descendant of Benedict Arnold to comment on the occasion. The vessel is now on display at the Smithsonian Institution.

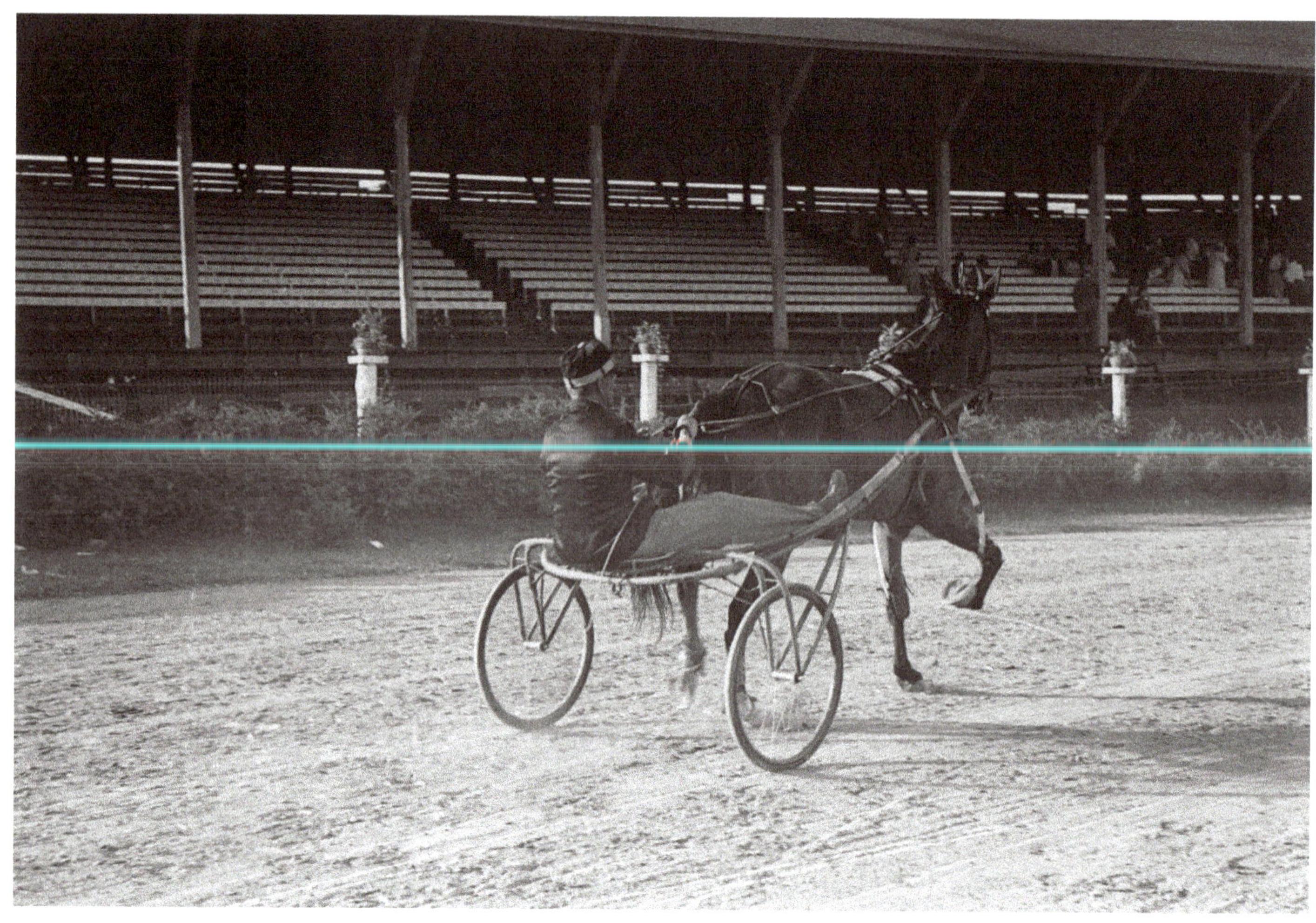

A harness race contestant at the Vermont State Fair in Rutland, 1937. When horse races first visited Vermont fairs, some worried that the excitement distracted onlookers from the event's more noble intent: to display the finest breeds to Vermont's farmers. Vermont's fairs also provided "edutainment" by showcasing other dramatic new technologies—among them bicycle races in the 1880s and a hot-air balloon launch in 1909.

An Arthur Rothstein view of the Craftsbury Fair, 1937. Rothstein worked for Franklin Roosevelt's Resettlement Administration, a New Deal program aimed at relocating farmers from unproductive lands slated for rehabilitation by the federal government. Despite support for the program from other constituents, state representative George Aiken vehemently opposed it, maintaining that Vermont should remain in charge of its own resources.

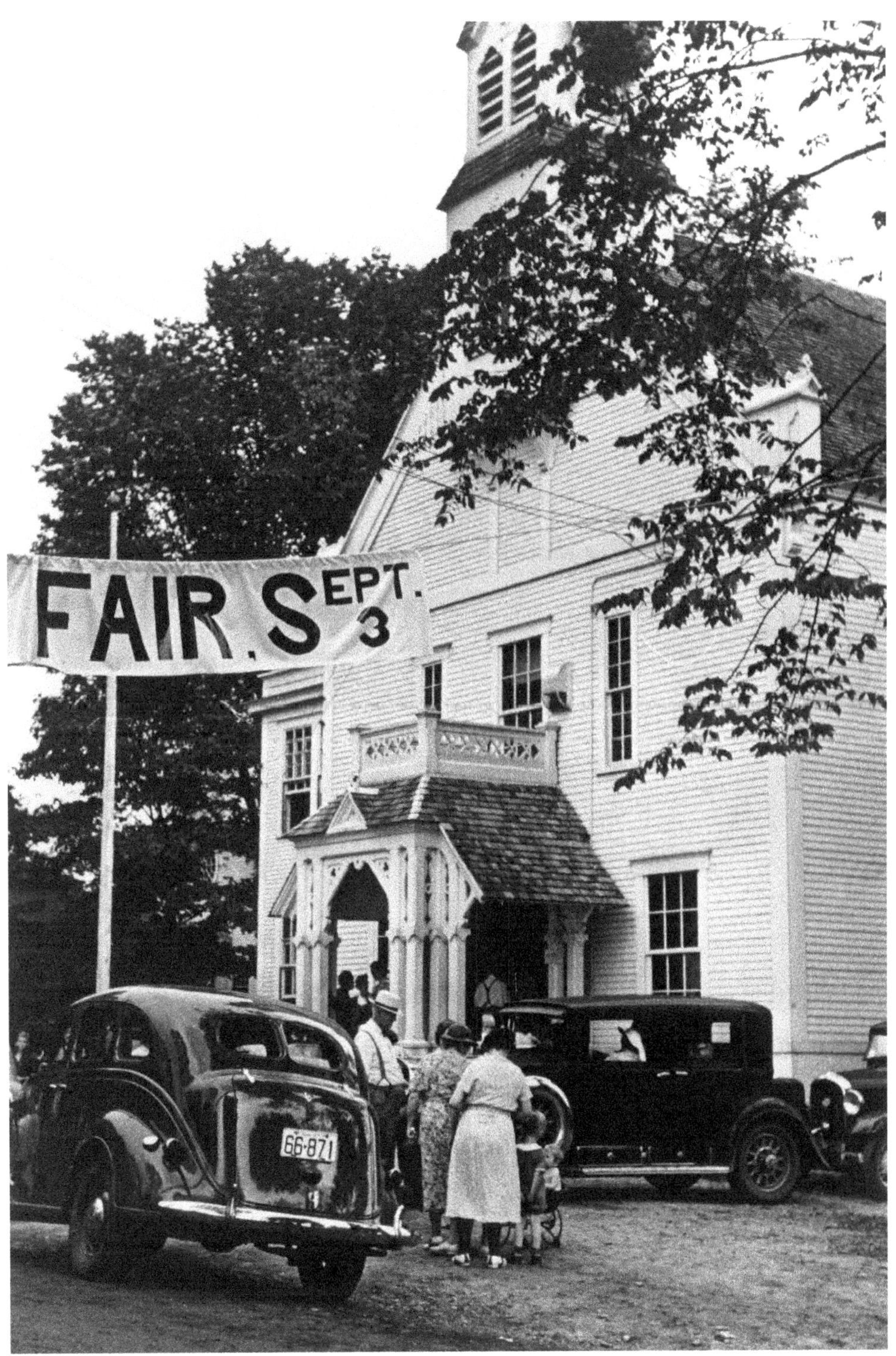

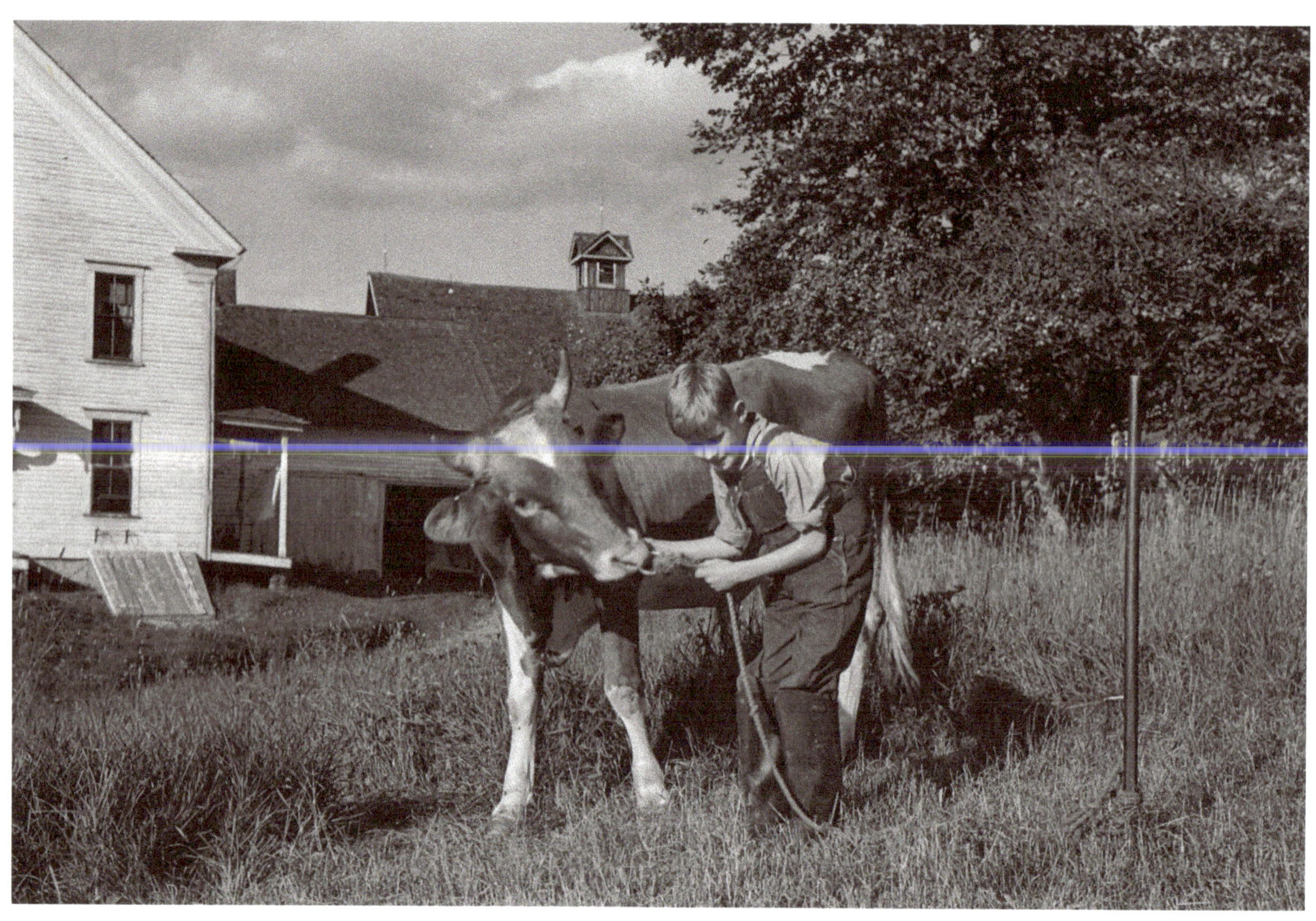

In 1937, Kirby farmboy Bob McNally demonstrates how to control a bull using a nose ring. By 1930, the state of Vermont hosted 450 active 4-H Clubs, a national organization intended to keep young people engaged in farming by way of club meetings, competitions, and affordable summer camps. Combined with the University of Vermont's Extension Service and traveling agriculture exhibits, 4-H represented state government's increasing role in supporting its farmers.

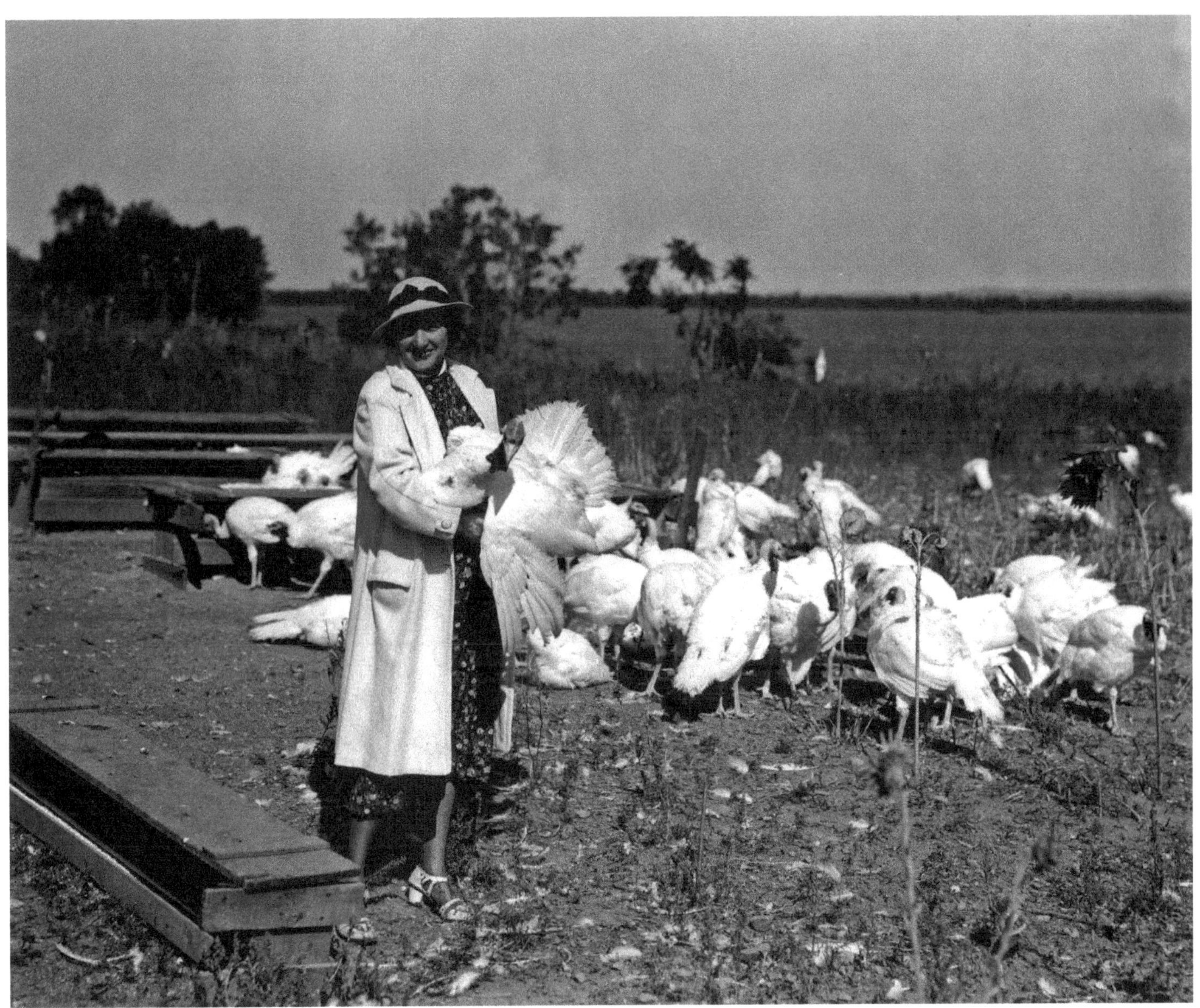

The Tabor farm, shown here in 1938, was one of many farms raising turkeys near Swanton. Through hard work and initiative, the Tabors took their family farm from a subsistence-level enterprise to a large-scale operation, rising from 3 birds to breeding more than 25,000. The farms shipped live turkeys to Boston and New York. By the 1970s the federal government had begun requiring farmers to slaughter out-of-state shipments in government-inspected slaughterhouses, putting Swanton's turkey farms out of business.

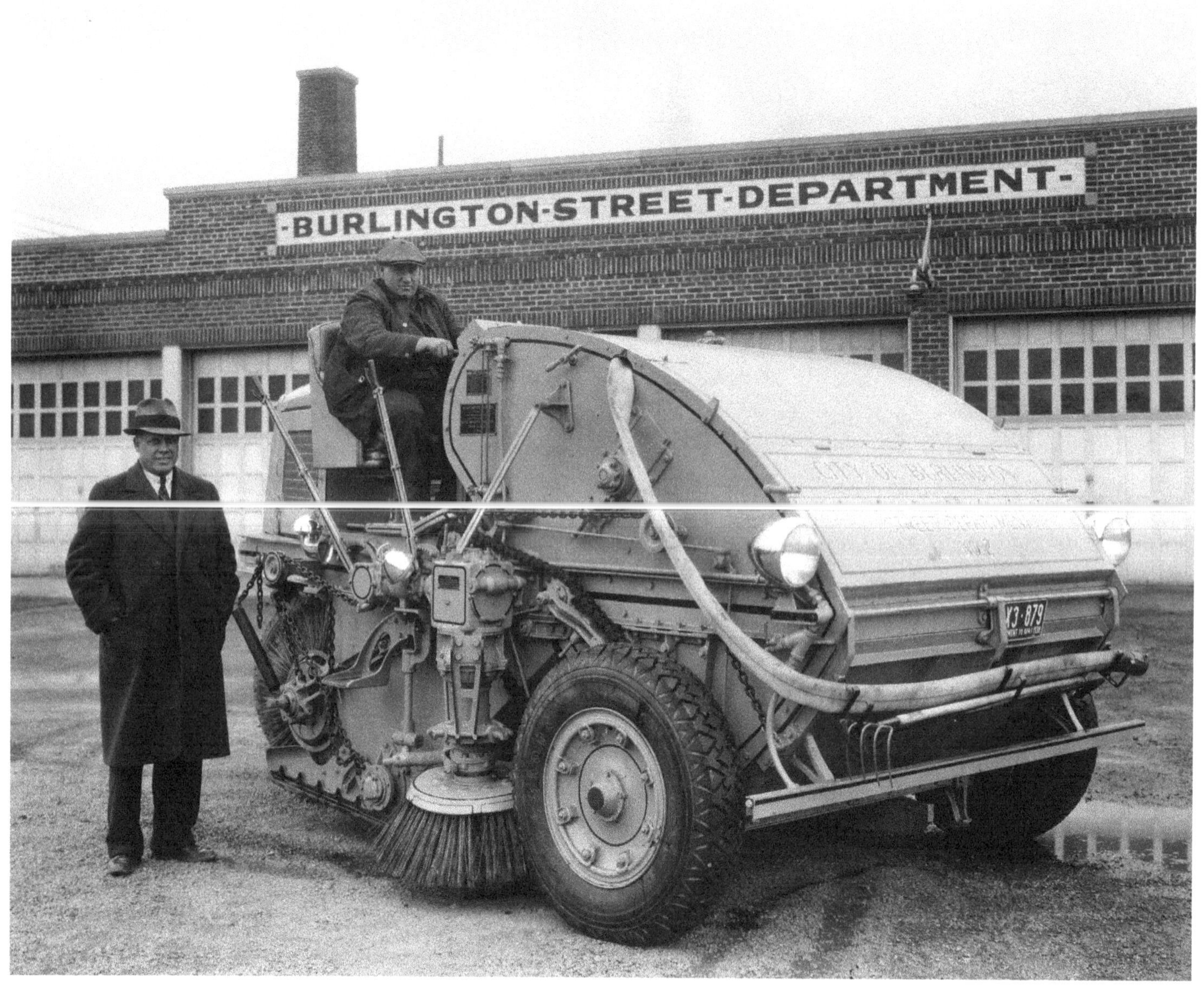

In 1937, the Burlington street department purchased a number of new pieces of machinery, including a sewer cleaning machine and a Sargent Heavy-Duty-Truck-Blade snowplow. Here, city employees pose with the new Elgin street sweeper, which the city bought for just over $6,700. Much of this new street equipment was used to keep the roads as passable in the winter months as they were in the summer.

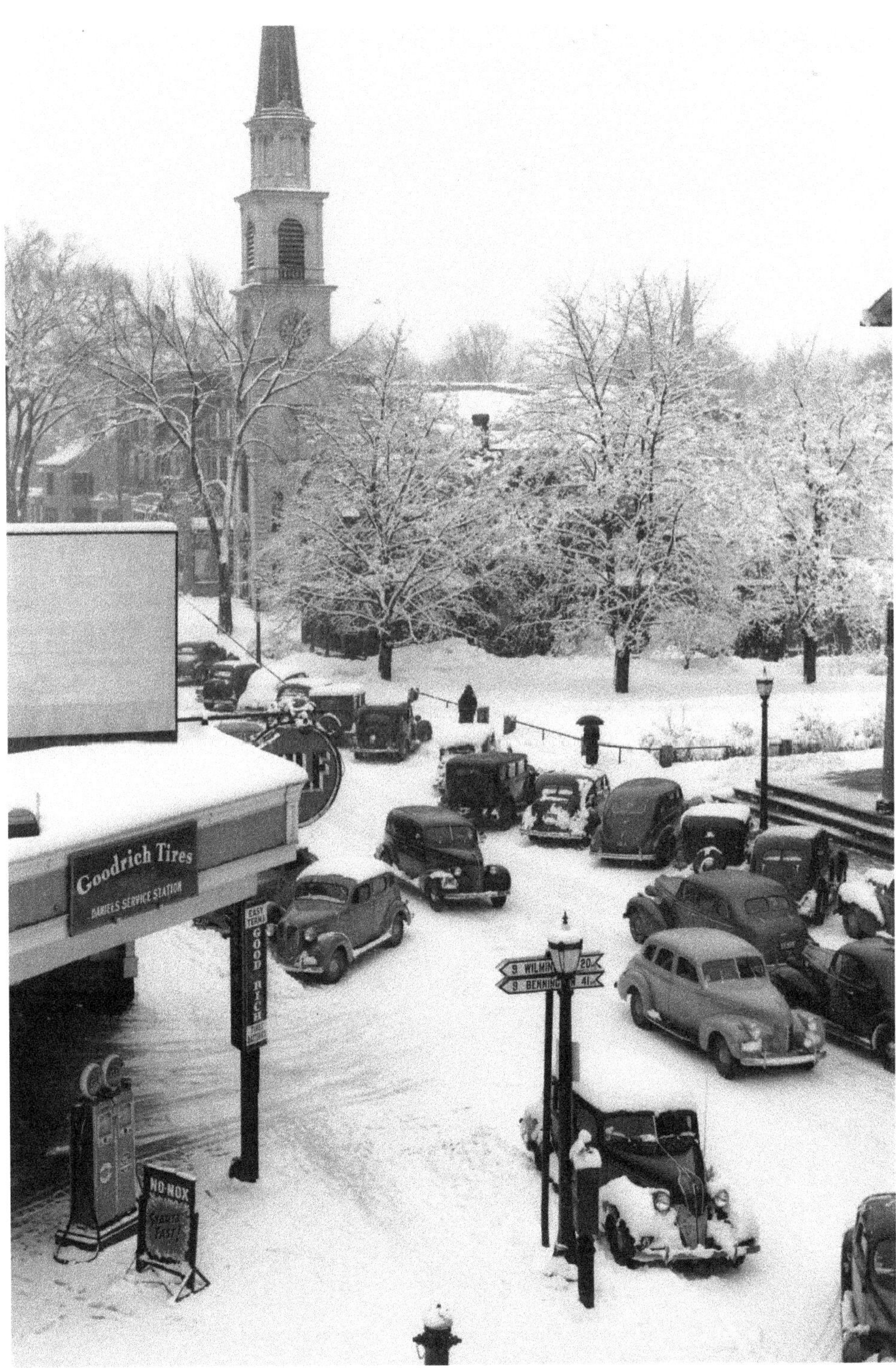

After a storm in Brattleboro, 1940. By March 1940, winter storms had left more snow than usual on the East Coast. Newfane postponed its town meeting owing to laborious travel conditions, and the storm took five lives as it moved up the Atlantic Seaboard. Brattleboro's newspaper anxiously speculated about the possibility of spring flooding—perhaps because of a concurrent investigation into the causes of a springtime flood four years earlier, in March 1936.

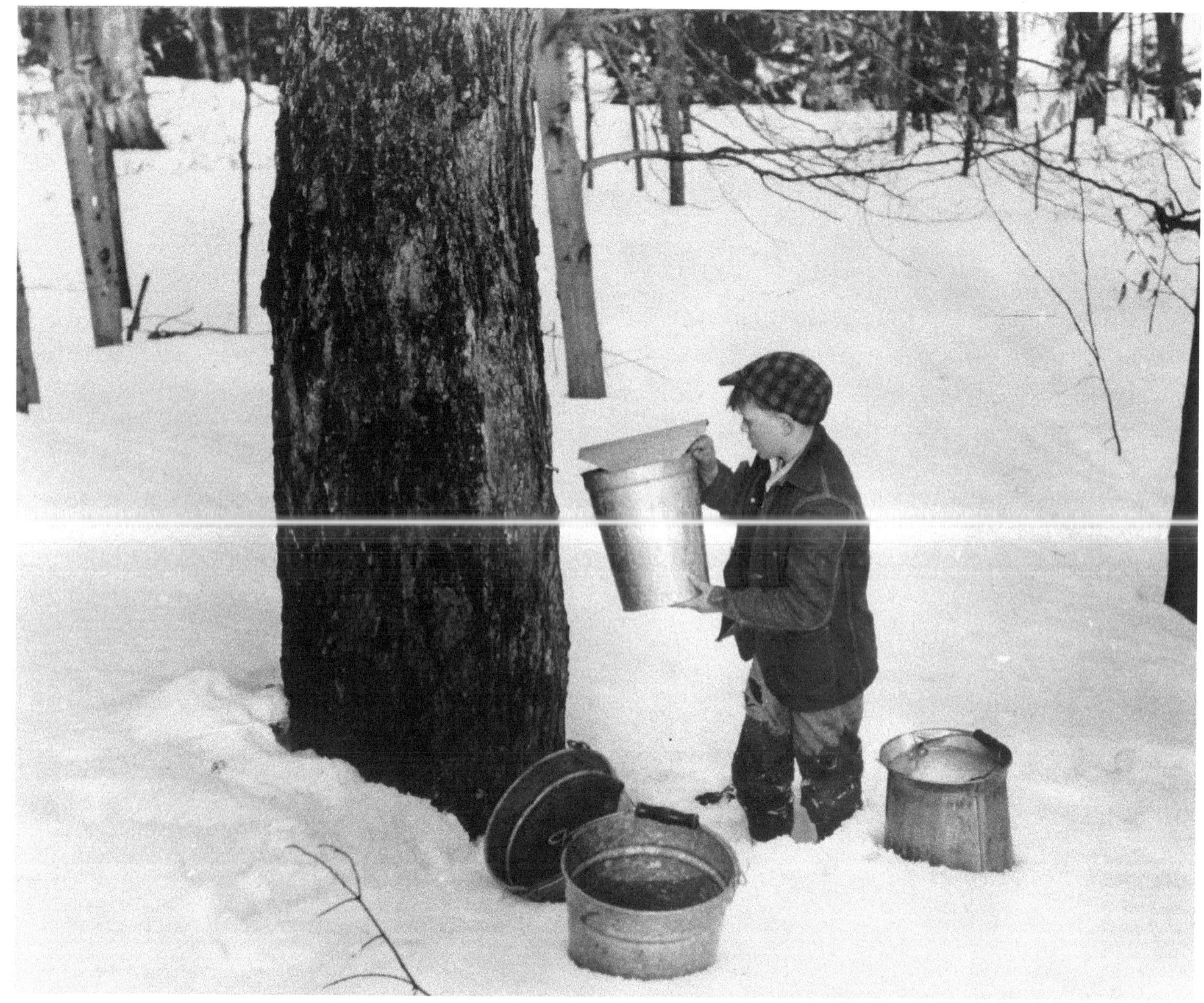

Frank Shurtleff's son collects sap on their 400-acre North Bridgewater farm in 1940. A family effort kept the farm running, and maple syrup production was one of the roles that farm youngsters could help fill. Children helped with many other farm chores. One Vermont farmer recalled how as a child he had lugged pails of water to the farmhouse, learning quickly the difference between heavy "wash days" and lighter "baking days."

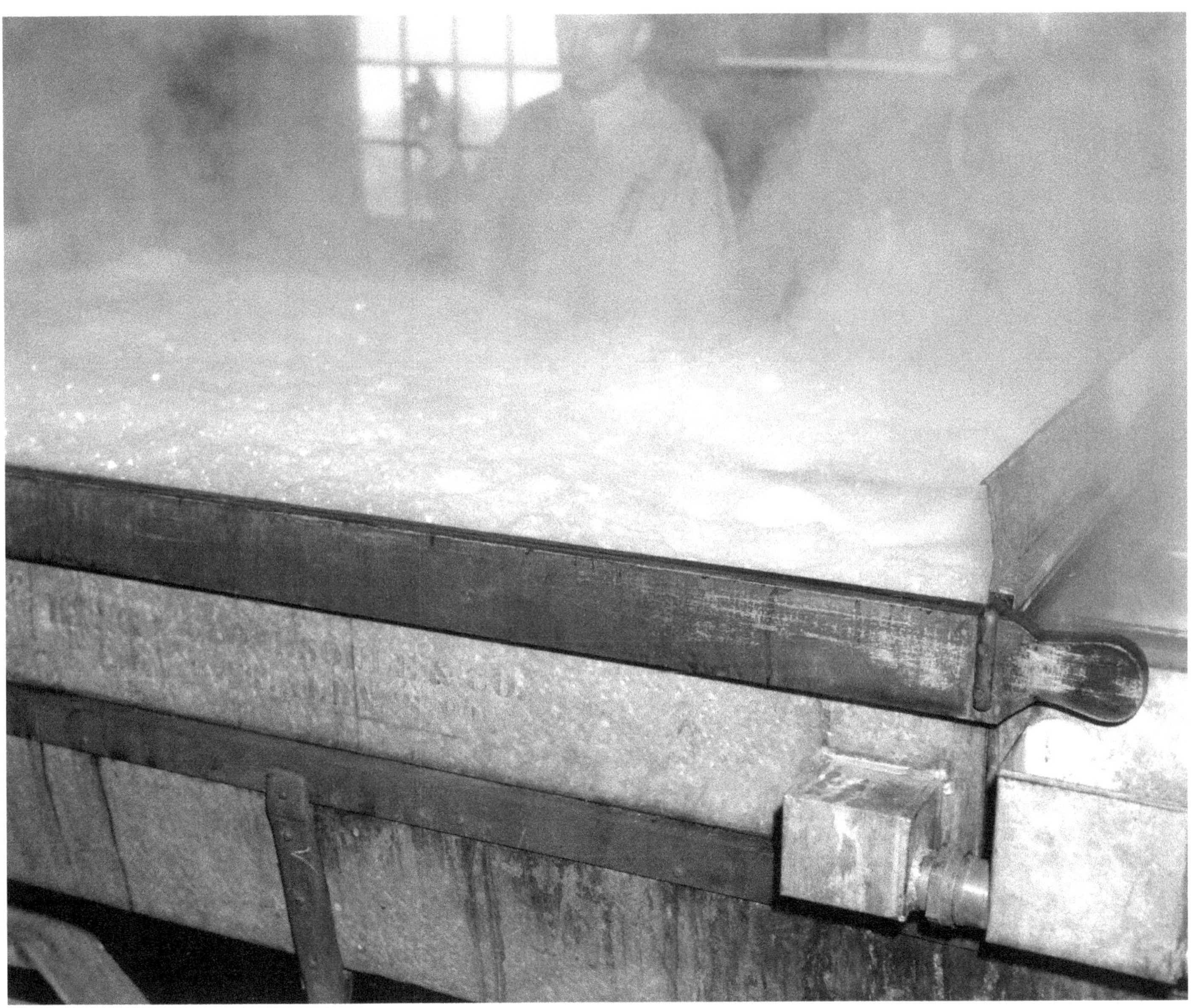

A vat of sap boils down at Walter Gaylord's house in Waitsfield in 1940. Before the introduction of labor-saving technologies, maple syrup production, or "sugaring," was sweet and hard work. Although methods have changed, the ratio has not: 40 gallons of sap are needed to yield 1 gallon of syrup. Like other farmers in the modern age, Gaylord diversified his farm to increase his profits. In addition to sugaring, which could fetch Vermont farmers from $500 to $1,000 a year, Gaylord raised beef cattle, poultry, and potatoes on his third-generation Vermont farm.

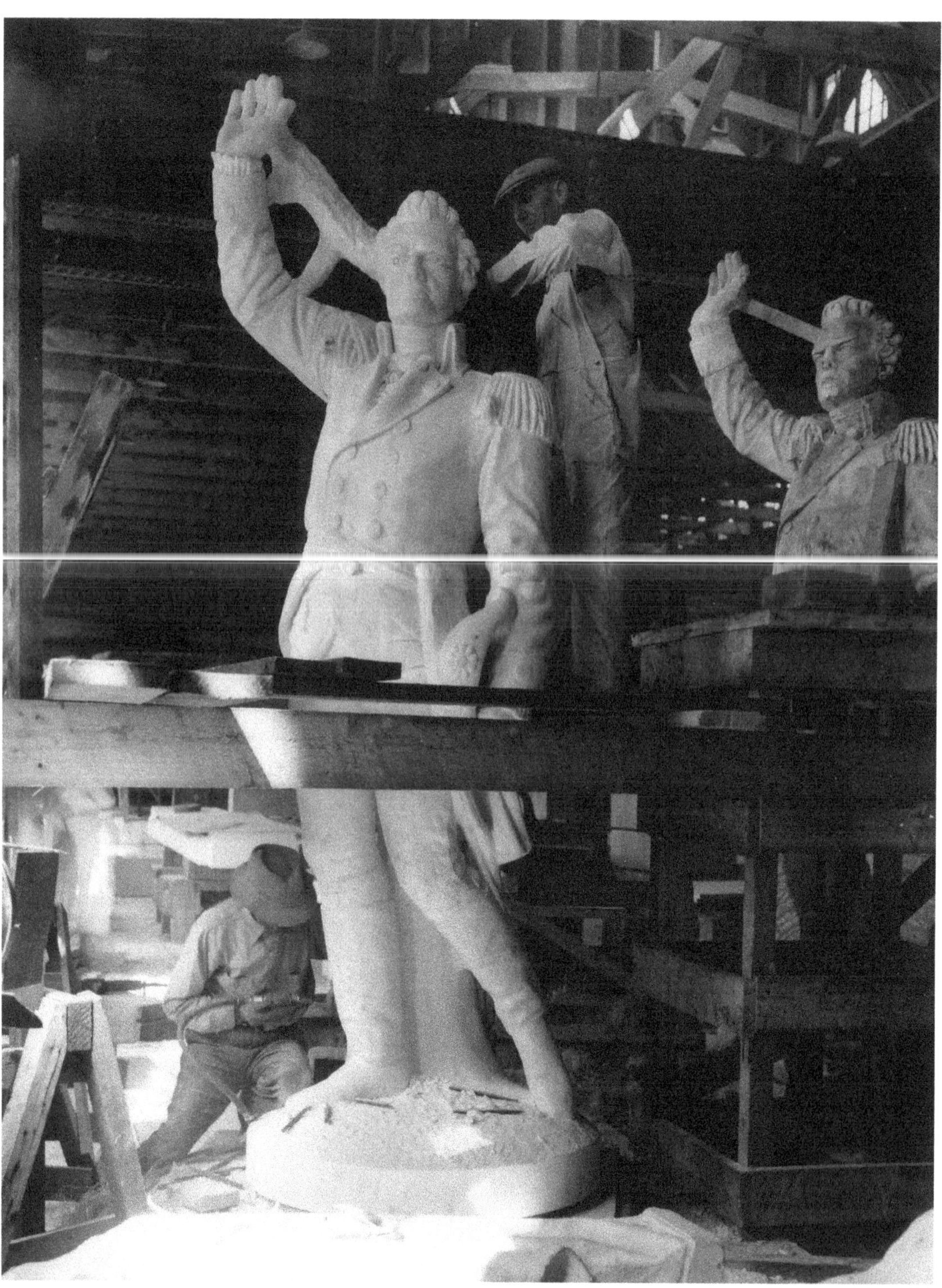

Vermont marble sculptors carve a replacement statue of Ethan Allen for Montpelier's State House in 1941. Beginning in the late nineteenth century, Vermonters revived their love for Revolution-era heroes with grand monuments and statues. In 1861, Civil War artist and Brattleboro sculptor Larkin G. Mead, Jr., completed a statue of Ethan Allen for the new State House in Montpelier. The statue was replaced with this one, credited to Rutland resident Aristide Piccini

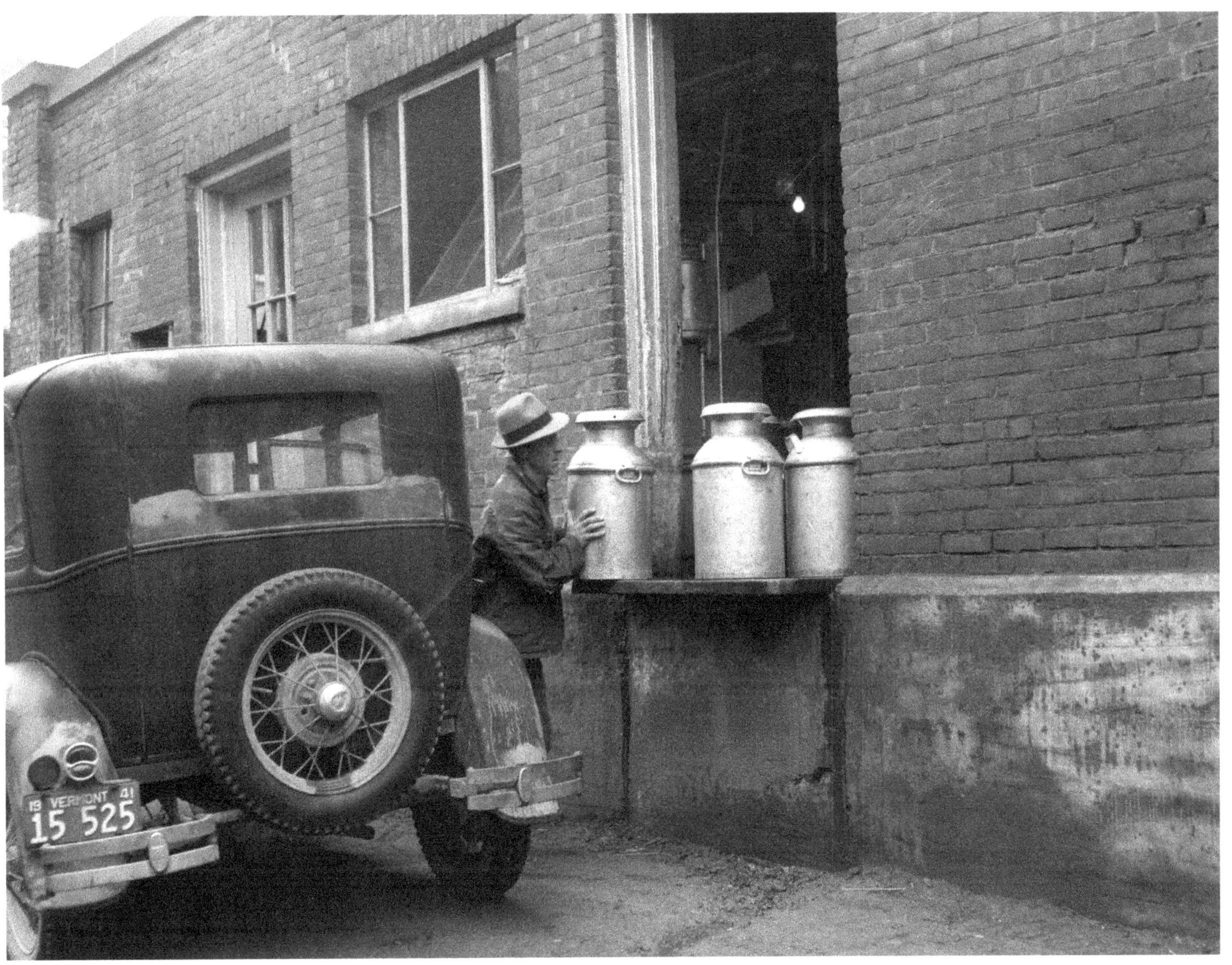

For farmers who did not live near a railroad depot, the journey from farm to railroad could prove costly since the milk could sour before it reached the train station. This was particularly worrisome in the days when milk was delivered by horse and wagon—and a problem greatly relieved by the advent of the speedier automobile. This farmer is bringing his milk to Burlington's cooperative bottling plant in 1941.

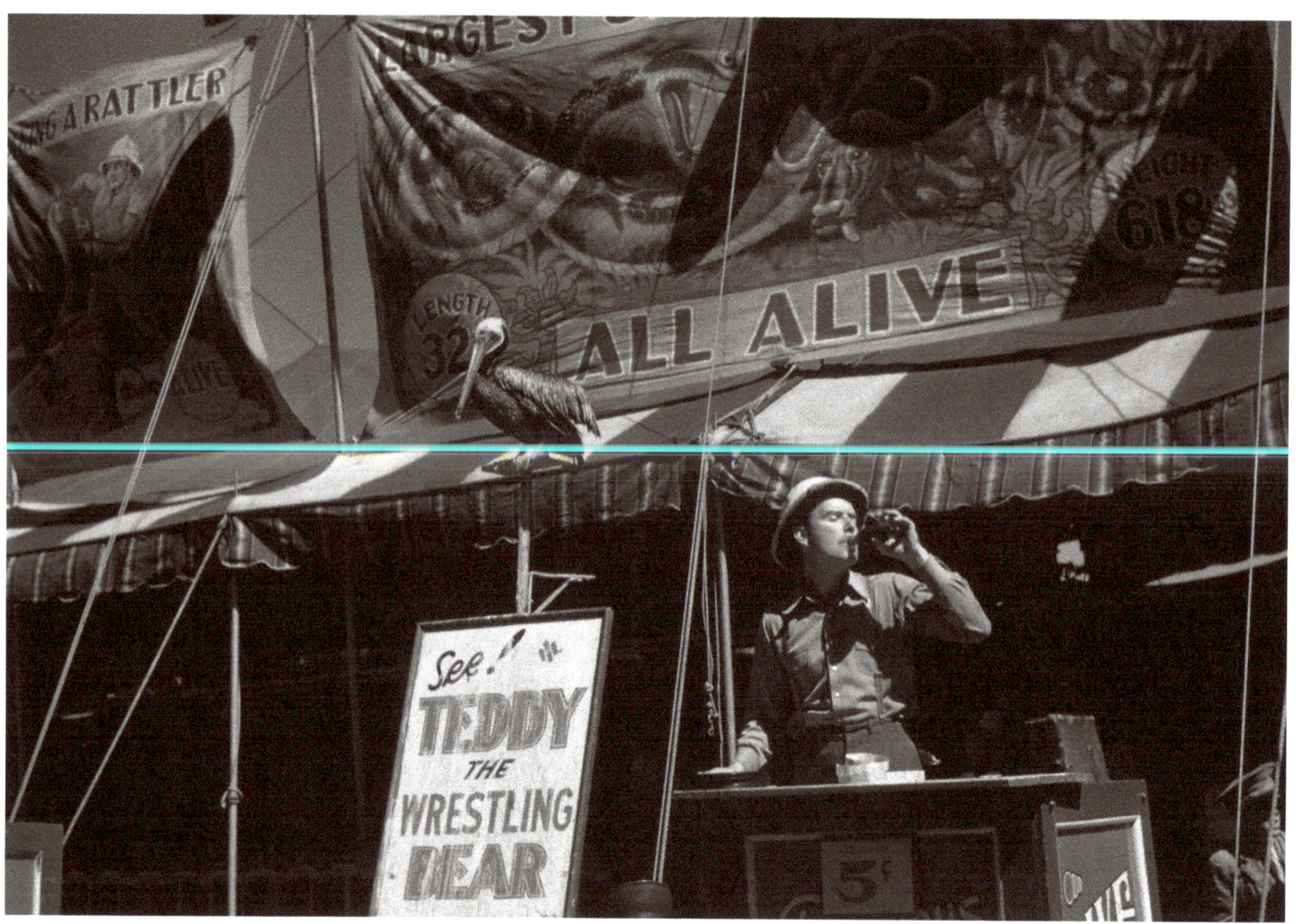

A barker at the Vermont State Fair, 1941. After stints in Middlebury and Castleton, the state fair moved to Rutland in 1852. Although its beginnings were agricultural, by the 1940s the fair had added a midway and carnival rides to satisfy the growing nonfarm crowds. In modern times, fairs have shifted away from educating farmers and toward educating the public about farming—an eye-opening experience for those of us who think that food comes from the grocery store.

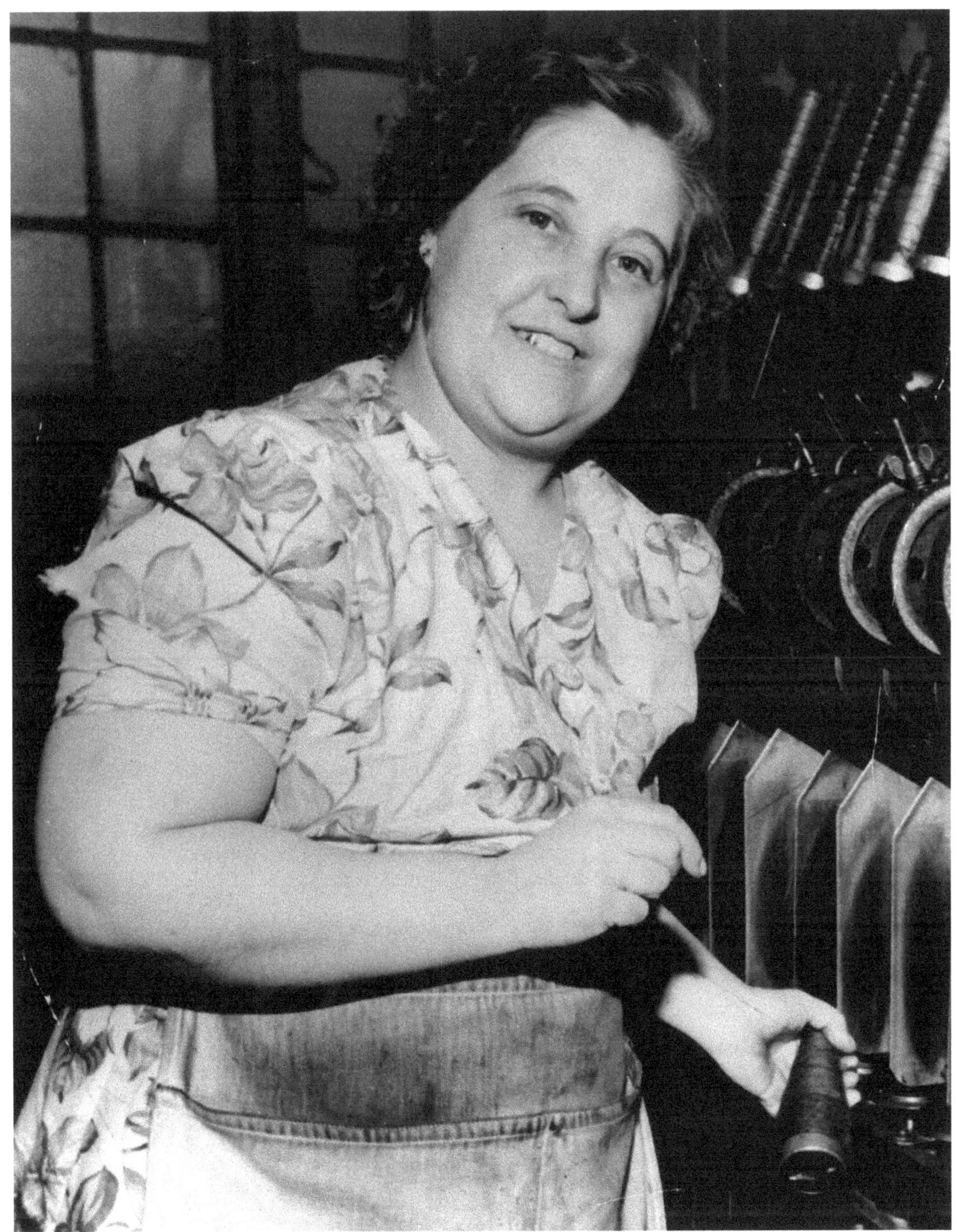

Dolly Kirby, a "twister" at American Woolen in Winooski. During the years of the Great Depression, American Woolen sold off company housing to keep itself afloat, but World War II brought a business boom to this Winooski-based mill. Orders for "fighting cloth"—white blankets for the navy, brown ones for the army, as well as overcoats and uniforms—arrived by the millions. In the 1940s, American Woolen became the largest single private employer in Vermont.

Following Spread: A scrap metal drive is under way at Park Street and Copley Avenue in Morrisville in 1942. Vermont state legislators declared the United States at war even before the federal proclamation—prompting bemused local references to a "London-Moscow-Montpelier Axis." In 1943, Vermonters gathered a per-capita average of 162.9 pounds of scrap metal for the war effort, the largest contribution in the nation for that year.

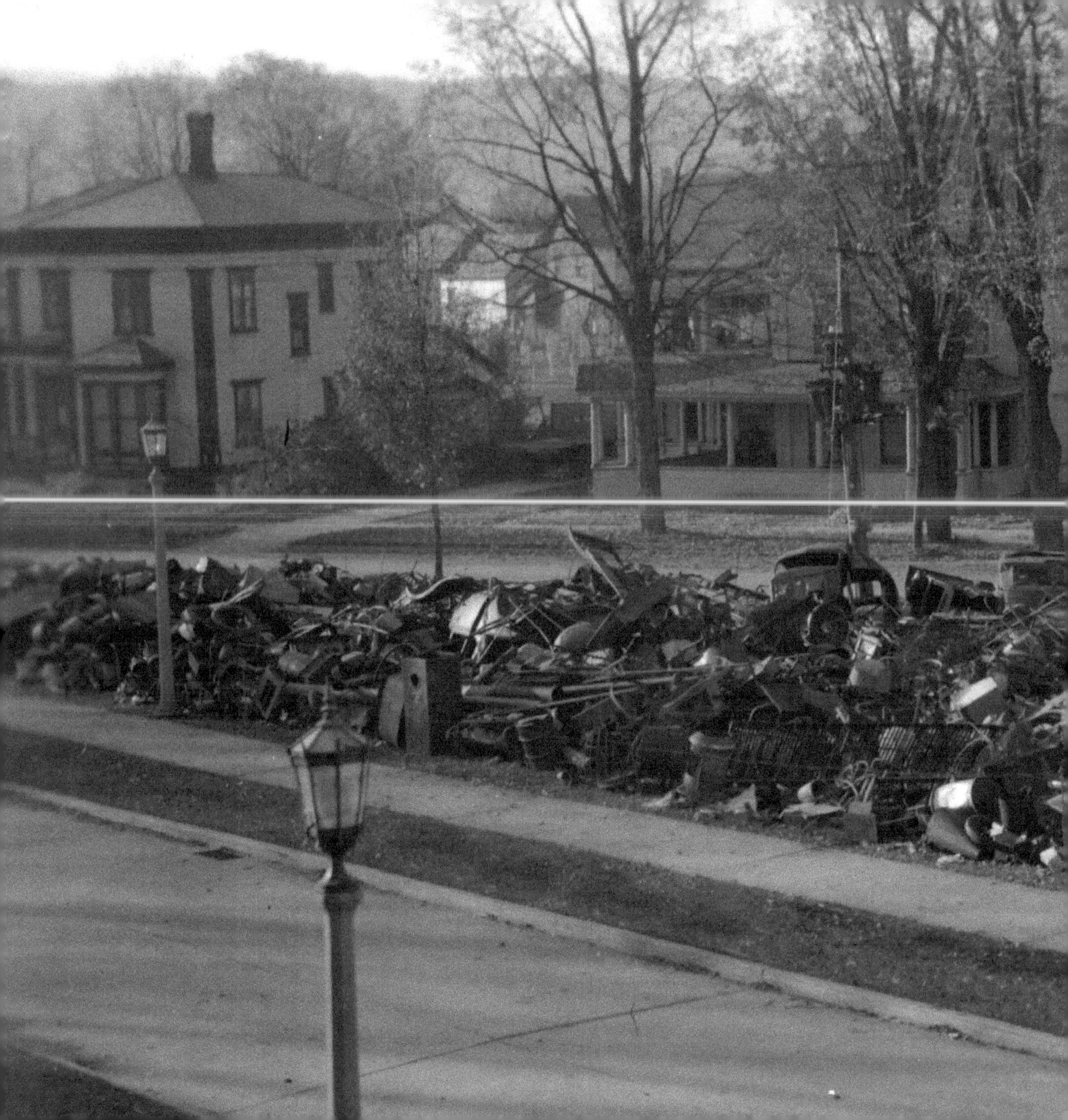

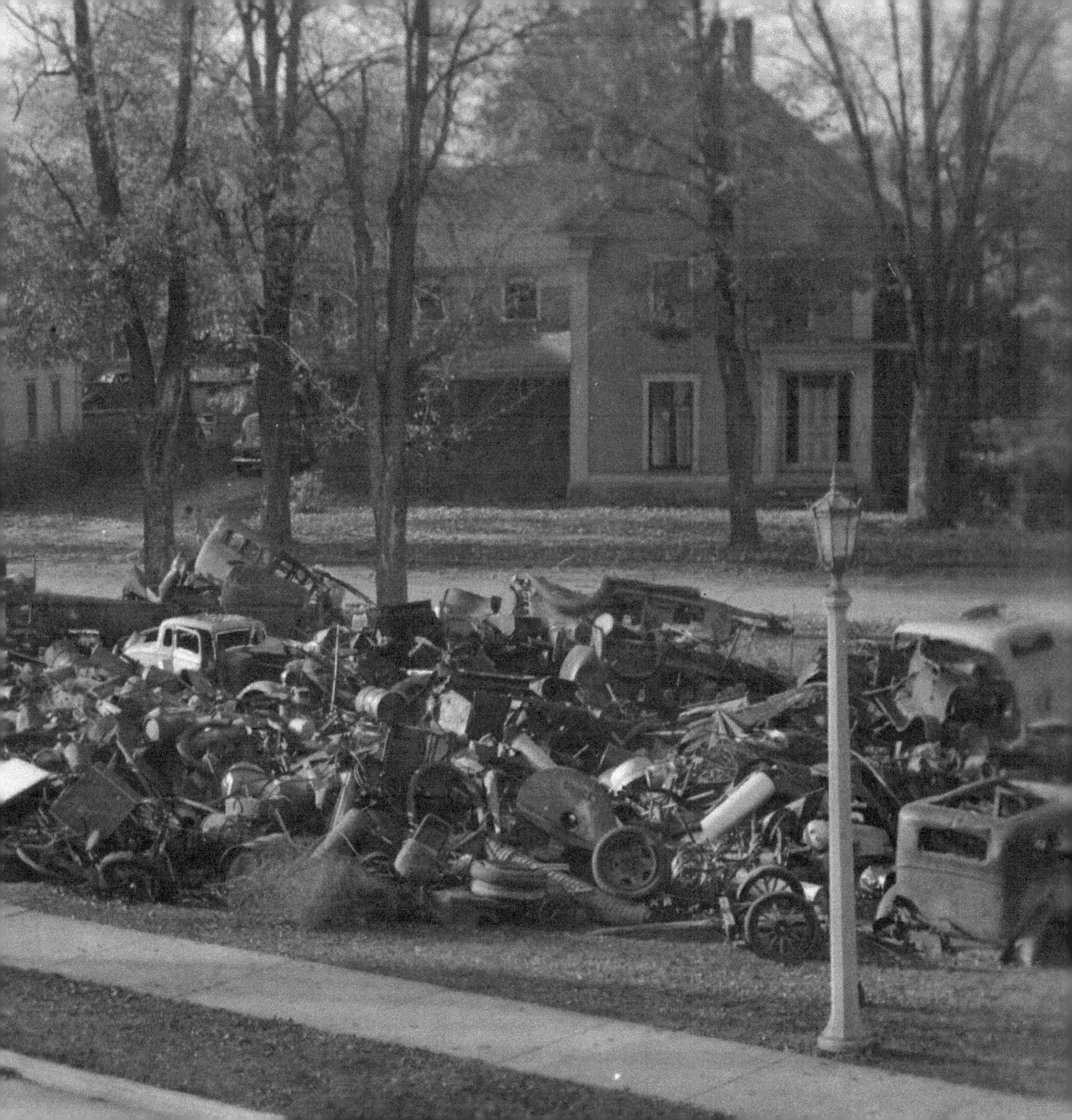

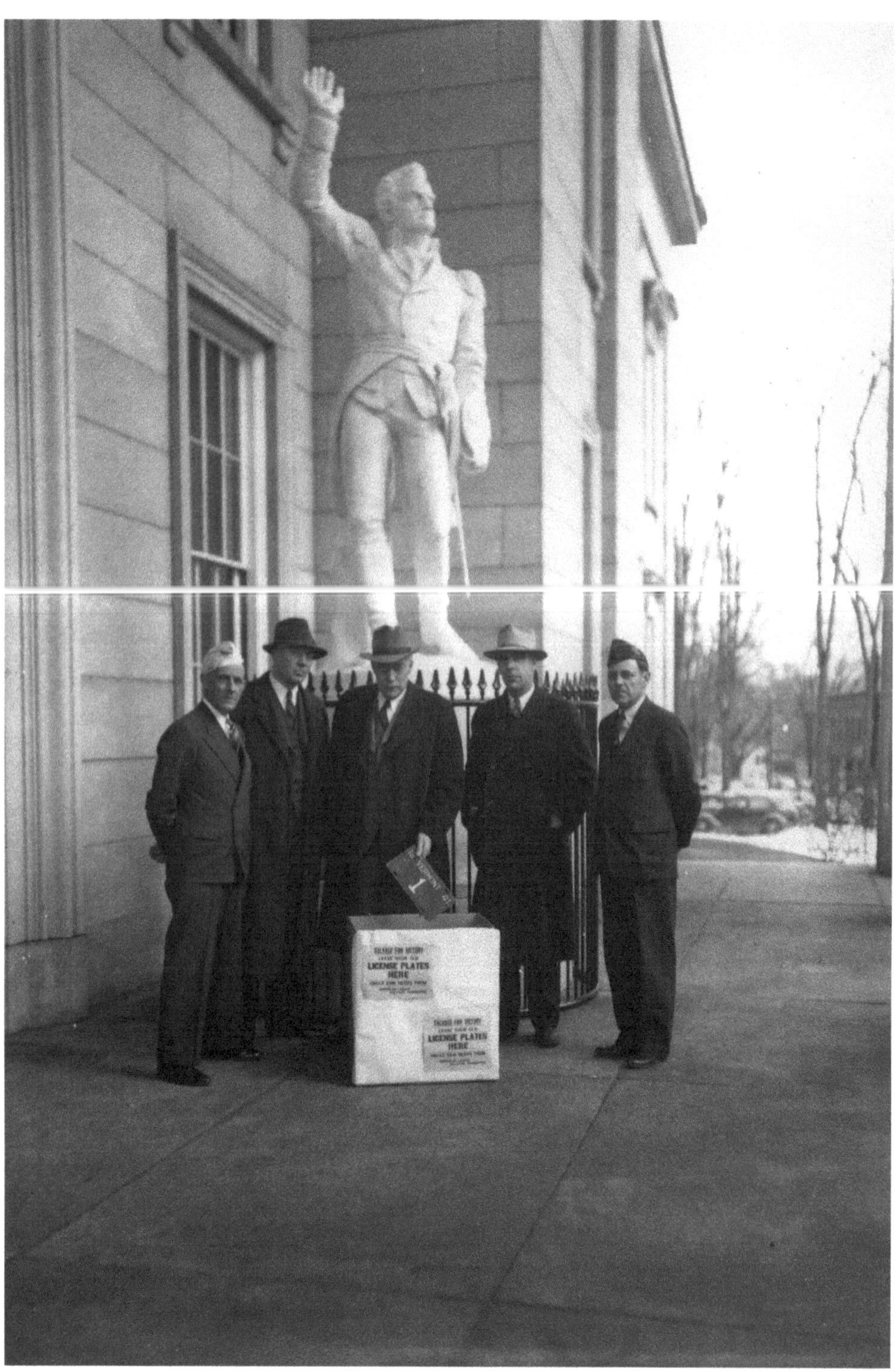

Vermont issued its first license plates in 1905 and established a Department of Motor Vehicles 22 years later. Drivers received new plates every year. Each year's plate was distinguished initially by color, and later by date. During World War II, plates were updated by attaching only a small metal tab to the previous year's plate, a result of the metal shortage. The tabs were made from the tin cans of state prisoners' food.

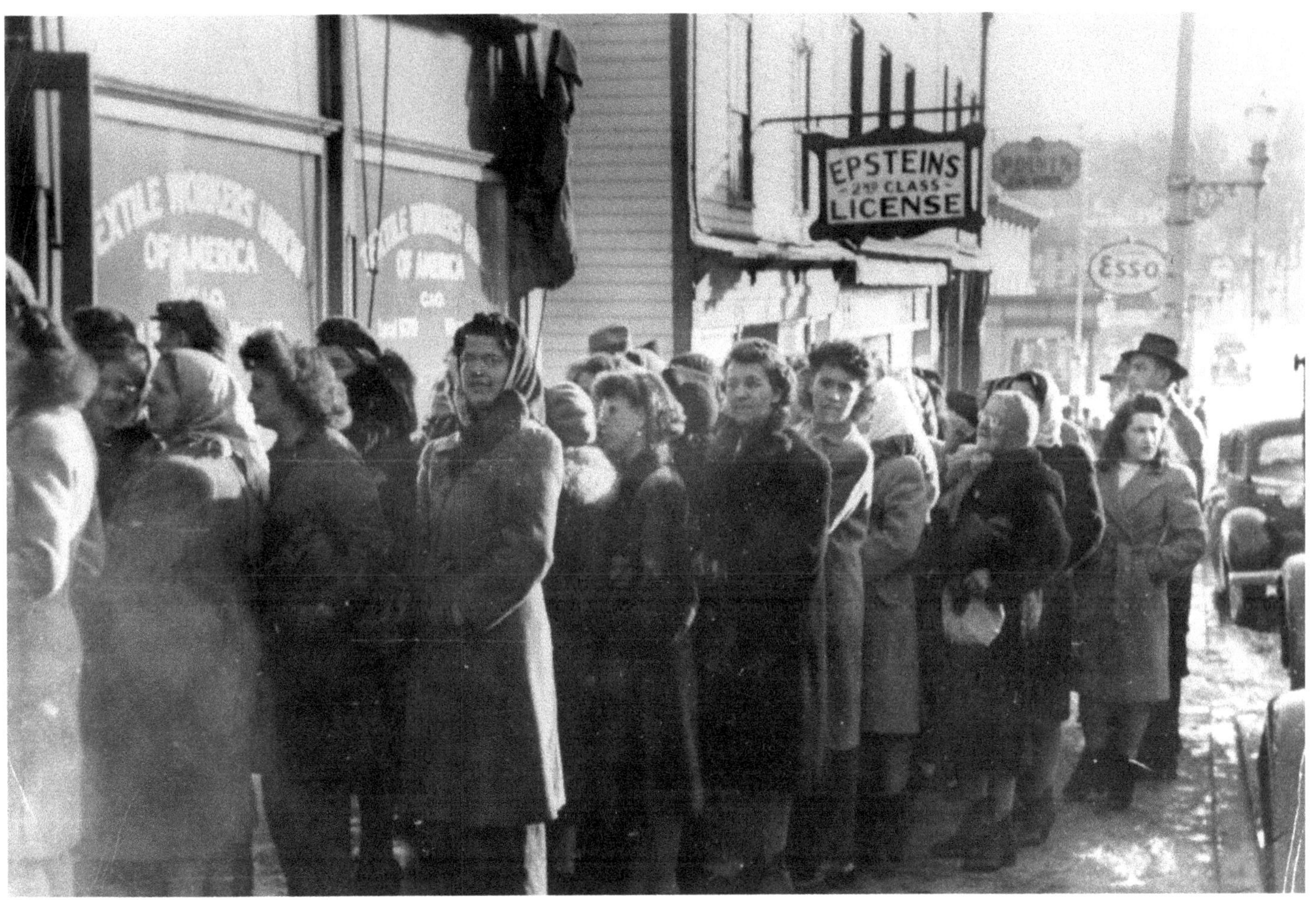

Workers line up on Main Street at Winooski's Union Hall in 1943. Employees at American Woolen historically opposed unionization, fearing that agitation would drive the large employer out of town altogether. In the summer of 1943 however, buoyed by wartime job stability, employees voted in favor of unionization. Winooski's vote set off a rash of organizing across the state: by year's end, seven new unions had appeared in Vermont.

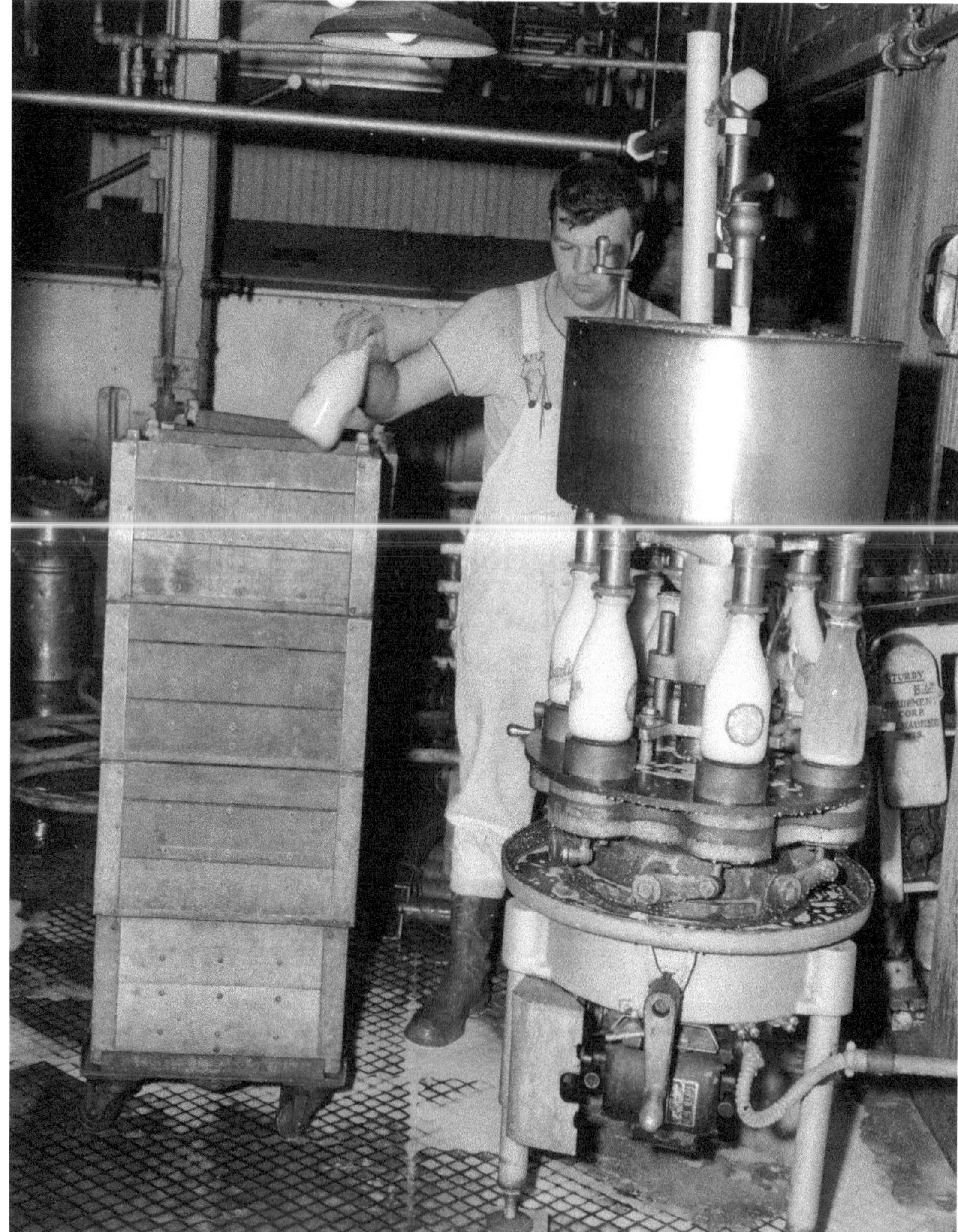

Milk bottling plant in Burlington. Patented milk bottles appeared by the 1880s, and by the 1910s there was talk of "single-service paper containers" for milk. The containers would eliminate the challenges of cleaning the bottles, sometimes reused by the public to store vinegar, gasoline, or kerosene. Cartons appeared on store shelves in the 1930s, but most home delivery continued to rely on glass bottles for years to come.

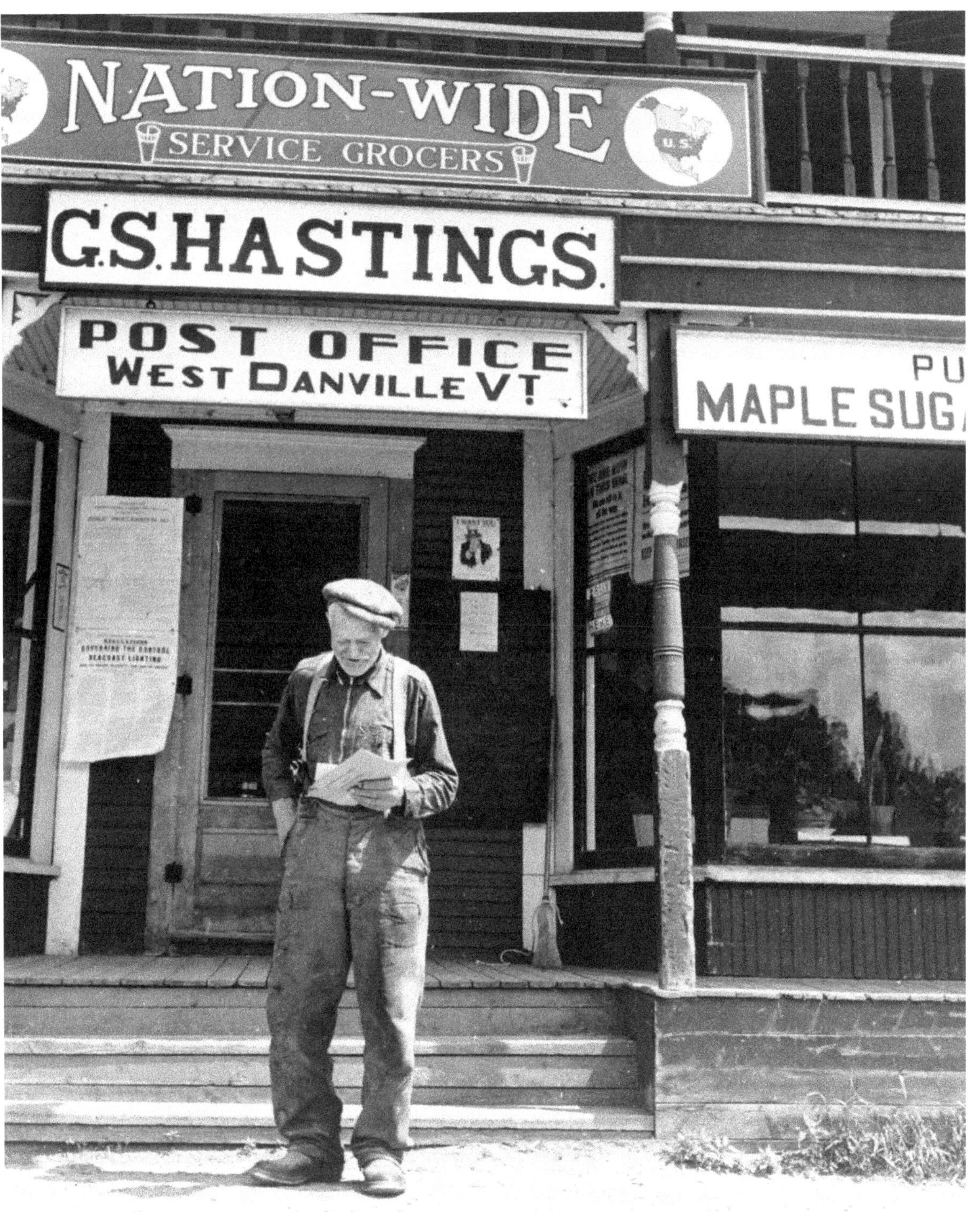

West Danville farmer Frank Goss stands reading a postcard in 1942. The postcard announced that last year's hired hand "won't be around for haying this year on account of he's in Californi' in the Navy." Since the mid–nineteenth century, Vermonters had felt the exodus of native-born sons to other states with more economic opportunity. Farms were particularly hard hit during World War II as America's finest headed abroad to defend the homeland.

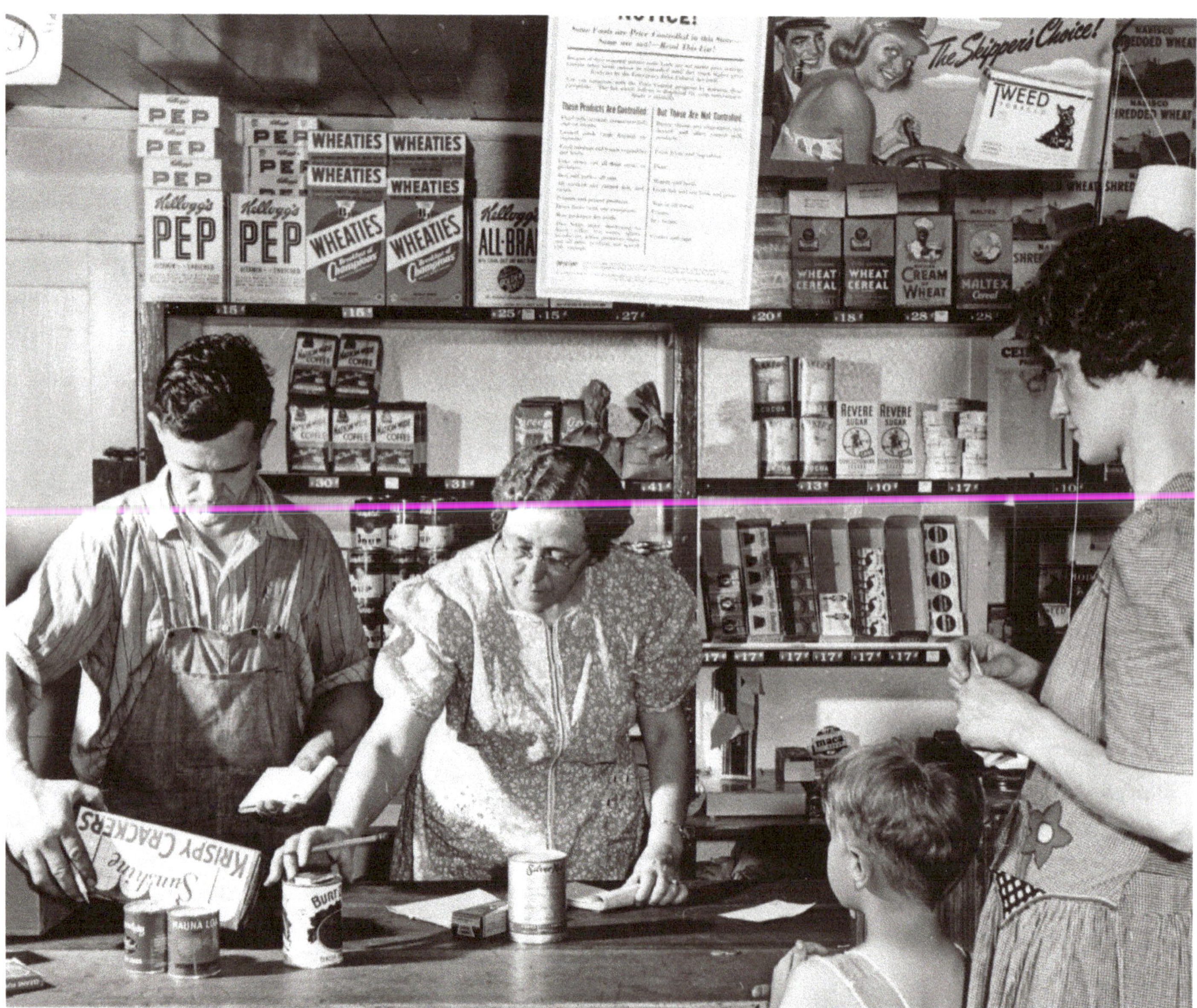

Hastings General Store, West Danville, 1942. When modernity visited Vermont's general stores, proprietors swapped their long counters for self-service shelves. The day Gilbert Hastings stocked his first case of commercially produced bread, he fretted that nobody would want it. To persuade customers to buy the product, he decided to put a whistle in every loaf. The idea worked: every kid in town wanted the bread so he or she could tweet a whistle.

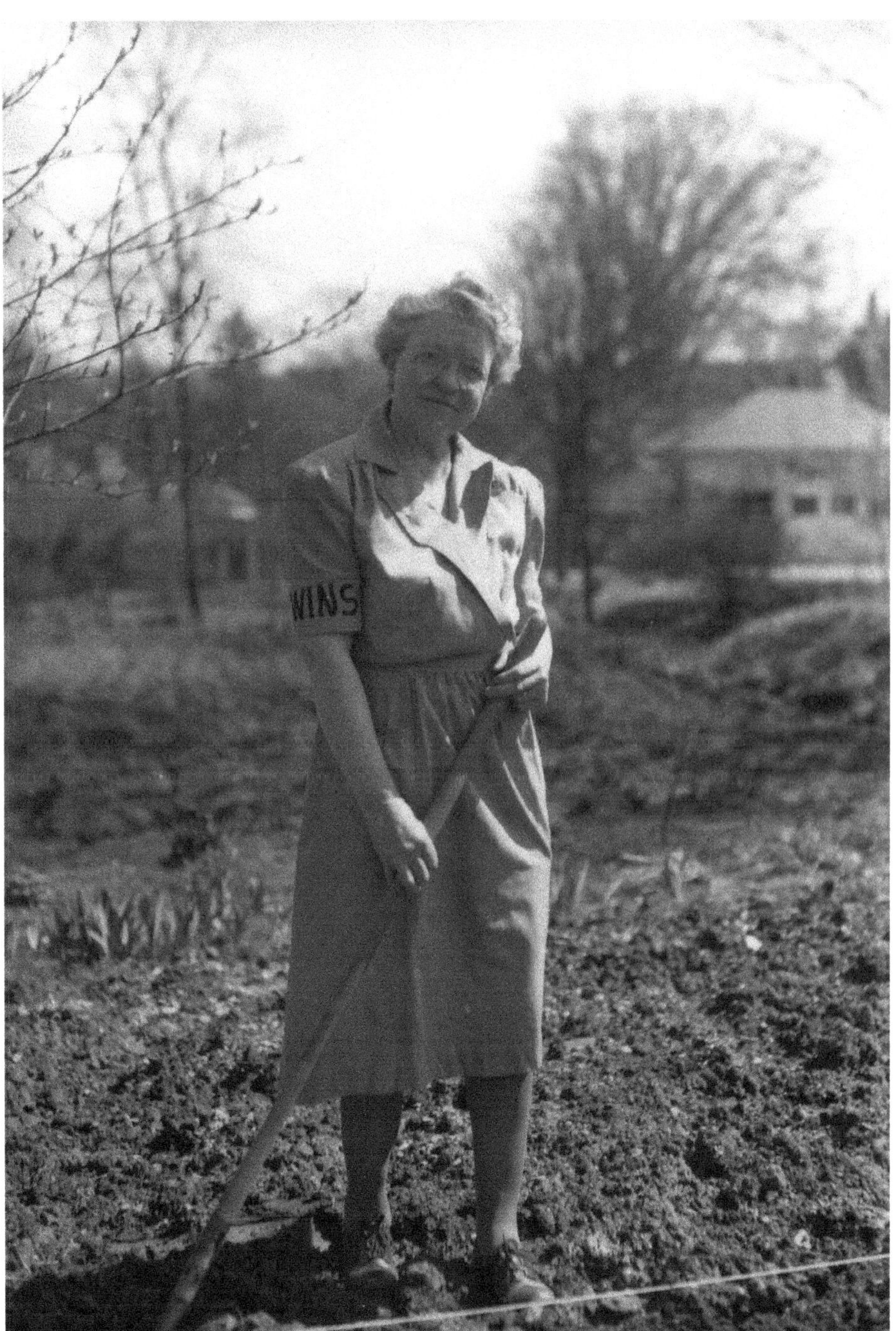

Helen Wills, wife of governor William Wills, tends a World War II Victory Garden. Reflecting on the war years, Mrs. Wills noted that "careful management in husbanding resources brought substantial surpluses for those days." Her husband worked hard to attract Vermont veterans back after the war, instituting the Soldier's Bonus and a spate of state-sponsored jobs for returning servicemen.

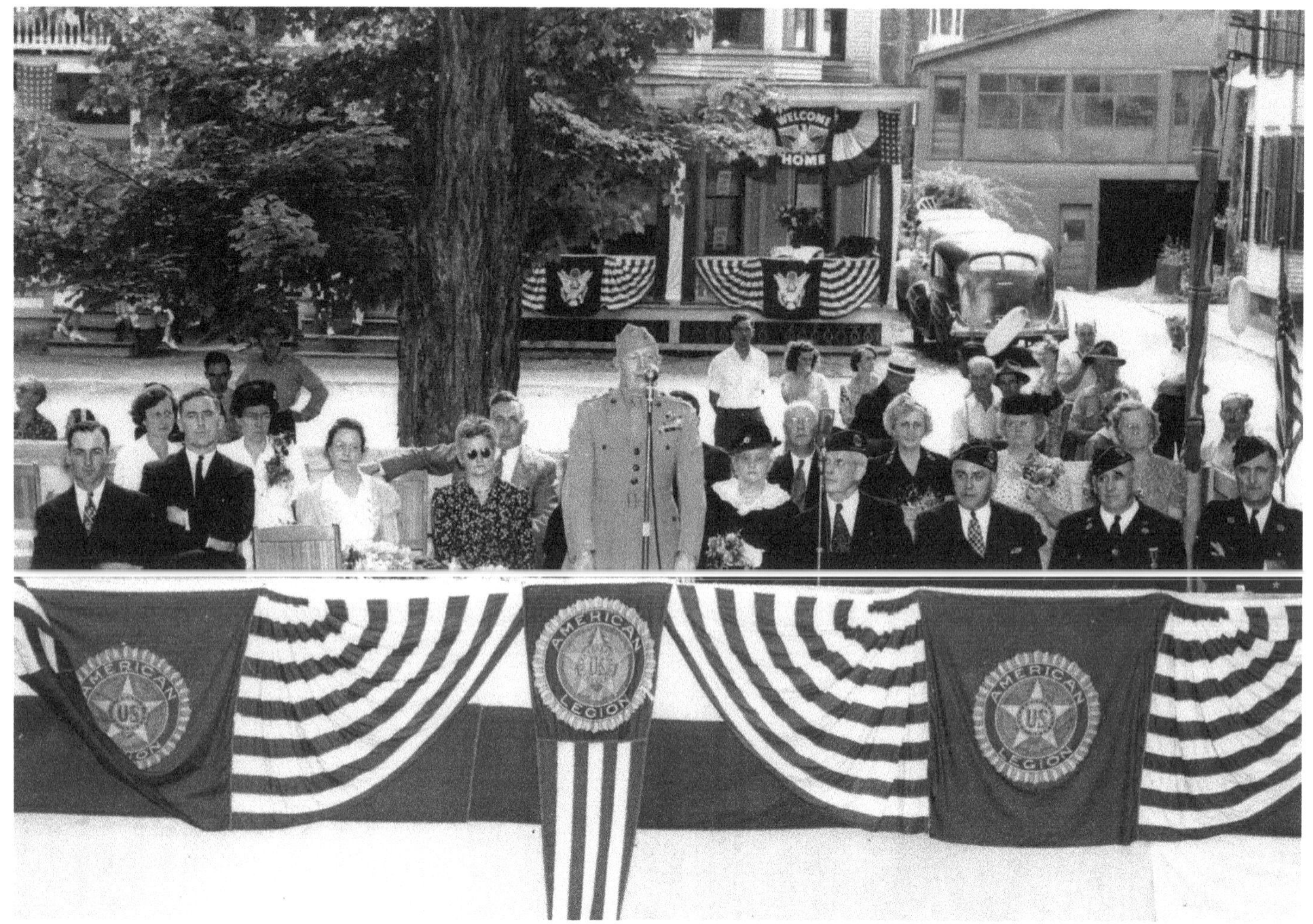

General Merritt Edson, known as "Red Mike," is best known for his participation at Guadalcanal during World War II. The only Vermonter to win the Medal of Honor during the war, Edson became Vermont's first public safety commissioner in 1947. He arrived to find troopers working 90-hour weeks and requested that the state double the size of the force. Vermonters celebrated Edson's no-nonsense manner—he once used his own car to chase down a young speeder—but they also questioned the spending increases associated with a state police force. In this image, Edson is speaking to a crowd at Winchester in 1944.

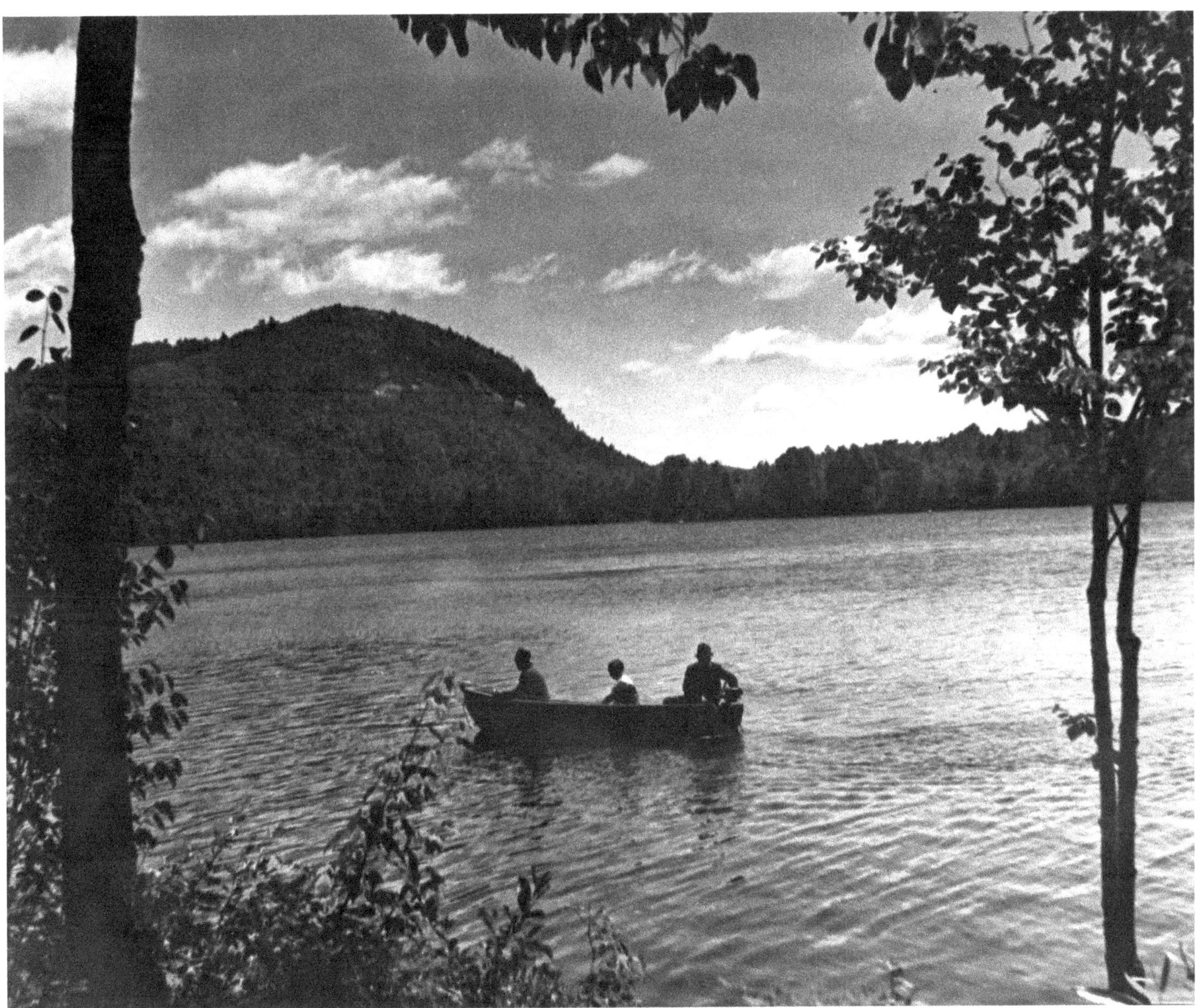

Following World War II, the solid economic footing of many Vermonters allowed them to purchase small pleasure boats. The development of reliable, inexpensive outboard motors permitted almost anyone to purchase a small runabout for recreational use upon the state's hundreds of lakes and ponds. With more people on the water, the state increased its involvement in water resource management by increasing the number of fish and game wardens and state police on the state's waters. This is a water's-edge view in Groton State Park.

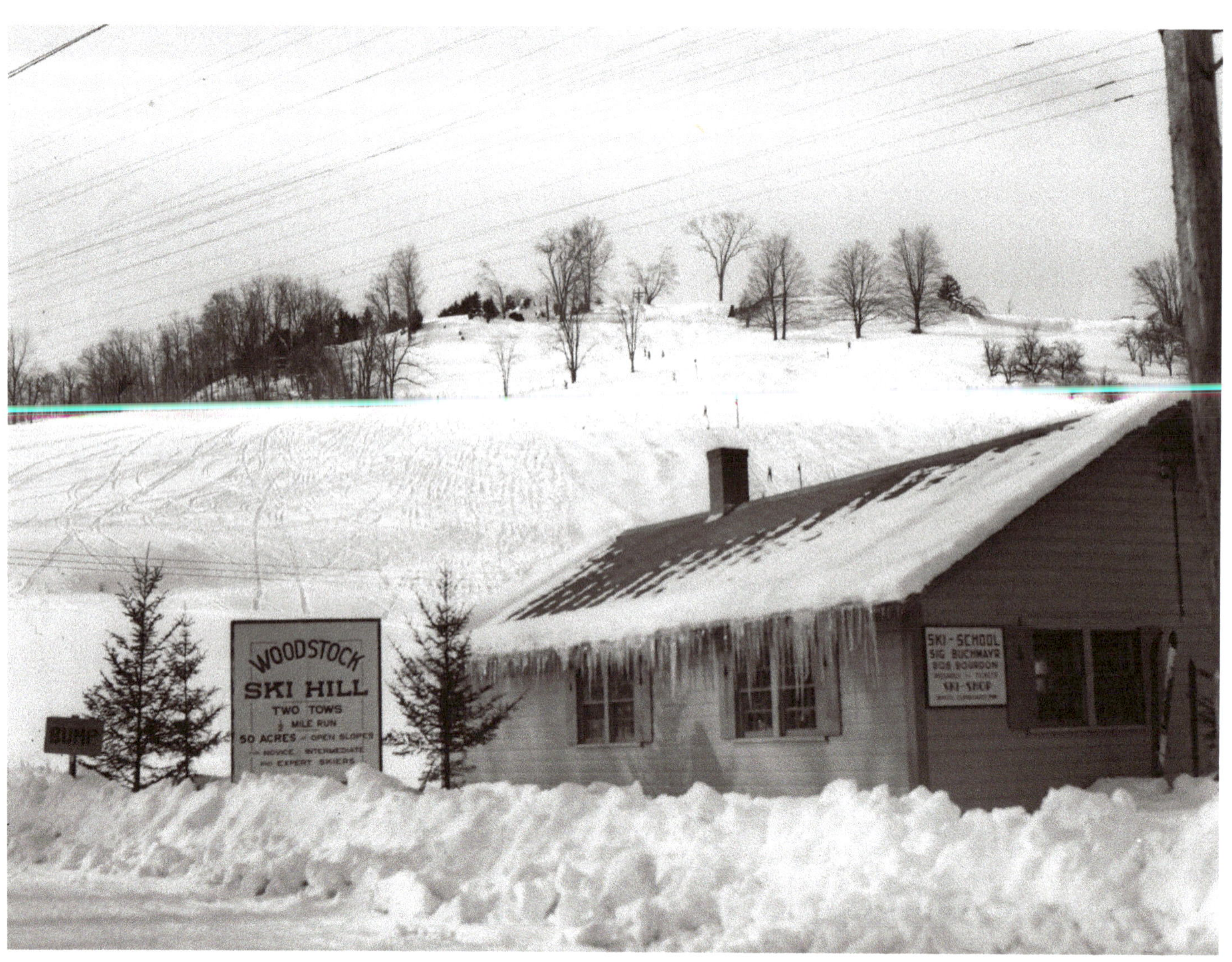

Ski enthusiasts built a rope tow on Clinton Gilbert's farm near Woodstock in 1934. Constructed with 1,800 feet of rope and a Ford Model T engine, the tow attracted more skiers, who supplemented Gilbert's farming income by 25 percent. Named the "Ski Way," the mechanism is said to have spurred the rope-tow era in the United States.

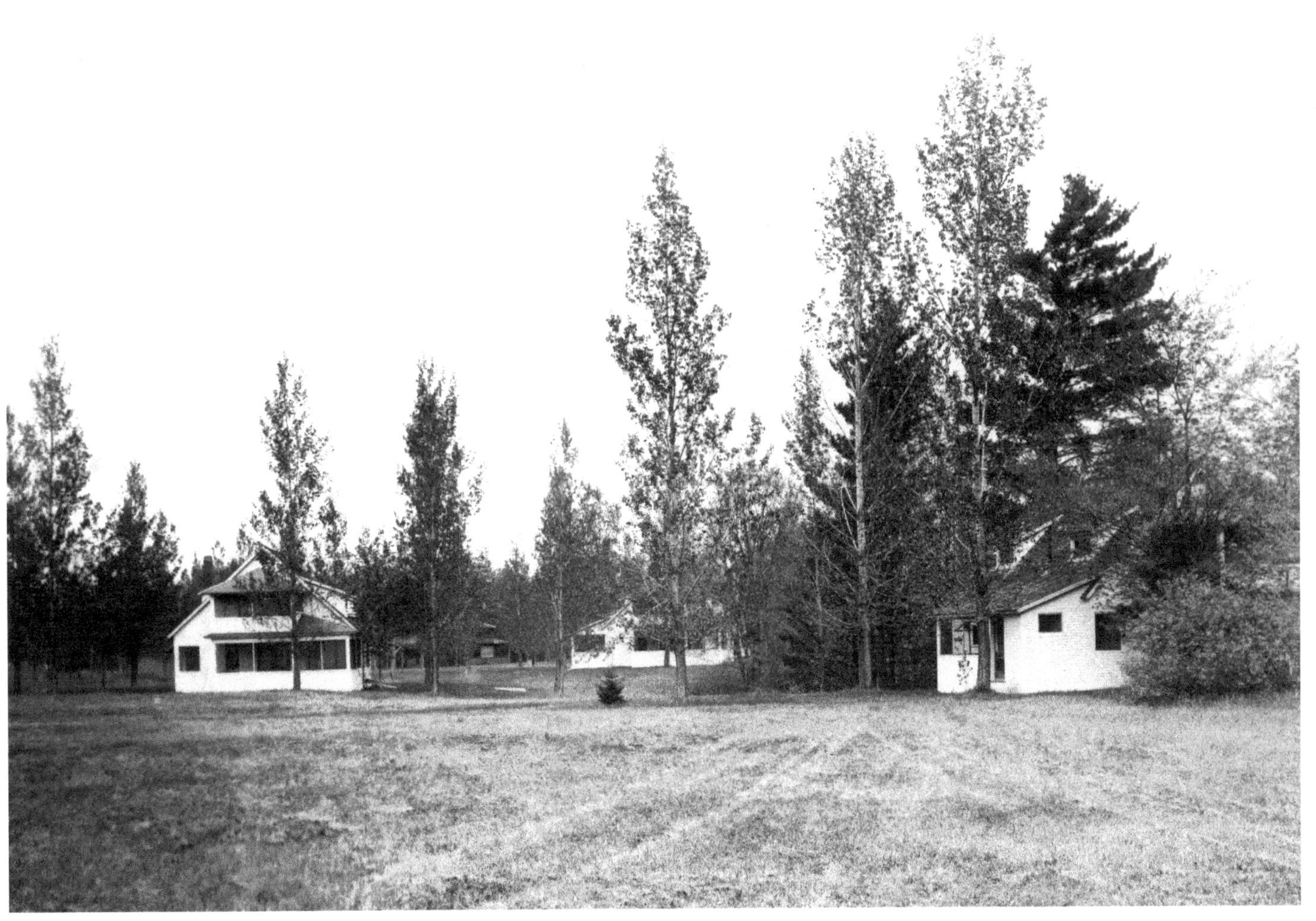

Around 1908, Dr. William Slayton converted his farmhouse into the first dwelling at a summer recreation community—later called Samoset Colony—on Morristown's Lake Lamoille. Slayton was one of many Vermonters to revitalize former farms into recreation spots. In the 1960s, the Coutures, also from Morristown, turned their LaPorte dairy farm first into the Farm Motel, and then into an 18-hole golf course.

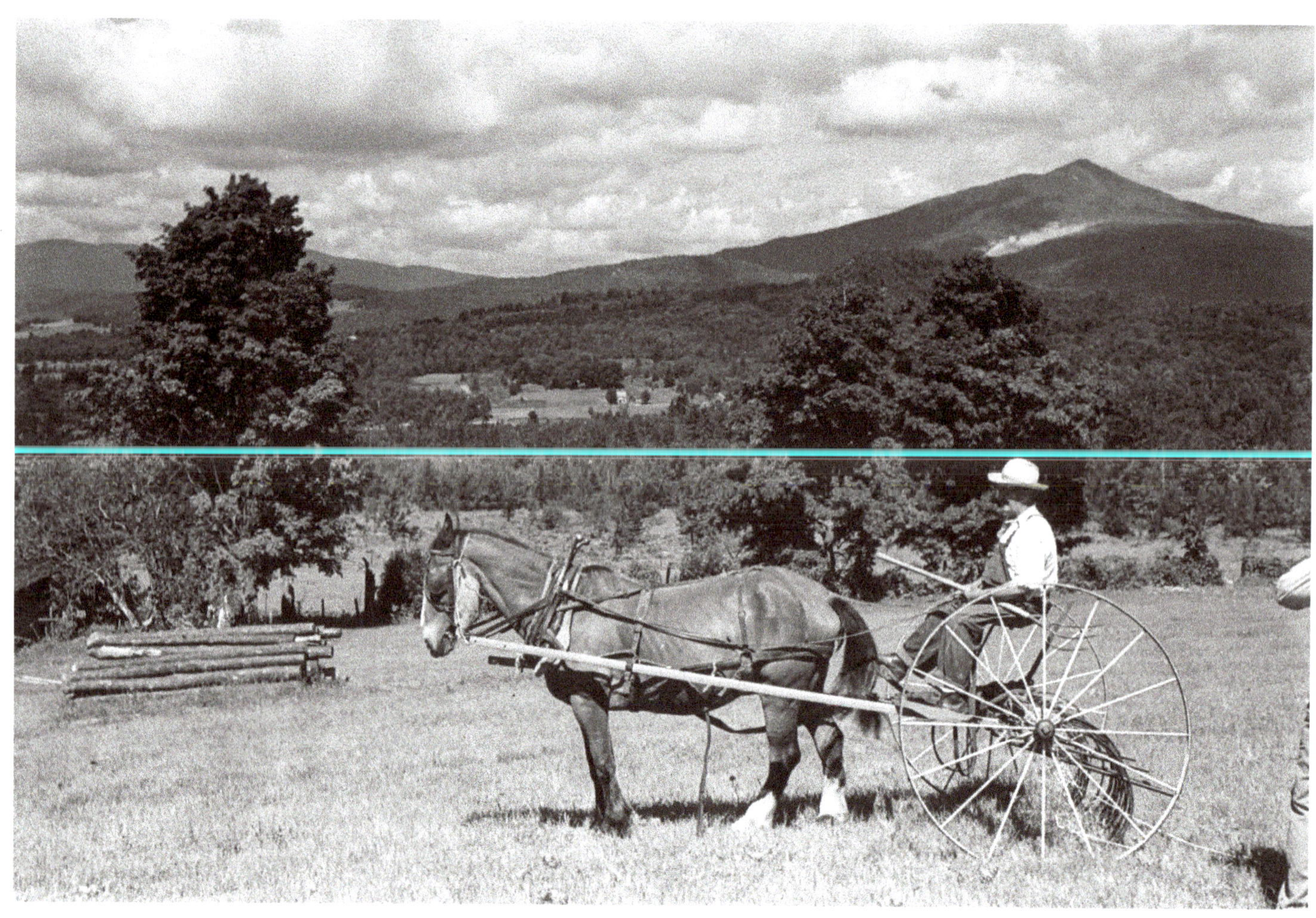

From its inception, Vermont's house of representatives had instituted a system of "one-town, one-vote" representation regardless of a town's population. This system resulted in a disproportionate number of farmer-politicians pushing legislation geared to rural interests. Although industrial and urban interests dominated senatorial representation, the U.S. Supreme Court ruled in 1965 that the traditional one-town, one-vote system did not appropriately represent Vermont's voters, and the system was immediately abolished.

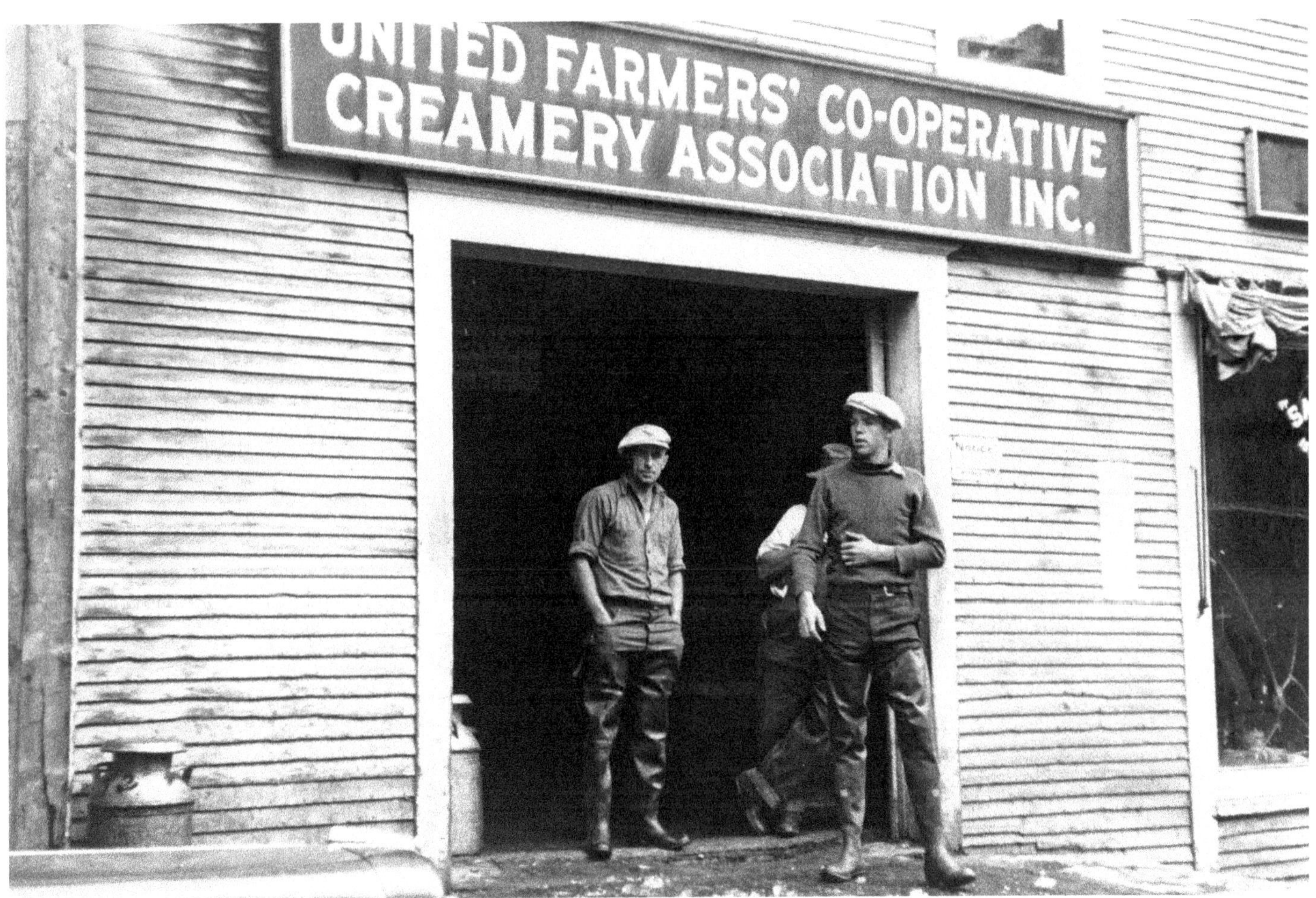

A milk cooperative in Hardwick. By 1930, Vermont dairy farms supplied two-thirds of the milk consumed in Boston. Many Vermont farmers had found themselves at a disadvantage in the Boston market, since large dealers controlled prices. In 1910, some farmers mounted an unsuccessful "milk war," holding two-fifths of the normal supply from the Boston dealers. Others formed cooperative creameries, which permitted them to ship milk themselves and to depend less on the large Boston dealers.

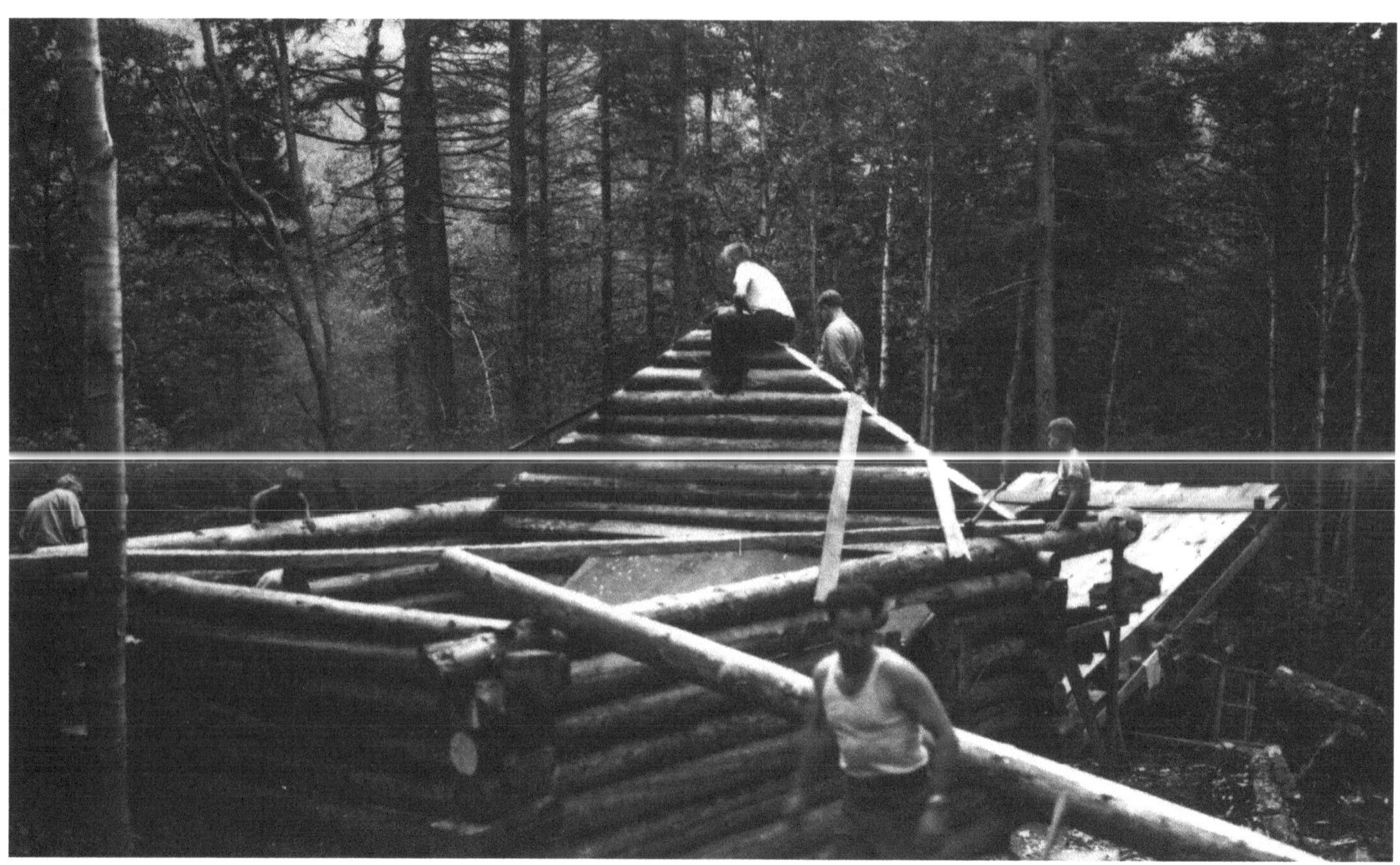

In the late 1940s, a group of Morristown residents organized the Sterling Section of the Green Mountain Club. One summer they met every Sunday to build the Beaver Meadow Lodge, a shelter that could accommodate 15 campers. A horse pulled the logs to the site, and the men dragged furnishings and a stove the two-and-a-half miles from the nearest access road. The new lodge replaced an older retreat on the trail.

THE BECKONING COUNTRY

(1950–1970s)

In December 1956, residents of Brattleboro received word that they were one of eleven U.S. towns to win the All-America City Award. The award celebrated "alert, hard-hitting action taken by citizens to meet pressing community problems." Brattleboro caught the eye of judges because of the town's community-wide effort to create Living Memorial Park, a municipally sponsored recreation area and tribute to residents who had served in World War II.

Brattleboro citizens celebrated with a great winter carnival, and the *Brattleboro Reformer* published a lengthy insert to celebrate the affair. Local companies placed full-page advertisements to salute the "mark of distinction," and the newspaper published a front-page article about the special community "triumph."

In writing of the award, the *Reformer*'s editor hinted at why the prize was so significant for Brattleboro. "It has brought much more than a citation and handsome banner," the editor wrote. "It has also brought nationwide publicity and no little fame." Brattleboro was now on the national map.

Indeed, by the 1950s the entire state of Vermont was vying for national attention—from potential tourists. Since the 1920s, Vermonters had been converting abandoned farmhouses into inns and unused pastures into golf courses. By the 1930s, ski areas, state parks, and the 270-mile Long Trail were attracting recreation-seekers to Vermont during both the cold winters and the warm summers. When Philip Hoff was elected governor in 1962, he updated the billboard slogans at the state borders from "Last Stand of the Yankees" to "the Beckoning Country." The state had stepped full-force into a marketing effort to promote Vermont as a tourist destination.

Brattleboro's All-America City Award also touched on Vermonters' fond feelings for their heritage. They embraced the award because it recognized the community spirit and Yankee initiative of native residents. For decades to follow, this would be the image Vermonters hoisted in efforts to boost state tourism. It was an image of good "Old Vermont": a self-sufficient community whose fate was in the hands of its citizens.

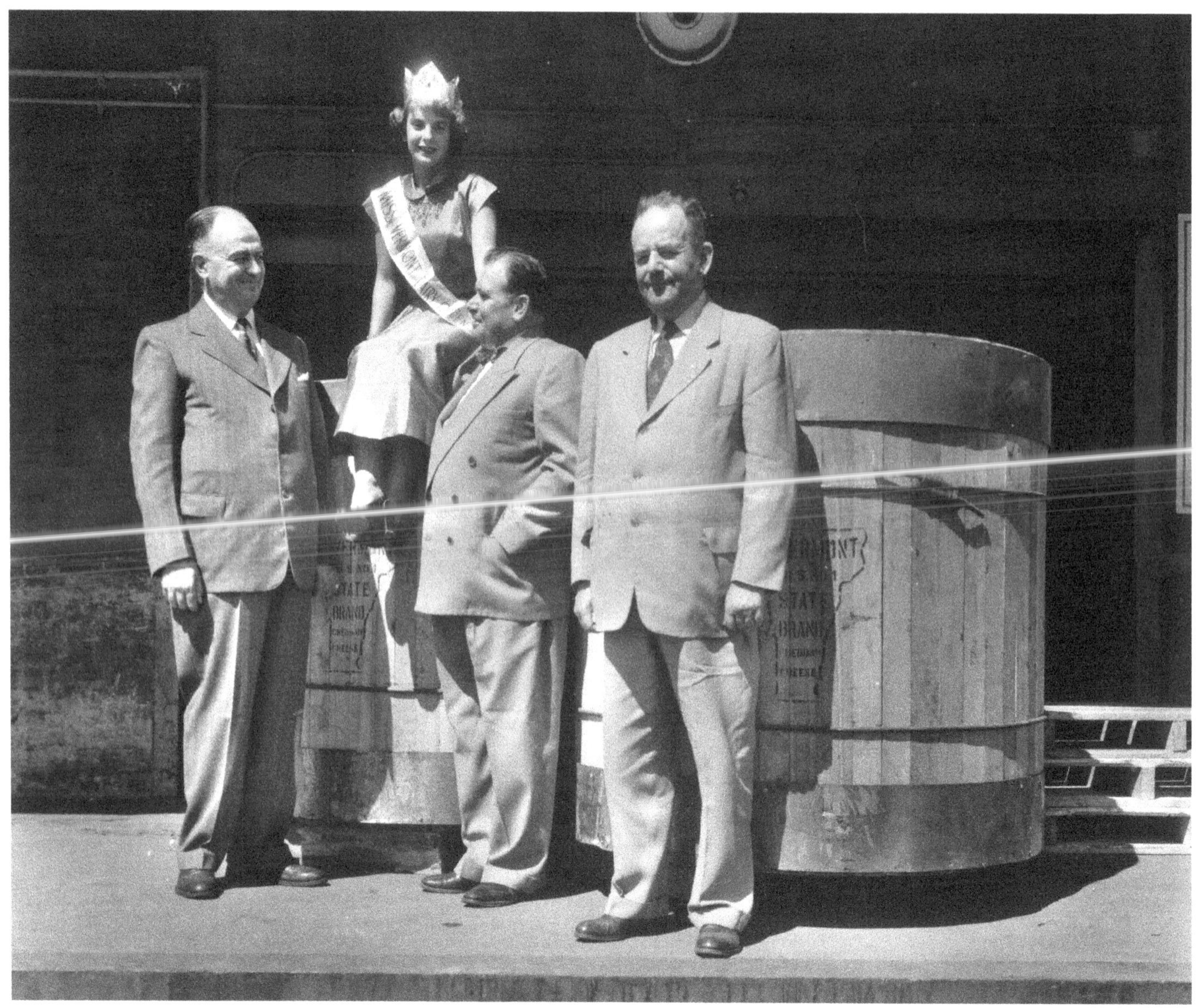

Five thousand pounds of Vermont cheddar at the Eastern States' Exposition in 1952. The exposition (the "Big E") began in Springfield, Massachusetts, in 1917 to showcase farm products and to stage competitions between producers from around New England. Employees from the Kraft Company cut the first slice of cheddar from one of these wheels, and it weighed nearly 300 pounds. Miss Vermont Dairy Queen, a young woman from Colchester, accompanied the delegation from Vermont.

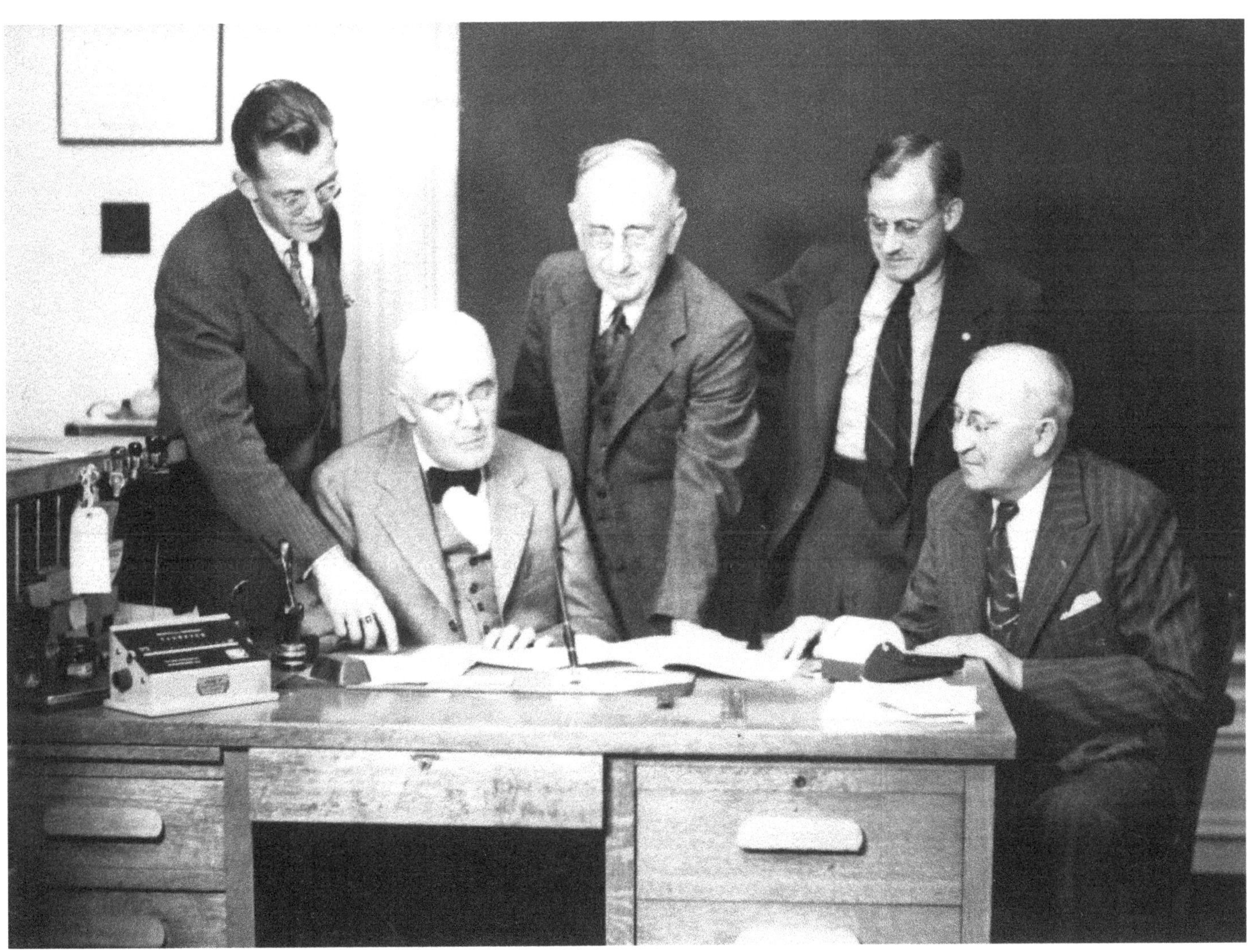

Morrisville's water and light commissioners, 1951. Morrisville provided water and electricity not only to its own residents but also to surrounding towns. Residents referred to the service as the village's "sugar daddy," particularly since out-of-towners paid higher rates. In 1934 and 1945, for example, the town enjoyed profits high enough to cover all the village's expenses—and the town's self-reliant citizens paid no taxes.

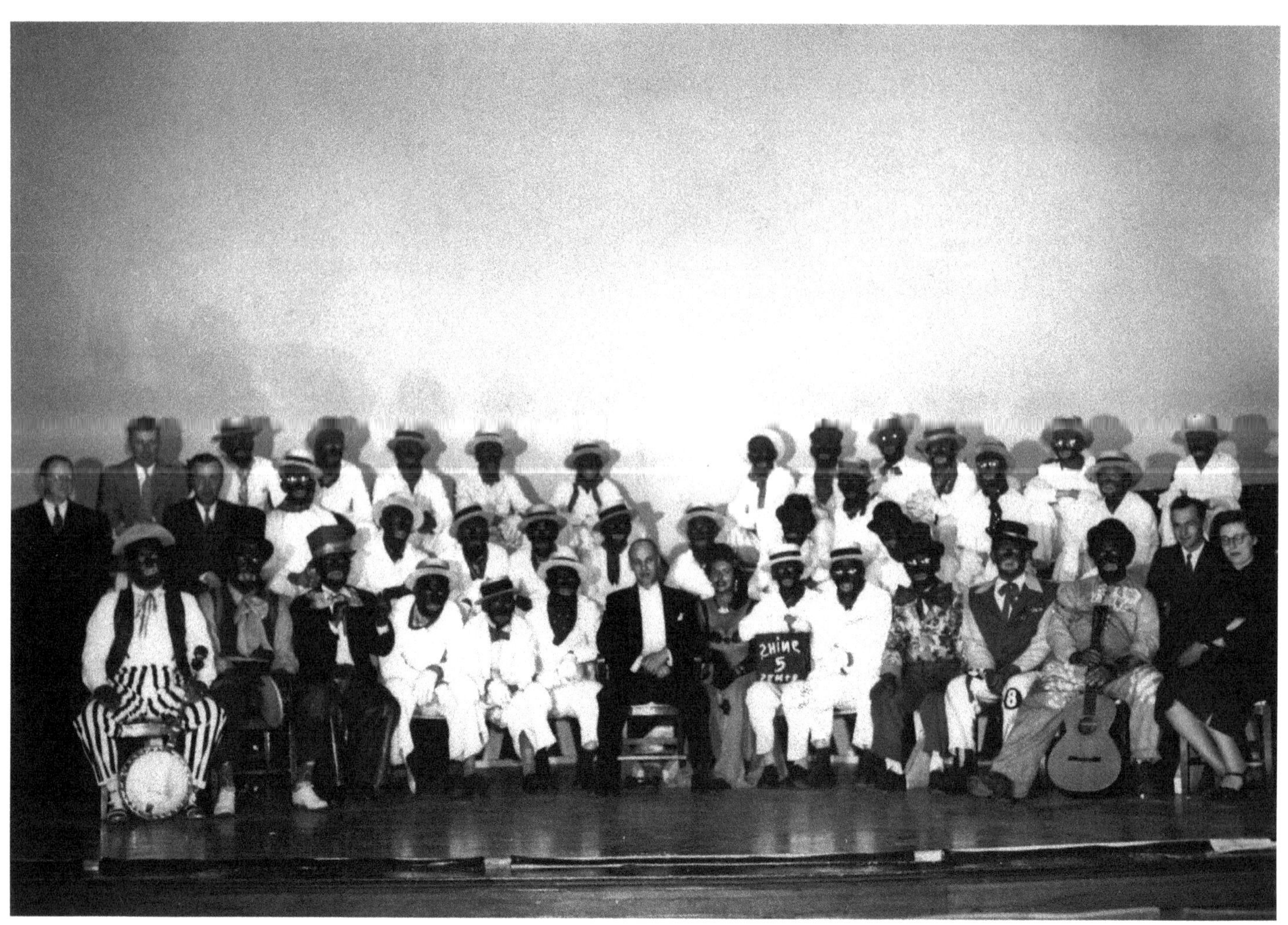

The Muddy River Minstrels perform to a packed house in Stowe in 1950. With a longstanding history of racial tensions—including an active Ku Klux Klan contingent in the 1920s—Vermont towns found audiences for minstrel shows at bandstands, opera houses, and university campuses. The University of Vermont's Kake Walk, a highly attended winter carnival event performed by students in blackface since 1893, garnered nationwide criticism in the 1960s. The performance "took the cake" for the last time in 1969.

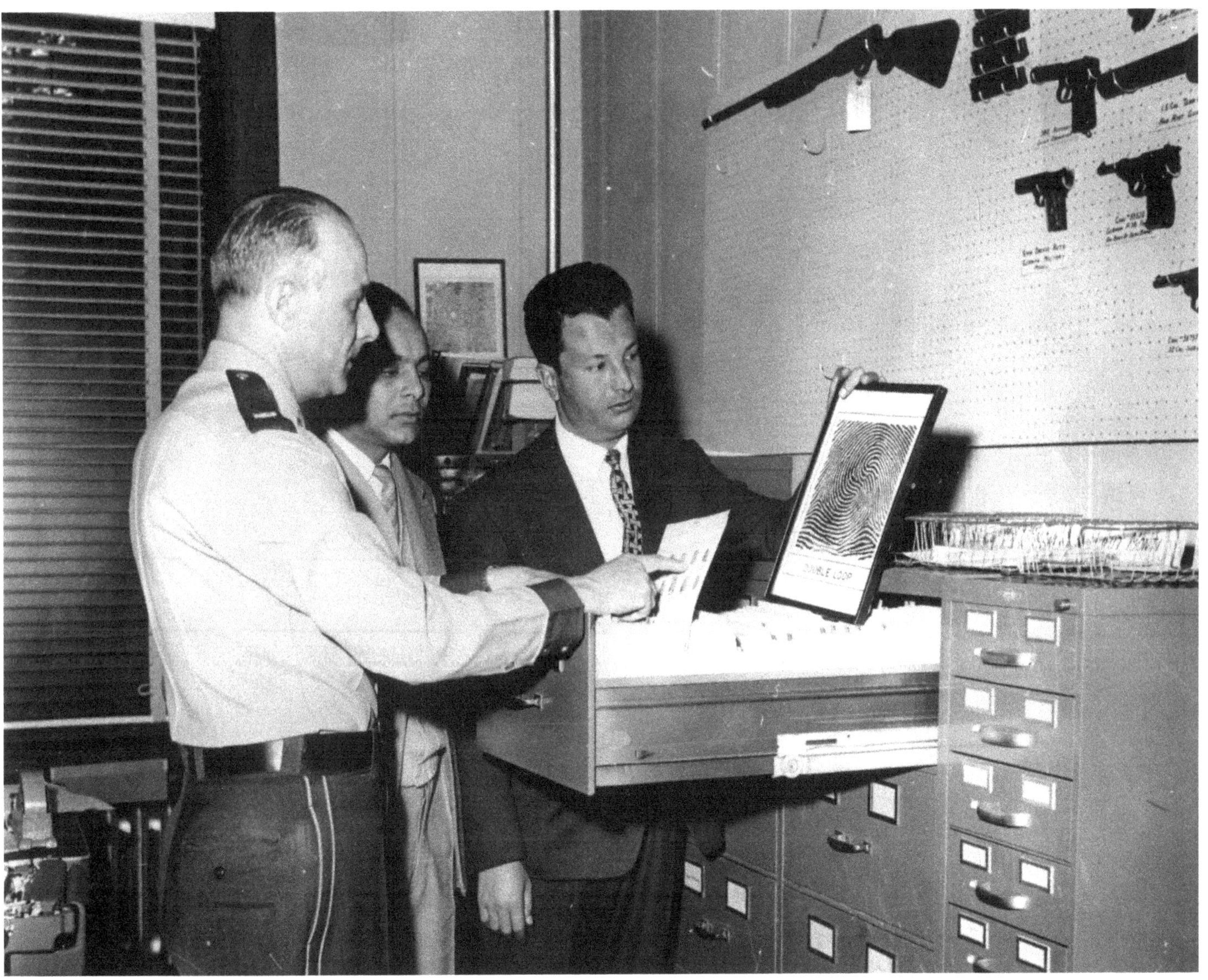

A police officer reviews a Vermont State Police fingerprinting file in 1953. New technologies such as Teletype, statewide radio, radar, and intelligence information made state police expenditures a concern to both the legislature and the public. The scrutiny was so pronounced that Governor Emerson, in office from 1951 to 1955, attempted to dissolve the newly formed state police force and fold it into the Department of Motor Vehicles.

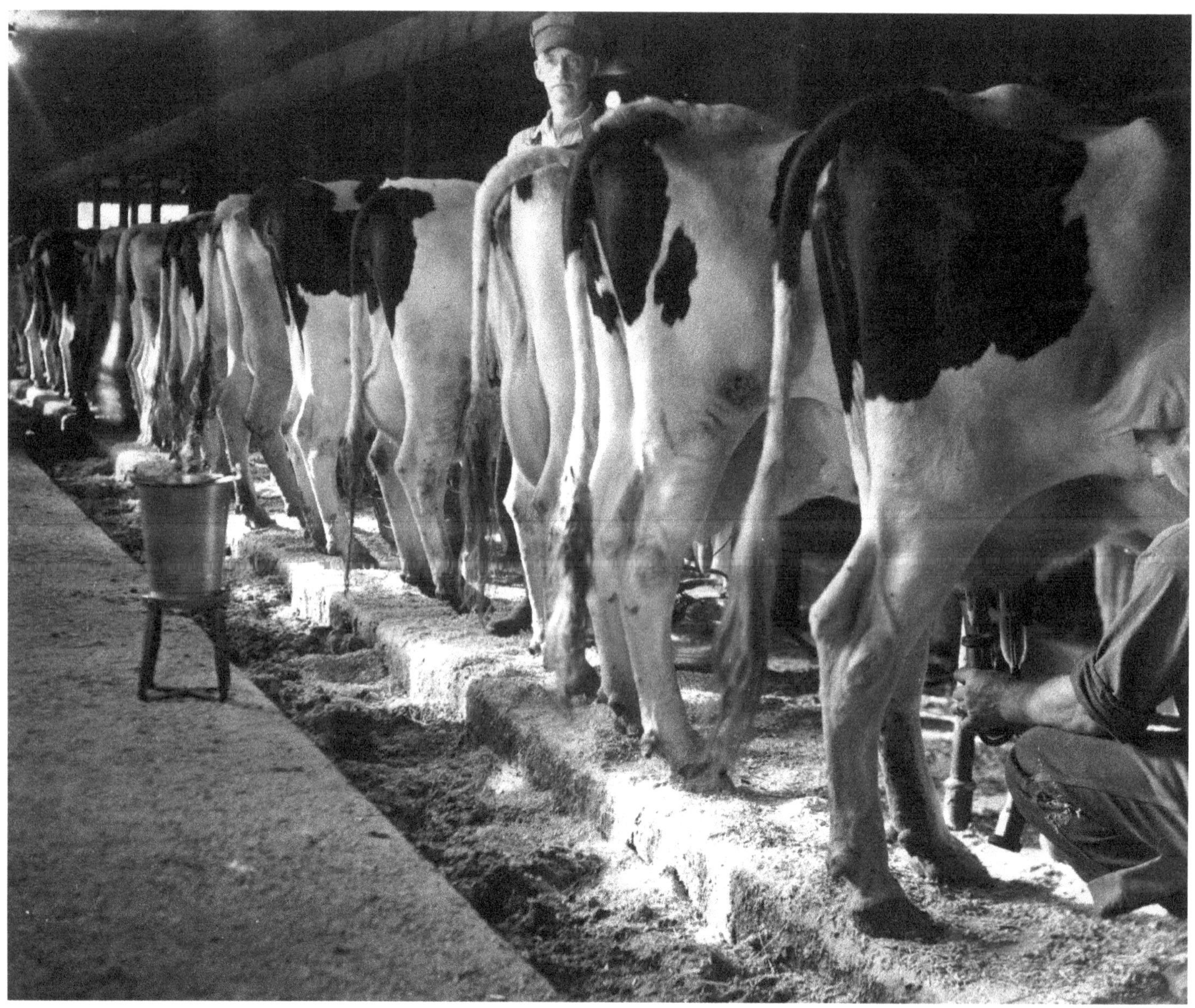

Throughout the nineteenth century and into the twentieth, a large herd for a dairy farmer consisted of roughly 20 cows. On average the farmer needed four hours daily to milk the herd. With the advent of rural electrification, farmers took advantage of milking machines and could now spend considerably less time milking. Mechanized milking machines, tractors, and automatic gutter cleaners also allowed individual farmers to increase their herd sizes to roughly 60 animals.

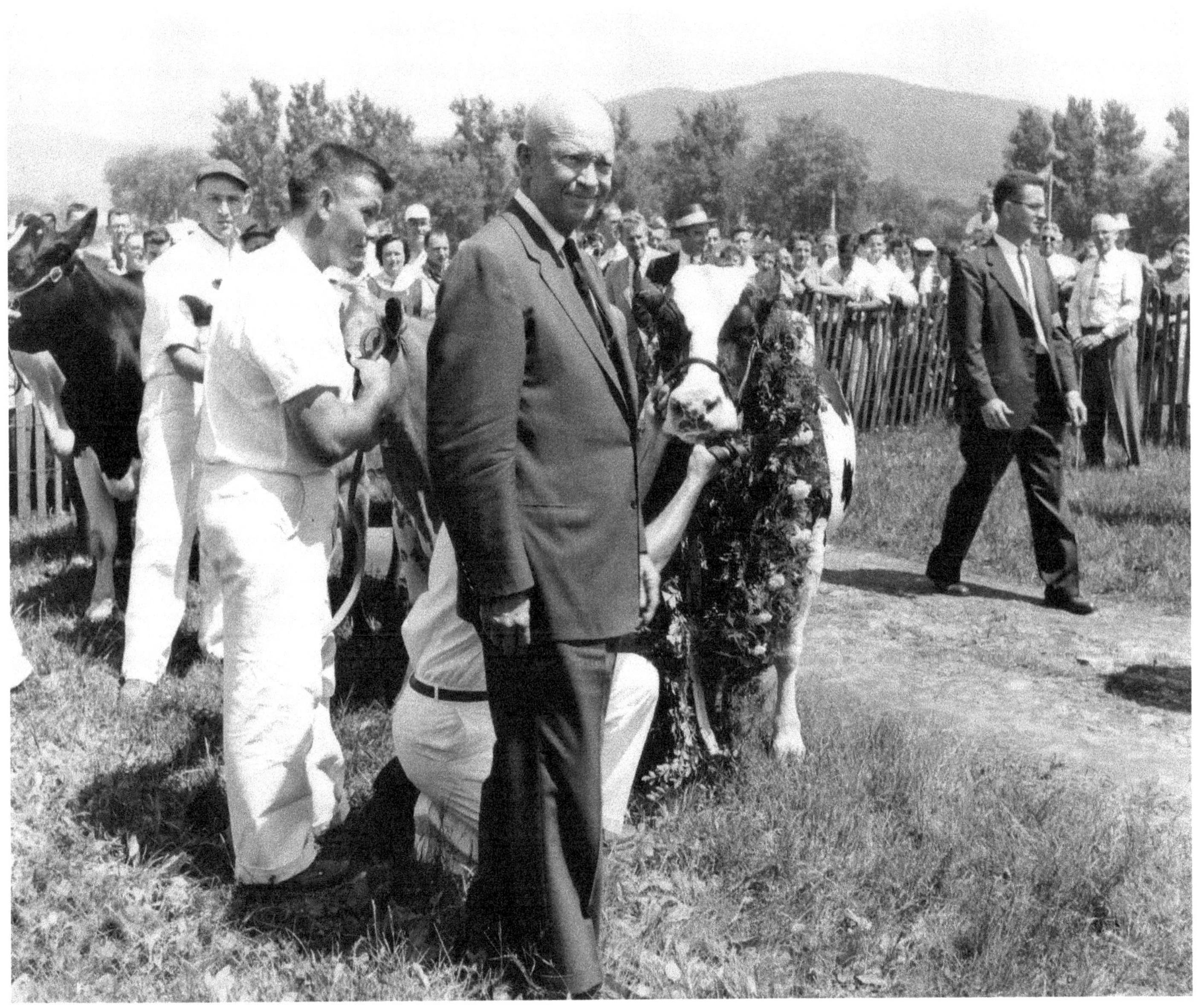

President Dwight Eisenhower at the first Vermont Dairy Festival in Rutland, 1955. Rutland hosted 50,000 visitors at this festival, to which the *Rutland Herald* noted that admission was free provided "you don't eat." President Eisenhower's visit was the highlight. Vermont Agriculture Commissioner Elmer Towne beat six other agriculture commissioners in the milking contest, and Eisenhower received a gift from the festival organizers when he arrived: a heifer that was shipped to his Pennsylvania farm.

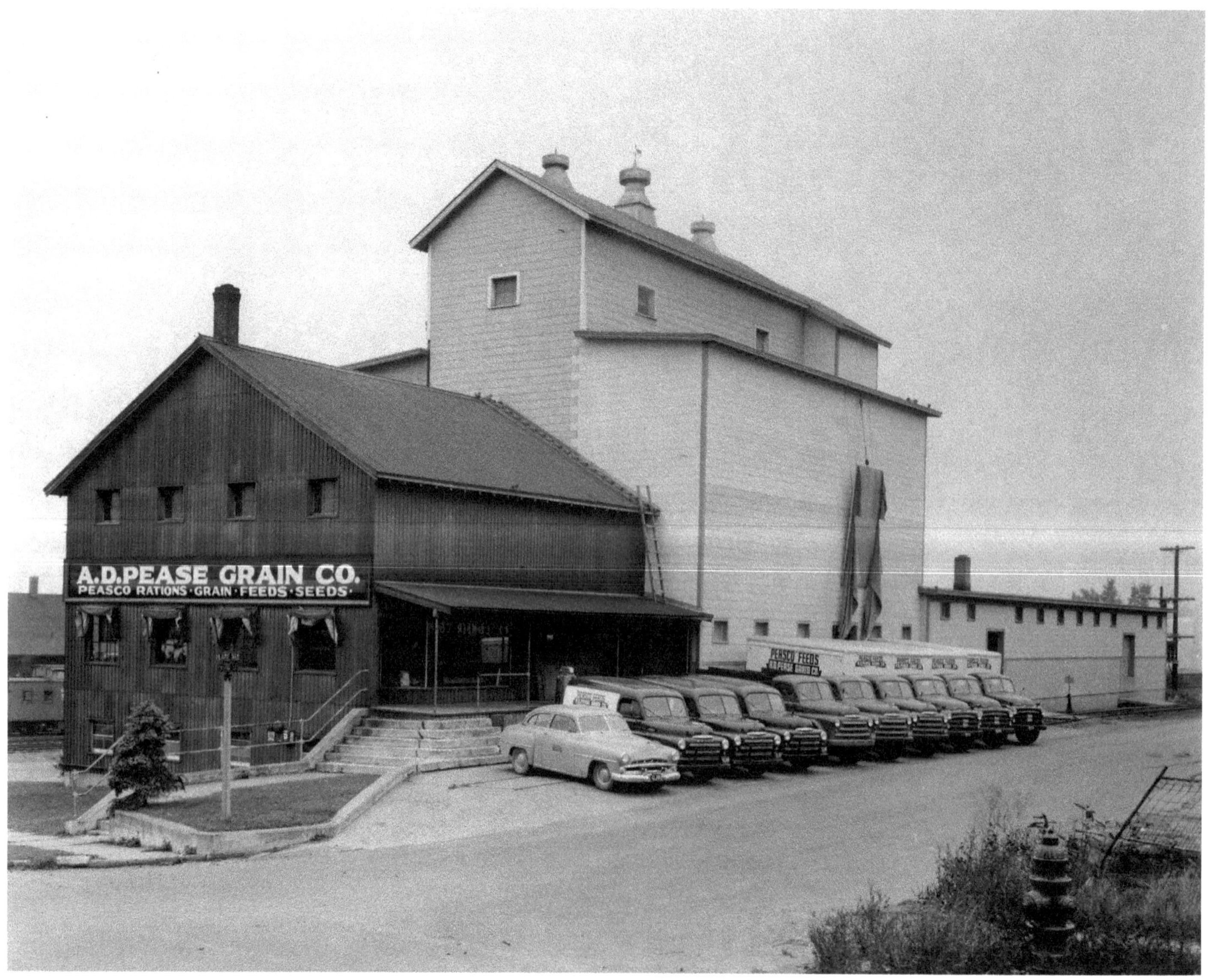

Pease Grain Company, Burlington. By the twentieth century, it had become more economical to ship livestock feed from the western United States than to produce it locally. Formerly located at 217 College Street, the Charles P. Smith Feed Company became the company of A. D. Pease around 1910. Eventually Pease Grain relocated to the corner of College and Lake streets, an advantageous location near the railroad.

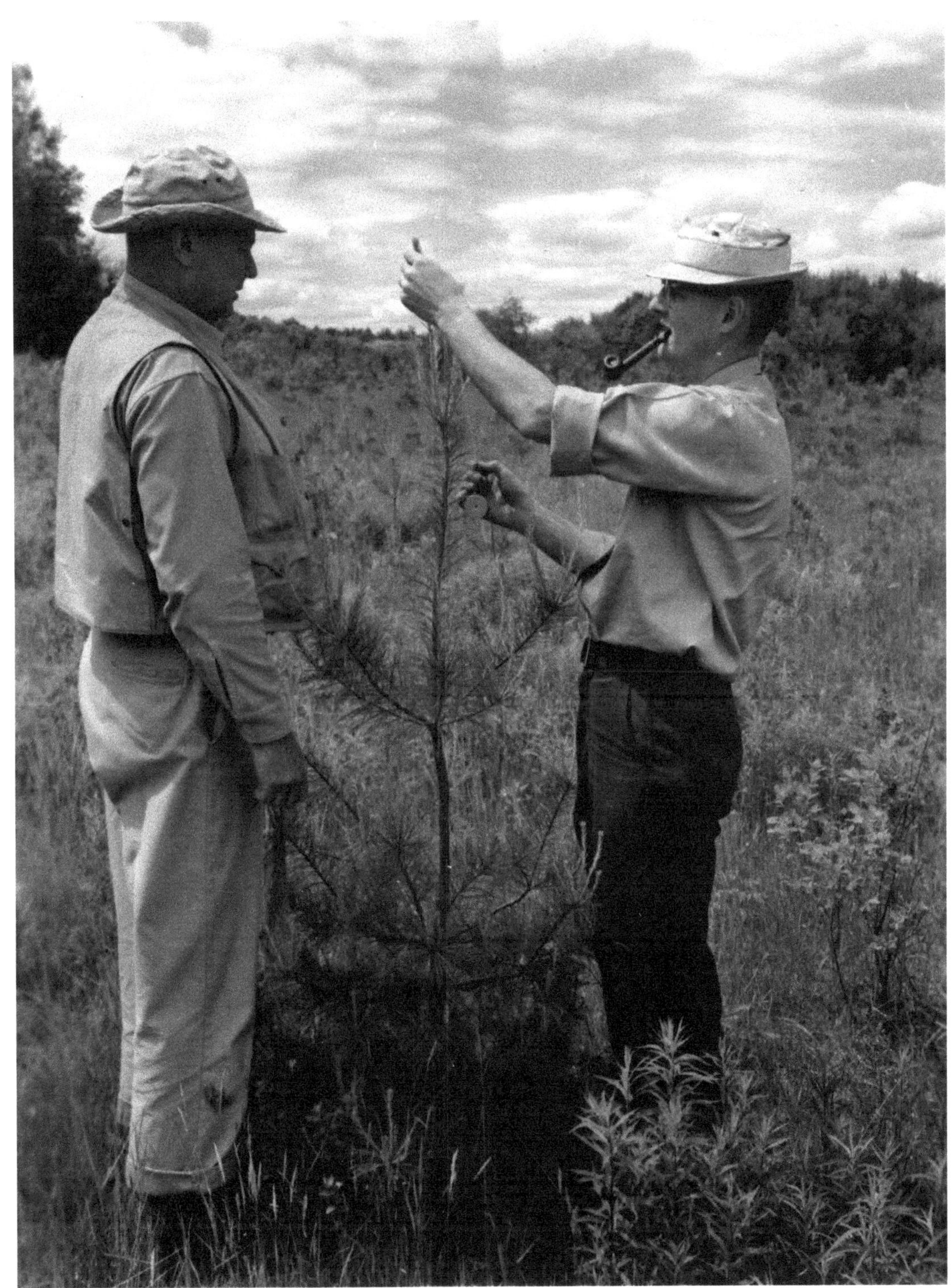

After military service in Korea and Germany, including work as a World War II spy, Arlo Sterner moved to Vermont and became Lamoille County's forester. Beginning in the 1950s, Sterner employed forest management practices at the Morrisville Village Forest, a 5,400-acre municipally controlled tract of land at Green River Reservoir. The forest protected surrounding lands from flooding and erosion. Sterner's work illustrates the steadily increasing role of the state in managing Vermont's natural resources.

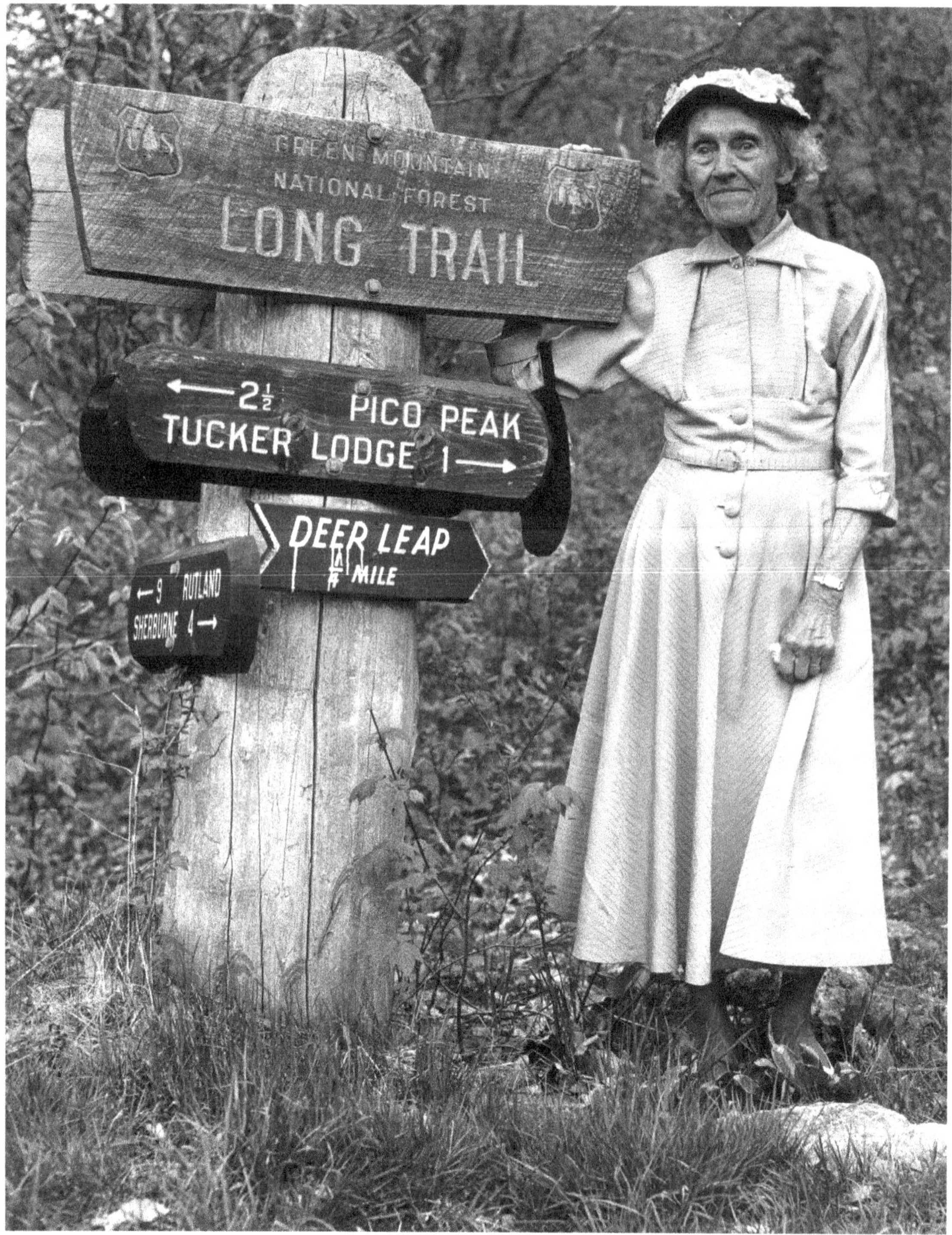

In 1910, Green Mountain Club founder James Taylor proposed a trail that could be enjoyed primarily by Vermonters. Once the trail was blazed, club members debated what colors to use for the trail markers that would be nailed to trees: the Appalachian Mountain Club recommended white, yellow, or blue markers, but discouraged red ones—while the Bennington group preferred red to all others. Volunteers donated tin can bottoms to test different marker sizes.

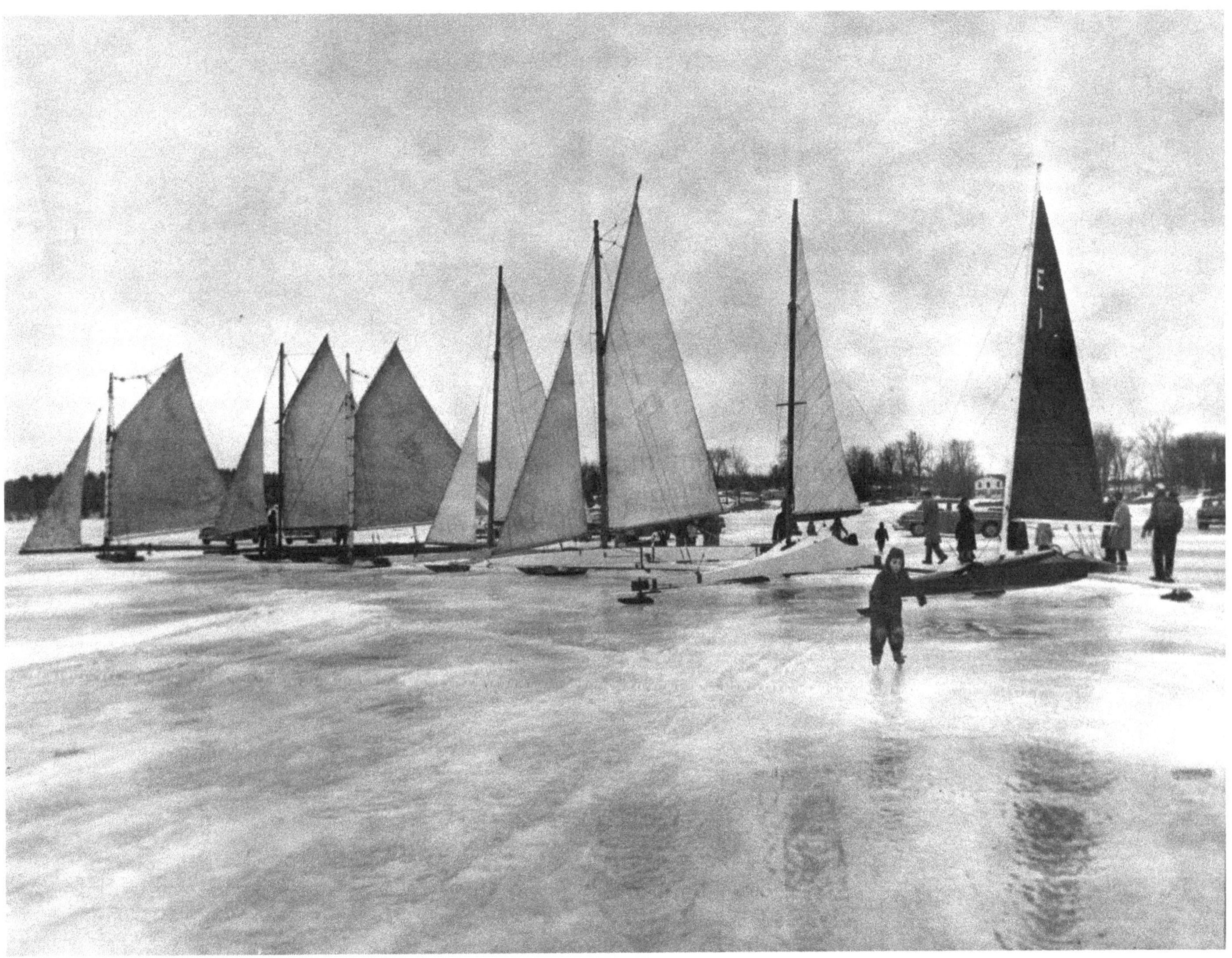

An 1881 newspaper proclaimed ice-boating to be the most "exhilarating winter sport" and Lake Champlain an "unsurpassed" venue for this pastime. Some families used iceboats for more than just pleasure sailing—fishing families transported their catch back home using the conveyance. Ice-boating clubs sprang up in the early 1900s, becoming very popular by the 1950s. In heavy winds, boat speeds can exceed 60 miles per hour.

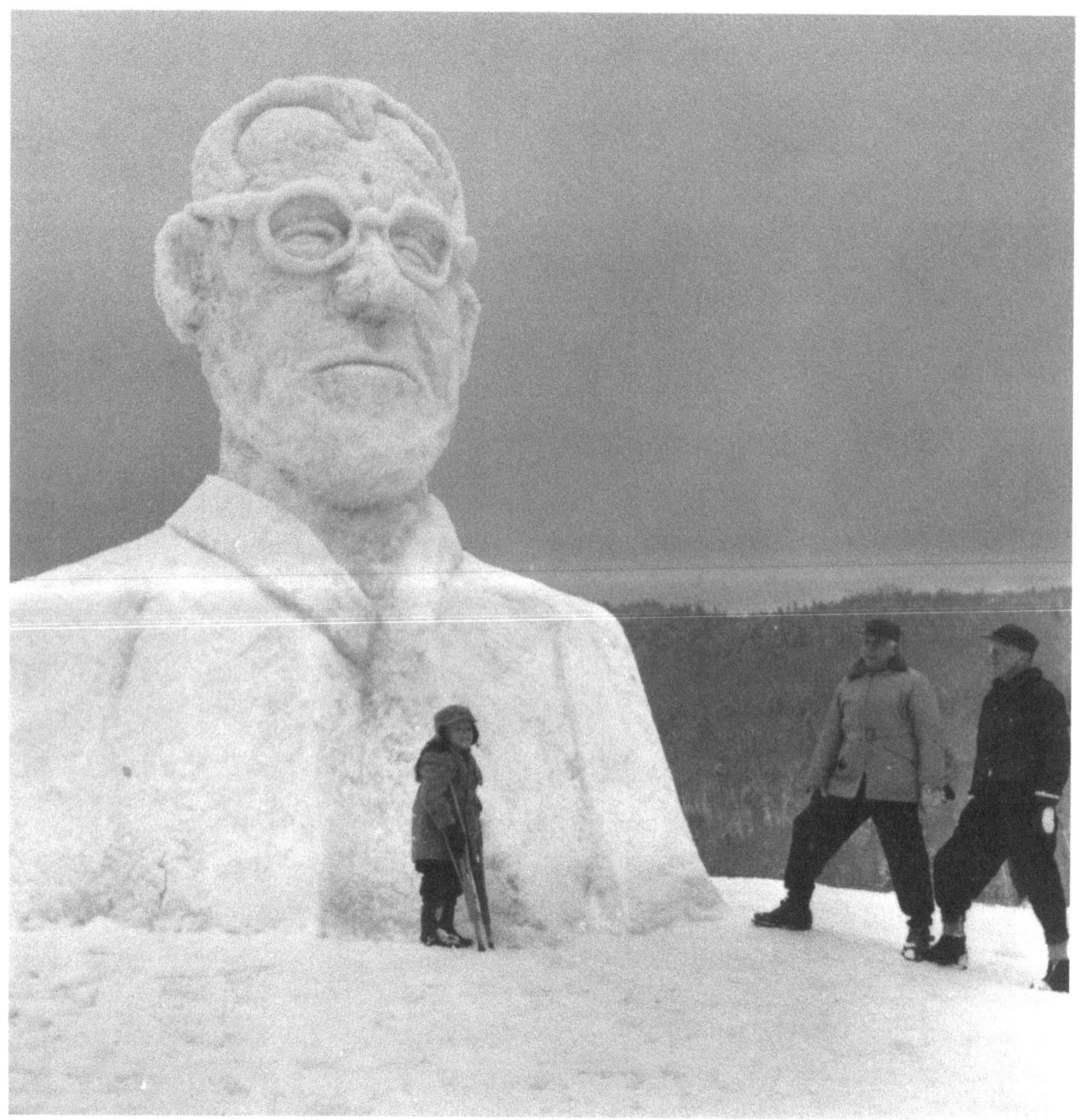

March of Dimes kickoff party on Mount Mansfield, 1956. In 1894, Vermont became the first state to experience a polio epidemic, with 132 cases diagnosed in Rutland County. The boy standing in front of the snow sculpture is the March of Dimes poster boy and the last person to contract the disease. The sculpture represents Jonas Salk, the developer of the polio vaccine in 1954.

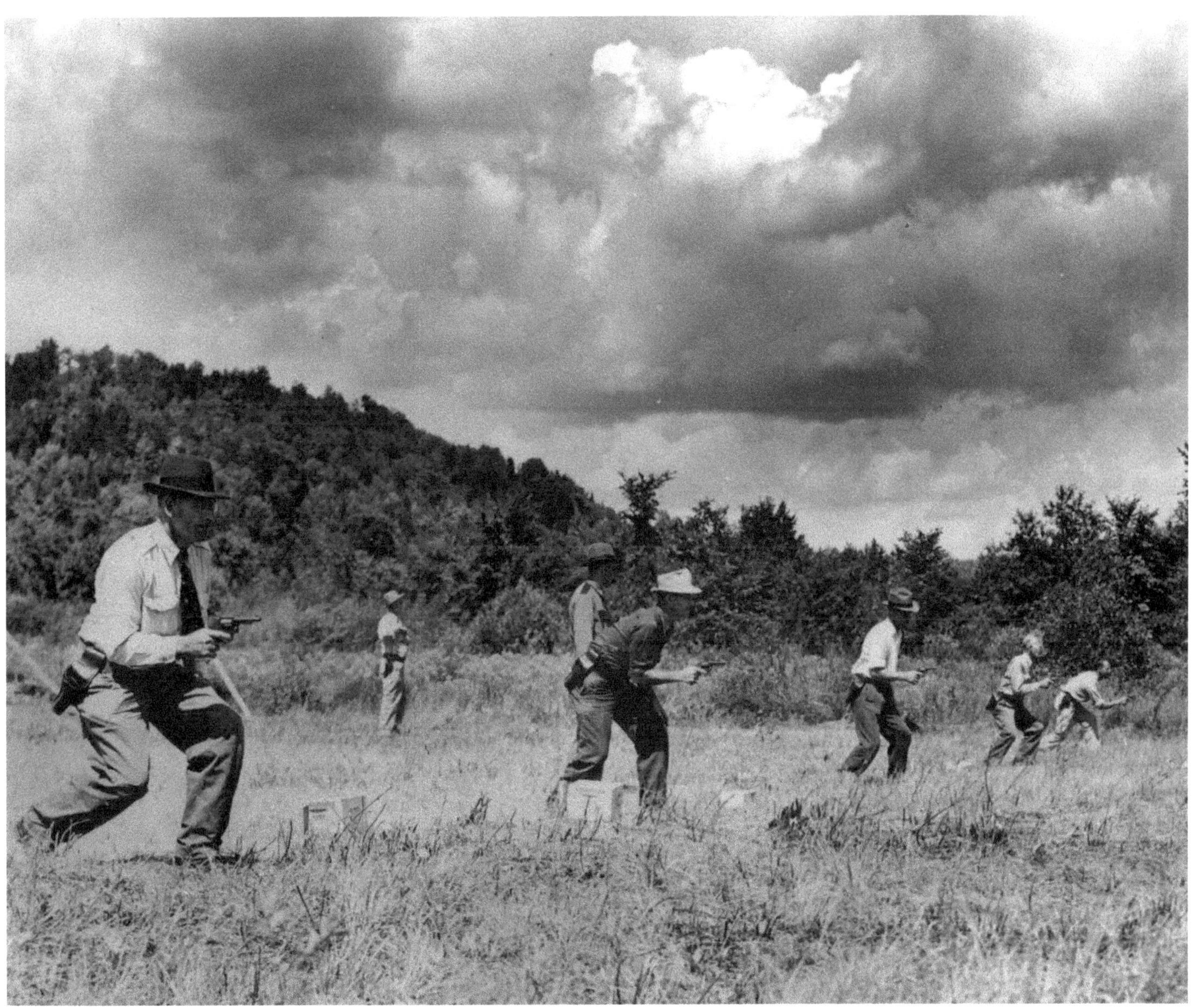

Freeze! State police participate in a firearms training class in 1956. The first wave of 55 state troopers attended a four-week training course coordinated by the Training Division's single staff member. Within two years, the Vermont State Police Training School had opened, and the training program had expanded from four weeks to four months. Housed at the Weeks School in Vergennes, 22 recruits entered the program and 16 graduated.

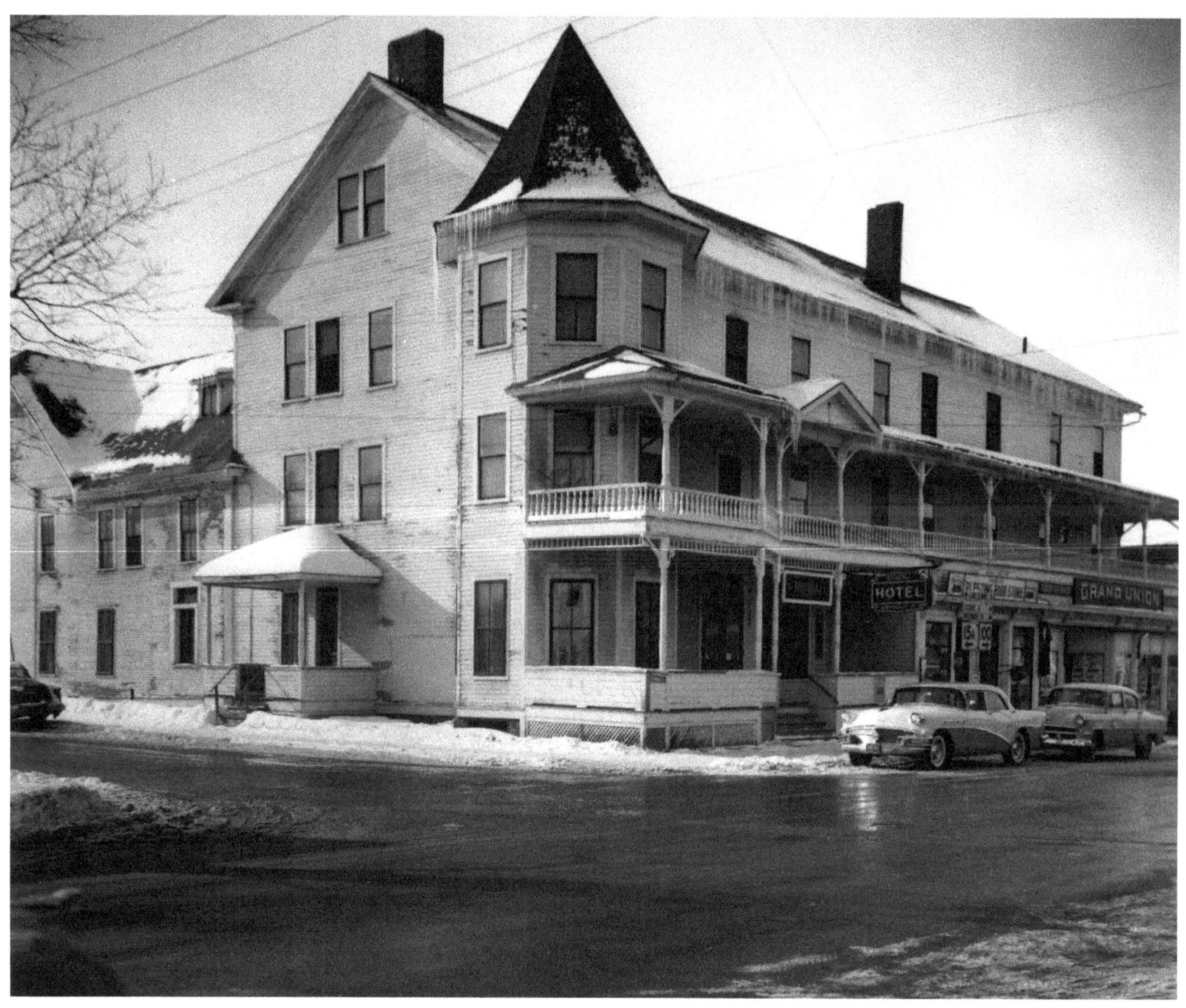

The Randall Hotel the year it was demolished, 1956. Erected during an economic boom in the early 1890s, the Randall Hotel was a centerpiece of Morrisville life. The inn served as a telephone office, celebration place for the World War I armistice, short-term living quarters for Vermont's chief justice, and the regular meeting place for the Rotary Club. Today a filling station stands on the site.

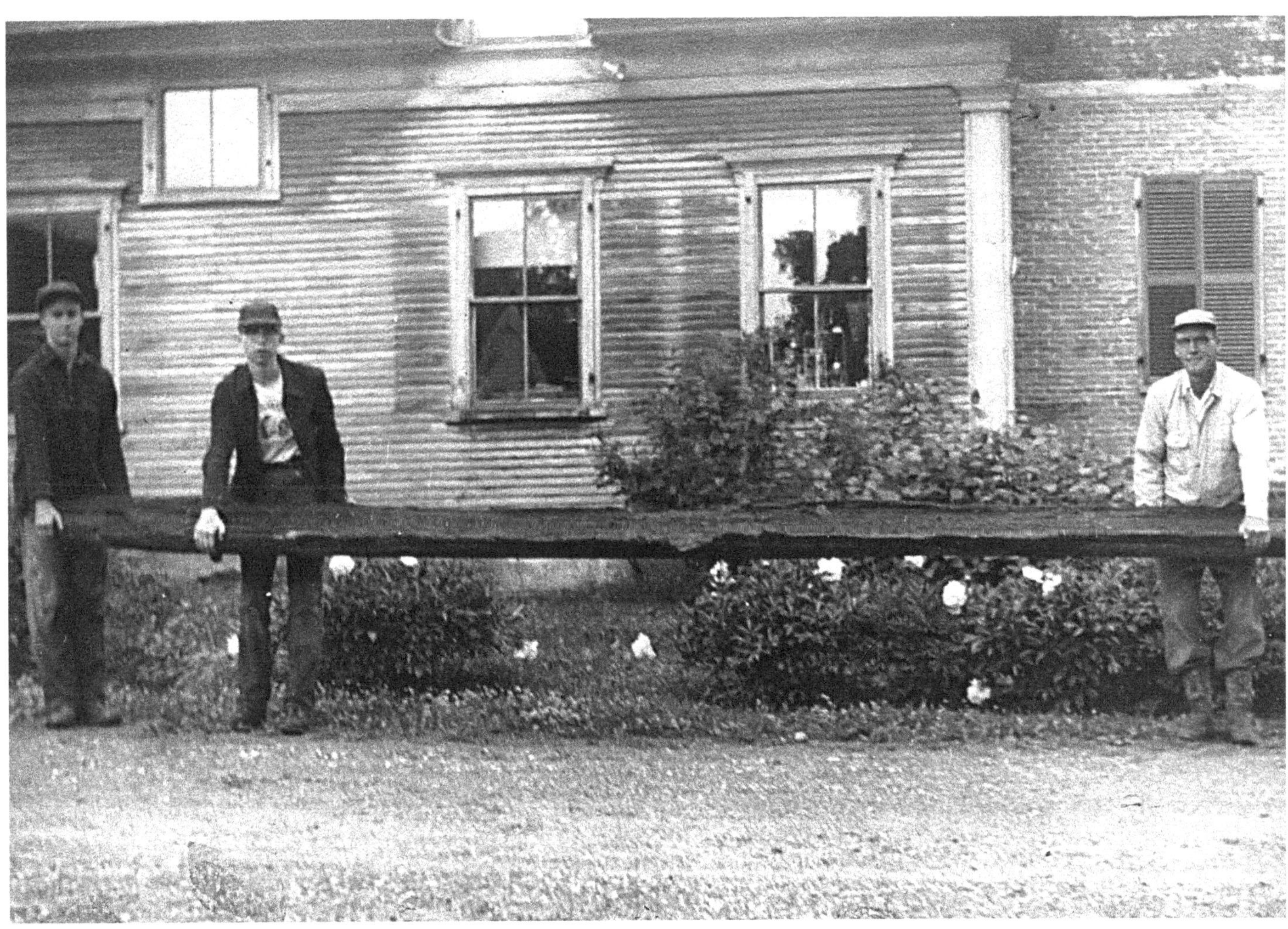

In 1956, three Lamoille County residents recovered this dugout canoe from Joe's Pond in Morristown. The vessel likely once belonged to Indian Joe and Molly, members of the Canadian Micmac who lived many years in exile in the Lamoille Valley. Joe acted as a scout during the Revolutionary War and was honored for his service by dinner with George Washington. Here the canoe is shown at Morristown's Noyes House Museum where it remains on display today.

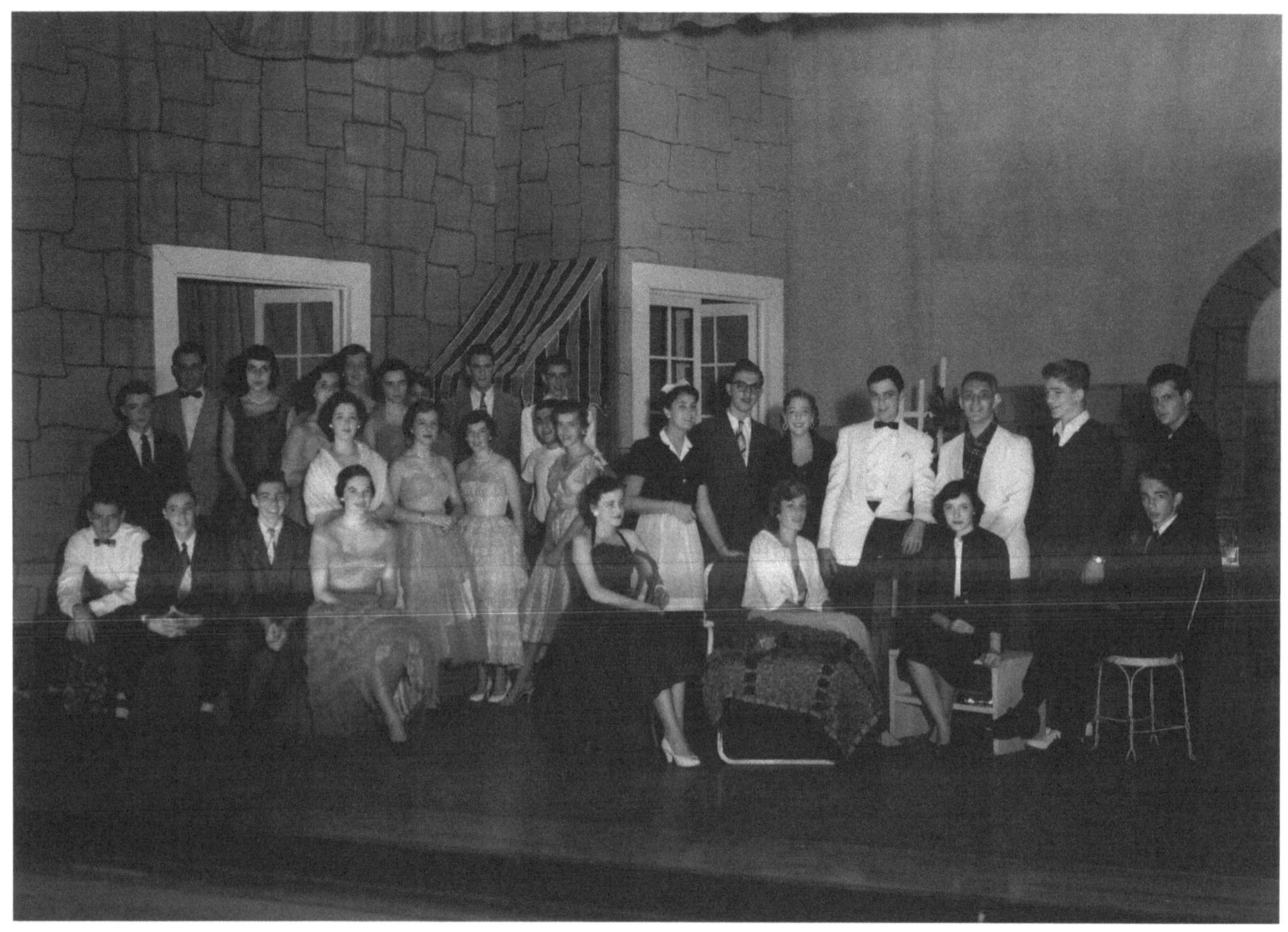

Theater production of *Sabrina Fair* at Burlington High School, 1956. Students from Burlington High School, located in the Edmunds building on Main Street until the 1960s, spent "many a lunch" eating ham-and-dill sandwiches at Mr. Farmer's shop on College Street. Reminiscing 50 years later, one graduate recalled how she and her friends gathered to read plays like *Hedda Gabler,* which she added, "I'm not sure we understood, but [we] had a great time."

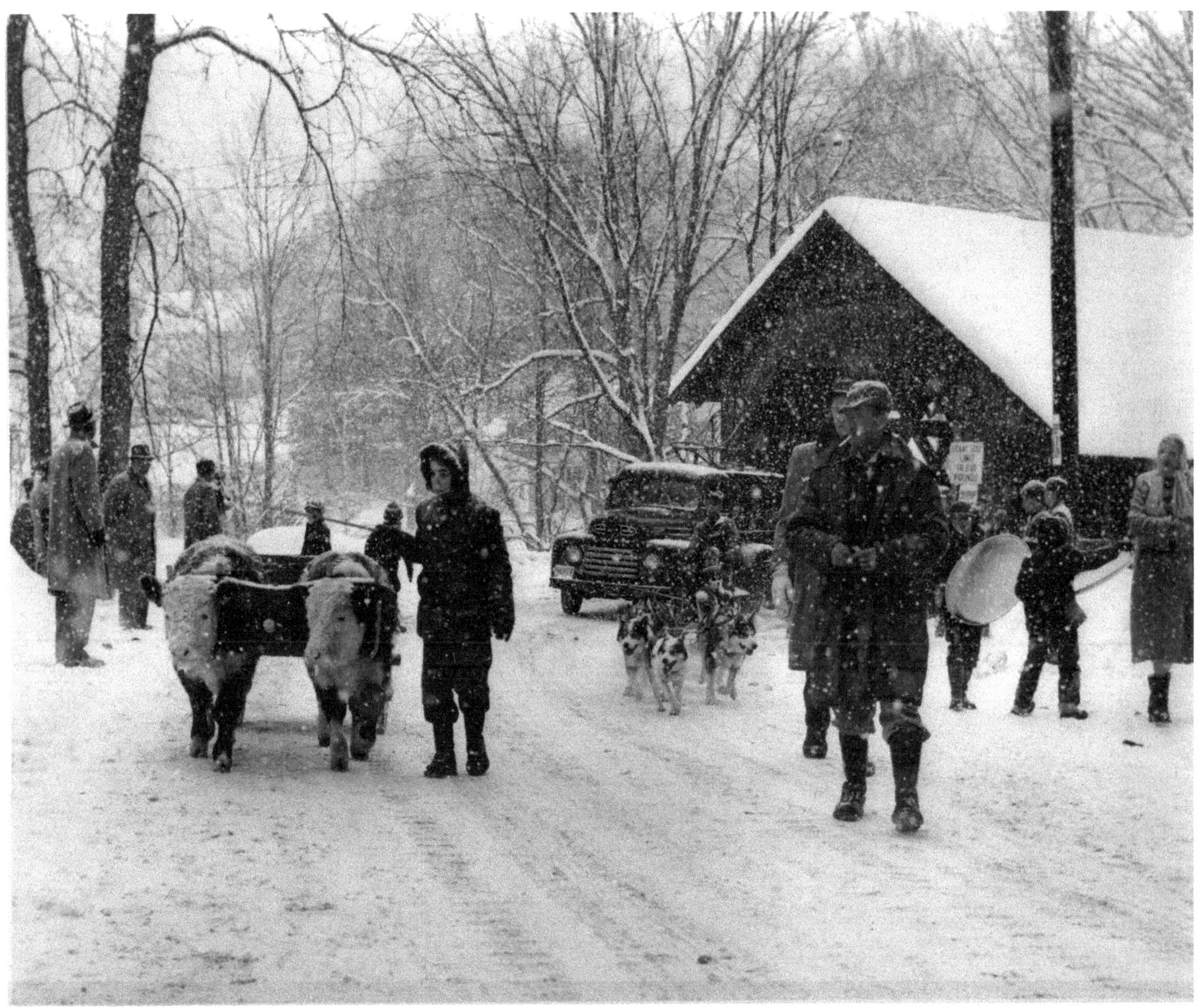

The All-America City Award Parade in Brattleboro, 1957. Honored for its municipally funded Living Memorial Park, Brattleboro is the only Vermont town ever to win this award. Festivities included 13 speakers and a procession of floats, including a Green Mountain Club entry with its own campfire. After the parade, children competed in skating competitions, uphill-downhill races, and more. The newspaper ran a special multi-page insert and reminded town residents, "This is *your* party."

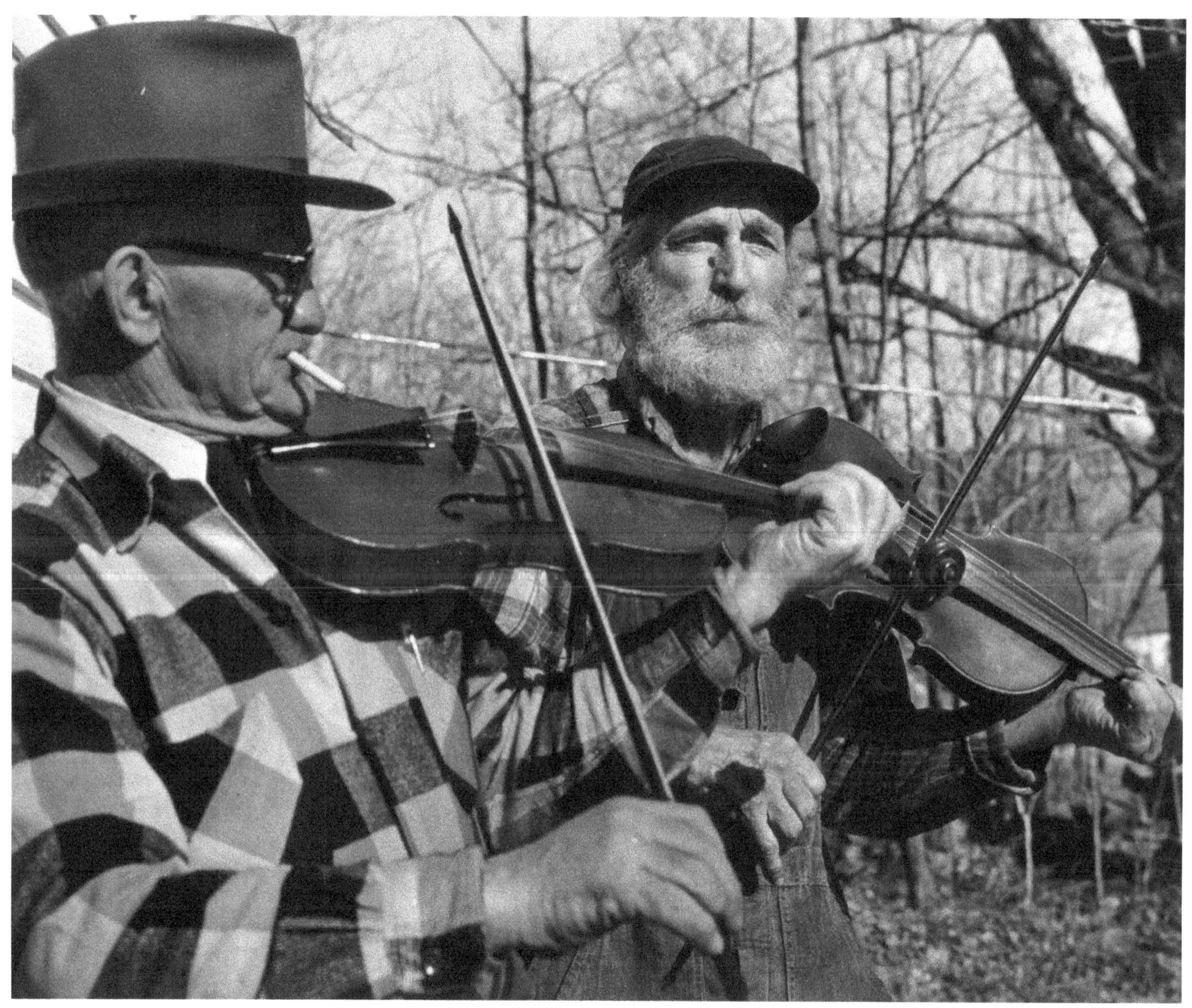

Fiddlers in Shrewsbury, 1957. From the "kitchen junket" to the barn dance, rural Vermont has provided a welcome home for folk music. Because the popularity of traditional fiddling had fallen off at midcentury, a revival was staged in the 1960s by a number of Vermont musicians. In 1965, staffers from Goddard College, along with Barre fiddler Clem Myers, helped to initiate the Northeast Fiddlers Association. They held their first event the following year in Hardwick.

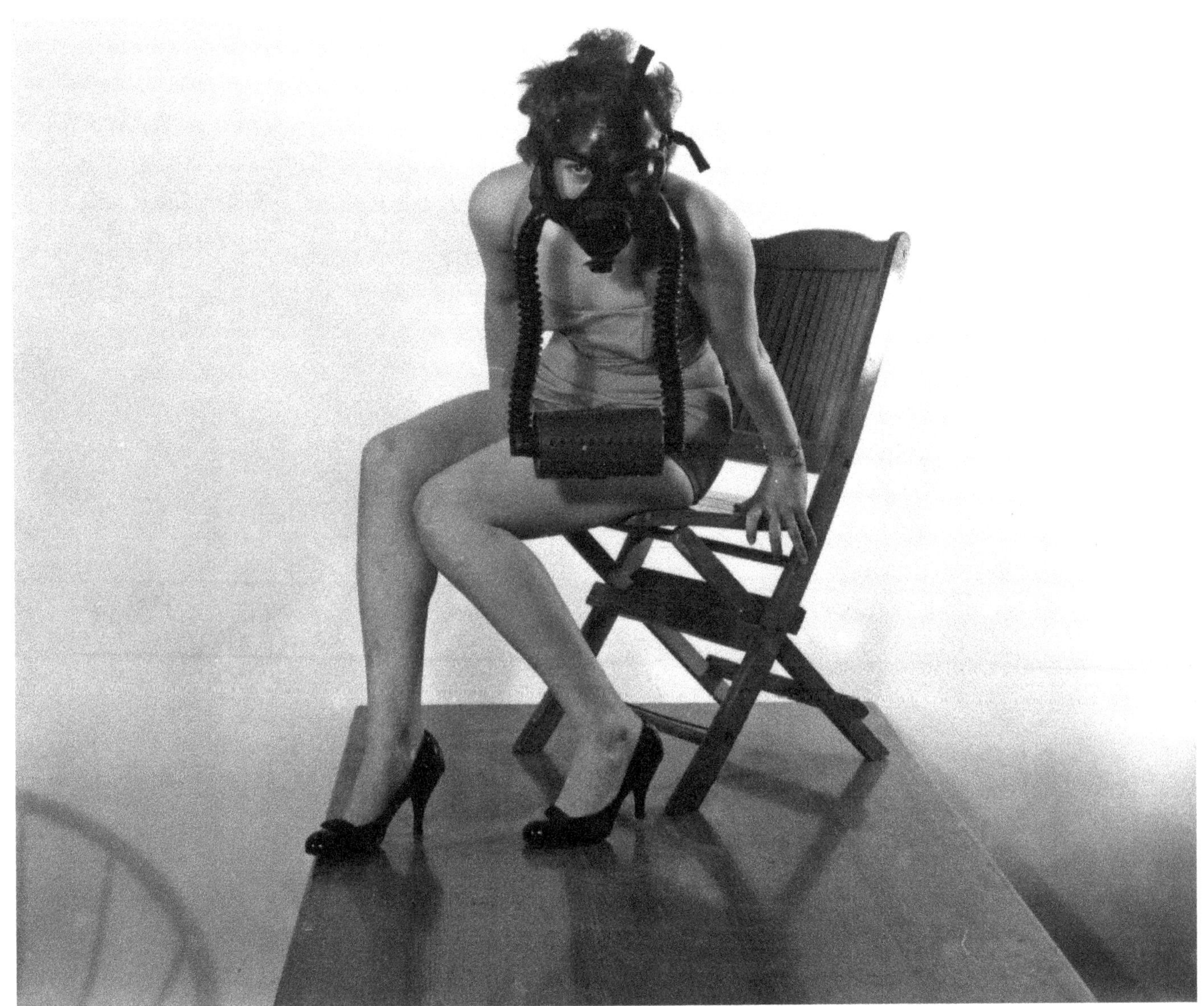

What was the photographer thinking? Clearly more inspired by fashion photography than by government literature, this photograph shows a model demonstrating a gas mask in 1958. Vermont did not escape repercussions of the cold war, which included accusations of communism directed at one University of Vermont professor and two former federal officials who owned property in the state. Barnet-born Senator Ralph Flanders compared communist-hunting Joseph McCarthy to the cartoon character Dennis the Menace, accusing him of dividing the nation, and finally calling for government censure of the Wisconsin senator. "In every country in which communism has taken over," he stated, "the beginning has been a successful campaign of division and confusion." Added Flanders, "One of the characteristic elements of communist and fascist tyranny is at hand as citizens are set to spy upon each other. . . . Were the junior Senator from Wisconsin in the pay of the communists, he could not have done a better job for them."

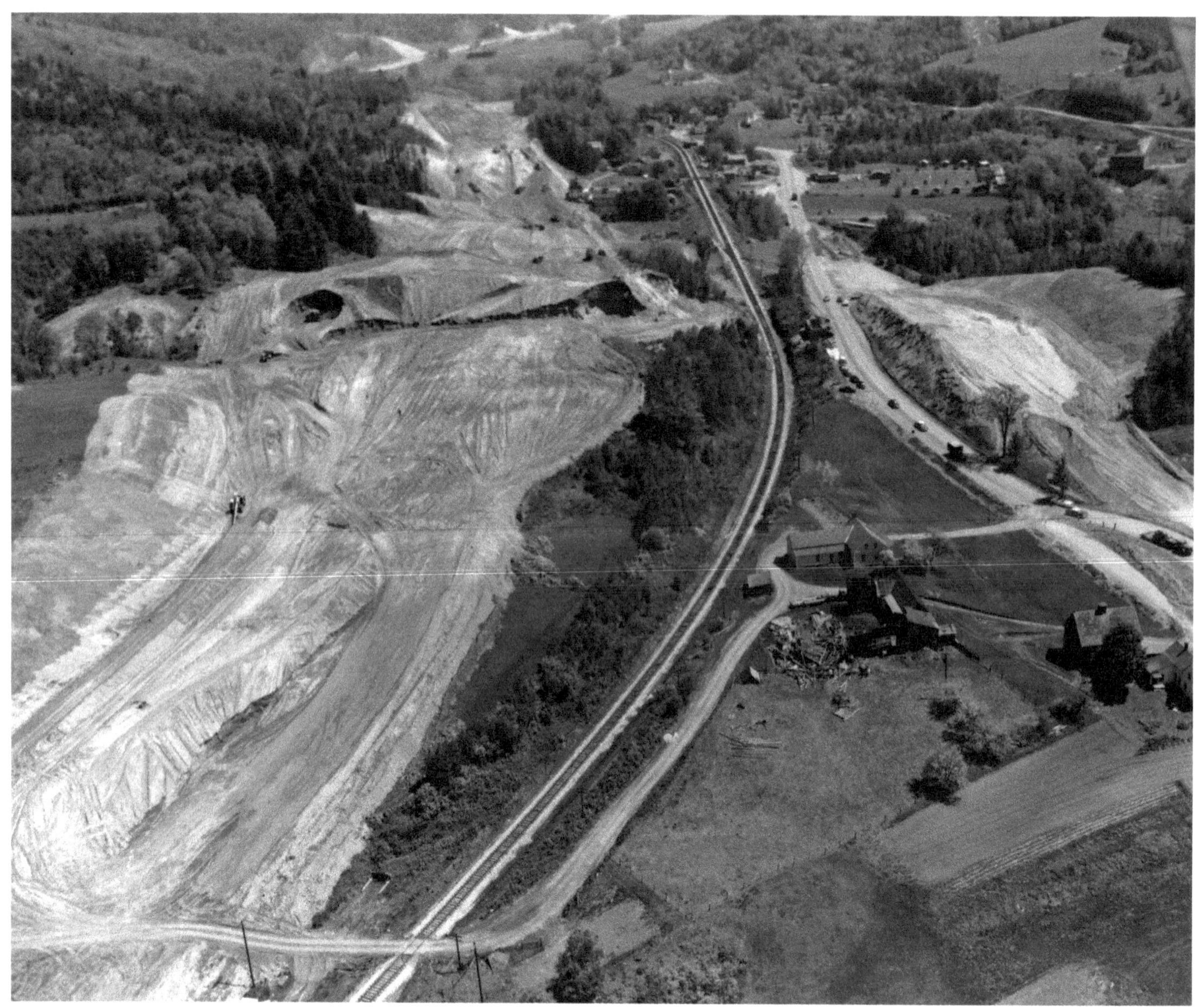

Construction of Vermont's interstate highway system cost roughly $1 million a mile. Many Vermonters resisted the project, and some felt betrayed by a state government that had once promised not to trade "one acre of good farmland" for development. With a total of 381 miles of four-lane highway, the project displaced many people from their homes, including Romaine Tenney. The Weathersfield resident burned his 150-year-old family farm—with himself inside—to avoid being forced to watch his home destroyed by the encroaching highway project.

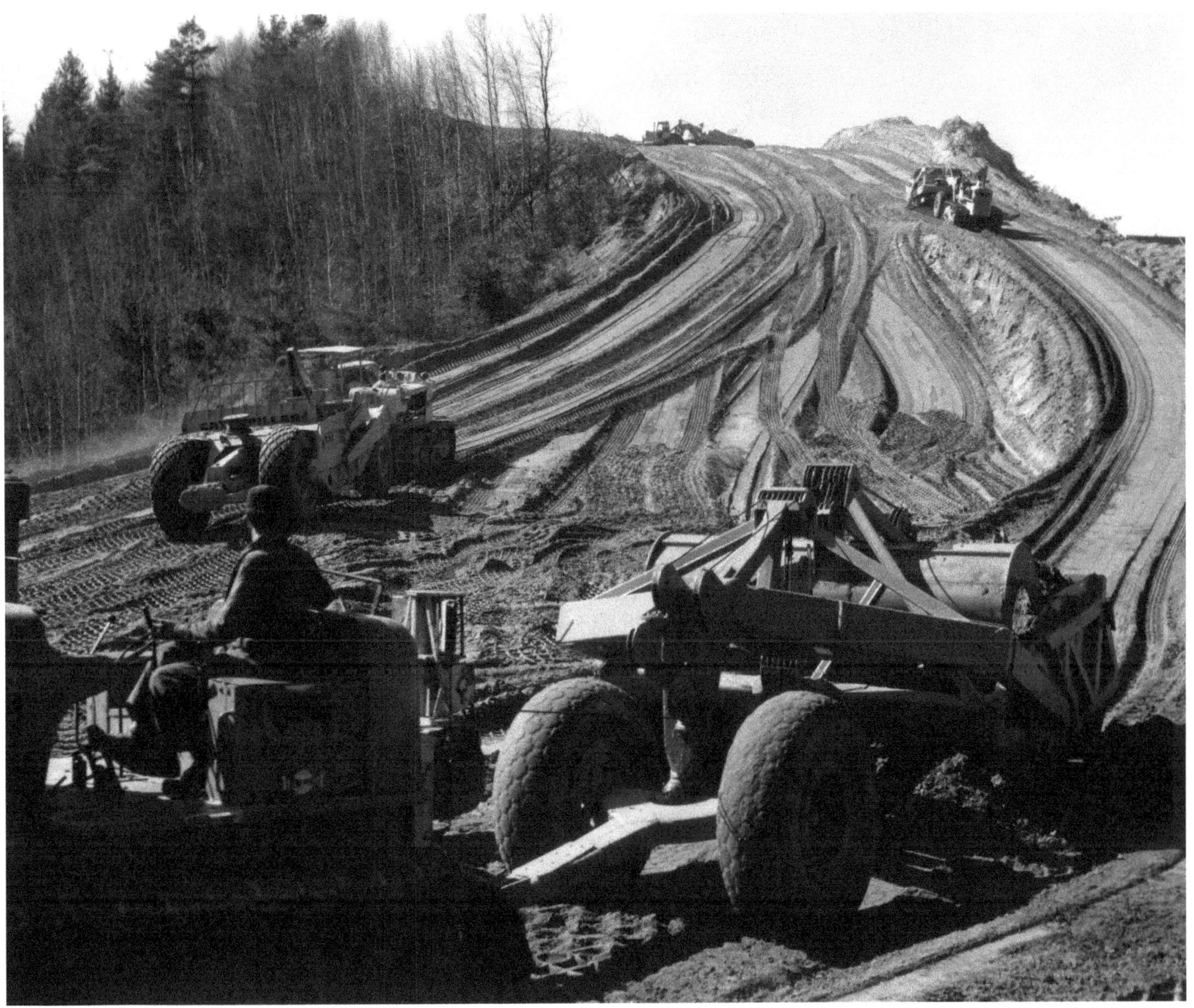

Interstate 89 construction near Middlesex, 1959. Begun in 1957, the Interstate Highway Program provided easy access to larger communities within the state. The program also stimulated the construction of many local roads, which improved travel within rural communities. The new transportation corridors fostered economic development, a housing explosion, and tourism. Many out-of-staters who purchased second homes in Vermont soon decided to become permanent residents, prompting a population boom within a decade.

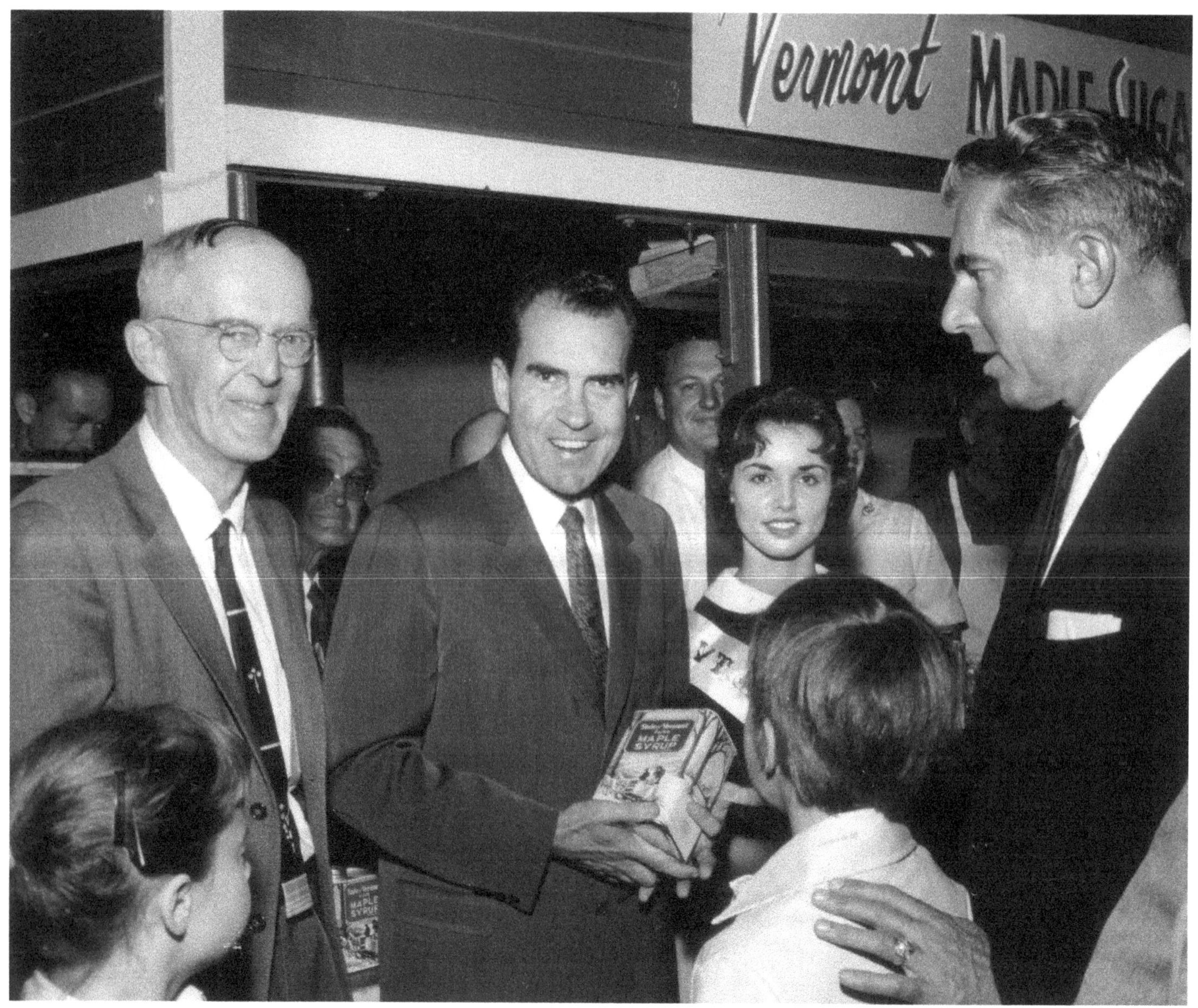

Vice-president Richard Nixon with Governor Robert Stafford (at right) around 1959. Stafford and Nixon were both campaigning for federal office in 1960: Stafford for the U.S. Senate and Nixon for the presidency against John F. Kennedy. When Nixon came to Burlington in September 1959, the *Burlington Free Press* reminded its readers that he was the first Republican presidential candidate to visit "this most Republican of all states" since 1912. Nixon is holding a can of State of Vermont Pure Maple Syrup.

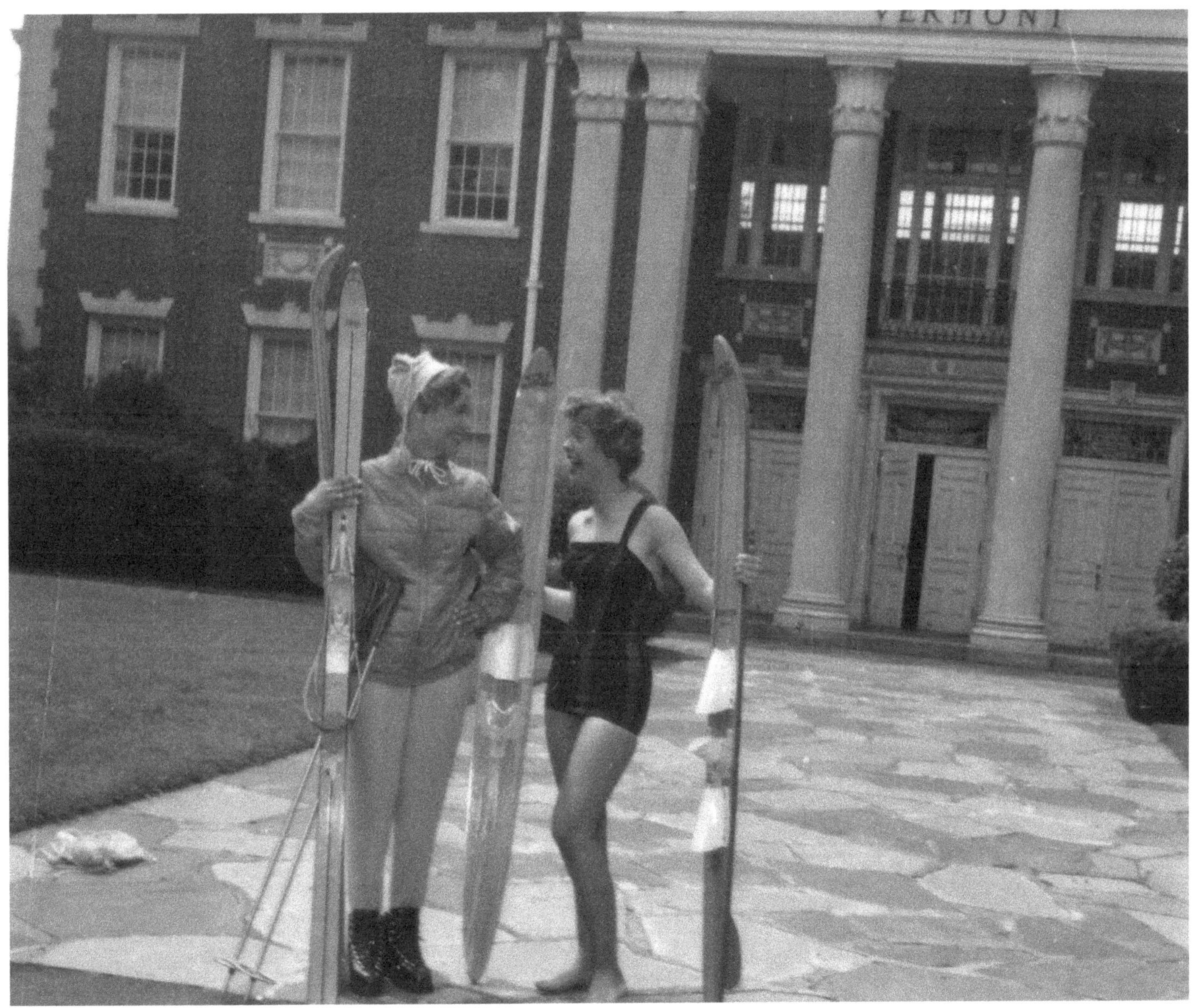

Twins model Vermont's vacation possibilities at the Eastern States Exposition in 1960. The exposition's Avenue of the States included a replica of the Boston State House and buildings to represent all of the New England states. In 1929, Vermont had added its contribution: a large colonial structure with marble columns and ornaments. This scene—with its emphasis on tourism instead of farming—underscores Vermont's changing economy after 1950.

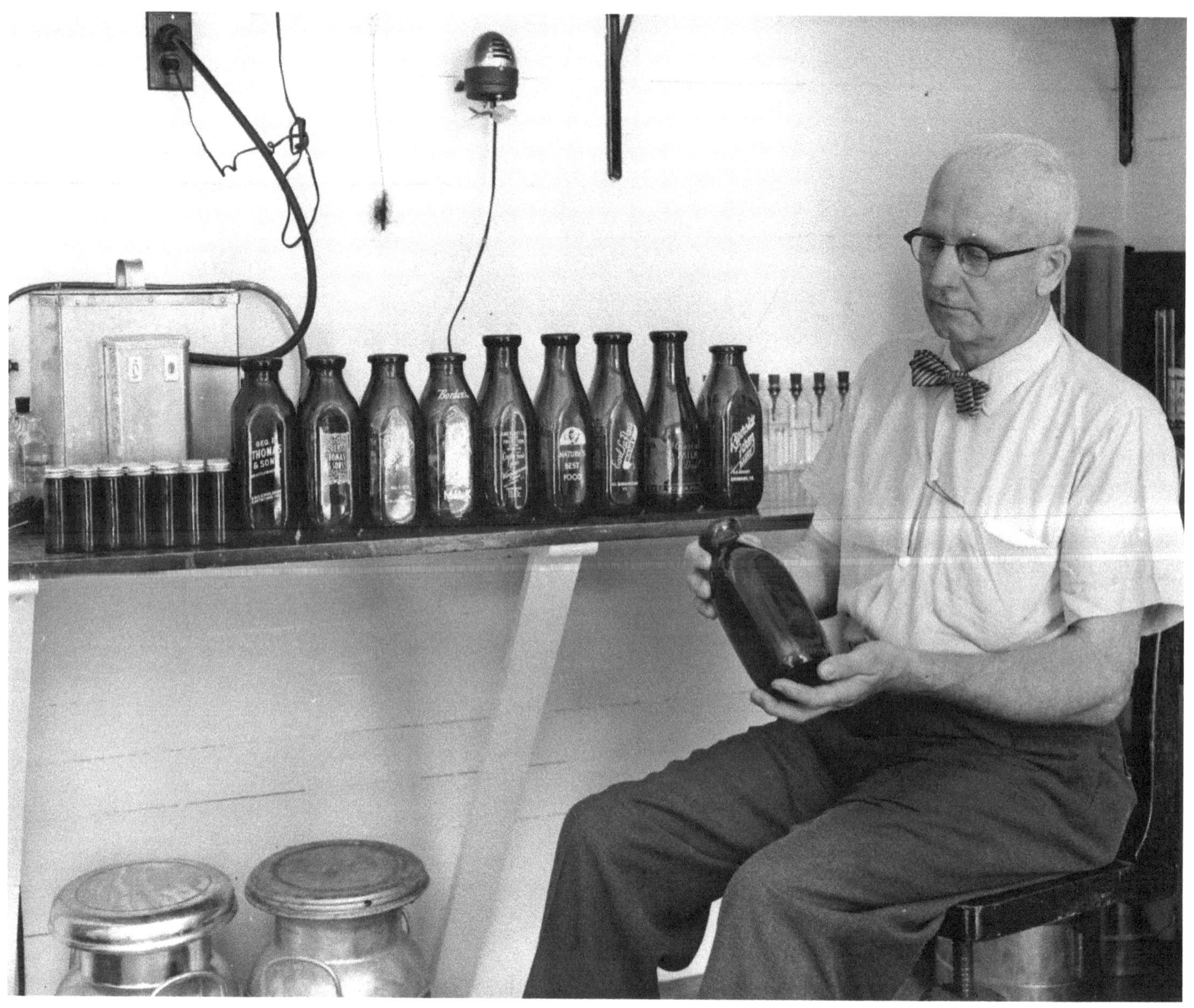

After World War II, the federal government increased regulations on farms in response to concerns about sanitation. By the mid-1950s, regulations demanded expensive investments such as concrete floors for barns, electricity, running water, and bulk tanks. In the wake of these new expenses, the state devised programs to support small farmers with new research and training. Here, Harold Clark, a specialist from the University of Vermont's Milk Flavor Program, inspects amber milk bottles in 1960.

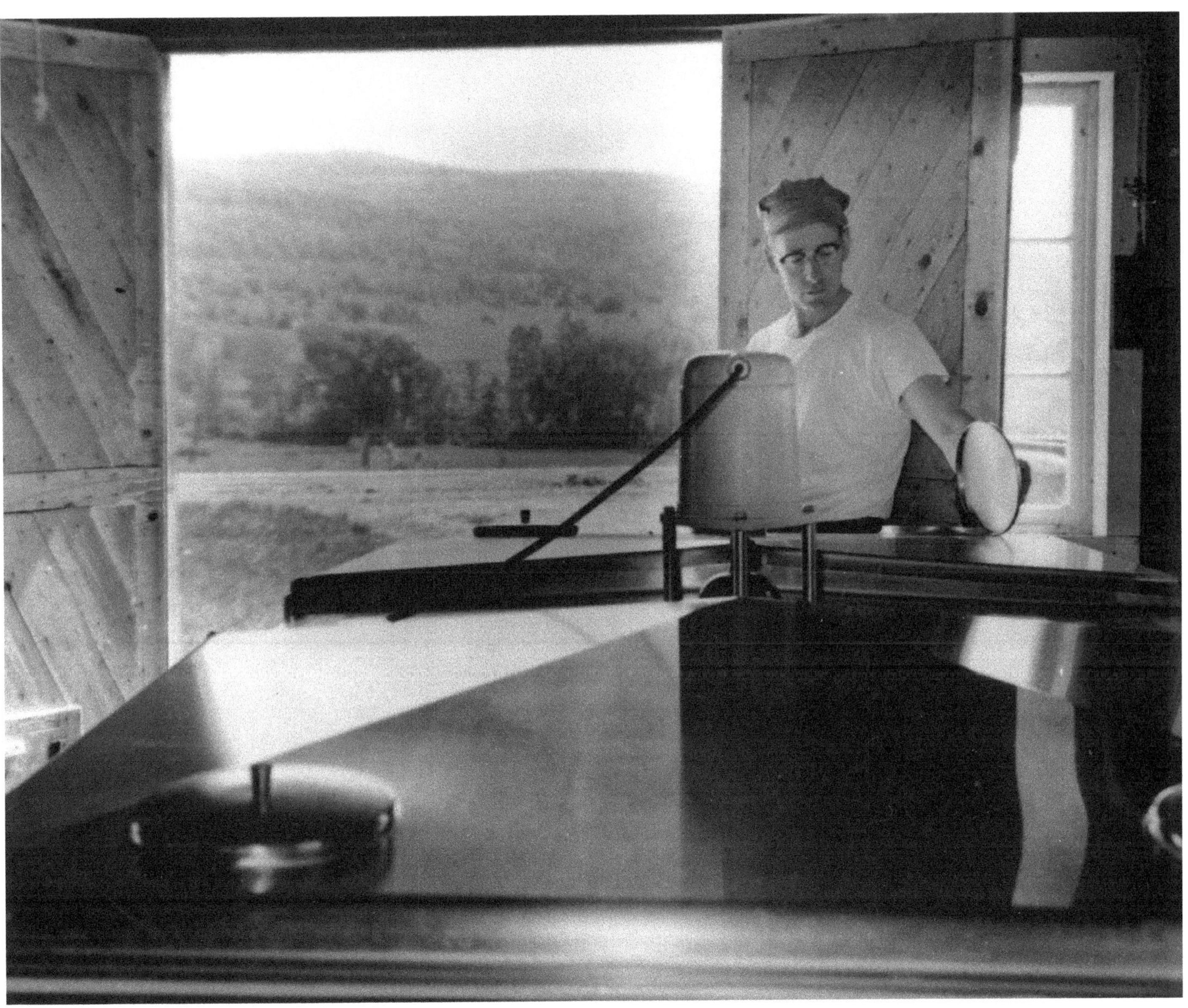

Bulk tanks for milk storage, 1960. Before the 1950s, the traditional practice was to store fresh milk in cans. After 1953, creameries began encouraging farmers to use the more expensive bulk tanks, eventually refusing to pick up from farmers who still used the cans. When the government began requiring the use of these expensive tanks, the number of Vermont dairy farms fell dramatically—and the size of those still in operation nearly tripled. This trend, in which only large-scale farms could hope to remain profitable, held true for farming in general and continues today.

Green River Reservoir, 1960. Starting in 1946, the village of Morrisville and the Public Electric Light Company of St. Albans built a reservoir that made possible controlled releases of water to their respective hydroelectric facilities. Water and Light Commission superintendent Willard Sanders noted that the last section of the dam was poured "without fanfare or ceremony." It was the county's largest civil engineering project to date.

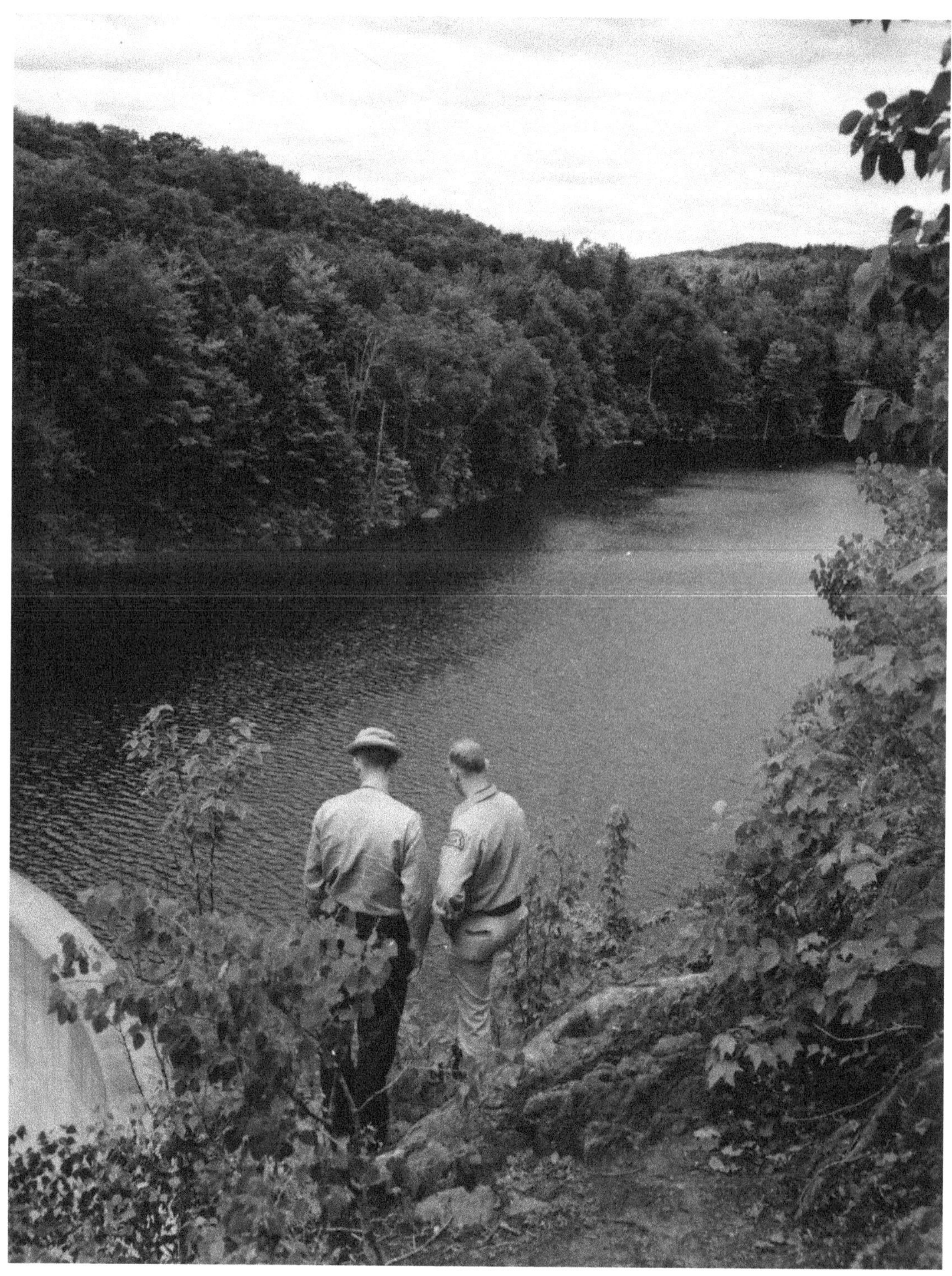

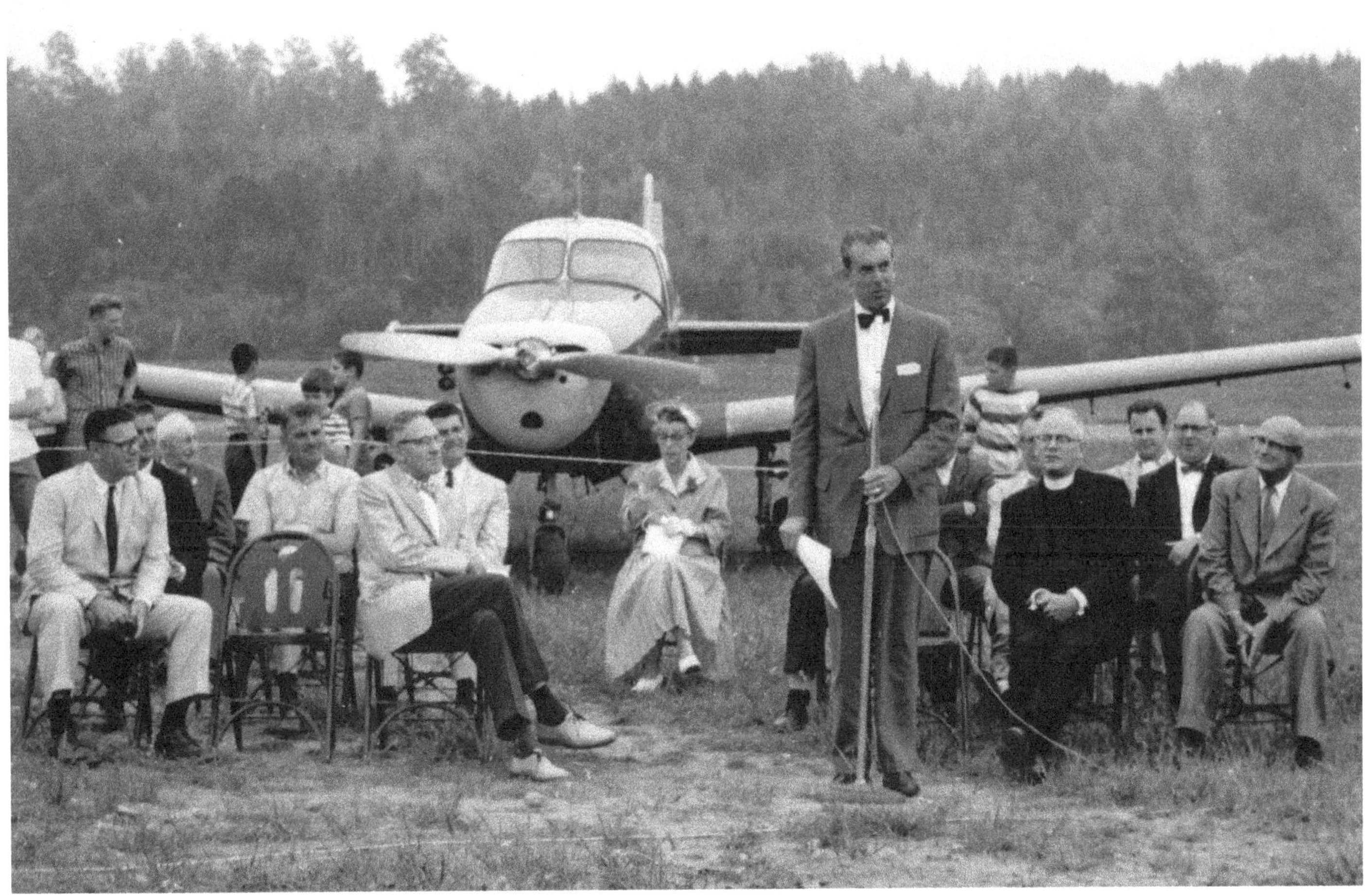

Governor Robert Stafford, in office from 1959 to 1961, speaks at an airport dedication in Morristown. The Morrisville-Stowe State Airport opened in 1960 as the first airport constructed and owned by the state of Vermont. The facility replaced Copley Airfield's two landing strips, which had simultaneously served as golf course fairways. One pilot, remembering having to steer through trees at takeoff, commented that safety at the original facility was "poor at best."

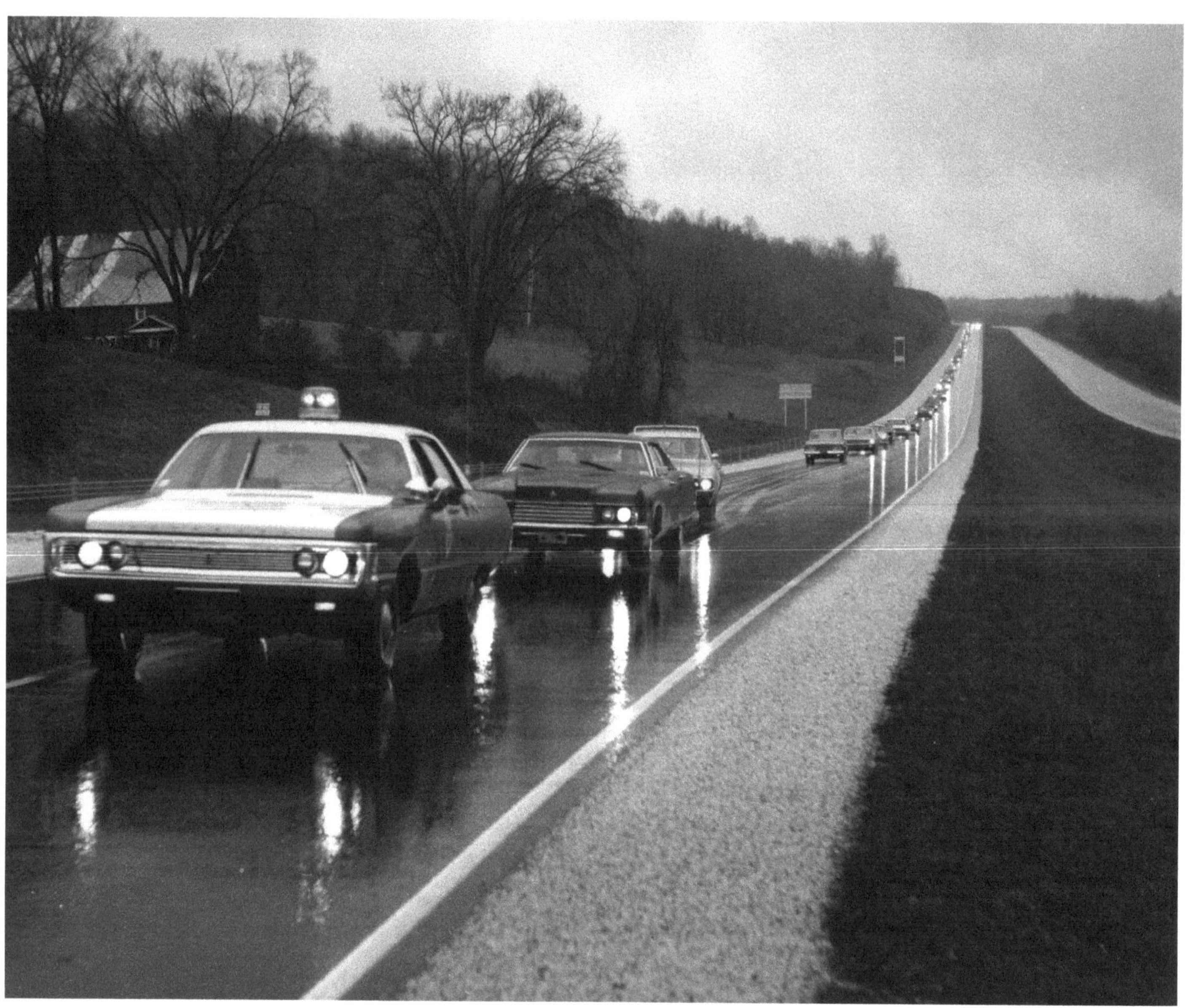

A police motorcade around 1960. Though opposition to the Vermont State Police continued well into the 1950s, Vermonters began to be confronted with an increasing number of reasons to support the force. By 1970, societal changes were contributing to a crime rate that was nearly double that of 1960. Drug-related crimes, including marijuana cultivation, played a role.

Walt Disney's *Those Calloways* portrayed a New England fur trapper who hoped to transform a nearby lake into a refuge for migrating geese. Filmed in Stowe while Philip Hoff was governor, the movie merged well with the administration's platform of promoting tourism and environmentalism. Hoff's administration changed the entry signs at Vermont's borders from "Last Stand of the Yankees" to "the Beckoning Country." The film helped portray Vermont as a peaceful, bucolic destination for visitors.

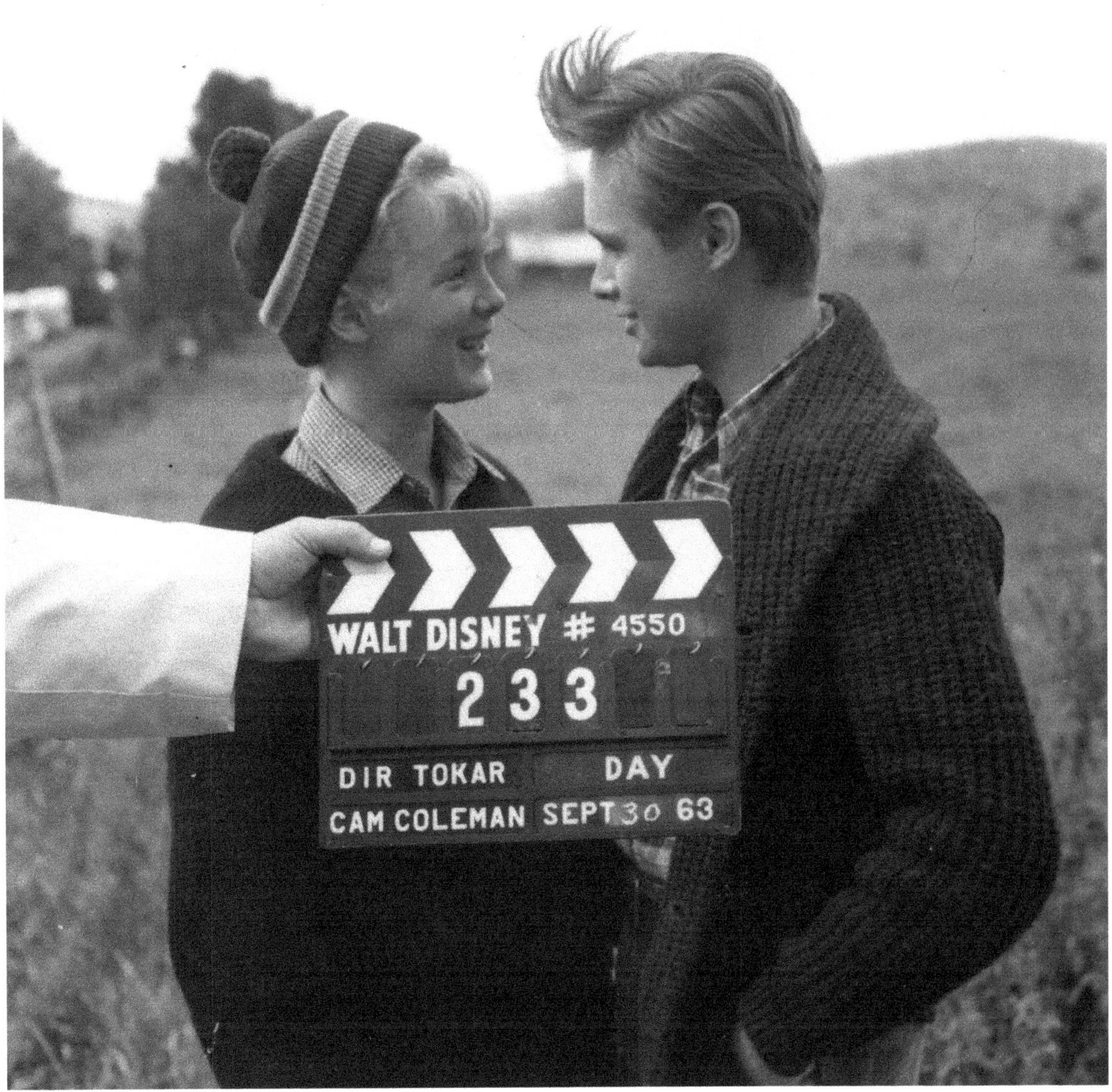

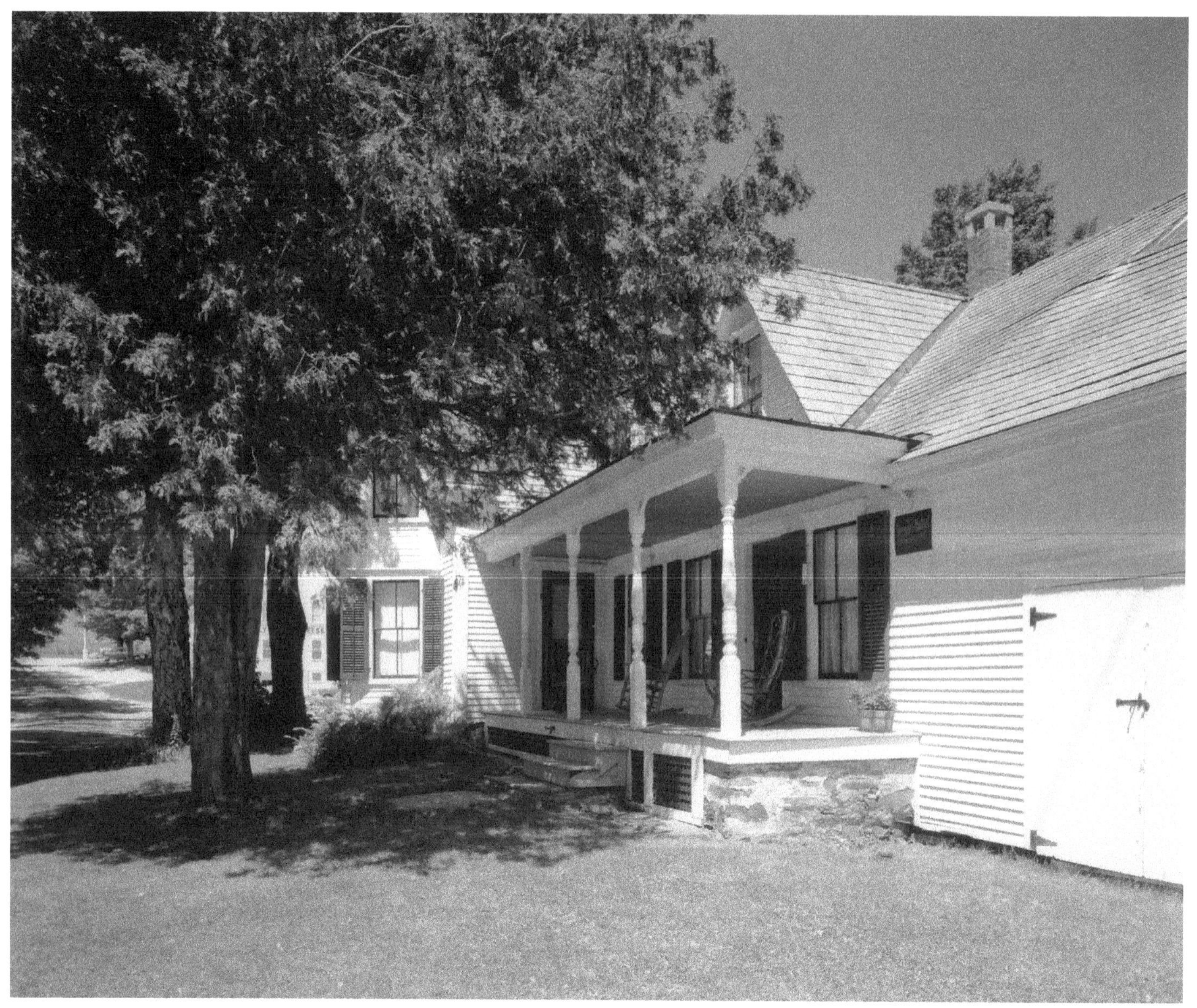

Calvin Coolidge homestead, 1961. Vermonters fell in love with the story of Coolidge's presidential inauguration, which took place one late night at this family home in Plymouth Notch. After learning of President Harding's death in 1923, Coolidge was quickly sworn in to the presidency by his father, a justice of the peace. In 1957, Coolidge's son deeded the homestead to the state, one of many historic properties that would help bolster Vermont tourism. Another Vermonter, Chester Arthur, preceded Coolidge to the nation's highest office, becoming the 21st United States president following the assassination of President James Garfield in 1881.

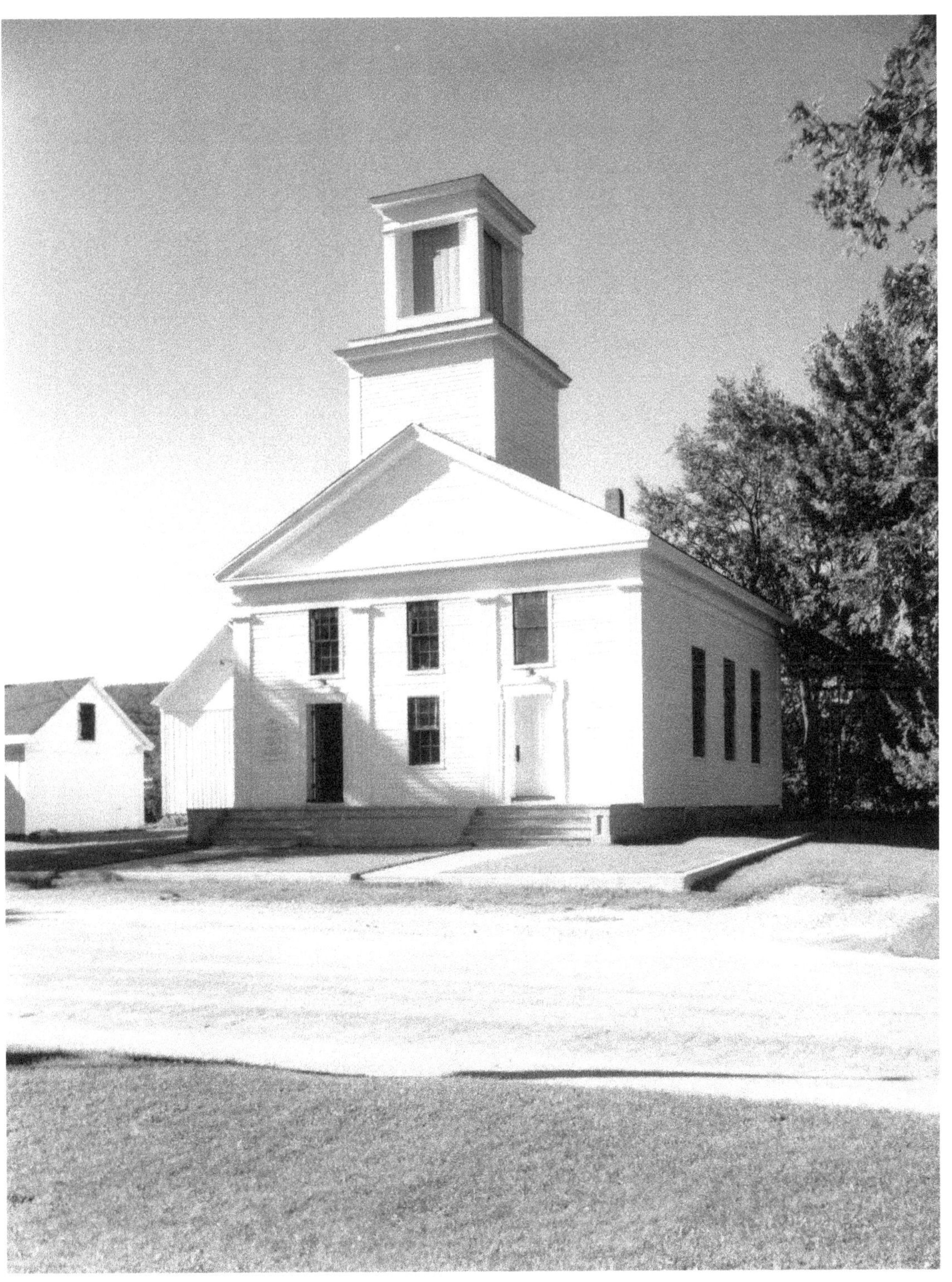

Union Church, 1961.
After the new president's "homespun inaugural," summer crowds quickly made a destination of the Coolidge homestead at Plymouth Notch. Hucksters reportedly set up on the lawn of this church, ready to make a quick dollar from the onlookers who had come to see the Coolidge home. Today the church building is one of 15 sites at Plymouth Notch celebrated for their historic importance. The church holds the Coolidge family pew.

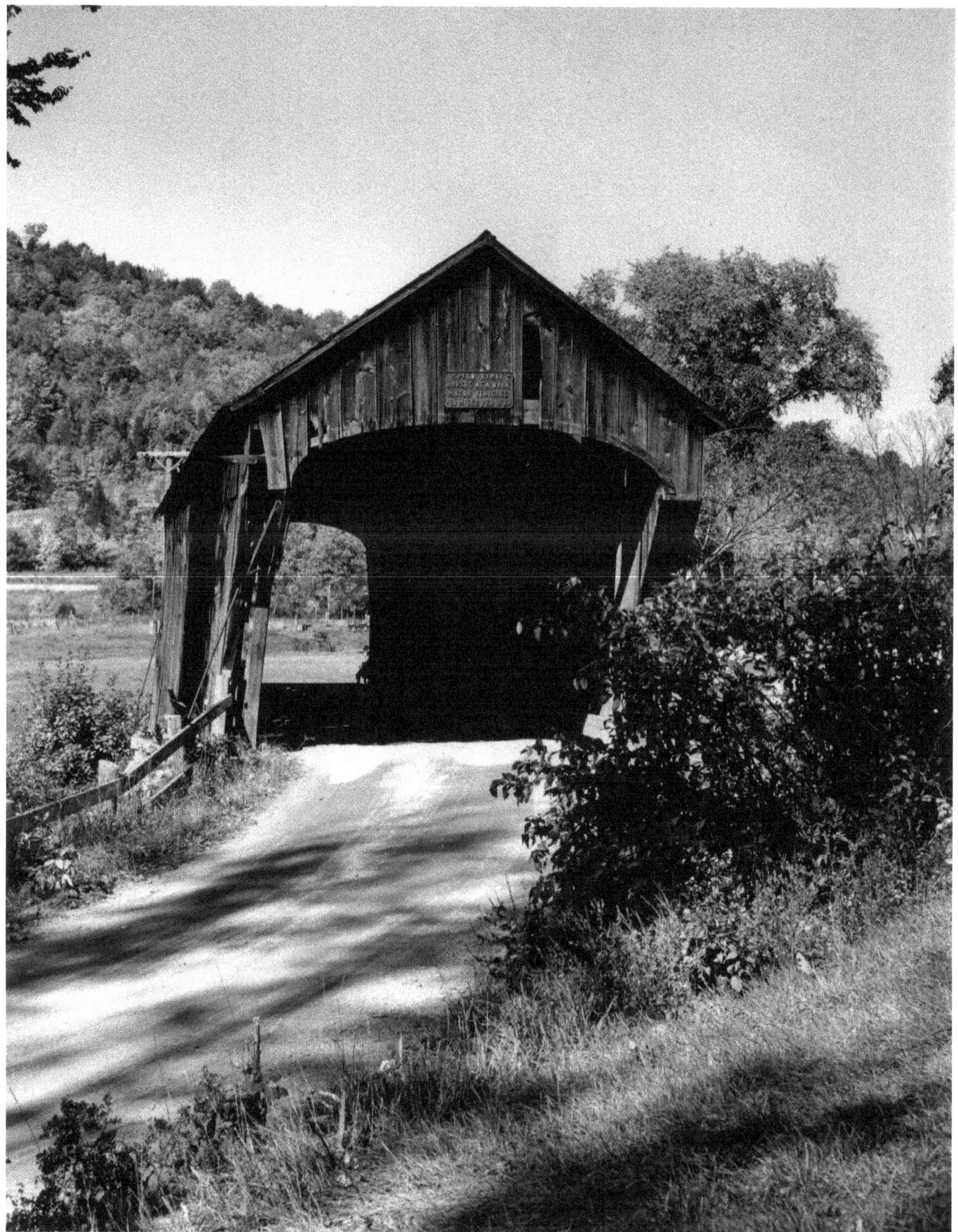

The Worrall Covered Bridge, Rockingham. Built in 1868 by Sanford Granger, this plank-lattice design used nearly a thousand hardwood pegs for every one hundred feet of bridge, and its hundreds of junctions eased concerns about any singularly weak plank. Today Vermont's covered bridges are a destination for tourists. The Worrall retains its historic flavor with the sign "Speed Limit, Horses at a Walk, Motor Vehicles 10 Miles Per H'r."

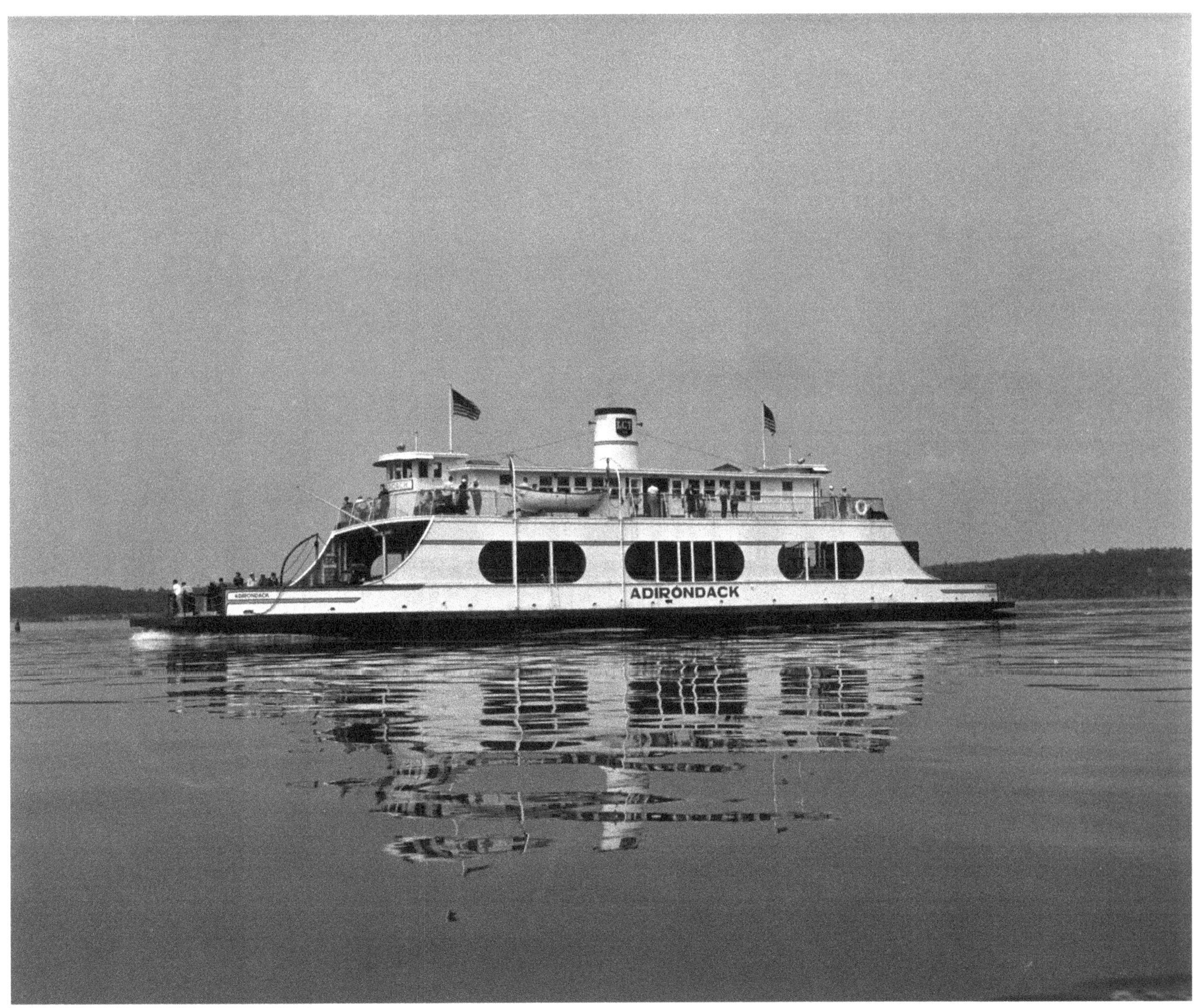

Built in Jacksonville in 1913, this ferry operated on the St. John's River in Florida, on the Delaware, on Manhattan's East River at 34th Street, and on the Chesapeake Bay. In 1954, the Lake Champlain Transportation Company purchased the vessel and renamed it *Adirondack.* It still operates on Lake Champlain as a ferry from Burlington to Port Kent and is the oldest double-ended ferryboat still in service in the United States.

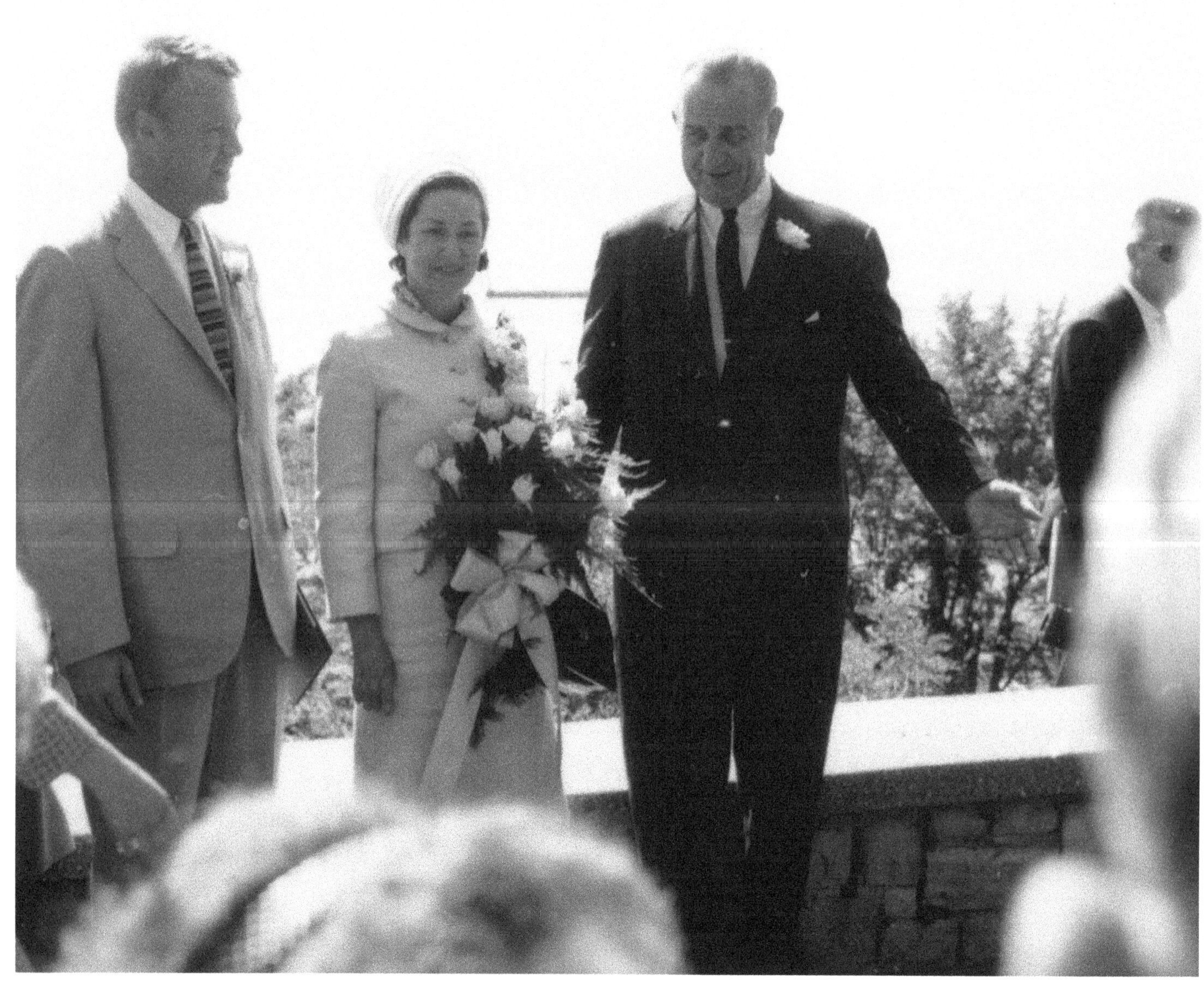

Governor Philip Hoff with Lyndon and Lady Bird Johnson. Until the 1960s, Vermont had a strong tradition of voting Republican. Hoff was the first Democratic governor since 1853, and Lyndon Johnson was the first Democratic president ever to carry the state. After Hoff's victory, the executive director of Vermont's Republican committee told Hoff that he would "never cease to marvel at the vigor and sincerity with which you campaigned. Unfortunately your effort paid off."

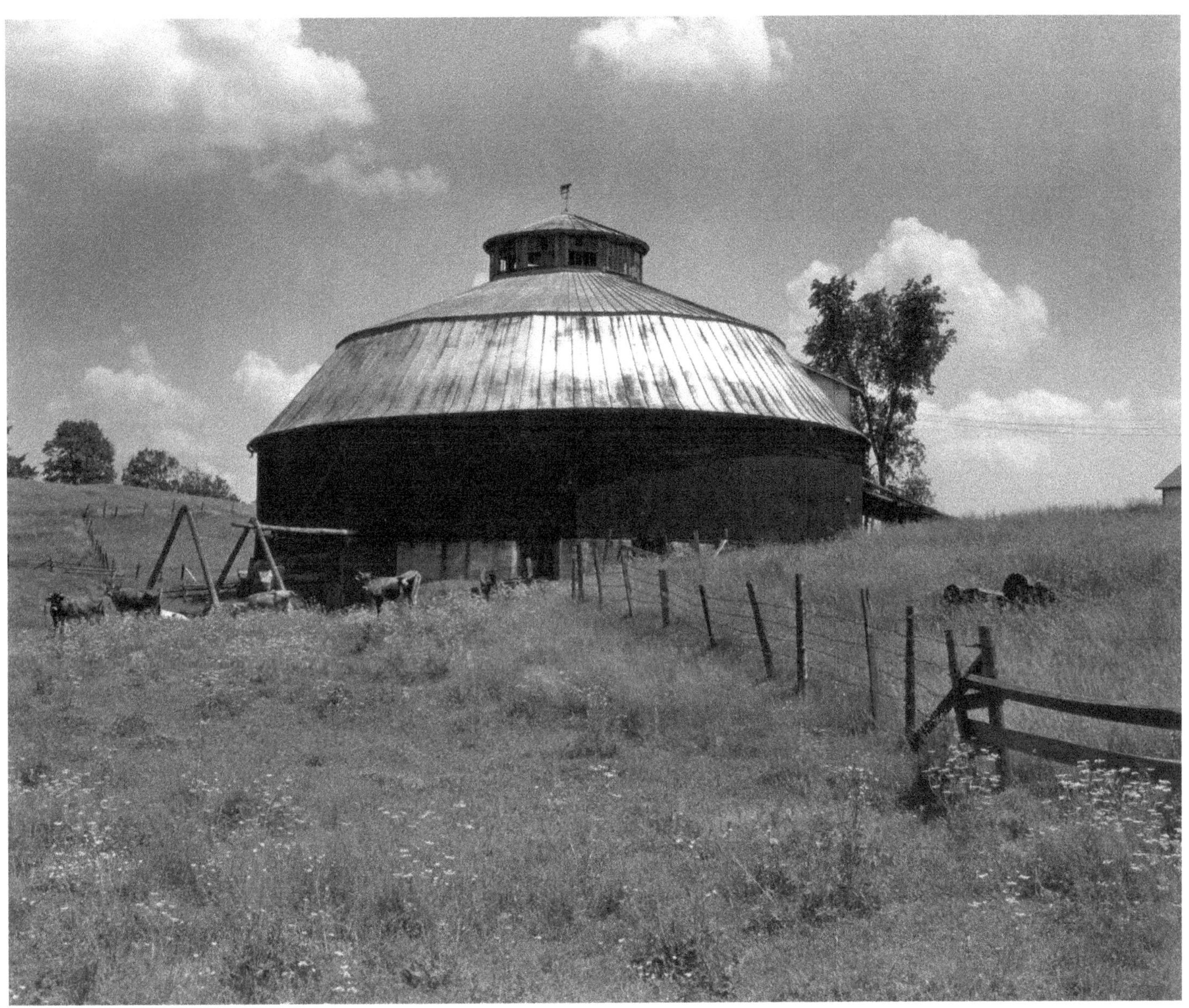

Round Barn in Enosburg, 1966. With the increase in dairy farming, barn architecture was adjusted to accommodate herds of cows. Farmers built multi-story "bank barns" into their hillsides, the slope providing a ready-made ramp for stacking hay on the upper floors. Round and polygonal barns, especially popular around 1910, also facilitated food storage, since a team of horses could enter the barn, circle a pathway, and exit without having to back up.

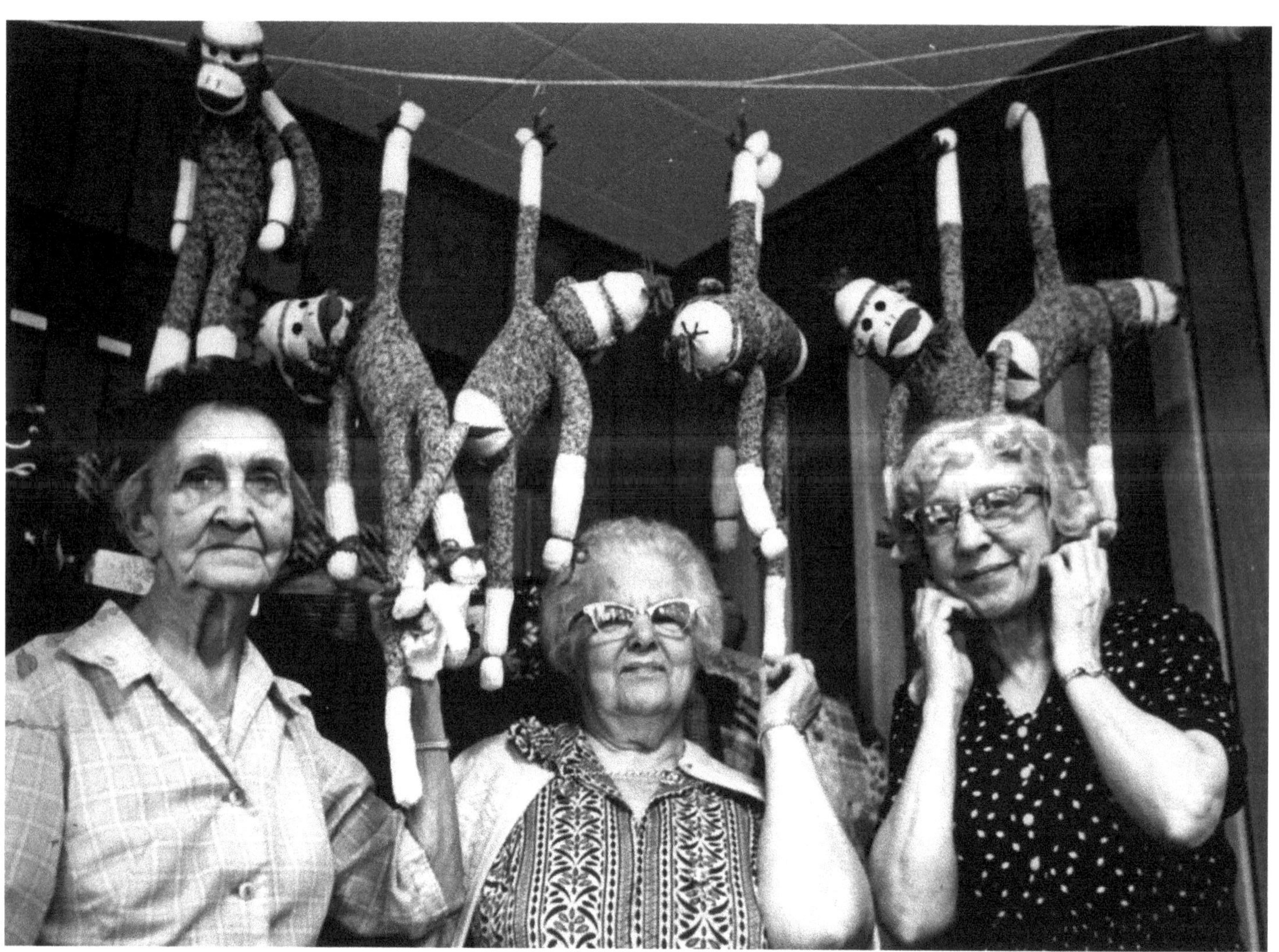

Residents at Dumont Manor, Morristown. During the early twentieth century, municipalities often hired nurses to care for their aged residents. The state also provided poor farms for impoverished Vermonters, many of whom were elderly. By 1975, the state had abolished the poor farms, and now hosted more than 50 nursing homes. These changes were a direct result of outward migration of young people as well as changing attitudes about care for the elderly.

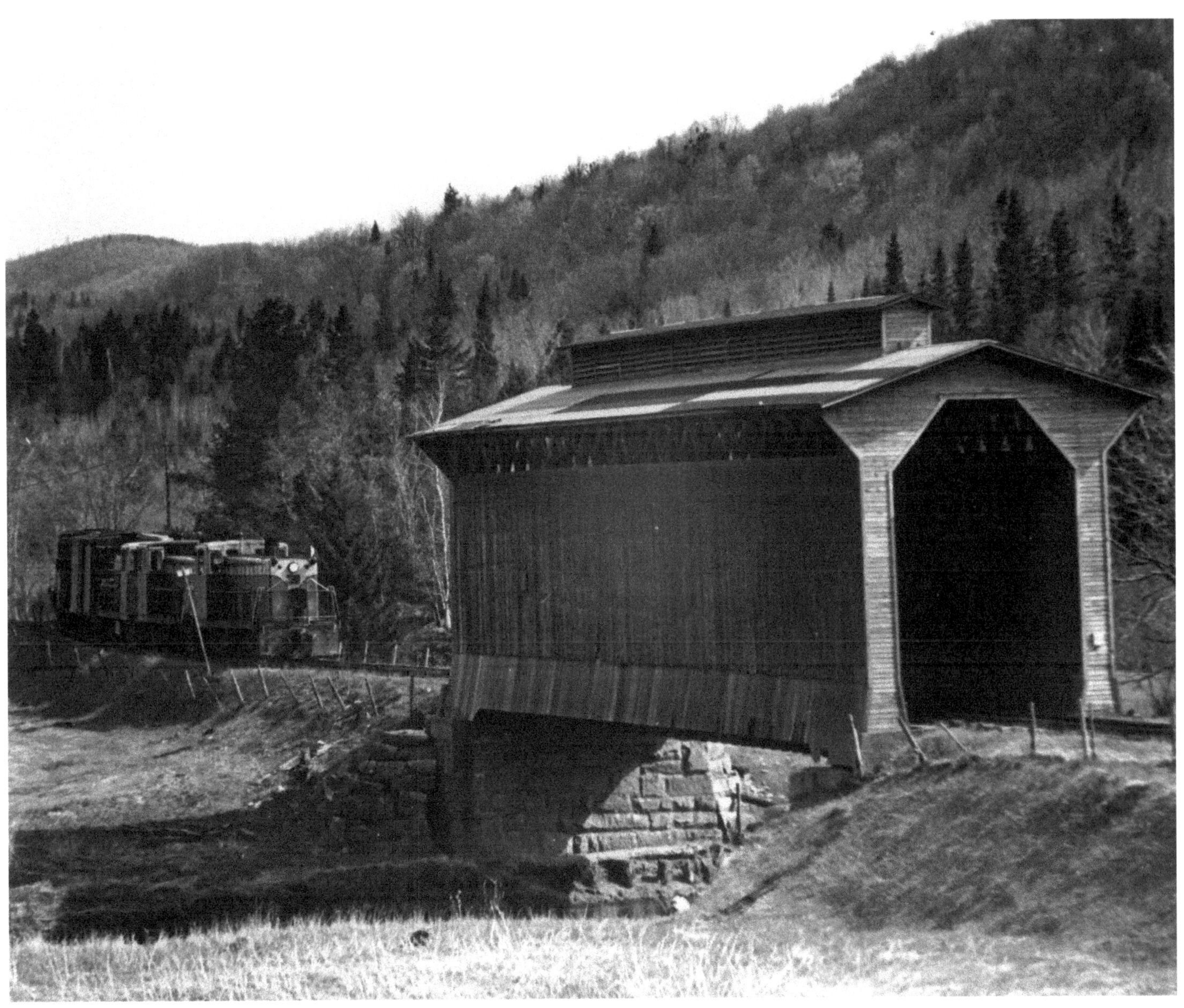

Fisher Bridge near Wolcott, 1967. Like many Vermont rail companies, the St. Johnsbury and Lamoille County Railroad reorganized, re-strategized, and reincorporated many times during the twentieth century. After filing for bankruptcy in 1945, the company changed ownership at least five times, with new headquarters located as far away as New York, Boston, and distant Idaho. Like many Vermont businesses, the company turned to tourism in the early 1980s, converting to a passenger excursion line which also failed to yield a profit.

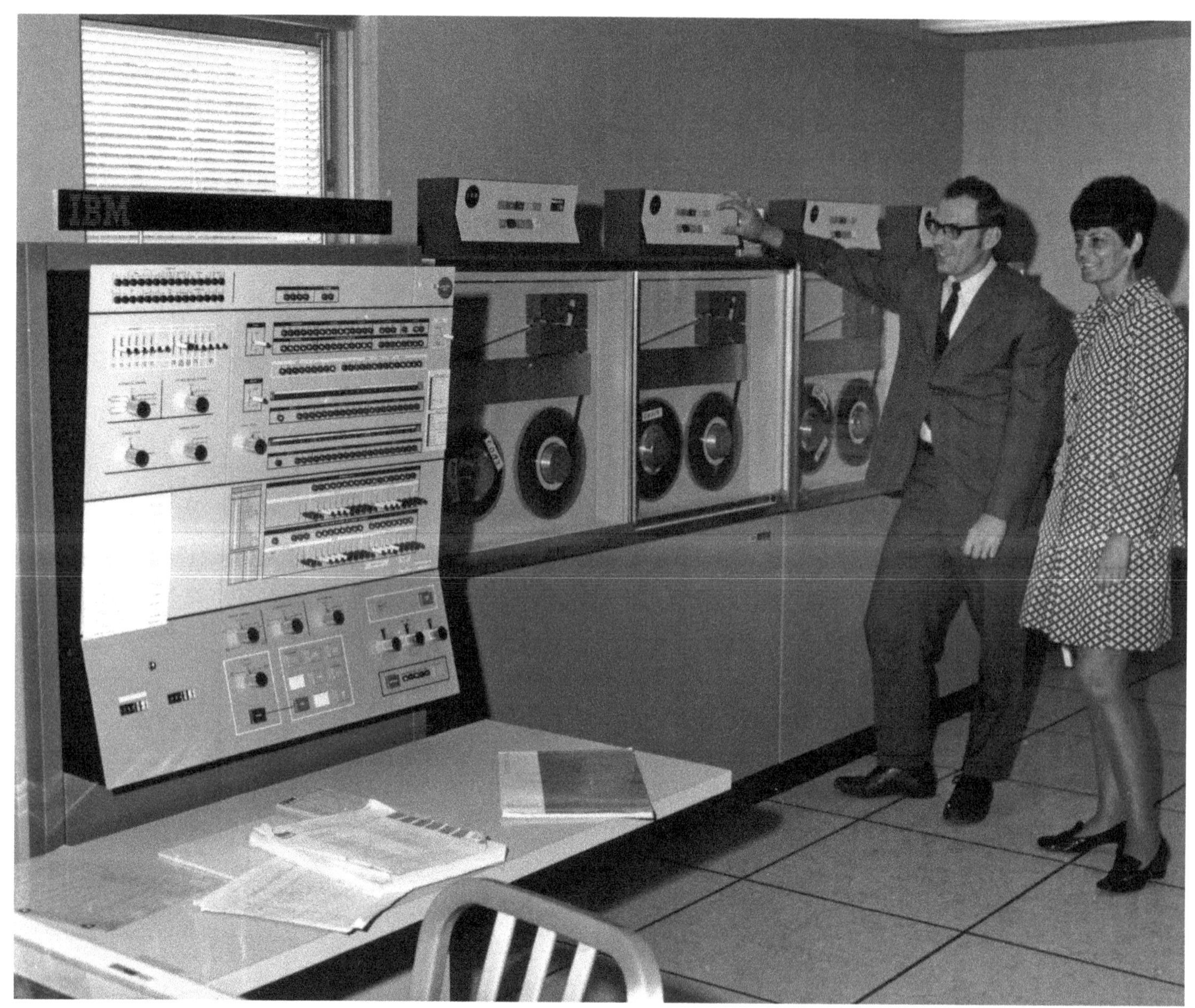

Mainframe computer used by the state, 1970. IBM opened a manufacturing plant in Essex Junction in 1957. By 1969, the company had become the state's largest industrial employer, attracting allied businesses and support services to Vermont. IBM's computers had a dramatic impact on state organization, including the manner in which government agencies collected and distributed information.

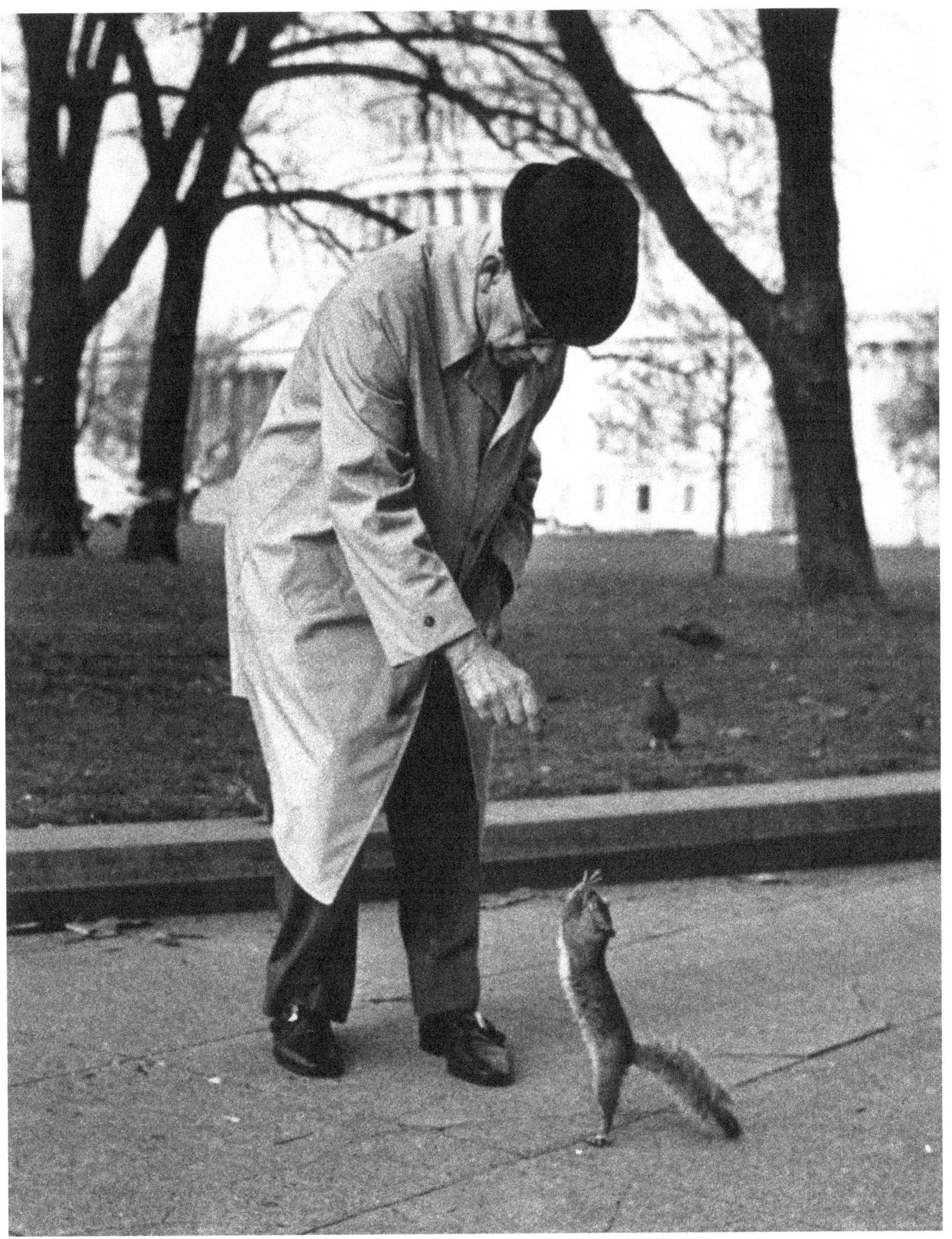

A very tame squirrel captures the attention of Senator George Aiken, on his way to work in Washington, D.C., in 1973. This farmer and wildflower lover from Poultney enjoyed a swift rise into politics, serving as state representative, lieutenant governor, governor, and finally 34 years as U.S. senator. Aiken always identified himself as a farmer, not as a politician, and some have noted that his popularity stemmed from this self-professed identity as "one of the people."

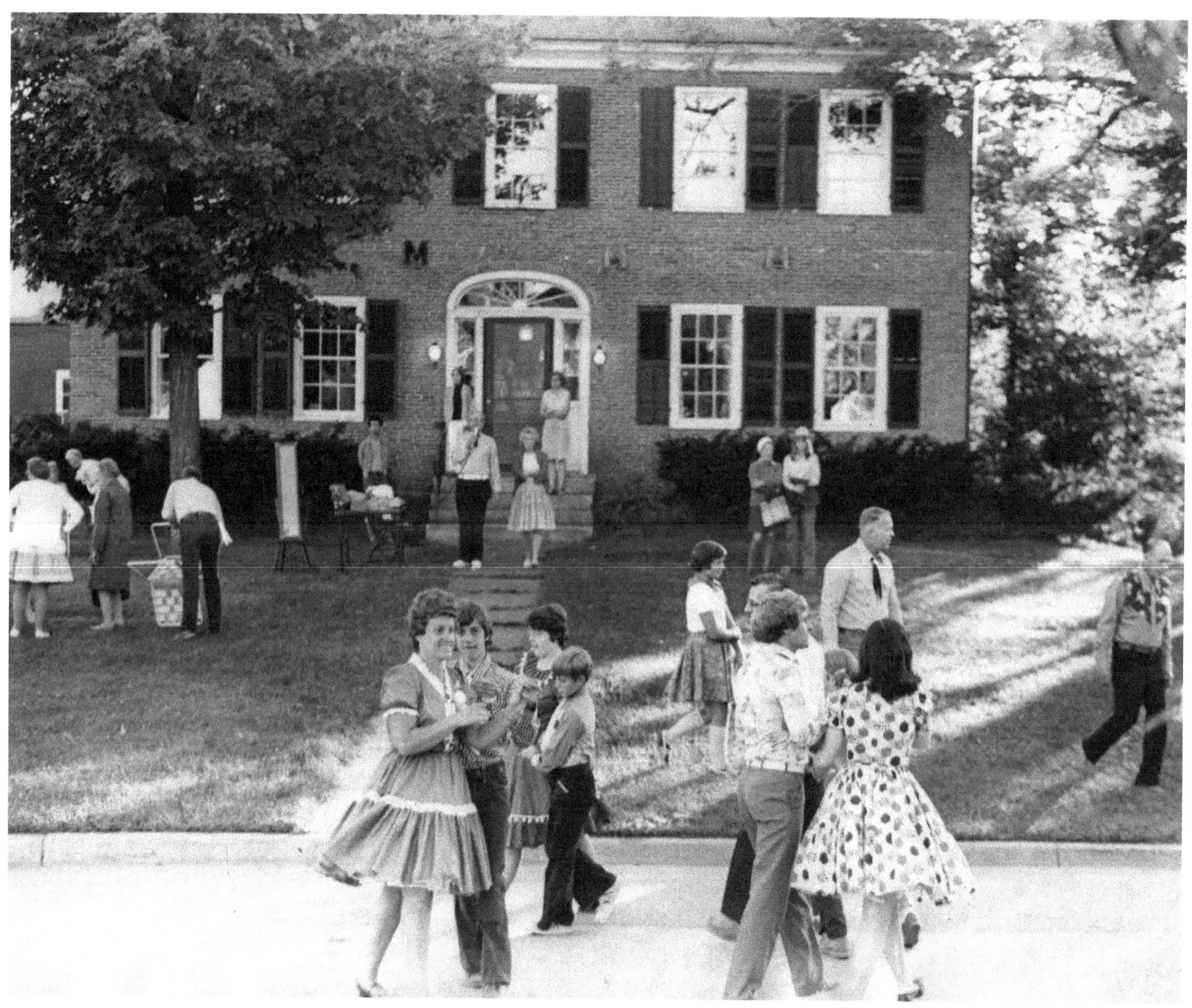

The Lamoille River Swingers at the Noyes House Museum's "Come and See Day," 1976. The nation's Bicentennial brought forth celebrations throughout Vermont, most of them sponsored by local historical societies. The festivities prompted many to update their town histories and arrange a roster of events to qualify as an official Bicentennial community. In Morrisville, residents installed several park benches around the village and baked a 500-pound birthday cake.

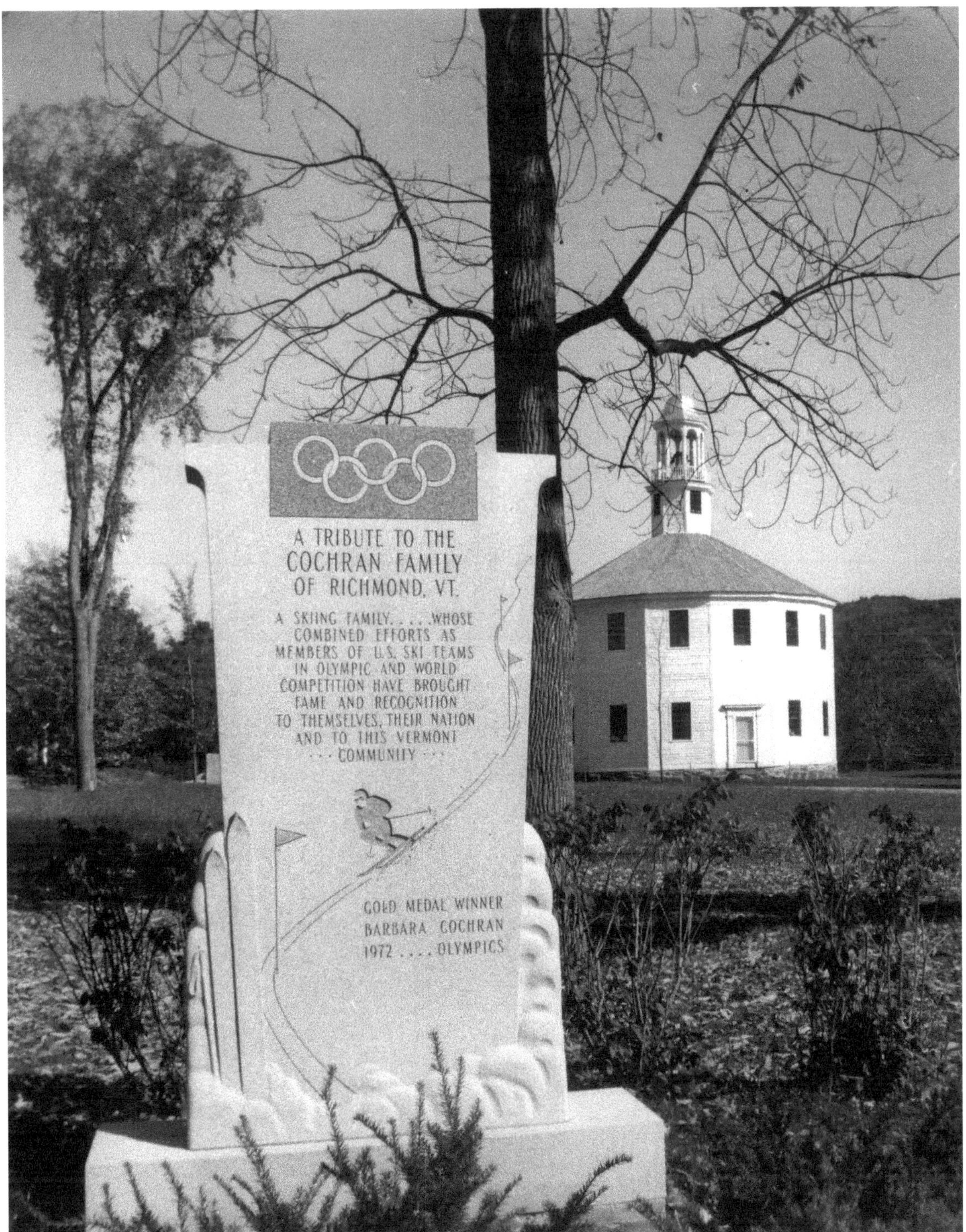

A tribute to the Cochran family near the Old Round Church, Richmond. In the 1950s, the Cochrans built a ski hill and rope tow in their backyard. By the 1970s, four Cochran children had won competitions around the world, including an Olympics gold medal. In 1969, *Vermont Life* celebrated the Cochrans as well as other top-ranking Vermont skiers from Manchester, Stowe, Rutland, Warren, Brattleboro, Norwich, and other communities. These champions became favorite mascots for the promotion of state tourism.

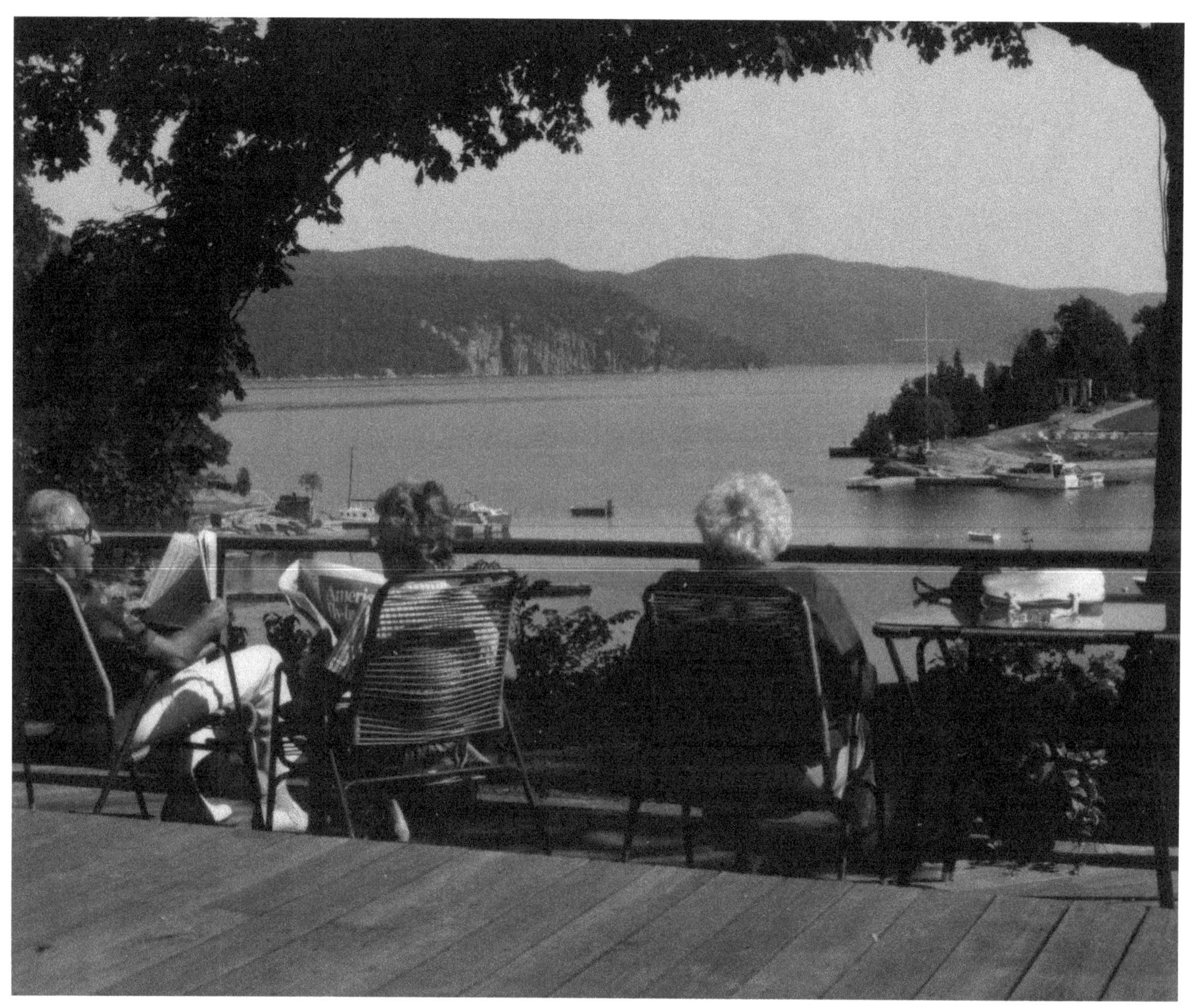

Basin Harbor Club, Ferrisburg. Once a farm that took in summer boarders, the Basin Harbor Club was developed into a tourist mecca—complete with its own steamboat landing—by Allen Penfield Beach. The club built a golf course in 1927 and added cottages in the 1930s. Beach was a conservationist who also embraced the value of development, and was an early advocate for Vermont tourism. Beach also funded the first issue of *Vermont Life* out of his own pocket.

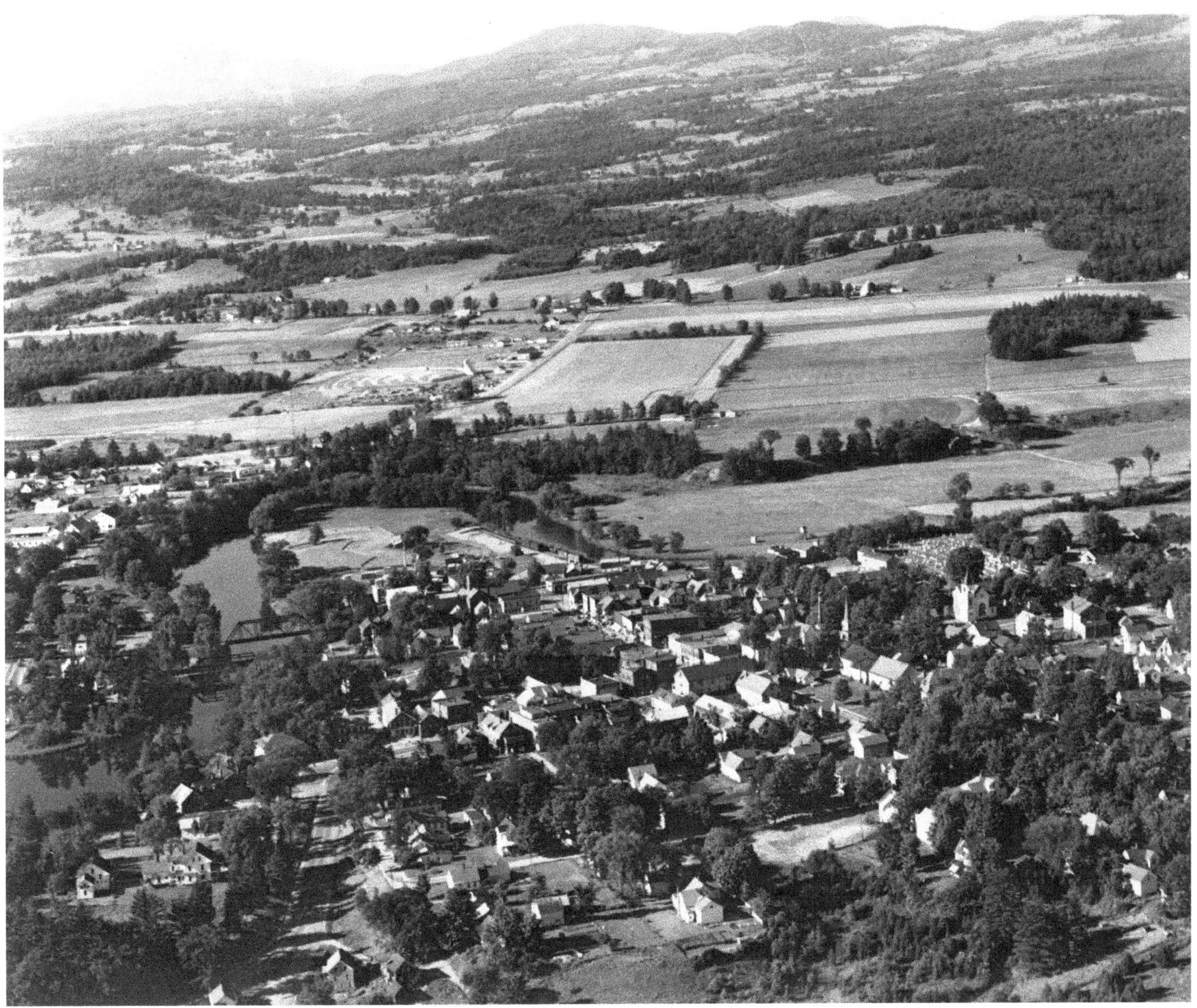

An aerial view of Lamoille County. Vermont's landscape has shifted to suit agriculture, ecological attitudes, and business. Farming created the rolling pastures we know today, as did an eager lumber industry that left a large portion of the state deforested. The trees have grown back, but the landscape still battles population sprawl. In 1993, the entire state was named one of the nation's "Most Endangered Historic Places," a reminder of how growth has affected the state's cultural heritage.

Notes on the Photographs

These notes, listed by page number, attempt to include all aspects known of the photographs. Each of the photographs is identified by the page number, a title or description, photographer and collection, archive, and call or box number when applicable. Although every attempt was made to collect all data, in some cases complete data may have been unavailable due to the age and condition of some of the photographs and records.

II **Village of Moretown**
Morristown Historical Society/Noyes House Museum
MoretownAlbum4

VI **Newport from West Derby**
UVM Bailey Howe Special Collections
BHSC037

X **Maple Sugaring**
Jericho Historical Society
1900.561

2 **Group at Summit House**
UVM Bailey Howe Special Collections
BHSC027

3 **Montpelier Flooded Street**
UVM Bailey Howe Special Collections
BHSC002

4 **Camping Party at Long Island**
UVM Bailey Howe Special Collections
BHSC040

5 **Old Catamount Tavern, Bennington**
UVM Bailey Howe Special Collections
BHSC001

6 **Water-powered Saw**
UVM Bailey Howe Special Collections
BHSC020

7 **Hiram Powers House**
UVM Bailey Howe Special Collections
BHSC033

8 **Stonecutters at Barre**
UVM Bailey Howe Special Collections
BHSC054

9 **Vermont Copper Mines at Vershire**
UVM Bailey Howe Special Collections
BHSC050

10 **Train on Pumpkin Hill Bridge**
Tennie Toussaint Photographs, Folder 6, Special Collections, University of Vermont Library

11 **Waterbury Reform School**
UVM Bailey Howe Special Collections
BHSC045

12 **Smuggler's Cave**
UVM Bailey Howe Special Collections
BHSC031

13 **Berlin Cascades**
UVM Bailey Howe Special Collections
BHSC008

14 **East Alburgh Bridge**
UVM Bailey Howe Special Collections
BHSC056

15 **Newport Steamboat Wharf**
UVM Bailey Howe Special Collections
BHSC038

16 **Croquet at Middletown Springs**
UVM Bailey Howe Special Collections
BHSC104

17 **Brickyard Pug Mill**
UVM Bailey Howe Special Collections
BHSC014

18 **Kids at Woodstock Railroad Cut**
UVM Bailey Howe Special Collections
BHSC025

19 **Brockway Mills Train Wreck**
UVM Bailey Howe Special Collections
BHSC301

20 **Philomene Daniels Ferry**
Bixby Memorial Library, Vergennes
Philomene2

21 **Burlington's City Hall Park**
UVM Bailey Howe Special Collections
BHSC300

22 **Moss Dealers**
UVM Bailey Howe Special Collections
BHSC017

23 **View from Montpelier State House**
UVM Bailey Howe Special Collections
BHSC006

24 **Jericho Reporter**
Jericho Historical Society
JCbs9

25 **Horse-powered Saw at Danville**
Tennie Toussaint Photographs, Folder 2, Special Collections, University of Vermont Library

26 **Breadloaf Inn at Ripton**
UVM Bailey Howe Special Collections
BHSC005

27 **Covered Bridge**
UVM Bailey Howe Special Collections
BHSC036

28 **Jericho Mills**
Jericho Historical Society
JCm2

29 **Martin Millinery**
Jericho Historical Society
JCbs24

30 **Rutland Marble Quarry**
UVM Bailey Howe Special Collections
BHSC009

31 **Hoisting Marble**
UVM Bailey Howe Special Collections
BHSC007

32 **Mount Mansfield Logging House**
UVM Bailey Howe Special Collections
BHSC026

33 **Soapstone Quarrymen at Grafton**
UVM Bailey Howe Special Collections
BHSC053

34 **Clarendon Springs Party**
UVM Bailey Howe Special Collections
BHSC035

35 **Child with Pets**
UVM Bailey Howe Special Collections
BHSC022

36 **Billings Library**
Library of Congress
LC-DIG-ppmsca-15376

37 **Aunt Sally Horton**
UVM Bailey Howe Special Collections
BHSC043

38 **Campground Boardinghouse**
Morristown Historical Society/Noyes House Museum
CA.01

39 **Morrisville Tannery**
Morristown Historical Society/Noyes House Museum
BS.79

40 **Williston's Old Brick Church**
Williston Historical Society
Old_Brick_Church_with_cornfield

41 **Morristown Parade**
Morristown Historical Society/Noyes House Museum

42 **Memphremagog House Band**
UVM Bailey Howe Special Collections
BHSC044

43 **Jericho Blacksmith Shop**
Jericho Historical Society
blacksmith

44 **Shoreham House Inn**
Shoreham Historical Society
Shoreham Inn

45 **Morrisville's Portland Street**
Morristown Historical Society/Noyes House Museum
BU.PS.19

46 **Barre Opera House Fire**
UVM Bailey Howe Special Collections
BHSC055

48 **Tucker Toll Bridge**
Library of Congress
LC-DIG-det-4a22310

49 **Barre Gravestone Artisans**
UVM Bailey Howe Special Collections
BHSC058

50 **The Thurlow Ploofs**
UVM Bailey Howe Special Collections
BHSC099

51 **Moses Pearson with Trout**
Cuttingville Historical Society
005a_Spring_Lake.Moses_Pearson

52 **Randolph Railroad Station**
Library of Congress
LC-USF33-T01-002578-M2

54 **RFD Delivery**
Cuttingville Historical Society
Pitts_Charles_c1900_001

55 **Nashville Road Maintenance Crew**
Jericho Historical Society
1900.611

56 **Brattleboro Kids on Skis and Snowshoes**
Brattleboro Historical Society
1223 skier & snowshoes

57 **The Better Farming Special**
Vermont Historical Society
fp6016

58 **Chittendon Mills**
Jericho Historical Society
Miller

59 **Morrisville Snow Roller**
Morristown Historical Society/Noyes House Museum
BS.35

60 **Rock Dunder**
UVM Bailey Howe Special Collections
BHSC013

61 **West Danville Couple with Phonograph**
Tennie Toussaint Photographs, Folder 3, Special Collections, University of Vermont Library

62 **Hunters with Deer**
Tennie Toussaint Photographs, Folder 6, Special Collections, University of Vermont Library

63 **Jericho's Church Street School**
Jericho Historical Society
JCps1

64 **Scene at Shrewsbury**
Cuttingville Historical Society
Northam_003

65 **Morrisville Business Directory**
Morristown Historical Society/Noyes House Museum
BS.59

66 **Rutland Railroad Employees**
UVM Bailey Howe Special Collections
BHSC068

67 **Barre Dressmaker**
UVM Bailey Howe Special Collections
BHSC057

68 **Bristol Manufacturing**
Bristol Historical Society
1979.3.49

69 **Clawson-Hamilton College Interior**
Brattleboro Historical Society
0252 Clawson-Hamilton

70 **Burlington City Hall Construction**
Louis L. McAllister Photographs, Box A02, Folder 03, Item 03, Special Collections, University of Vermont Library

71 **Traveling Ministers**
Morristown Historical Society/Noyes House Museum
PE.GP.10

72 **Bennington's Holden-Leonard Company**
Library of Congress
LC-DIG-nclc-01836

73 **Pin Boys at Bowling Academy**
Library of Congress
LC-DIG-nclc-03374

74 **Hickok Lumber Company**
Library of Congress
LC-DIG-nclc-04590

75 **Barn Raising at North Danville**
Tennie Toussaint Photographs, Folder 1, University of Vermont Library

76 **Lee River Road Farmhouse**
Jericho Historical Society
JCh1

77 **Jericho Milk Delivery**
Jericho Historical Society
JCT1

78 **Bertha McLaughlin**
McLaughlin Family Private Collection
Bertha

79 **Vermont Youngsters**
UVM Bailey Howe Special Collections
BHSC023

80 **Covered Bridge at Jericho**
Jericho Historical Society
JCB3

81 **Paul Crown in Toy Car**
Brattleboro Historical Society
1206 boy in toy car

82 **Mount Sinai Shriners**
Morristown Historical Society/Noyes House Museum
0.00.09

83 **Shelburne Shipyard Marine Railway**
UVM Bailey Howe Special Collections
BHSC101

84 **Roosevelt at Barre**
Morristown Historical Society/Noyes House Museum
PE.MR.23

85 **Telephone Company Switchboard Crew**
Morristown Historical Society/ Noyes House Museum
BS.21

86 **Jericho School Bus**
Jericho Historical Society
JCT 6

87 **Vermont Tourists**
Library of Congress
LC-USZ62-28546

88 **Lake Champlain Ferry**
UVM Bailey Howe Special Collections
BHSC096

89 **Burlington Auto Accident**
Louis L. McAllister Photographs, Box A05, Folder 15, Item 06, Special Collections, University of Vermont Library

90 **Estey Organ Truck**
Brattleboro Historical Society
0259 estey organ truck

91 **Asian Wedding**
Brattleboro Historical Society
0255 chinese wedding

92 **Bentley Cows**
Jericho Historical Society
JHSun02

93 **Cemetery Superintendents Convention at Barre**
Library of Congress
LC-USZ62-52839

94 **Fort Ethan Allen**
UVM Bailey Howe Special Collections
BHSC094

95 **Fort Ethan Allen Training Camp**
UVM Bailey Howe Special Collections
BHSC090

96 **Lakeside Garage in Morrisville**
Morristown Historical Society/Noyes House Museum
BS.22

97 **Hydroelectric Plant in East Montpelier**
UVM Bailey Howe Special Collections
BHSC109

98 **Street Paving in Winooski**
UVM Bailey Howe Special Collections
BHSC078

99 **Steam Pumper**
UVM Bailey Howe Special Collections
BHSC076

100 **Fisk Bicycle Club**
Brattleboro Historical Society 0326 fisk bicycles

101 **Girls' Basketball Team**
Morristown Historical Society/Noyes House Museum
PA.BK.03

102 **Winooski Whirlwinds Football**
UVM Bailey Howe Special Collections
BHSC079

104 **Randolph's Green Mountain Band**
UVM Bailey Howe Special Collections
BHSC067

105 **Bennington Beekeepers**
Library of Congress
LC-DIG-nclc-00316

106 **Vermont Fur Dealers and Mrs. Coolidge**
Library of Congress
LC-DIG-nclc-13191

108 **Flood-ravaged Home in Waterbury**
Library of Congress
LC-USZ62-119412

109 **Flood-splintered Railroad at Slip Hill**
Library of Congress
LC-USZ62-101981

110 **Winooski Pontoon Bridge**
UVM Bailey Howe Special Collections
BHSC080

111 **Burlington Main Street #2**
Louis L. McAllister Photographs, Box A05, Folder 16, Item 21, Special Collections, University of Vermont Library

112 **Burlington's Church Street**
Louis L. McAllister Photographs, Box A04, Folder 05, Item 01, Special Collections, University of Vermont Library

113 **Burlington Rapid Transit Bus**
Louis L. McAllister Photographs, Box A06, Folder 02, Item 01, Special Collections, University of Vermont Library

114 **Vermont Coastal Freighter**
UVM Bailey Howe Special Collections
BHSC098

115 **Cutting Hay in Windsor County**
Library of Congress
LC-USF33-T01-002590-M2

116 **Improvements to Potash Brook Bridge**
Louis L. McAllister Photographs, Box A1, Folder 13, Item 10, Special Collections, University of Vermont Library

117 **Hyde Park Farm Machinery**
Library of Congress
LC-USF33-T01-00741-M4

118 **Cabot Creamery's Rosedale Truck**
Cabot Historical Society
cabotcreamery'srosedaletruck_1931

119 **St. Albans Silage**
Vermont State Archives
VSA09

120 **Burlington Lakefront Utility Workers**
Louis L. McAllister Photographs, Box A 03, Folder 01, Item 06, Special Collections, University of Vermont Library

121 **Little River Dam at Waterbury**
Vermont State Archives
VSA18

122 **Vermont Youngsters, 1930s**
Vermont State Archives
H322

123 **WPA Street Construction**
Louis L. McAllister Photographs, Box A 04, Folder 06, Item 03, Special Collections, University of Vermont Library

124 **Montpelier Bookwagon**
Vermont State Archives
H729_bookwagon

125 **Women Legislators, 1930s**
Vermont State Archives
women_legislators_1935

126 **Wheelbarrow Race at Albany Fair**
Library of Congress
LC-USF33-T01-000759-M2

127 **Officer at Albany Fair**
Library of Congress
LC-USF33-T01-000761-M4

128 **Biplane Wreckage**
Louis L. McAllister Photographs, Box A 01, Folder 2, Item 1, Special Collections, University of Vermont Library

129 **Burlington Airport**
Louis L. McAllister Photographs, Box A1, Folder 21, Item 03, Special Collections, University of Vermont Library

130 **Hyde Park Auction**
Library of Congress
LC-USF33-T01-000761-M4

131 **Salvage of the Philadelphia**
UVM Bailey Howe Special Collections
BHSC102

132 **Rutland State Fair Harness Race**
Library of Congress
LC-USF33-T01-002597-M4

133 **Craftsbury Fair, 1937**
Library of Congress
LC-USF33-T01-002591-M3

134 **Kirby's Bob McNally with Bull**
Library of Congress
LC-USF33-T01-002607-M2

135 **Tabor Turkey Farm near Swanton, 1938**
Vermont State Archives
VSA01

136 **Elgin Street Sweeping Machine**
Louis L. McAllister Photographs, Box A 03, Folder 10, Item 7, Special Collections, University of Vermont Library

137 **Brattleboro Winter Storm**
Library of Congress
LC-USF34-53018

138 **Collecting Sap at North Bridgewater**
Library of Congress
LC-USF33-030893-M4

139 **Boiling Sap at Waitsfield**
Library of Congress
LC-USF34-53627

140 **Ethan Allen Sculpture**
Library of Congress
LC-USZ62-093235

141 **Milk Delivery to Burlington Co-op**
Library of Congress
LC-USF34-45580

142 **Barker at State Fair**
Library of Congress
LC-DIG-fsac-1a33917

143 **Dolly Kirby at American Woolen**
UVM Bailey Howe Special Collections
BHSC086

144 **Scrap Metal Drive, 1942**
Morristown Historical Society/Noyes House Museum
SE.26

146 **War Years License Plates**
Vermont State Archives
VSA17

147 **Unionization of Women at Winooski**
UVM Bailey Howe Special Collections
BHSC085

148 **Milk Bottling Machinery**
Library of Congress
LC-USF34-45594

149 **West Danville Farmer Frank Goss**
Library of Congress
LC-USW3-05385-E

150 **Hastings General Store, 1942**
Library of Congress
LC-USW3-053820-E

151 **Helen Wills with Victory Garden**
Vermont State Archives
VSA19

152 **General Merritt Edson**
Library of Congress
LC-USZ62-106894

153 **Boating in Groton State Park**
Vermont State Archives
VSA03

154 **Gilbert Ski Hill at Woodstock**
Library of Congress
LC-USF34-53134

155 **Samoset Colony at Lake Lamoille**
Morristown Historical Society/Noyes House Museum
0.00.20

156 **Vermont Farmer**
Library of Congress
LC-USF33-T01-02619-M1

157 **Milk Cooperative at Hardwick**
Library of Congress
LC-USF33-T01-000815-M4

158 **Green Mountain Club Project**
Morristown Historical Society/Noyes House Museum
0.00.01

160 **Vermont Cheddar at Exposition**
Vermont State Archives
VSA07

161 **Morrisville Water and Light Commissioners**
Morristown Historical Society/Noyes House Museum
MG.WL.19

162 Muddy River Minstrels
Morristown Historical Society/Noyes House Museum
MU.MMB.03

163 Fingerprinting
Vermont State Archives
VSA12

164 Farmer Milking Cows
Morristown Historical Society/Noyes House Museum
A.G.05

165 Eisenhower at Dairy Festival, 1955
Vermont State Archives
AG2037

166 A. D. Pease Grain Company
Louis L. McAllister Photographs, Box A 01, Folder 01, Item 01, Special Collections, University of Vermont Library

167 White Pine Plantation
Morristown Historical Society/Noyes House Museum
0.00.06

168 Green Mountain Club Trail Markers
Vermont State Archives
VSA10

169 Ice Boats
UVM Bailey Howe Special Collections
BHSC100

170 Jonas Salk Ice Sculpture
Vermont State Archives
VSA13

171 State Police Training Class
Vermont State Archives
VSA11

172 Randall Hotel, 1956
Morristown Historical Society/Noyes House Museum
BS.100

173 Dugout Canoe Recovery
Morristown Historical Society/Noyes House Museum
O.MHS.02

174 Burlington High School Play
Louis L. McAllister Photographs, Box A 02, Folder 12, Item 05, Special Collections, University of Vermont Library

175 Brattleboro All-America City Award Parade
Vermont State Archives
DCA2025

176 Shrewsbury Fiddlers
Vermont State Archives
DCA2027

177 Cold War Fashion Statement
Vermont State Archives
VSA14

178 Interstate Construction
Vermont State Archives
AOT1319

179 I-89 Construction near Middlesex, 1959
Vermont State Archives
AOT3183

180 Nixon with Maple Syrup
Vermont State Archives
DCA2006

181 Twin Tourism Models
Vermont State Archives
DCA4098

182 Amber Milk Bottle Inspection, 1960
Vermont State Archives
VSA06

183 Bulk Milk Tanks
Vermont State Archives
VSA05

184 Green River Reservoir
Morristown Historical Society/Noyes House Museum
MG.WL.21

185 Morristown Airport Dedication
Morristown Historical Society/Noyes House Museum
SE.02

186 Police Motorcade
Vermont State Archives
AOT3249

187 Disney Filming
Vermont State Archives
VSA23

188 Calvin Coolidge Homestead, 1961
Library of Congress
LC-G613-77174

189 Union Church at Plymouth Notch
Library of Congress
LC-G613-77162

190 Covered Bridge at Rockingham
Vermont State Archives
DCA4112

191 Adirondack Ferry on Lake Champlain
UVM Bailey Howe Special Collections
BHSC097

192 Hoff with the Johnsons
Vermont State Archives
ABT_10_Johnson_Aug_1966

193 Round Barn at Enosburg
Vermont State Archives
AOT2353

194 Dumont Manor Residents
Morristown Historical Society/Noyes House Museum
BS.16

195 Fisher Bridge near Wolcott
Morristown Historical Society/Noyes House Museum
BR.07

196 Mainframe Computer
Vermont State Archives
VSA16

197 Senator Aiken and Squirrel
UVM Bailey Howe Special Collections
BHSC087

198 Bicentennial Celebration at the Noyes House
Morristown Historical Society/Noyes House Museum
O.MHS.18

199 Cochran Family Tribute
Morristown Historical Society/Noyes House Museum
OldRoundChurchCochran

200 Basin Harbor Club at Ferrisburg
Vermont State Archives
DCA3678

201 Lamoille County Aerial
Morristown Historical Society/Noyes House Museum
BU.OV.11

HISTORIC PHOTOS OF VERMONT

Rolling green hills, cozy villages, covered bridges, maple trees—these are the images that have made Vermont. Residents and visitors alike appreciate Vermont for its old-time values that have steered clear of the modern world. Yet this image of Vermont has not come easily. Vermont's old-time values have been challenged, tested, adapted—and even consciously sculptured.

Vermonters have shown great creativity and adaptability in preserving the past while admitting the new. Integral to Vermont's story of creativity are people like Ara Griggs, a one-man patrol who enforced state laws on 15,000 miles of roads. Or Gilbert Hastings, who put a toy whistle in every loaf to move bread off his grocery shelves. Or Philomene Daniels, who earned her steamboat pilot's license to help keep the family business afloat—and was the first woman to do so.

Historic Photos of Vermont tells the story of the nation's 14th state in nearly 200 striking black-and-white photographs, all printed in an attractive and handsomely bound format. Take this journey into the past and discover why Vermonters cherish the land they call home.

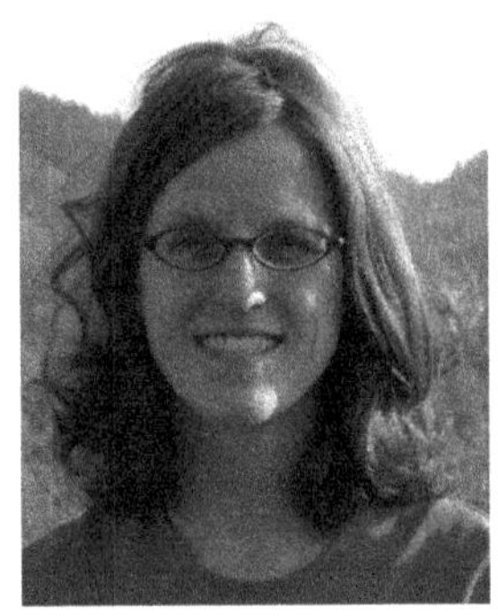

Ginger Gellman holds a master's degree in history from the University of Vermont and an undergraduate degree from Princeton University. She has worked as a freelance archivist for the Jericho Historical Society and has served as a summer guide for Vermont's preeminent Underground Railroad site, the Rokeby Museum in Ferrisburg. Currently, Gellman is researching the history of Burlington's early development from 1790 to 1810.

Gellman works at the Burnham Memorial Library in Colchester, Vermont, and sings with Social Band, an *a cappella* chorus specializing in Old World and American shape note music. She lives in Jericho with her cat Angus.

WWW.TURNERPUBLISHING.COM